Volu

# EARTH
## OUT OF ORBIT

*Royals & Majesties*

# SANCTUS EST ADONAI

Earth Out of Orbit 3

© 2016 Sanctus est Adonai

All rights reserved. No part of this publication may be reproduced, stored in a retrieval system, or transmitted in any form or by any means—electronic, mechanical, photocopying, recording, or any other—except for brief quotations in printed reviews, without the prior written consent of the copyright owner or publisher. Any unauthorized publication is an infringement of the copyright law.

All Scripture quotations are taken from the King James Version (KJV) of the Bible.

ISBN-13: 978-1-4866-1273-4

Front cover: the goddess Athena, Louvre Museum/Paris, and King Alexander the Great, Bode Museum/Berlin [images source: author].

Back Cover: the god Apollo, and a cameo belonging to Emperor Augustus, Louvre Museum/Paris [images source: author].

Printed in Canada.

# Contents

**Introduction** ..... xi

## CHAPTER ONE

## TIME ON EARTH

**Wake Up, You Dead Majesties!** ..... 1
   The Prince of This World ..... 1
   Edit: Can You See Water with Your Eyes? ..... 2
   Water Everywhere ..... 2
   How Did Moses Know? ..... 4
   Can You See the Ozone Layer with Your Naked Eyes? ..... 4
   How Did Moses Know? ..... 5
   Do You See Black Holes with Your Naked Eyes? ..... 5

**Show Us Your Old Records** ..... 6
   The Greatest Loss of All ..... 9

**A Shining Star** ..... 10
   The Kid's Father ..... 12

**The Sea Roars** ..... 15
   Leading Up to the Great Tribulation ..... 178
   The Earth Will Shake ..... 18
   All Alone ..... 18
   The Three Builders ..... 189
   An Unprecedented Earthquake ..... 20

**What Time Is It On Earth Today?** ..... 212
   Celestial ..... 27
   Edit: Silver and Gold Paradises ..... 28
   Paradise Virgins ..... 28
   Selling and Buying in Paradise ..... 29

**The Greatest Two Events** ..... 31
   The Last and Final Interview ..... 32

**The Ruler of Planet Earth** ..... 33
   End of the World ..... 35
   An Island in the Sea ..... 35

**My Friend** ..... 40

**Good News and Bad News** ..... 42
   Endless Hatred ..... 45

## CHAPTER TWO

## HAIL TO THE KING OF EGYPT, WHO SHINES LIKE THE SUN

   Make Us Wise ..... 52

**1436 BC Exodus** ..... 53
   Skipping Ahead ..... 54

## IV—EARTH OUT OF ORBIT

| | |
|---|---|
| **1398/1397 BC Long View from Pisgah** | **55** |
| **1397–1004 BC Running from Slavery to Poverty** | **59** |
| **1004 BC A Reddish-Haired King and Musician** | **60** |
| Wonderful Are Thy Works | 63 |
| **931 BC Break Up** | **63** |
| **A False Prophet of a Poor Copy** | **64** |
| Kissing Stones | 66 |
| **Big Trouble! I am Rich** | **67** |
| Heroes & Future Kings | 69 |

## CHAPTER THREE

## FIRST 666 – COMING ALIVE

| | |
|---|---|
| **746/745 BC Assyria** | **71** |
| **Remarkable! Land of Shinar—666** | **72** |
| **745 BC By Armageddon** | **75** |
| **A Child Shall Be Born** | **78** |
| Unto You and Unto Us | 79 |
| **727–722 BC King Shalmaneser V—Samaria** | **84** |
| **722 BC King Sargon II & the Lost Ten Tribes** | **84** |
| Bit-Humria | 87 |
| **705–681 BC King Sennacherib** | **89** |
| What Is in a Name? | 95 |
| **The Black King of Egypt** | **96** |
| From Peak to Abyss | 97 |
| **Jerusalem All Alone** | **100** |
| **No, Not All Alone—Nature Came** | **102** |
| A Future Repeat | 104 |
| Fiery and Noisy Nuclear Holocaust? | 107 |
| **Forty-Seven Years in Advance** | **110** |
| **Revolt in Transition Time** | **113** |
| **The Summit of Power** | **117** |
| **715 & 711 BC The Changing Face of Israel—Immigrants** | **122** |
| **I Will Make Your Grave** | **124** |
| Everyone Hates Us | 125 |
| **Do You See Any Difference?** | **125** |
| Same Ally Then and Now | 126 |
| A Great Marvel | 127 |
| **The House of the Lions** | **134** |

CONTENTS—V

## CHAPTER FOUR

## BABYLON THE GOLDEN

| | |
|---|---|
| The Land of Shinar | 140 |
| **612 BC** | **141** |
| **The Valley of Megiddo** | **142** |
| **Rage Ye War Chariots** | **145** |
| **Jerusalem! Jerusalem!** | **150** |
| A Prince and a Prophet | 151 |
| **597 BC** | **153** |
| Jehoiachin's Rations Tablets | 155 |
| **596 BC First Punch in the Twilight** | **160** |
| **A Second and a Third Punch** | **163** |
| **586 BC A Year for the Count** | **164** |
| Missing Smoke Signals | 166 |
| **Another Man of Mystery** | **167** |
| **582 BC How Can We Sing the Lord's Song?** | **169** |
| One Hundred Years in Advance | 170 |
| By the Rivers of Babylon | 174 |
| Remarkable – 1290 & 666 | 174 |
| Events Leading to the Dome of the Rock | 175 |
| The Dome of the Rock | 1767 |
| Confirming the Date of the Dome of the Rock – 1290 & 666 | 1778 |
| First Date | 170 |
| Second Date & Confirmation | 178 |
| And So It Is Today | 179 |
| Wait No More! It Is Certainly Him – April 3, 31/33 AD | 179 |
| 666 and Gold | 180 |
| **It Shall Come to Pass** | **182** |
| Servants Defeat Masters | 183 |

## CHAPTER FIVE

## THE UNEQUAL TWO HORNS OF IRAN

| | |
|---|---|
| **A Grandson Against A Grandfather** | **189** |
| Iran Against Iraq | 193 |
| **As Rich as Croesus** | **200** |
| **Total Indifference** | **204** |
| **Dance the Night Away** | **205** |
| Why the Third? Why Not Second? | 207 |
| **539 BC In Writing** | **214** |
| The Wisdom of Compromising | 216 |
| The Cylinder | 219 |
| Unimaginable Today | 221 |

## VI—EARTH OUT OF ORBIT

**Little Earth Covers My Body** — 224

**THE PERSIAN EMPIRE SPREAD ITS WINGS** — 226

**Cambyses II 530–522 BC** — 226
**525 BC Lashing with Whips** — 227
    A Bridge Over Hell — 229
    Mystery Solved? — 234
**522 BC Tonyoaxarces —The King Has no Ears** — 236
**530–525 BC Meanwhile, in Jerusalem** — 241
    The Golden Opportunity — 242
**The Good Samaritan** — 244
**522 BC Seven Nobles** — 247
**522–520 BC Two Years** — 250
**520 BC Reinstating** — 2521
**520 BC Troublous Times** — 254
**516 BC Do the Math** — 255
    Past and Future Threats — 259
**516 /515 BC A Year for the Counting!** — 260
**Joy—Wait No More** — 263
    The Wait Is Over – It Is Him — 265
    Hava Nagila, Wait No More — 266
    The Apple of God's Eye — 267
    The Spirit of God — 270
    Christian Teacher Dies — 273
    Beautiful White — 277
    Divine — 279
    A Daily Miracle! — 279
    One Becomes Two — 280
    A Daily Miracle — 280
    The Son of Mary — 2810
**585 BC Europe Ties the Knot with Iran** — 281
**547/546 BC As Rich as Croesus** — 284
**499–494 BC Greek Uprisings Everywhere** — 289
**494 BC Master, Remember the Athenians** — 292
**490 BC A Word for the Ages** — 294
    The Olympic Games — 297
**Joy. We Won. Now Die.** — 301
**By the Memory!** — 303
**486-465 BC We Shall Own the Borders of God** — 306
**August/September 480 BC The Last Stand** — 310
    Worse than a Woman — 322
    Hell is Full of Them — 323
    The Back of the Bus — 323

| | |
|---|---|
| **September 480 BC Salamis Says It All** | 327 |
| Xerxes, Husband of Esther? | 330 |
| 483 BC Final Days of Celebration | 332 |
| 480 BC | 333 |
| **479 BC Foreign Trash** | 333 |
| You Are Not Equal | 335 |
| **Plataea and Mycale** | 336 |
| | |
| **MONEY IS MIGHTIER THAN THE SWORD** | 342 |
| | |
| **465-424 BC Artaxerxes I** | 342 |
| **458 BC** | 342 |
| **445 BC A Counting Date** | 344 |
| **Remarkable!** | 345 |
| Sixty-Two and Seven | 348 |
| **424–423 BC A Year of Upheaval and Mayhem** | 348 |
| **423–405 BC** | 348 |
| **404–358 BC** | 349 |
| The Sea, the Sea | 350 |
| **The Sunset of the Kings of the World** | 351 |
| **Reminiscing** | 353 |

## Chapter Six

## Past and Present Abominations

| | |
|---|---|
| **The Only Two Men in the World Who Count** | 357 |
| **334 BC Let Us Share** | 361 |
| From the West … and Touched Not the Ground | 362 |
| **I Will Find You Wherever You Hide** | 363 |
| **I Am Not Parmenio** | 365 |
| **331 BC** | 367 |
| **In the Palace of Nebuchadnezzar** | 372 |
| **June 10, 323 BC** | 372 |
| **Four Royal Houses: First and Second** | 378 |
| **The Third Kingdom—Macedonia** | 384 |
| Misunderstanding | 388 |
| **The Fourth Kingdom—Anatolia [Asia Minor]** | 389 |
| **The Final Count** | 395 |
| **Marriages and Divorces Peace and War** | 397 |
| Egypt Takes Israel | 399 |
| 320 BC | 400 |

## VIII—EARTH OUT OF ORBIT

| | |
|---|---|
| **280 BC Who Owns Israel?** | **400** |
| The Greatest Library of the Ancient World – Home of the Book of Daniel in Greek | 402 |
| **September 246 BC Greater Than His Father** | **410** |
| **246 BC The Gods Came Home** | **413** |
| **Another Great One** | **417** |
| **Royals in Review** | **419** |
| **King Alexander the Great** | **419** |
| **Ptolemy II of Egypt [His Daughter Marries King of the North]** | **419** |
| **Ptolemy III of Egypt [Attacks the North to Revenge his Sister]** | **420** |
| **219/218 BC – The Fight to Own Israel** | **423** |
| **The Battle of Raphia—June 13–22, 217 BC** | **430** |
| **205 BC The Delinquent Gone** | **432** |
| **205–186 BC The Egyptian Secession** | **433** |
| The Great Egyptian Rebellion | 437 |
| **198 BC Battle of Panium—The Tide Turns** | **439** |
| **Why Not King of Europe Too?** | **445** |
| Forever Kings in Roman Times | 445 |
| Be Very Ambitious | 446 |
| **195–193 BC An Astonishing Move** | **447** |
| **Hot Gates Again—Thermopylae** | **458** |
| **188 BC A Debt to Pay** | **459** |
| **187 BC The Great Has Fallen** | **461** |
| **Pillaging Temples** | **463** |
| **187–175 BC The Tax Collector** | **465** |
| **Family Feud in Israel** | **468** |
| **The Nephew Is Unhappy** | **470** |
| **170 BC The King Is Taken Hostage** | **472** |
| **A Shifty Lawyer Destroys by Peace** | **473** |
| **A Vile Person—Cheap, Flashy and Base** | **476** |
| **170 BC Incomplete Victory** | **480** |
| **The Bank** | **485** |
| **Thieves and Robbers** | **487** |
| **170 BC A Date to Remember** | **488** |
| **168 BC Round Two—A Line in the Sand** | **489** |
| Grain to Rome | 490 |
| **168 BC No Handshakes** | **493** |
| **168/167 BC He Is Alive** | **496** |

## ABOMINATION, TRIBULATION, AND DESOLATION — 499

**167 BC A Year for the Counting** — 499
**Abomination of Desolation** — 500
    National Superstition — 507
**The Maccabees – Pushing Back** — 509
**167 BC A Guerrilla Warfare** — 510
**164 BC Short Calculation Hanukkah** — 512
**164 BC Dust to Dust** — 515
**Farewell, My Lords** — 516

BIBLIOGRAPHY AND NOTES — 521

# Introduction

The author began writing the manuscript of *Earth Out of Orbit* more than fifteen years ago.

The large size of the manuscript necessitated dividing it into several volumes.

The first two volumes have been already published. They, as well as the future volumes, are and will be made available on the Internet, free of charge.

It was assumed that this present volume would have in fact become volume number seven, according to the chronological order of the manuscript.

However, mindful of the events taking place on the world stage at the present time, the author decided to leapfrog publishing volumes three, four, five, and six—and instead publish the current volume.

The question he then faced was what number to give this volume.

He eventually settled on calling it "volume three," even though it is out of the chronological order.

The next volume, which deals with the future prophecies, shall therefore be called "volume four."

Should the time allow it, the author will then attempt to publish the four sidelined volumes.

- All biblical quotes in this book are taken from the King James Version, unless otherwise specified.

- All blue background pages are Christian editorials.

- All Islamic quotes in the book are cut and pasted from the sacred Islamic books of the Koran and Hadith. The quotes were not edited for spelling, grammar, or punctuation.

- All the comments and contents of the parentheses in the Islamic quotes are strictly and solely made by Islamic scholars.

- All green background pages are Islamic editorials.

- The underlining in all the quotes in the book is an added editorial emphasis.

- All [comments] contained in square brackets are made by the author.

- All non-museum images are presumed to be what they proclaim.

## LIST OF ABBREVIATIONS

ARAB:  *Ancient Records of Assyria and Babylonia* by Daniel David Luckenbill.

AROE:  *Ancient Records of Egypt*, translated and edited by James Henry Breasted, University of Illinois Press, 1906

ANET:  *The Ancient Near East*, edited by James B. Pritchard

WC:  Wikipedia Commons

For the purpose of copyrights, it should be noted that the entire costs of producing this series of books are undertaken by the author.

However, the entire proceeds of the series, should there be any, are assigned to registered charities, or the reprinting of *Earth Out of Orbit*.

# Chapter One

# Time on Earth

## Wake Up, You Dead Majesties!

My lords, why is the small nation of Israel so important?

Why does it attract the world's attention?

And why do some hate her so intensely, while others love her so passionately?

My lords, every single man and woman in the world needs Israel. Her enemies and her friends alike—they all need her, your majesties. They need Israel if they wish to know the future.

Israel's past and present, my sovereigns, unlock the secrets of the future.

We need Israel, my lords, like a man needs a timepiece to know what time of the day it is. We need the nation of Israel, your majesties, in order to know what time it is today on our beautiful but doomed planet.

Israel is the future-teller of the world, my lords.

Hard days are in store for Israel and for the world. Days of sorrow are approaching steadily towards Israel, my lords, month after month. The prince of this world is loaded against her. And no one, king or president, shall succeed to help. And no nation, great or small, shall be able to save the world from what shall begin in Israel.

### *The Prince of This World*

In the final years of the earth, the prince of this world shall change his strategy from deception to a global display of astounding power and violence. Knowing that his end is near, he no longer shall turn people away from God through deception. The savage wolf shall no longer come in sheep clothing.

*2 Thess 2:8 And then shall that Wicked be revealed*
*Rev 12:12 Woe to the inhabitants of the earth ... [the prince of the world] having great wrath, because he knoweth that he hath but a short time.*

## 2—EARTH OUT OF ORBIT

ABOVE: The prince of this world, Louvre Museum, Paris (image source: author).

The world shall be in a state of emergency. The earth shall be on a heightened alert. And while the prince of this world begins to display his awesome power, God shall restrict His judgment for a time.

Lk 22:53 *This is your hour, and the power of darkness.*

As a result, the world shall be tempted to believe that God stands helpless before the extremely powerful and violent prince of this world. Indeed, the world shall lose its trust and confidence in God. And so encouraged by God's seeming weakness, many shall trust their future to the prince of darkness. And they shall clinch their fists against the sky in defiance to God.

Lk 18:8 *When the Son of man [Christ Jesus] cometh, shall he find faith on the earth?*

## Edit: *Can You See Water with Your Eyes?*

Moses and Job, two men from the children of Israel, knew mysteries that took place millions of years before their day and ours.

The man Moses was not an astronomer. He was not a scientist. And he was not a physicist. Moses was born in Egypt nearly 3,500 years ago. There were no power telescopes in his day. And there were neither space observatories in his time, nor were there radio dishes well placed around the world to solve any of the mysteries of the universe—the heavens.

Yet Moses made an extraordinary claim. And he did so without hesitation.

His claim was and still is an extraordinary claim because it could not have been reached by simple or careful observation of the skies above us. No man, neither in his time nor now, intelligent or otherwise, can make the same claim that Moses made without specialized space observatories properly placed on high mountains.

### *Water Everywhere*

Look up to the sky on a clear night. Can you see water amongst the stars—the mansions of the heavens?

Scientists equipped with highly sophisticated and technologically advanced observatories can. And he too, Moses, could.

On July 22, 2011, two teams of scientists published a paper on NASA's website confirming the existence of huge amounts of water everywhere in the universe—everywhere. Can you see any?

They not only claimed that water "permeates" the universe in large quantities, a trillion times more than that on Earth, but that water was there at the very dawn of time, or shortly after the "Big Bang."

Can you see this water that permeates the heavens?

The Milky Way, Stennis Space Center (SSC), Mississippi, USA (image source: author).

The following quotes are taken from NASA's website:[1]

> "Two teams of astronomers have discovered the largest and farthest reservoir of water ever detected in the universe. The water, equivalent to <u>140 trillion times all the water in the world's ocean</u>, surrounds a huge, <u>feeding black hole, called a quasar</u>, more than 12 billion light-years

---

[1] http://www.nasa.gov/topics/universe/features/universe20110722.html

away," said Matt Bradford, a scientist at NASA's Jet Propulsion Laboratory in Pasadena, California.

"It's another demonstration that <u>water is pervasive throughout the universe, even at the very earliest times,</u>" said Matt Bradford.

"His team's research is partially funded by NASA and appears in the Astrophysical Journal Letters.

Astronomers expected water vapor to be present <u>even in the early, distant universe, but had not detected it this far away before.</u> There's water vapor in the Milky Way … most of the Milky Way's water is frozen in ice."

"Bradford's team made their observations starting in 2008, using an instrument called 'Z-Spec' at the California Institute of Technology's <u>Submillimeter Observatory,</u> a 33-foot (10-meter) telescope near the summit of Mauna Kea in Hawaii. Follow-up observations were made with the Combined Array for Research in Millimeter-Wave Astronomy (CARMA), an array of radio dishes in the Inyo Mountains of Southern California."

"Because the light we are seeing left this quasar more than 12 billion years ago, we are seeing <u>water that was present only some 1.6 billion years after the beginning of the universe,</u>" said study co-author Alberto Bolatto, of the University of Maryland, in a statement. "This discovery pushes the detection of water one billion years closer to the Big Bang than any previous find."

## *How Did Moses Know?*

Now the prophet Moses of Israel wrote the following sentences nearly 3,500 years ago in the biblical book of Genesis:

> Gen 1:1 *In the beginning God created the heaven and the earth.*
> Gen 1:2 *And the earth was without form [molten, thus without shape], and void [no water and no vegetations or animals]; and darkness was upon the face of the deep. And the Spirit of God moved upon the face of the waters [in the universe, not on the earth].*

## *Can You See the Ozone Layer with Your Naked Eyes?*

Once again, this same prophet Moses, who was neither a physicist nor had a spectrophotometer 3,500 years ago, did also write of the ozone layer, which was discovered as recently as 1913.

The depth of this ozone layer, or firmament, is about 20–30 kilometers. And it engulfs the stratosphere above the earth in order to shield it from the bombardment of many harmful rays. Indeed, this firmament is what makes life on the surface of the earth possible.

## *How Did Moses Know?*

> Gen 1:6 And God said, Let there be <u>a firmament</u> in the midst of the waters [which permeates the universe], and let it [the firmament] divide the waters from the waters [let the firmament sandwich itself in the middle of the waters].
> Gen 1:7 And God made the firmament, <u>and divided the waters which were under the firmament from the waters which were above the firmament [which permeates the universe above us]</u>: and it was so.
> Gen 1:8 And God called the firmament Heaven.
> Gen 1:9 And God said, <u>Let the waters under the heaven be gathered together unto one place, and let the dry land appear: and it was so</u>.
> Gen 1:10 And God called the dry land Earth; and the gathering together of the waters called he Seas: and God saw that it was good.

## *Do You See Black Holes with Your Naked Eyes?*

Look up at the night skies. Can you see black holes with your eyes?

Of course, you cannot because they are not actually black; rather, they are invisible. Yet their gravity is so extreme that even energy cannot escape their grip.

It took modern science, with all its sophisticated equipment, to determine the existence of black holes, such as the one in the article above, and near where the water reservoir was found.

Yet two biblical prophets, John and Jude, over two thousand years ago, spoke of the existence of these black holes. And they too have said that black holes can indeed chain energy.

For now, one should remember that angels, including fallen angels, are celestial beings. And as such they are nothing but energy. Indeed, the biblical text, for the lack of the word "energy" at the time, calls them flaming fire.

> Heb 1:7 he ... maketh his angels <u>spirits ... a flame of fire</u>.

Neither of these two men, John or Jude, was an astronomer or a trained scientist, or had special equipment to inform them of the existence of such black holes, or of their strong grip on energy.

How did they know? Is the biblical text extended beyond its meaning?

## Show Us Your Old Records

Wake up, you dead. Wake up, you highest ranking citizens of the kingdom of dust, you, the great ones. "The chief ones of the earth," as the old prophet calls you.

Talk to us, you mighty dead, for you are the ones who know exactly what past prophecies you yourselves have fulfilled.

You, my lords, were born, fed, and raised to fulfill the great prophecies of the world. But as you may or may not know, the prophets of old say that it was all in God's plan in order to testify of His plan and timetable to the peoples of the earth before the day of judgment takes them by surprise.

Is this correct, your majesty King David?

> PS 33:11 *The counsel [the plan] of the LORD standeth for ever, the thoughts of his heart to all generations.*
> ISA 42:9 *Behold, the former things are come to pass [past prophecies], and new things [prophecies of new events] do I declare: before they spring forth I tell you of them.*
> JN 13:19 *Now I tell you before it come, that, when it is come to pass, ye may believe*

The questioning minds amongst us, my lords, do indeed trust you, my sovereigns, because you wrote your records without realizing that you were fulfilling prophecies. And so the questioning minds amongst us, my lords, need to have a good look at your records in order to verify the prophecies—the prophecies, which the prophets of Israel made years in advance before you fulfilled them.

Speak up, you great ones! Break your silence. We intend today to mine the truth from your clay-baked journals of old, which are still with us today and which we have learned to read.

We have deciphered your ancient languages, your majesties. We indeed can read your old journals.

We have learned the hieroglyphic language of Egypt. And we can read the cuneiform documents of Iraq, of Assyria, of Babylon, and of Persia [Iran]. We can read ancient Greek and Roman documents.

You cannot escape your own files, my lords. Today, it is too late for you to alter your old writings and your ancient records, which you have even carved on the murals of the walls of your palaces.

We need these ancient documents of yours, my lords, in order to interpret the past prophecies of the prophets of Israel.

> PROV 22:21 *That I might make thee know the certainty of the words of truth*

TIME ON EARTH—7

Above is a small section of the ancient Egyptian *Book of the Dead*. British Museum, London (image source: author).

The Egyptian kings began a program to destroy and exterminate the Israelites by killing all Israelite newborn boys. Others would later follow their example and attempt to obliterate Israel, the clock of the world.

Above is one of many ancient Assyrian Iraqi inscriptions, which were carved on the murals of the walls of Nineveh's palace. The mural above shows Assyrian (Iraqi) King Tiglathpileser (whose number is 666 as shall be seen) under a parasol; the inscription above him details one of his campaigns, 730–727 BC; British Museum, London (image source: author).

## 8—EARTH OUT OF ORBIT

Above is an inscription of Assyrian King Sargon II (721–705 BC), who destroyed the city of Samaria, the capital of the northern half of Israel, and began the legend of the lost ten tribes. This destruction of his was the first step of nearly exterminating the entire population of Israel and bringing it to an end. But yet, against all odds, Israel rose again from the ashes.

The inscription was found in the inner court of King Sargon's palace at Khorsabad, Iraq; Vatican Museum, Rome (image source: author).

A Greek Papyrus fragment of Book X of Homer's Odyssey, late 2nd–early 3rd AD; Archaeological Museum, University of Pennsylvania, Philadelphia, USA (image source: author).The mighty Greeks in their heyday, they too, wanted to put an end to Israel as the preacher of the plan of God. Later, the Romans would attempt to do the same.

My lords, we have prepared our luggage. We have put on our travelling clothes. Our determined feet will trace your steps everywhere you went, up and down the prophecy highway, far and near. We shall track you down the ancient highways and byways and bobbing lanes of the seas. We shall follow you from France to Spain, from Germany to Britain, from Italy to Greece, from Cyprus and Rhodes Island to Syria, Israel, Jordan, and Egypt.

Our dogged search shall not tire or become weary until we know how the prophecies of the past were fulfilled and what will happen to us in the coming years.

Indeed, we cannot wait to go to Vienna, the exile city of that famous governor who is now sitting amongst you, my lords. We see you there, sir. We need to talk to you because prior to your exile to Vienna, you were in charge of the city of Jerusalem during the fulfillment of one of the two most important prophecies of the world, and on which the fate and future of every single soul rests, as the prophets say. And there is nothing more precious than one's own life, my lords—is there?

## The Greatest Loss of All

MAT 16:26 *For what is a man profited, if he shall gain the whole world, and lose his own soul? or what shall a man give in exchange for his soul?*
ECCL 12:1 *Remember now thy Creator*

And we shall demand, my lords, that the august Roman senate hand us its archived files so that we can find out what some of you have done when you sailed the crashing waves of the Mediterranean with noisy huge fleets of fearful warships full of tough warriors, all unaware, yet were on their way to fulfill prophecies.

And talking about the Roman senate, my lords, where is the great one whose people described as having "intelligence ... while he had good looks, too, and a certain dignity of manner"?[2]

Yes, there you are, sir. But, no, do not come out just yet, my lord, the emperor. Stay where you are for now, and wait for your chronological turn. We shall travel a long distance up the highway of past world prophecies before we ask you to speak out. Stay put for now, your majesty.

---

[2] Tacitus, *Histories*, Kenneth Wellesley [translator], London: Penguin Books, 81.

## 10—EARTH OUT OF ORBIT

Emperor Titus, 79-81 BC, The Numismatic Museum of Athens, Greece (image source: author).

Whatever you be, my lords, criminals or greats, you have unknowingly fulfilled the past prophecies and set the stage for the modern ones. And, yes, the masses did adore you, my lords, and the masses did abhor you.

One of you honorable gentlemen is called "the darling of the nation." Are you there, sir? Yes, there you are.

And another one of you a certain group of people would not as much as spit out his name—and you know who you are sir—unless they first mouthed the curse "may his bones be crushed." No, not us, sir, for we shall put your bones together and talk to you. We need to hear your explanations and track the prophecies you fulfilled.

The Emperor Hadrian, "may his bones be crushed," Louvre Museum, Paris (image source: author).

## A Shining Star

And if any of you, my lords, wishes to know who of your exclusive club of great men and women stands out the most in our modern mind? Our answer, no offense to the rest of you, my lords, is his majesty the kid.

The name of this young man, the kid, my lords, is a well-known name to the people of our modern day.

How this handsome youngster could look to his right and find himself hugely overwhelmed, and then look to his left and register how vastly he was outnumbered, and then look straight ahead to face a huge number of fighters armed to the teeth, and yet in cool command, his majesty the kid turned the table around with decisive knock-outs.

My lords, his majesty the kid put an end to two hundred long years of hard work achieved by great men much older than him. And he did so, my lords, in just three rounds of battles.

How, my lords, was the kid able to accomplish such a great feat in such a little time and become the ruler, the king of the world?

The answer, your majesties, is that the kid had a destiny rolled out for him to fulfill. He was born, fed, and raised to fulfill old prophecies delegated to him according to the plan and timetable of the earth.

Your majesty the kid, we shall examine your old record very carefully, sir.

As for now, please go ahead, prophet Daniel of Israel, and tell their majesties your prophecy concerning the kid.

> DAN 8:5 *And as I was considering, behold, an he goat [the army of the kid] came from the west on the face of the whole earth, and touched not the ground [very fast]: and the goat had a notable horn between his eyes [the kid].*
> DAN 8:6 *And he came to the ram that had two horns [the Persian Empire of Iran], which I had seen standing before the river, and ran unto him in the fury of his power.*
> DAN 8:7 *and smote the ram [Iran], and brake his two horns [the two horns are the kingdoms of Media and Persia—today, Iran]: and there was no power in the ram [Iran] to stand before him, but he cast him down to the ground, and stamped upon him: and there was none that could deliver the ram [Iran] out of his hand.*
> DAN 8:8 *Therefore the he goat [the kid] waxed very great: and when he was strong, the great horn was broken [the kid died at the height of his power]; and for it came up four notable ones toward the four winds of heaven.*

My lords, it is said that his majesty the kid was shown what the prophets of Israel had written about him hundreds of years in advance.

Is it true, your majesty? Did they, your majesty the kid, show you the old prophecies concerning you when you came upon Jerusalem, the city of Israel?

We don't think that you will answer us, sir. But what a prophecy it was! It revealed so many future secrets. And it still does today and shall reveal more secrets yet tomorrow for those who have eyes to read and hearts to understand, or so the prophets of Israel say, my lords.

As for us, your majesties, we want to see. We want to see eternity with wide-open eyes. We do not want to come short.

Carry on with your prophecy, please, prophet Daniel.

> DAN 12:9 *And he said, Go thy way, Daniel: for the words are closed up [the meaning of the prophecy is hidden] and sealed [kept secret] <u>till the time of the end</u>.*
> DAN 12:4 *But thou, O Daniel, shut up the words, and seal the book, <u>even to the time of the end</u>: many shall run to and fro, <u>and knowledge shall be increased</u>.*

12—EARTH OUT OF ORBIT

## *The Kid's Father*

The kid's father was also known as an intelligent, lighthearted, witty, and innovative army general. There are a couple of recorded incidents that speak to his lightheartedness and wit:

It is recorded that following one of his military victories, he was, as customary, occupied in selling his prisoners of war to the slave dealers.

One of the prisoners drew his attention when he shouted, "Spare me, sir. I was your father's friend."

The kid's father, somewhat surprised by the claim, asked the prisoner for details. The prisoner replied that he could not speak of his claim publically. The general therefore permitted the prisoner to approach near him.

The prisoner did so and whispered into the general's ear to pull down his cloak, as his crotch was showing. The general grinned and of course it is easy to imagine the outcome correctly concerning the fate of the prisoner.

It is also said that he coined the famous witty reply to his barber's question: "How would you like your hair cut, Sir?"

"In silence!"

Young and old King Philip II, 359-336 BC, the father of the kid, Wien Museum, Vienna, Austria (images source: author).

# TIME ON EARTH—13

Two famous members of the club of the great rulers of the earth who have fulfilled past prophecies: (L) Alexander the Great, c.300 BC, marble, discovered in Cairo, Egypt, the Louvre Museum, Paris (image source: author); (R) The famous Queen Cleopatra, Altes Museum, Berlin (image source: author).

King Herod, who wanted to kill the infant Christ, also wished to murder the famous Queen Cleopatra, the lover of Mark Antony and Julius Caesar, as shall be seen.

And, yes, your majesties, we shall be patient. For we know that we can only meet the kid after we have first met the great Iranian majesty who today sits on the roster of your exclusive club, my lords.

Your Iranian majesty King Cyrus, you are, sir, the great man who launched the first attack against Europeans and won.

May we speak to you, your majesty, and tell you that your victory of that day has started a fight with Europe, which lasted a few hundred years after you entered the earth! And that your people of Iran, sir, not only fulfilled old prophecies but shall yet fulfill more prophecies, which have not happened yet.

And did you know, your majesty, that a prophet had mentioned you by name, years before you came along marching down the highway of prophecy? We are just wondering, sir, if you knew!

But the irony of it all, sir, is that you, your great Iranian majesty King Cyrus, you had attacked Europeans but yet saved the important nation of Israel from a final death and total extermination. Your Iran saved Israel, sir.

On the other hand, your majesty the kid, you had indeed saved Europe from the Iranians but one of your own successors, sir, intended to exterminate Israel, which his great Iranian majesty had saved.

What a difference it is today, sirs? Today the very opposite is true.

All of this aside, we do wish also to tell you, your majesties, the "lions of the nations," as the old prophet called you, that you shall not be the only illustrious speakers before us, as you have seen so far.

Indeed, the questioning minds amongst us, my lords, insist that along with you, we should also question and cross-examine the eyewitnesses of your reigns.

And so without offense, your majesties, we shall also present to you Pilo of Alexandria and Josephus of Jerusalem. We shall bring in the Roman senator Tacitus, along with Thucydides, and the Greek historian Herodotus, and their companions—Xenophon, Arrian, and Plutarch.

We shall bring them all in, my lords, along with whoever else we may find up and down the highway of prophecies.

And, yes, my lords, we shall not fail also to call upon the false prophet, the Antichrist, and give him a chance to speak up and explain his number "666." He shall be unmasked, my lords.

"Behold, you are a butcher whose delight is slaughter,
And the mutilation thereof means nothing to him,'" says the ancient Egyptian.[3]

(L) The ancient Greek historian Herodotus (b, circa 490–480 BC), National Museum of Italy, Rome (image source: author). (R) Fragment from Herodotus' Histories, Book VIII on Papyrus Oxyrhynchus 2099, dated to early second century AD, Papyrology Rooms, Sackler Library, Oxford. (Image source: WC).

---

[3] *The Literature of Ancient Egypt*, translated and edited by Robert K. Ritner, Vincent A. Tobin, Edward F. Wente Jr., and William Kelly Simpson, Yale University, 35.

## The Sea Roars

At any rate, my lords and majesties, "whales of the seas," as the prophet again calls you, we hope that your ancient records coupled up with the extensive surviving files and journals of the ancient historians will not only verify the old prophecies, but will also help us decipher the future warnings of the time of the end.

These warnings of the time of the end, my lords, range from roaring seas to the great tribulation, falling asteroids and meteorites, earth out of orbit, Armageddon, and the following day of judgment.

May we introduce to you, your majesties, the Christian apostle Luke!

Go ahead please, apostle Luke, and tell their majesties what you recorded about the days of the end.

> LK 21:25 *there shall be signs in the sun, and in the moon, and in the stars; and upon the earth distress of nations, with perplexity; <u>the sea and the waves roaring</u>;*
> LK 21:26 <u>*Men's hearts failing them for fear*</u>*, and for looking after those things which are coming on the earth: for the powers of heaven [asteroids and meteorites] shall be shaken [regarding asteroids and meteorites falling, NASA once said in a statement, "We believe anything larger than one to two kilometers (about 0.6 to 1.2 miles) could have worldwide effects." These large sizes of asteroids are called "earth crushers" or "doomsday asteroids."].*
> MK 13:24 *But in those days, after that tribulation, the sun shall be darkened, and the moon shall not give her light,*
> MK 13:25 <u>*And the stars of heaven shall fall*</u>*, and the powers that are in heaven shall be shaken.*
> LK 21:11 *fearful sights and great signs shall there be from heaven.*
> REV 6:15 *And the kings of the earth, and the great men, and the rich men, and the chief captains, and the mighty men, and every bondman, and every free man, hid themselves in the dens [caves] and in the rocks of the mountains;*

So now, my lords, we do hesitantly wish to begin our journey on the highway of past prophecies.

We do so hesitantly, my lords, because in our minds we are still struggling to see if we can have a short cut to the future prophecies of tomorrow. We struggle to see if we can understand the warnings of the time of the end without having to go back to the past prophecies. The time of the end, my lords, is the final stage of the plan of God before His invitation comes to an end, as His preachers of Israel proclaim.

16—EARTH OUT OF ORBIT

"The seas and the waves roaring," increasing fears of global warming and rise of sea levels, polar bear, the Academy of National Sciences of Philadelphia, USA (image source: author)

Where is the prophet Daniel? Here you are, sir.

Go ahead, please, prophet Daniel, and tell their majesties something about the time of the end. Go ahead and speak of the great tribulation. Tell their majesties of the false prophet, the Antichrist, and tell them of the number of years between these troubling events, which you said shall take place before the dawn of the day of judgment.

And let us see, sir, how much their majesties would be able to understand, how much they can gleam of your prophetic words.

We are afraid, my lords, that you shall glean but little from his prophecies. Let us see.

Go ahead, please, prophet Daniel.

> *DAN 12:1 And at that time [the time of the end] … there shall be a time of trouble [a worldwide time of trouble, the great tribulation], <u>such as never was since there was a nation</u> even to that same time: and at that time thy people shall be delivered, every one that shall be found written in the book.*
> *DAN 12:2 And many of them that sleep in the dust of the earth shall awake [the resurrection], some to everlasting life, and some to shame and everlasting contempt.*
> *DAN 12:3 And they that be wise shall shine as the brightness of the firmament; <u>and they that turn many to righteousness as the stars for ever and ever</u> [God's shinning stars, which He harvested throughout the ages from the populations of the earth].*
> *DAN 12:4 But thou, O Daniel, shut up the words, and seal the book, even to the time of the end: many shall run to and fro, and knowledge shall be increased.*

TIME ON EARTH—17

DAN 12:6 ... *How long shall it be to the end of these wonders?*
DAN 12:7 ... *it shall be for a time, times, and an half;* and when he [who is "he"? Has he already come or is he yet to come? And what exactly is he to do?] shall have accomplished to scatter the power of the holy people [Israel?], all these things shall be finished.
DAN 12:8 And I heard, but I understood not: then said I, O my Lord, what shall be the end of these things?
DAN 12:9 And he said, Go thy way, Daniel: for the words are closed up [shall remain a mystery hard to understand] and sealed till the time of the end [when it shall be easy to understand].
DAN 12:10 Many shall be purified, and made white [cleansed], and tried [tested]; but the wicked shall do wickedly: and *none of the wicked shall understand; but the wise [the knowledgeable] shall understand.*
DAN 12:11 *And from the time that the daily sacrifice [offered in Israel's temple, which was built by King Solomon and destroyed by the Babylonian Iraqi Nebuchadnezzar but rebuilt again by the permission of the Iranian King Cyrus the Great] shall be taken away, and the abomination that maketh desolate set up [has it been already set up?], there shall be a thousand two hundred and ninety days.*
DAN 12:12 *Blessed is he that waiteth [is it our generation?], and cometh to the thousand three hundred and five and thirty days.*
DAN 12:13 But go thou thy way till the end be: for thou shalt rest, and stand in thy lot at the end of the days.

These are puzzles and mysteries, Daniel. But we do know that we must understand them, sir.

And so, my lords, we have no option but to go back to the beginning of the highway of prophecies and its calendar— – the prophecies' calendar.

We must, my lords, get on the highway of prophecy near where it started in order to be sure about our findings. There are no shortcuts for certainty, my lords. We need to unlock God's calendar and understand His amazing and wonderful plan for mankind.

Indeed, my lords, God had kept a great secret in mind, even before He created the world. And He only revealed this great secret about two thousand years ago. We shall in the fullness of time behold the One who revealed the secret, my lords—a secret of joy and grace.

## Leading Up to the Great Tribulation

Several important questions that deal with a series of major events, which shall plague the earth in our own modern day, will be answered once Daniel's prophecies, among others, become clear and well understood.

One of these major events is what the Bible calls the great tribulation. And the question is: What would trigger it? What would trigger the great tribulation?

## The Earth Will Shake

Will an Israeli attack on Iran cause a major earthquake, which would produce universal horrors? Will the Dome of the Rock, Al-Aksa Mosque, the Islamic shrine in Jerusalem, shake and tumble? Or will the contention for its site between Israel and the Islamic countries of the world trigger an Iranian-led war?

Will Iran, and huge mobs of eastern armies, invade Israel across the marches of southern Iraq, as prophesied in the Bible?

## All Alone

They will gather, says the Bible. Israeli's neighbors and enemies of old shall gather and besiege Jerusalem. And Jerusalem, city of Israel, shall fall to the Islamic armies and mobs. Israel shall stand alone, abandoned by all and helpless. The Islamic armies and mobs shall triumph. Doubts shall shake the hearts of many believers. When shall all of these happen?

The biblical prophecies give the answer as Armageddon draws near.

(L): Russian president Vladimir Putin with Israeli Prime Minister Benjamin Netanyahu at the Jewish Community Centre in Moscow. www.kremlin.ru/events/photos/2000/12/132815.shtml.
(R): Russian president Vladimir Putin with the president of Iran (edit: then), Mahmoud Ahmadinejad (image source: WC, Presidential Press and Information Office).

## *The Three Builders*

If the interpretation of the biblical prophecies is correct, then we are indeed to understand that three countries—Germany, Russia, and perhaps North Korea—were destined to greatly empower Iran in the final years of the earth.

The Bible identifies Russia by location.

And it identifies Germany as the nation that would attempt to exterminate the children of Israel in the last days.

As for North Korea, the Bible speaks of the people who cut their hair in a certain manner.

Indeed, the Iranian Bushehr nuclear plant [opened in 2010 and put on stream in September 2011] was first built by Germany—the exterminator of the Jews, or the children of Israel.

However, following the Western sanctions on Iran, the nuclear plant, which was started by Germany, was then completed by Russia.

Thus, both countries, Germany and Russia, aided Iran in building its nuclear capabilities.

As for the third country, North Korea, the following quotation is taken from a recent article featured in *The Christian Science Monitor* and written by Jamey Keaten of the *Associated Press* on December 7, 2010. The article has been featured in several international newspapers and news outlets as well.

> "A former Iranian diplomat who defected to the West this year said Tuesday he saw North Korean technicians repeatedly travel to Iran, which Western officials fear is trying to develop nuclear weapons.
>
> Mohammad Reza Heydari, who resigned in January from his post as Iranian consul in Norway, said he's "certain" the cooperation is continuing between his home country and North Korea.
>
> The comments at a Paris think tank conference come amid rising international concerns that North Korea, which has already staged atomic tests, is cooperating with Iran on its nuclear program.
>
> Heydari said that from 2002 to 2007, when he headed the Iranian Foreign Ministry's office for airports, he saw many technicians from North Korea travel to Iran.
>
> "I witnessed repeated roundtrips of North Korean specialists and technicians — given that I was right there at the border — who came to collaborate on the Iranian nuclear program," he said through a translator.
>
> Heydari said their visits were handled "in a very discreet way, so they could come through unnoticed."
>
> Heydari said he also had contacts then with officials from Iran's Revolutionary Guards, and "it was clearly said that Iran was concentrating on two objectives ... the first was to build the range of

> surface-to-surface missiles, the second was to get a nuclear weapon with North Korea's help."
>
> ...
>
> A U.S. intelligence assessment — published among the flood of classified U.S. State Department memos obtained by WikiLeaks — concluded that Iran received advanced North Korean missiles capable of targeting Western European capitals and giving Iran's arsenal a significantly longer reach than previously disclosed."
>
> However, it should be mentioned that Iran denies recruiting North Korean scientists and technicians or purchasing North Korean hardware.
>
> But if the above statements by the Iranian diplomat are true, then they confirm the prophecies regarding the involvement of Germany, Russia, and North Korea in empowering Iran, the deadliest enemy of Israel. As a result of Iran's nuclear abilities, Israel lives in fear of blackmail and even an Iranian nuclear strike.
>
> Again, if the biblical interpretation is correct, based on one of Daniel's prophecies, threatened Israel would in time attack Iran. This is a momentous event that may result in nuclear retaliation by Iran and a series of events that include earthquakes, volcanoes, and plagues. All of these events would ultimately lead to the period of years called the "great tribulation."
>
> It should be understood that the end of the world is not a one-day event. And the great tribulation covers a specified number of years.

## *An Unprecedented Earthquake*

A powerful earthquake is one of the events that would bring about this period of years, the great tribulation. Now it is very difficult for seismologists to predict an earthquake far ahead in time. However, we are told of a number of specific and clear-cut events that should take place before this mighty and unprecedented earthquake strikes.

We are also told clearly of the length of this coming great tribulation, and of the never-seen-before events that shall occur during its predetermined number of years.

But the great tribulation is not the end of the world. It will be followed by specific events: first resurrection, then the millennium, which will ultimately lead to the second resurrection, the day of judgment, and the dawn of new and different heavens and earth.

But first it shall be the earthquake and the siege of Jerusalem, where the eagles shall gather around dead corpses. Jerusalem shall be overcome by its longtime enemies. But then another mighty earthquake shall strike.

> Lk 21:20 *And when ye shall see Jerusalem compassed [surrounded] with armies, then know that the desolation [its population abandoning the city] thereof is nigh [the siege of Jerusalem happened before and will happen again].*

> Lk 21:22 *For these be the days of vengeance, <u>that all things which are written [prophecies] may be fulfilled</u>.*
> Lk 21:25 *And there shall be signs in the sun, and in the moon, and in the stars; and upon the earth distress of nations, with perplexity; the sea and the waves roaring;*
> Lk 21:26 *Men's hearts failing them for fear, and for looking after those things which are coming on the earth: for the powers of heaven shall be shaken.*
> Luke 21:27 *And then shall they see the Son of man [Christ the Lord] coming in a cloud with power and great glory.*
> Lk 21:28 *And when these things begin to come to pass, then look up, and lift up your heads; for your redemption draweth nigh [getting near].*

What will trigger this unprecedented and powerful earthquake, which shall literally rock our planet in its orbit? Shall it be a nuclear explosion? Or shall it be a natural collision of the tectonic plates?

One thing is clear: the earth shall rock and wobble, and sail back and forth in unchartered territory, and collide with a stream of asteroids and meteorites, which may have been previously out of the way and harmless. And the catastrophic events, which the bombardment of the asteroids and meteorites will trigger, shall be disastrous new events in the history of mankind. But yet, the end shall be anything but catastrophic.

> Acts 17:31 *Because he [God] hath appointed a day, in the which he will judge the world*
> Heb 9:27 *it is appointed unto men once to die, but after this the judgment:*
> Rev 14:7 *Fear God, and give glory to him; for the hour of his judgment is come: and worship him that made heaven, and earth, and the sea, and the fountains of waters.*
> Rev 20:12 *And I saw the dead, small and great, stand before God; and the books were opened: and another book was opened, which is the book of life: and the dead were judged out of those things which were written in the books, according to their works.*
> Rev 20:13 *And the sea gave up the dead which were in it; and death and hell delivered up the dead which were in them: and they were judged every man according to their works.*
> Rev 16:10 *And the fifth angel poured out his vial upon the seat of the beast; and his kingdom was full of darkness; and they gnawed their tongues for pain,*
> Rev 16:11 *And blasphemed the God of heaven because of their pains and their sores, and repented not of their deeds.*

All of these events shall be made clear in the course of the journey up the highway of prophecy.

## What Time Is It On Earth Today?

The nation of Israel, the nation of the Savior of the world, acts as a clock of God's timetable of our temporary earth.

Above is the reliable Big Ben clock of the British Parliament, London (image source: author).

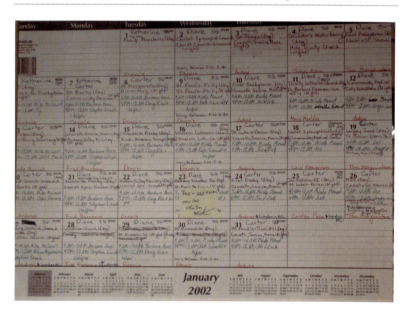

The above is a calendar of volunteers attending to the recovery of workers post-9/11, St Paul's Chapel, New York (image source: author).

The nation of Israel is like a calendar of scheduled and foretold events, whicht tell the world where we are in God's timetable-- the countdown to the new heavens and earth.

Your majesties, as we have already mentioned to you at the start, the small nation of Israel is an important nation and very much needed in this world of ours.

Hate her or like her, my lords, the world, her enemies, and her friends did and still need this small nation of Israel. And the reason the enemies and the friends need her, my lords, is because the routine of the earth does not change.

Allow us, your majesties, to explain our meaning in a short while.

But the very fact that Israel exists at all, my lords, gives assurance that there is indeed a plan that is being followed, and that there is indeed a timetable that moves along towards the day of judgment and the dawn of a new and lasting world to come—tomorrow's amazing world.

Some of you, your majesties, may not be aware that once upon a time, this tiny nation of Israel was but a single family—a single family that had over the years raised many godly men and prophets, and became the nation of God's prophets, as they say.

And not only did it become the nation of God's prophets and thus, my lords, the preacher nation of the world, and the nation of the timekeepers of the timetable of God, but it is also the nation from which was to come Shiloh, the Messiah, the grace of God, the hope of all generations, our one and only hope, as they say, for life after death—life eternal in the stretched-out heavens of heavens, and in the stars of our future and permanent home.

> GEN 49:10 *The sceptre [royalty] shall not depart from Judah [one of the twelve tribes of Israel], nor a lawgiver [governor/king] from between his feet, <u>until Shiloh come</u>; and unto him shall the gathering of the people be.*

Look at the routine of the earth, my lords. Our world carries on from day to day with absolutely no change, none whatsoever.

The sun rises, my lords, and the sun sets down in the same way every day—in your day it did so as it does in our day today. Nature's routines remain the same with no change and with no interruption since your time, my lords, and even before your time.

And so we can safely say, my lords, that there is really no end in sight to this beautiful earth of ours. Our earth is a permanent house of humanity; it always was and it always shall be. And this in turn, my lords, means that there is no plan or a schedule with a start day and a finish day. People die and new people are born, and no end in sight. Our earth, our present house in space, may last yet for thousands of years for all we know, my lords. Sure, we ourselves may not last for tens of years, but our lasting earth, my lords, shall carry on with its repeated routines years and years after we are dead and far gone. Nothing in nature, my lords, nothing indicates a drastic change is about to happen anytime soon. Ours then, my lords, is not a doomed earth.

Was not this your earliest conclusion, your majesty, King Solomon? There you are, sir.
Would you please, your majesty, tell your follow sovereigns what you yourself have meditated upon, sir!

> ECCL 1:4 <u>One generation [of humanity] passeth away, and another generation cometh: but the earth abideth [remains] for ever.</u>
> ECCL 1:5 <u>The sun</u> also ariseth, and the sun goeth down, and hasteth [hurries] to his place where he arose.
> ECCL 1:6 <u>The wind</u> goeth toward the south, and turneth about unto the north; it whirleth about continually, <u>and the wind returneth again according to his circuits</u>.
> ECCL 1:7 All <u>the rivers</u> run into the sea; yet the sea is not full; unto the place from whence the rivers come, thither they return again.
> ECCL 1:9 The thing that hath been, it is that which shall be [nature repeats its routine]; and that which is done is that which shall be done: and there is no new thing [change] under the sun.

The earth from space, Stennis Space Center (SSC), Mississippi, USA (image source: author).

No drastic and unusual change in sight

It is hard, my lords, to convince anyone that this ancient, unchangeable routine of our earth could soon come to an end.

And there, my lords, there is the great need. And there where the nation of Israel comes in to do its assigned task. There it is where the nation of God's prophets and His Messiah is needed, my lords.

Israel is needed to tell all of us, all the races of the peoples of this present world, what time it is on earth. For according to the prophets, my lords, our seemingly permanent earth is actually a temporary home and shall wind down and come to a fiery end in a predetermined manner, and on a predetermined date, and in predetermined fashion.

The nation of Israel, which you fulfilled its prophecies, my lords, is the one and only designated clock of the world. Nothing, as they say, happens haphazardly to Israel. Everything that happens to Israel was foreseen in advance in order to tell the high and low of all the peoples of all the nations of the earth how much time is left until the day of judgment and the destruction of our temporary cottage in the great universe of million mansions.

Indeed, my lords, the prophets did also prophesize that as the days draw near towards the determined end of the earth, many people and many thinkers would poke fun of anyone speaking of any change to the present routine of our seemingly eternal earth.

Go ahead please, apostle Peter, and tell their majesties what you have foreseen two thousand years ago.

> 2 PET 3:3 there shall come <u>in the last days</u> scoffers [sarcastic mockers], walking after their own lusts,
> 2 PET 3:4 And saying, <u>Where is the promise of his coming</u> [second coming of Christ]? for since the fathers fell asleep [since our ancestors died], <u>all things continue as they were from the beginning of the creation</u>.

And so, my lords, the prophets, the timekeepers of the plan of God, tell us that the timetable of the earth is made up of a chain of events, a sequel of important events that did and also shall befall the nation of Israel, the nation of the prophets, the nation of the Christ.

Sometimes, these events would be good events, as your Iranian Majesty King Cyrus did for Israel.

And sometimes the events shall be terrible ones as the man of the pig, your famous successor, your majesty, the kid, had inflicted upon Israel.

Nonetheless, all these major events, which would befall Israel, my lords, are nothing but signposts, markers in the timetable of the earth. And all these markers in Israel's life, past and future events, my sovereigns, do tell us how close we are to the major event, which they call the day of rapture. This day of rapture, my lords, was established in advance by the owner of heavens and earth. It is the day in which the door to join the Kingdom of Heaven, to join the nation of God, shall be closed. That day, the day of the rapture, my lords, shall be the last day when no longer citizens will be accepted into the eternal heavens above. The opportunity for every man and woman to become a member of the future royal family of God will in that day be lost for good your majesties.

And remember, my lords, what the preachers of Israel say; they say that the purpose of life is eternal life, eternal life in the heavens.

Go ahead please, apostle Titus, and tell their majesties of God's promise.

> *TITUS 1:2* In hope of eternal life, which God, that cannot lie, <u>promised before the world began</u> [it was God's intention right from the beginning that man would live forever, in a new and celestial body];

So then according to them, my lords, the purpose of life, my lords, is life eternal. The purpose of life, my sovereigns, is transformation from humans to celestials.

And accordingly, my lords, there shall be winners and losers. And the losers would have turned down the gift of grace that was offered them. They thought little of it, as the prophets of Israel preach, my lords.

The first shall be last and the last shall be first.

Go ahead, please, apostle Paul, and tell their majesties of the unbelievable future of those who love God.

> *1 COR 15:50* Now this I say, brethren, that flesh and blood [human body] cannot inherit the kingdom of God [the space of the heavens]
> *1 COR 15:51* Behold, I shew you a mystery ... <u>we shall all be changed</u>,
> *1 COR 15:40* There are also celestial bodies, and bodies terrestrial
> *2 COR 5:1* For we know that if our earthly house of this tabernacle [our temporary body is like a tent] were dissolved, we have a building of God [a new permanent body], an house not made with hands [not human], eternal in the heavens.
> *2 COR 5:5* Now he that hath wrought us [created us] for the selfsame thing [for this exact purpose] is God
> *1 COR 2:9* Eye hath not seen, nor ear heard, neither have entered into the heart of man, the things which God hath prepared for them that love him.

But one day, my lords, this nation of Israel was no more than an old husband who had no children. This nation of Israel, my lords, the calendar of the earth, was one day but thousands of poor slaves working as maidservants and construction workers in the land of the one and only superpower of the world at the time.

And then major events, my lord, made them a nation. Major events broke them into two nations, and major events threw both of them out of their homelands and then brought them back as one united nation. Shall we begin, my lords, to see how this people became the timeline of the earth?

How far have we come, and what is ahead around the corner? Botanic Garden, University of Cambridge, UK (image source: author).

## *Celestial*

The Lord opens the door slightly so we could glance into a different world—unimaginable world. Nothing in it is natural, earthly natural—all is amazing.

What is life like in a celestial body?

What shall the transformed children of God be doing in the space of the heavens?

The simple answer is: if man can hardly understand many of the mysteries of what he sees on earth, how can he at all understand or believe what life would be like in a celestial body. How can one understand the celestial rules where time as we know it on earth shall no longer exist?

The very idea that time shall no longer exist is unfathomable to even highly educated men and women outside the physics field of Einstein and his likes and equals. Science has become hard even for scientists.

> Jn 3:12 *If I have told you earthly things, and ye believe not, <u>how shall ye believe, if I tell you of heavenly things</u>?*
> Rev 10:6 *And sware by him that liveth for ever and ever, who created heaven, and the things that therein are, and the earth, and the things that therein are, and the sea, and the things which are therein, <u>that there should be time no longer</u>:*
> 1 Jn 3:2 *Beloved, now are we the sons of God, and <u>it doth not yet appear what we shall be</u>: but we know that, when he [Christ the Lord] shall appear, <u>we shall be like him; for we shall see him as he is</u>.*

## Edit: *Silver and Gold Paradises*

Yet many men have speculated as to how life would be like in heaven, or to use their language, "Paradise."

The following are quotes from the Islamic prophet Muhammad. The quotes, as in all of this manuscript, are cut and paste from Islamic sources. And all bracketed comments, if any, are made by Islamic scholars and by them only. However, the underlining is that of the author.

The letters "pbuh" are an abbreviation of the words "peace be upon him," which sincere and devoted Muslims say each time whenever the name of their Islamic prophet is mentioned.

Finally, all Islamic edits in this manuscript are written on light green background; whereas Christian editorials are written on blue background.

*Bukhari*, 9, 536

The Prophet said, "(There will be) <u>two Paradises</u> of silver and all the utensils and whatever is therein (will be of silver); and two Paradises of gold, and its utensils and whatever therein (will be of gold)

*Muslim*, 40, 6798

Jabir reported: I heard Allah's Apostle (pbuh) as saying that <u>the inmates of Paradise would eat and drink but would neither spit, nor pass water, nor void excrement</u>, nor suffer catarrah.
It was said: Then, what would happen with food?
Thereupon he said: <u>They would belch and sweat (and it would be over with their food)</u>, and their sweat would be that of musk and they would glorify and praise Allah as easily as you breathe.

## *Paradise Virgins*

The maidens in Paradise, or the "houris," according to the Koran, are very special virgins who become virgin again after each intercourse. They have large eyes and large breasts.

*Bukhari*, 4, 544

Allah's Apostle said, "The first group of people who will enter <u>Paradise</u> ... and those who will follow them ... <u>will not urinate, relieve nature, spit, or have any nasal secretions</u>. Their combs will be of gold, and their sweat will smell like musk. The aloes-wood will be used in their centers. Their wives will be houris. All of them will look alike and will resemble their father Adam (in statute), sixty cubits tall. [100 ft or 32 m]"

*Qudsi*, 1, 91

Allah's Messenger (PBUH) said ... Allah has made in Paradise a wide valley in which He has created dunes of white musk. When it is Friday, Allah will

descend to it. The pulpits of gold are kept there for the Prophets and chairs made of pearl are arranged for the martyrs and the maidens with big lustrous eyes will get down from their upstairs rooms. They all praise Allah and glorify Him.
The Prophet said: Then Allah will say: Cloth My slaves. So they will be dressed. He will say: Feed My slaves. So they will be fed. He will say: Make them drink. So they will be made to drink. He will say: Perfume My slaves. So they will be perfumed. Then He will ask: What do you want? They will say: O' our Lord! We want Your pleasure. The Prophet said: Allah will say: I am pleased with you. Then He will order them to disperse.
So they will deport. And the maidens with big lustrous eyes ascend to the upstairs rooms, which are made of green emerald and red ruby.

## *Selling and Buying in Paradise*

*Muslim*, 40, 6792

Anas b. Malik reported that Allah's Messenger (pbuh) said: In Paradise there is a street to which they would come every Friday. The north wind will blow and would scatter fragrance on their faces and on their clothes

The Islamic prophet was superstitious about days. Nonetheless, Friday was a propitious day. It is the day the market opens in paradise.

*Muslim*, 32, 6222

Abu Huraira reported Allah's Messenger (pbuh) as saying: The gates of Paradise are not opened but on two days, Monday and Thursday.

*Dawud*, 14, 2599

It was rarely that the Apostle of Allah (pbuh) set out on a journey on any day but on a Thursday.

*Dawud*, 3, 1078

The Prophet (pbuh) disapproved of the offering of prayer at the meridian except on Friday. The Hell-fire is kindled except on Friday.

*Dawud*, 28, 3852

The Prophet (pbuh) said: If anyone has himself cupped on the 17th, 19th and 21st it will be a remedy for every disease.

*Muslim*, 1316

Allah's Apostle (PBUH) said: In Paradise there is a market to which they would come every Friday.

The Arabian prophet did also speak about farming as well as vegetation in Paradise.

*Bukhari, 9, 610*

The Prophet said, "<u>A man from among the people of Paradise</u> will request Allah to allow him to cultivate the land Allah will say to him, 'Haven't you got whatever you desire?'
He will reply, 'Yes, but I like to cultivate the land.' (Allah will permit him and) he will sow the seeds, and <u>within seconds the plants will grow and ripen and (the yield) will be harvested and piled in heaps like mountains</u>

*Bukhari, 3, 538*

Once the Prophet was narrating … "<u>One of the inhabitants of Paradise</u> will ask Allah to allow him to cultivate the land. Allah will ask him, 'Are you not living in the pleasures you like?' He will say, 'Yes, but I like to cultivate the land.' " The Prophet added, "When the man (will be permitted he) will sow the seeds and the plants will grow up and get ripe, ready for reaping and so on till it will be as huge as mountains <u>within a wink</u>.

*Sunan Ibn Majah, 14, 2306*

that the Messenger of Allah (saw) said: "Sheep are among the animals of Paradise.'"

*Bukhari, 54, 474*

The Prophet said, "There is a tree in Paradise (which is so big and huge that) if a rider travels in its shade for one hundred years, he would not be able to cross it."

He also spoke of other enjoyments in Paradise, specifically those granted to men.

The Apostle of Allah (pbuh) said: if anyone suppresses anger when he is in a position to give vent to it, Allah, the Exalted, will call him on the Day of Resurrection over the heads of all creatures, and ask him to <u>choose any of the bright and large eyed maidens he wishes</u>.

*Bukhari, 6, 402*

Allah's Apostle said, "<u>In Paradise</u> there is a pavilion made of a single hollow pearl sixty miles wide, <u>in each corner of which there are wives who will not see those in the other corners; and the believers will visit and enjoy them.</u>

*<u>Al-Tirmidhi, 1482</u>*

The Prophet (peace be upon him) said, "In Paradise the believer will be given such and such power to conduct sexual intercourse." He was asked whether he would be capable of that and replied that he would be given the capacity of a hundred men.

# The Greatest Two Events

Indeed, my lords, God's timetable of the earth has two major events.

The prophets, my lords, give us the exact year of the first great event.

But they do not tell us the year of the second event. They only tell us the signs that show that the event is getting close.

The timetable of God, my lords, gives us the exact year of the death and resurrection of God's gift to man. And in doing so, my lords, the date leaves no one in doubt that indeed the One we beheld was indeed the Lamb, the sacrifice of God that takes away the sin of the world.

Go ahead, please, prophet Isaiah, and tell their majesties of the Lamb of God, the sacrifice of God that takes away the sins of their majesties and qualifies them for the life eternal.

> IS 9:6 *unto us a child is born, unto us a son is given: and the government shall be upon his shoulder: and his name shall be called Wonderful, Counsellor, The mighty God, The everlasting Father, The Prince of Peace.*
>
> IS 9:7 *Of the increase of his government and peace there shall be no end … from henceforth even for ever.*
>
> IS 53:5 *But he [Christ the Lord] was wounded for our transgressions, he was bruised for our iniquities: the chastisement of our peace was upon him; and with his stripes we are healed.*

Prophet Daniel, my lords, prophesied of the exact year Christ would appear amongst us—His first coming.

But we caution you, my lords, that Daniel's prophecy would seem difficult to understand at this time. Yet it shall become very clear, my lords, later on as we slowly walk to its station on the highway of prophecy.

Go ahead, please, prophet Daniel.

> DAN 9:24 *Seventy weeks are determined upon thy people [490 years] and upon thy holy city, to finish the transgression, and to make an end of sins, and to make reconciliation for iniquity [to bring about God's pardon of sin through the sacrifice of His son Christ Jesus], and to bring in everlasting righteousness [pardon], and to seal up the vision and prophecy [to fulfill the prophecies about the first coming of Christ to give His life a ransom for all], and to anoint the most Holy [Christ Jesus the Lord].*

> DAN 9:25 *Know therefore and understand, that from the going forth of the commandment [by whom? We shall soon understand, my lords] to restore and to build Jerusalem unto the Messiah the Prince shall be seven weeks, and threescore and two weeks [476 years]: the street shall be built again, and the wall, even in troublous times.*
>
> DAN 9:26 *And after threescore and two weeks shall Messiah be cut off [crucified], but not for himself [not because of His sins]: and the people of the prince that shall come [the Romans] shall destroy the city [Jerusalem] and the sanctuary [the temple, 70 AD]; and the end thereof shall be with a flood [the children of Israel scattered all over the world as carried away by a flood], and unto the end of the war desolations [Israel deserted] are determined.*

However, my lords, God's timetable, which gave the exact year of the birth of Christ, the exact year of the destruction of the temple, and its related 666 keeps the date of the second major event on the calendar of the earth absolutely secret—the day in which Christ the Lord returns again to earth, the day of rapture, of which we have already spoken, my lords. The day when the access to the heavens is shut close.

> MAT 25:10 *and the door was shut.*
>
> LUKE 13:25 *and ye begin to stand without, and to knock at the door, saying, Lord, Lord, open unto us; and he shall answer and say unto you, I know you not whence ye are:*
>
> LK 13:29 *And they [the children of God] shall come from the east, and from the west, and from the north, and from the south [from all races and nations]*
>
> MAT 25:34 <u>*Come, ye blessed of my Father, inherit the kingdom prepared for you from the foundation of the world:*</u>

The timetable keeps this day secret, your majesties, so that we, the people of the earth, should always be ready to meet with the God of the whole inhabitable universe, as the preachers of Israel say, my lords.

## *The Last and Final Interview*

> Am 4:12 *Therefore ... prepare to meet thy God*

Try as much as we wish, my lords, we shall never be able to nail down the date of the second coming of the son of God. We shall only be able to tell, my lords, whether the day is far in the future or near at hand.

Is this understanding correct, apostle Matthew?

MAT 24:33 *ye, when ye shall see all these things [these events happen], <u>know that it is near, even at the doors</u>*

Now, my lords, it is this secret date of the second appearance of Christ, the day the door is closed, is the date that the majority of the people consider to be the date of the end of the world.

Go ahead, please, apostle Matthew and apostle Peter, and speak to their majesties of what you have been told regarding the day of closing the door to the kingdom of God.

MAT 24:36 *of that day and hour knoweth no man, no, not the angels of heaven, but my Father only.*
MAT 24:37 *But as the days of Noe [Noah] were [in the ancient days leading to the flood of Noah's time], so shall also the coming of the Son of man be [Christ Jesus].*
MAT 24:38 *For as in the days that were before the flood they were eating and drinking, marrying and giving in marriage, until the day that Noe entered into the ark,*
MAT 24:39 *And knew not until the flood came, and took them all away; so shall also the coming of the Son of man be.*
MAT 24:40 *Then shall two be in the field; the one shall be taken, and the other left.*
MAT 24:41 *Two women shall be grinding at the mill; the one shall be taken, and the other left.*
MAT 24:42 *Watch therefore: for ye know not what hour your Lord doth come.*
MAT 24:44 *Therefore be ye also ready: for in such an hour as ye think not the Son of man cometh.*
2 PET 3:10 *the day of the Lord will come as a thief in the night; in the which the heavens shall pass away with a great noise, and the elements shall melt with fervent heat, the earth also and the works that are therein shall be burned up.*

## The Ruler of Planet Earth

But Israel, the nation of the prophets, the calendar of the world, and of whom the savior of the world was to come, my lords, has an enemy. Israel has a very intelligent and a very powerful enemy. Israel's enemy, my lords, was and is absolutely determined to exterminate her and end its message of the future.

More than that, my lords, Israel's enemy, knowing full well that he cannot defeat the Messiah, the child of Israel, came up with a wise and different strategy. His strategy, my lords, was and still is centered on spotting and helping as many antichrists and false prophets as he could find in order to muddle and confuse the people of the world by the millions. He has succeeded so far, my lords.

And his efforts, your majesties, shall intensify in the final stages of the world as he becomes aware that his end is near. The events, which shall befall Israel shall also, my lords, show him that his time is soon up. And so at that time, my lords, he shall be allowed to drop his mask and shall act in an open way and with great violence as he bestows his incredible power on his false prophet, and his false prophet's followers.

Indeed, my lords, he shall enable the followers of his false prophet to bring fire down from heaven— nuclear power.

Please, go ahead, apostles Matthew, Mark, and John, you know what we are referring to here.

> MK 13:22 *false Christs and false prophets shall rise, and shall shew signs [miracles] and wonders, to seduce, if it were possible, even the elect.*
> REV 13:13 *And he doeth great wonders, so that <u>he maketh fire come down from heaven on the earth in the sight of men</u>,*
> REV 13:14 *And deceiveth them that dwell on the earth by the means of those miracles which he had power to do in the sight of the beast; saying to them that dwell on the earth, that they should make an image to the beast, which had the wound by a sword, and did live.*
> REV 13:18 *Here is wisdom. Let him that hath understanding count the number of the beast: for it is the number of a man; <u>and his number is Six hundred threescore and six</u> [666, a number, which soon the prophecy shall show who it is associated with].*
> MK 13:23 *But take ye heed: behold, I have foretold you all things.*

At that time, my lords, a war in the heavens, a war in space shall take place, and space shall be on fire as the world nears its end.

Carry on, please, apostle John.

> REV 12:7 *And there was war in heaven*
> REV 12:12 *[the prince of this world] <u>having great wrath, because he knoweth that he hath but a short time</u>.*

## End of the World

Many have speculated about the end of the world while mixing up many unrelated events.

But even though their speculations were the result of their own imaginations, they still proclaimed themselves to be prophets.

And so the warning came: Be fair to yourself; do not lay your eternal future to their trust. What else can be more important than securing the future—the irreversible future? Be fair to yourself.

> Deut 18:22 When a prophet speaketh in the name of the LORD, if the thing follow not [if his prophecy does not happen], nor come to pass, that is the thing which the LORD hath not spoken [it is not a prophecy from the Lord], but the prophet hath spoken it presumptuously [made it up]: thou shalt not be afraid of him [he is a false prophet].

## An Island in the Sea

According to the Bible, an antichrist would do a major harm during the period of the great tribulation. And so many have speculated who is this particular Antichrist would be, and whether he has already come or he is yet to come.

The Islamic prophet Muhammad, having also heard about the Antichrist, went on to include him in his preaching.

To begin, Saudi Arabia in his time was in the middle of converting from paganism to Judaism and then to Christianity.

Indeed, a cousin of the Arabian prophet's first wife was a literate man who read the Bible, became a Christian, and went on to preach his new faith to his fellow Arabs, who, unlike him, were mostly illiterate.

In the course of time, Muhammad went to his relative to learn about the Bible.

The events of the end of the world left a strong impression on Muhammad. The middle-aged man became extremely frightened, so much so that he indeed attempted a couple of times to commit suicide by jumping from a mountain near Mecca, where he originally lived.

Failing to commit suicide, he then returned home and wrapped himself up while shivering in sweat and fever.

Later on, he ran away from Mecca and came to Medina [c.622 AD], a town whose population was under the Jewish influence, and whose population traded with one of the largest Jewish communities in Saudi Arabia of the time.

This large Jewish community lived in the Fortress of Khaibar for hundreds of years [For supporting quotes, see *Earth out of Orbit, Volume 1, the Past and Future Prophecies of the World* as well as *Earth out of Orbit, Volume 2, The Apocalypse of the Great Tribulation and Armageddon*. Both volumes can be found on the Internet free of charge.

For the balance of this manuscript, these two previous volumes will be abbreviated as: EOO01 and EOO02].

The middle-aged Muhammad aspired to do as his relative and teach what he learned from the Bible to his fellow Arabs. However, as he was an illiterate man, he could only recite that which he was told. And so when he later on began to add his own stories and teachings, he was no longer accepted by the Jewish rabbis or the Christian preachers. From that time on, he turned on both.

One of his teachings included those about the Antichrist, which is called *Dajjal* in Arabic.

The following Islamic quotes are taken from the Islamic sacred books of the Hadith of the Islamic prophet Muhammad. The quotes once again are cut and pasted without any editing or commentary other than the bracketed ones, which are made by Islamic scholars.

*Bukhari, 4, 55, 553*

Once Allah's Apostle stood amongst the people, glorified and praised Allah as He deserved and then mentioned the Dajjal saying, "I warn you against him (i.e. the Dajjal) and there was no prophet but warned his nation against him ... but I tell you about him something of which no prophet told his nation before me. You should know that <u>he is one-eyed</u>".

*Dawud, 37, 4306*

The Prophet (pbuh) said: I have told you so much about the Dajjal (Antichrist) that I am afraid you may not understand. <u>The Antichrist is short, hen-toed, woolly-haired, one-eyed</u>, an eye-sightless, and neither protruding nor deep-seated.

Presumably two Rhode Island Red Hens in Bangkok, the image shows their toes, which are the same as the toes of the Antichrist, according to the Islamic prophet Muhammad, Thailand, March 2014 (image source: WC, dshlfred).

The Arabian prophet, basing his faith on a story by a Christian convert, whose name is Tamim Dari, and thirty Jewish sailors from the two Jewish tribes of Bani Lakhm and Bani Judham, also preached that the Antichrist has already come and was indeed spotted in his day.

There were a number of Christian and Jewish Arabs who had converted to Islam. Some did so superficially in order to escape beheading or financial mistreatment.

This was not the only incident that the Arabian prophet based his teachings on Jewish traditions and legends. Indeed, there are numerous other incidents such as that of the flying horse. In fact, the Arabian prophet learned of the flying horse from his child-wife Aisha, who in turn had learned about it from a Jewish woman [see EOOO.1].

A silver coin, stater, from Corinth represents Pegasus, c. 500 BC, Archaeological Museum of Cambridge, UK (image source: author).

Pegasus on coins from Thyrrheion and Corinth, Numismatic Museum of Athens, Greece (image source: author). In Greek mythology, Pegasus went to heaven to meet with Zeus, king of the gods. The Islamic prophet Muhammad preached that he was carried on a flying horse from Jerusalem up to heaven in order to meet with Allah, God.

*Dawud*, 37, 4311

The Apostle of Allah (pbuh) once delayed the congregational night prayer. He came out and said: The talk of Tamim ad-Dari detained me. He transmitted it to me from a man who was on one of the islands of the sea. All of a sudden he found a woman who was trailing her hair. He asked: Who are you?
She said: I am the Jassasah. Go to that castle.
So I came to it and found a man who was trailing his hair, chained in iron collars, and leaping between Heaven and Earth.
I asked: Who are you?
He replied: <u>I am the Dajjal (Antichrist)</u>. Has the Prophet of the unlettered people come forth now?
I replied: Yes. He said: Have they obeyed him or disobeyed him?
I said: No, they have obeyed him.
He said: That is better for them.

*Muslim*, 41, 7028

When Allah's Messenger (pbuh) had finished his prayer, he sat on the pulpit smiling and said: Every worshipper should keep sitting at his place.
He then said: Do you know why I had asked you to assemble?
They said: Allah and His Messenger know best.
He said: By Allah. I have not made you assemble for exhortation or for a warning, but I have detained you here, for Tamim Dari, a Christian, who came and accepted Islam, told me something, which agrees with what I was telling, you about the Dajjal.
He narrated to me that he had sailed in a ship along with thirty men of Bani Lakhm and Bani Judham and had been tossed by waves in the ocean for a month. Then these (waves) took them (near) the land within the ocean (island) at the time of sunset. They sat in a small side-boat and entered that Island.
There was a beast with long thick hair (and because of these) they could not distinguish his face from his back. They said: Woe to you, who can you be?
Thereupon it said: I am al-Jassasa.
They said: What is al-Jassasa?
And it said: O people, go to this person in the monastery as he is very much eager to know about you.
He (the narrator) said: When it named a person for us we were afraid of it lest it should be a Devil. Then we hurriedly went on till we came to that monastery and found <u>a well-built person there with his hands tied to his neck and having iron shackles between his two legs up to the ankles.</u>
We said: Woe be upon thee, who are you?
And he said: You would soon come to know about me. but tell me who are you.
We said: We are people from Arabia and we embarked upon a boat but the sea-waves had been driving us for one month and they brought as near this island. We got into the side-boats and entered this island and here a beast met us with profusely thick hair and because of the thickness of his hair his face could not be distinguished from his back. We said: Woe be to thee, who are you? It said: I am al- Jassasa. We said: What is al-Jassasa? And it said: You go to this very person in the monastery for he is eagerly

waiting for you to know about you. So we came to you in hot haste fearing that that might be the Devil.
He (that chained person) said: Tell me about the date-palm trees of Baisan.
We said: About what aspect of theirs do you seek information?
He said: I ask you whether these trees bear fruit or not.
We said: Yes
Thereupon he said: I think these would not bear fruits. He said: Inform me about the lake of Tabariyya? We said: Which aspect of it do you want to know?
He said: Is there water in it?
They said: There is abundance of water in it.
Thereupon he said: I think it would soon become dry.
He again said: Inform me about the spring of Zughar. They said: Which aspect of it you want to know? He (the chained person) said: Is there water in it and does it irrigate (the land)?
We said to him: Yes, there is abundance of water in it and the inhabitants (of Medina) irrigate (land) with the help of it,
He said: Inform me about the unlettered Prophet; what has he done?
We said: He has come out from Mecca and has settled In Yathrib (Medina).
He said: Do the Arabs fight against him?
We said: Yes.
He said: How did he deal with him?
We informed him that he had overcome those in his neighbourhood and they had submitted themselves before him.
Thereupon he said to us: Had it actually happened?
We said: Yes. Thereupon he said: If it is so that is better for them that they should show obedience to him. I am going to tell you about. myself and I am Dajjal <u>and would be soon permitted to get out</u> and so I shall get out and travel in the land, and will not spare any town where I would not stay for forty nights except Mecca and Medina as these two (places) are prohibited (areas) for me and I would not make an attempt to enter any one of these two. An angel with a sword in his hand would confront me and would bar my way and there would be angels to guard every passage leading to it; then Allah's Messenger (pbuh) striking the pulpit with the help of the end of his staff said:
This implies Taiba meaning Medina. Have I not, told you an account (of the Dajjal) like this?
'The people said: Yes, and this account narrated by Tamim Dari was liked by me for it corroborates the account which I gave to you in regard to him (Dajjal) at Medina and Mecca.
<u>Behold he (Dajjal) is in the Syrian sea (Mediterranean) or the Yemen sea (Arabian sea). Nay, on the contrary, he is In the east, he is in the east, he is in the east, and he pointed with his hand towards the east.</u>

According to the prediction of the Islamic prophet the end of the world should have taken place one hundred years after his death. He died June 632 of our era. Thus the end of the world should have taken place around the year 732 AD.

> Furthermore, according to him, there would be nothing of all creatures alive after the year 732 AD, that is, nothing at all; no man, no animal and no trees should have remained alive for the last 1,250 years.
>
> *Muslim:* 31. 6165
>
> Abu Sa'id reported that when Allah's Apostle (pbuh) came back from Tabuk they (his Companions) asked about the Last Hour. Thereupon Allah's Messenger (pbuh) said: <u>There would be none amongst the created beings living on the earth (who would survive this century)</u>.
>
> *Muslim,* 31, 6162
>
> Jabir b. 'Abdullah reported: I heard Allah's Messenger (pbuh) <u>as saying this one month before his death</u>: You asked me about the Last Hour whereas its knowledge is with Allah.
> I, however, <u>take an oath</u> and say that none upon the earth, the created beings, would survive at the end of one hundred years.
>
> *Bukhari,* 8, 73, 188
>
> Narrated Anas:
> A bedouin came to the Prophet and said, "O Allah's Apostle! When will The Hour be established?"
>
> In the meantime, a slave of Al-Mughira passed by, and he was of the same age as I was. The Prophet said, "<u>If this (slave) should live long, he will not reach the geriatric old age, but the Hour will be established</u>."

## My Friend

My lords, we must now travel back in time to visit the events that made Israel the nation of the prophets and the calendar of the earth.

Nearly 3,500 years ago, my lords, lived a very wealthy man by the name of Abraham. In his day, the people knew him as Abraham, but later the prophets called him the "friend of God" because this is what God Himself had called him.

> IS 41:8 *Abraham my friend.*

My lords, God put Abraham through trials and tests, and taught him of His future plan for mankind— God's family – salvation, resurrection, transformation, and eternal life in the vast universe.

> LK 20:35 *they which shall be accounted worthy to obtain that world [the new world to come], and the resurrection from the dead*
> LK 20:36 *Neither can they die any more: for they are equal unto the angels; and are the children of God, being the children of the resurrection.*

God, my lords, taught Abraham, His friend, that this earth is an inn, a motel. It is not home; it is a foreign land. And that Abraham was only travelling on this foreign land on his way to the home of God, the city of God, the celestial cities of tomorrow.

> HEB 13:14 *For here have we no continuing city, but we seek one to come.*

Abraham grew convinced, my lords and sovereigns, that the purpose of life is heaven—the future home of those who loved God.

And so your majesties, Abraham walked, strolled, lived, and breathed in heaven because it was there that his heart lived. Abraham, my lords, raised cattle on earth, dug water wells, planted, harvested and did all the things that people do to live and prosper, but his heart was always amongst the stars, his future home.

Is this interpretation correct, apostle Paul?

> HEB 11:8 *Abraham*
> HEB 11:9 *By faith he sojourned in the land of promise, as in a strange country, dwelling in tabernacles [tents] …*
> HEB 11:10 *For he looked for <u>a city which hath foundations [eternal city – not temporal like tents], whose builder and maker is God</u>.*

Abraham, your majesties, saw the heaven of heavens clearly from afar. He stood one foot below it, and so while his feet walked on earth, his mind and soul lived in the kingdom of heaven, the immense city of God with all its houses and stars.

And so this faith, and this great joy, my lords, made Abraham grow closer to the Lord, "the most high God, the possessor [owner] of heaven and earth." And indeed the Lord God, the owner of the country of heaven and earth, loved him, called him "my friend," and promised him: You shall never walk alone. "Fear not, Abram: I am thy shield [protector], and thy exceeding great reward [I am your great prize]."

Carry on please, apostle Paul, and speak to their majesties of the world to come—the world without end.

> HEB 11:13 *having seen them afar off [God's promises], and were persuaded of them, and embraced them, and confessed that they [he and his family] were <u>strangers [foreigners] and pilgrims on the earth</u>.*
> HEB 11:14 *For they that say such things declare plainly that <u>they seek a country</u> [homeland].*

HEB 11:16 *But now they desire <u>a better country</u>, that is, <u>an heavenly</u> [country]: wherefore God is not ashamed to be called their God: for he hath prepared for them a city.*
LK 10:20 <u>*rejoice, because your names are written in heaven.*</u>
1 JN 2:25 *And this is the promise that he hath promised us, even <u>eternal life</u> [in the heavens].*

## Good News and Bad News

Sadly, your majesties, this very wealthy and aged man Abraham, who had a very beautiful wife by the name of Sarah, was childless. Abraham had no heir, no sons or daughters to inherit his vast possessions. More importantly, my lords, Abraham had no heir who could preach his faith and joy to the following generations. Yet, my lords, the preacher of the world was indeed born out of this barren and infertile beginning.

The processor and owner of heavens and earth made Abraham a Promise: Abraham, you shall have a son even in your and your wife's old age, for there is nothing impossible for me—is there?

"Is anything too hard for the LORD? At the time appointed I will return unto thee, according to the time of life [within nine months], and Sarah [your wife] shall have a son," went the promise.

And the Lord told Abraham to name his promised son "Isaac," meaning laughter or joy.

This was the first part of the prophecy, my lords: joy.

Abraham, you and your very aged wife will start a family, a family that will give birth to many godly men and prophets. But more importantly, Abraham, your family shall give birth to the Messiah, the "Lamb of God," the sacrifice of God, which pays for the sins of the people of the earth—joy to the world!

> ROM 9:5 *of whom [of Abraham] as concerning the flesh Christ came, who is over all, God blessed for ever. Amen.*

One day, my lords, Abraham climbed up the mount of Moriah with the intention of sacrificing his one and only son. Why? He wanted to do so as a proof for his love to God.

No, Abraham.

Stop.

I know your love.

It is now for me Abraham to prove my love to you and to Isaac by sacrificing my one and only begotten son. I shall do so in the fullness of time,

Abraham. But for now I provide you with a lamb. He is the symbol of "the Lamb of God who takes away the sins of the world."

And so, my lords, when Isaac, the promised son, up on the mountain asked his father, "Father, where is the sacrifice?" his godly father gave his son a prophetic answer.

May we now, your majesties, ask the prophet Moses to tell you what answer did Abraham give his one and only son? Go ahead, please, prophet Moses.

> GEN 22:8 *Abraham said, My son, God will provide himself a lamb [the lamb of God]*

There, my lords, there in this lands of Moriah, and up on one of its hills, there one day a temple, the house of God was to be built, to be destroyed, to be rebuilt, and destroyed once more.

And each time this happens, a date is set on the calendar of God—dates, which would explain, among others, the number 666 of the Antichrist.

Indeed, my lords, prophet Daniel, who has already testified before you, shall later on prophecy to you that one day a building shall be built on that same spot where the Lamb, which God provided, the Lamb of God, was slain. This building, thus occupying the same spot, shall therefore prevent the rebuilding of the house of God for a third time.

My lords, this building stands there today. And it is called the Dome of the Rock. And it was built in the exact year the prophecy calculated—666.

The Islamic Dome of the Rock sits on the site of the house of the Lord and prevents rebuilding it. The date of its construction explains the number is 666 of the false prophet, as shall be seen (image source: Wikipedia).

This then was good news for Abraham, your majesties; he shall leave a godly son and a family to keep the message of the plan and timetable of God alive.

But there was also bad news, my lords.

Abraham, your offspring, your grandchildren, your future family, the prophets and preachers of the world, shall become slaves.

How can the family of an exceedingly wealthy man who has his own army and a large number of servants become slaves?

They shall be enslaved, imprisoned in a foreign and powerful country, Abraham.

But then they shall be freed from their harsh slavery and return to the land of Canaan, where you are residing today, Abraham. And with their miraculous deliverance from slavery and imprisonment, I shall, Abraham, build a reputation for myself amongst the surrounding nations, so that the world may begin to know me, call upon me, and receive my gift of eternal life through the sacrifice of my son.

And then, your majesties, the prophecy carried on to tell Abraham that 430 years shall pass from the day he arrived to the land of Canaan, the present land of Israel, my lords, until his grandchildren would miraculously break away from where they were kept in slavery.

And so this is the second part of the prophecy, my lords: enslavement and then freedom and return home.

And indeed in the course of time, my lords, Abraham became the father of Isaac. And Isaac became the father of Jacob, whose name was changed to Israel, for a good reason, my lords.

> *HEB 11:12 Therefore sprang there even of one, and him as good as dead [old and barren], so many as the stars of the sky in multitude, and as the sand which is by the sea shore innumerable.*

And so in the course of time, my lords, Jacob Israel's children, the children of Israel, went down to a foreign land, Egypt, ahead of a famine, which plagued the land of Canaan where they lived.

They went down to Egypt, my lords, to "the beautiful garden of Osiris," as the ancient Egyptians called their homeland. And this, your majesties, was the start of what would become the nation of the prophets and the calendar of the earth.

## *Endless Hatred*

The aging Abraham was egged along by his wife Sarah to take one of her maiden servants, an Egyptian woman by the name of Hagar, as a wife in order for Abraham to secure an heir for his wealth.

This indeed took place nearly four years prior to the prophecy that he would have a son, Isaac, by his own aging wife Sarah.

And so in due time, the Egyptian servant Hagar bore Abraham a son. And Abraham named him "Ishmael."

As time went by, this older child Ishmael, son of the Egyptian servant Hagar, took advantage of his age and beat and mistreated the younger Isaac, the legitimate heir of wealthy Abraham, born of his wife Sarah.

And again in the course of time, this Ishmael would become the ancestor of the tribes that lived in northern Arabia.

And the hatred that young Ishmael bore against Isaac was a prototype of the hatred that carried on throughout all the past ages and still carries on even today, a perpetual hatred, between Arabs and Israelites.

> Gal 4:29 *But as then he that was born after the flesh [Ishmael] persecuted him that was born after the Spirit [Isaac], <u>even so it is now</u>.*
> Ezek 35:5 *thou hast had <u>a perpetual hatred</u>, and hast shed the blood of the children of Israel by the force of the sword*

Indeed, according to the prophecy, as shall be seen, much of Arabia's wealth shall, at the time of the end, go up in flames as burning bitumen. Iran shall rejoice for it.

## Chapter Two

# Hail to the King of Egypt, Who Shines Like the Sun

Your majesties, the years had passed. And then the exact date for fulfilling the second part of the prophecy, the freedom from Egypt, had arrived.

My lords, the timing for fulfilling the freedom prophecy could not have been any worse—it was the very worst of times.

Indeed, my lords, in the eyes of the children of Israel at that time, there was absolutely no way that the prophecy of their freedom could be fulfilled. The timing was the most unlikely of times and the most unsuitable times by far.

But the prophecy was fulfilled, my lords.

Go ahead, please, prophet Moses, tell their majesties of the events on the calendar.

> GEN 15:13 *And he [the Lord] said unto Abram, Know of a surety that thy seed [offspring] shall be a stranger in a land that is not theirs [Canaan and Egypt], and shall serve them; and <u>they shall afflict them four hundred years [430 years of slavery minus 30 years of tolerance during the reign of an Israelite by the name of Joseph]</u>;* GEN 15:14 *and afterward <u>shall they come out with great substance</u> [freed but also enriched].*

This exodus of the beaten and helpless Israelite slaves from Egypt, my lords, took place, not in the days of a weak Egyptian king as one would have expected, but rather—and as unbelievable as this may sound to you your majesties—the exodus and the freeing of the long-held Israelite slaves took place in the years when Egypt was at its summit of power, right after the rule of its greatest king ever, bar none, my lords.

Not only that, my lords, but their exodus took place in the nick of time as the Egyptian pharaohs had already begun a pogrom intended to exterminate and destroy the race of the children of Israel by killing all their newborn males.

Incidentally, your majesties, this genocide was but one of several future attempts to exterminate the nation of the prophets, the nation of the Savior from the face of the earth. Many more would follow this first attempt, my lords, and even to our modern day. The prince, the ruler of our world, has and is always looking for the opportunity to destroy and exterminate Israel, God's clock, and his greatest worry.

But Israel, my lords, was rescued. It was rescued by a prince, a prince, my lords, who was raised in the very same palace of the most powerful man on earth. The prince's name my lords, is Moses, who stood before you several times already.

Please reflect on this for a minute, my sovereigns. The children of Israel were rescued in the nick of time, by an unexpected man, and on the heel of the reign of the most powerful man on earth. A mighty hand was working behind the scene, my lords.

Where is His Majesty King Thusmosis III?
Here you are, sir.
Hail to the king of Egypt, who shines like the sun!

Is it true, my sovereign, King Thusmosis III, lord of sunlight? Is it true that you owned the largest swath of the Middle East that no pharaoh before you ever owned sir?

Is it true, your majesty, that you became king of countries: king of Iraq, Syria, Lebanon, Jordan, Israel, Palestine, Arabia [home of the sand crossers], Libya [of the feather-wearing barbarians], and the Sudan [the country of the gum eaters]. Or are you exaggerating your unbelievable achievements and the boundaries of your great worldly empire, my lord?

Would you please, your majesty, read to my lords a bit of your record, which your scribes had chiseled out upon the walls of the Karnack Temple in Luxor, your ancient capital city!

> "I have not uttered exageration, in order to boast of that which I did, saying: 'I have done something' although my majesty had not done it ... I have done this for my father [the god Amon] ... I swear as Re loves me, as my father [Amon] praises me, as my nostrils are filled with satisfying life, I have done this."[1]

Yes, my sovereign, "that is correct a million times", as your expression goes, sir.

---

[1] *Ancient Records of Egypt*, James Henery Breasted, University of Illinois Press, 2001, V. 2, 570, 226.

King Thutmose III smiting Canaanite enemies on the seventh pylon at Karnack describing the Battle of Megiddo (the future location where the Moslem armies and mobs of the east shall in the future gather to besiege Jerusalem city), 15th Century BC (image source: WC, Markh).

But may we also tell you, my sovereign King Thusmosis III, that not only before you, sir, but even till this morning of today, no other Egyptian pharaoh, king, or president has ever ruled over so many nations and countries as you did, sir! "By your face, my great lord," you are the greatest of them all, even greater than your successor His Majesty King Ramses the Great.

Edit: For surprising archaeological Egyptian discoveries, see EO00.1 and EO00.2

The might of the 18th Egyptian dynasty, which included the great King Thusmosis III and Queen Hatshepsut (the adopted mother of Moses), and during which dynasty Moses freed the children of Israel from their slavery in the lands of the superpower Egypt, British Museum (image source: author).

50—EARTH OUT OF ORBIT

RIGHT: King Thutmose III, before whom Moses fled to the desert of Sinai, where he stayed for forty years before finally returning to Egypt upon the death of the king. At that time, Egypt was at the summit of its power, Wien Museum, Vienna, Austria (image source: author).

Ex 2:15 Now when Pharaoh (Thutmose III) heard this thing (Moses' rebellion), he sought to slay Moses. But Moses fled from the face of Pharaoh, and dwelt in the land of Median (in the Sinai desert)

Ex 2:23 And it came to pass in process of time, that the king of Egypt (Thutmose III) died: and the children of Israel sighed by reason of the bondage (slavery), and they cried, and their cry came up unto God by reason of the bondage.

ABOVE LEFT: Queen Htshepsut, the adopting mother of biblical Moses; thus, Moses was a contestant for the throne of Egypt following her death, Berlin Alts Museum (image source: author).

"I will cause it to be said to prosperity: "How beautiful is she," wrote her father, King Thutmose I. "My sweet daughter, my favorite," proclaimed the god Amun-Re.

ABOVE RIGHT: Gold sandals, Toe and Finger Stalls, t belong to a minor wife of King Thutmose III, Metropolitan Museum of Art, NY (image source: author).

# HAIL TO THE KING OF EGYPT—51

ABOVE: A recent discovery (2007) of the mummy of Queen Hatshepsut, the adoping mother of biblical Moses, Cairo Museum (image source: unknown).

Baskets from Moses' time. The Metropolitan Museum, NY, USA (image source: author).

Ex 2:5-10 And the daughter of Pharaoh (Princess Hatshepsut) came down to wash herself at the river; and her maidens walked along by the river's side; and when she saw the ark (basket) among the flags (reeds), she sent her maid to fetch it. And when she had opened it, she saw the child: and, behold, the babe wept. And she had compassion on him ... and he became her son. And she called his name Moses (See EOOO.1 and EOOO.2 for evidence)

## Make Us Wise

See EO001 for the mysterious Egyptian official, the intimate of Queen Hatchepsut, who was most likely the biblical Moses, the man who led the children of Israel out of Egypt.

Moses was a highly educated man and a man of many talents. He may have been in fact the archatict who most likely built the Egyptian temple most visited by tourists in our modern times. He was also a military man who presumably had led the Egyptian armies into the Sudan.

But then at the peak of his power, he suddenly and mysteriously disappeared.

Later on, as he began to assess his life and his achievements, he had to face a sobering reality: whether we are powerful or ordinary folks, our days on earth are short.

And so he prayed:

God, make us wise in how to use our short days on earth. God, teach us to make our life worthwhile. Make it count.

An innovative ecryptogram designed by Moses. An ecryptogram is a statue whose components spell a name. In this case it spelled the name of his adoptive mother, Queen Hatshepsut, c.1478-1458 BC, found in Armant of southern Egypt, Brooklyn Museum, NY (image source: author).

*Ps 90:12 So teach us to number our days, that we may apply our hearts unto wisdom.*

And this Moses is the man whom many church preachers today end their sermons by quoting the loving words he used to bless the children of Israel.

*Num 6:23 Speak unto Aaron [Moses' brother] and unto his sons, saying, On this wise ye shall bless the children of Israel, saying unto them,*
*Num 6:24 The LORD bless thee, and keep thee:*
*Num 6:25 The LORD make his face shine upon thee, and be gracious unto thee:*
*Num 6:26 The LORD lift up his countenance upon thee, and give thee peace.*

Now, my lords, when your great companion, His Egyptian Majesty King Thusmosis III, "penetrated the sky, being joined to the sun disk"—that is to say he died—he was succeeded by His Majesty King Amunhotep II.

## 1436 BC Exodus

And so it was, my lords, that this great event in the timetable of God, which is called the Exodus, took place at the peak of Egypt's power and under the rule of its youthful and arrogant King Amunhotep II.

It took place on the exact day God had foretold His friend Abraham—April 15, 1436 BC. This is a date, my lords, that shall be used to calculate other future dates. It is a day to remember.

Go ahead, please, apostle Luke and prophet Moses.

> ACTS 7:17 <u>But when the time of the promise [according to God's timetable] drew nigh [near]</u>
> EX 12:41 *And it came to pass at the end of the four hundred and thirty years, <u>even the selfsame day it came to pass, that all the hosts of the LORD [the children of Israel] went out from the land of Egypt</u>.*
> EX 12:42 <u>It is a night to be much observed</u> *unto the LORD for bringing them out from the land of Egypt: this is that night of the LORD to be observed of all the children of Israel in their generations.*

The preacher nation of the world, my lords, has survived the extermination and emerged out of Egypt and came home, a central location, to preach holiness, and to preach God's plan and His timetable to the world——a plan and a timetable that was entrusted to them and their godly prophets, one single and clear voice from Israel to the world.

King Amunhotep II, circa 1426-1400 BC. He is the king of Exodus who refused to let the children of Israel leave Egypt, Brooklyn Museum, New York (image source: author).

## 54—EARTH OUT OF ORBIT

RIGHT: Moses of the biblical Exodus, the Metropolitan Museum, New York (image source: author). See EOOO1. Moses, who was in line of the throne of Egypt, preferred the future over the present.

Heb 11:24 By faith Moses, when he was come to years, refused to be called the son of Pharaoh's daughter (her heir to the throne of Egypt);
Heb 11:25 Choosing rather to suffer affliction with the people of God, than to enjoy the pleasures of sin for a season (the short present)
Heb 11:26 Esteeming the reproach of Christ greater riches than the treasures in Egypt: for he had respect unto the recompence of the reward (the future reward).
Heb 11:27 By faith he forsook Egypt, not fearing the wrath of the king (King Thutmose III): for he endured, as seeing him who is invisible (as if seeing God).

ABOVE: Is this the mummy of King Amenhotep II? Boils are found on the mummy of the king of the Exodus. Boils were one of the ten plagues that afflicted Egypt during the days of the Exodus (image source: unknown).

Ex 9:11 And the magicians could not stand before Moses because of the boils; for the boil was upon the magicians, and upon all the Egyptians.

Some of the plagues, the natural disasters, so to speak, that struck Egypt, shall strike the earth in its last years.

## *Skipping Ahead*

A few hundred years following their freedom and return to their homeland, the preacher nation Israel was then uprooted, and exiled to southern Iraq, home of the Shiite Muslims of today.

> And from there, they were dispersed in Syria, Iraq [Babylon], and Iran—the lands of their enemies.
>
> This exile would become their first exile as a nation, and it is known as the Babylonian exile.
>
> Now exiled and scattered in Iran and Iraq [Babylon], they were naturally expected to integrate, die off, and perish as a race. But yet they survived and even returned home from a near and complete extermination.
>
> It was another miraculous event. Thy were saved by the king of their prisoners and jailors.
>
> At that time, the time of their return from the Babylonian exile, began the countdown to another major event in the life of the preacher nation. For once again, and for the second time, Israel was to be uprooted and chaesd away from its homeland. And in this second exile, they were not to be displaced to Egypt, Babylon, and Iran only; they were to be despersed and fanned out all over the world. Now this second and last exile is called the Roman exile.
>
> But, once again, from a near complete disappearance from the surface of the earth, they were to return a second and last time from their worldwide exile.
>
> It happened.
>
> And once again they were saved by the most powerful. This time they were saved by the rulers of Western Europe and America.
>
> Israel survived extermination, once, twice, and three times.
>
> Now, this second and last return, which happened only a few years ago, is scheduled to open a chain of major events, including the worldwide great tribulation.

# 1398/1397 BC
# Long View from Pisgah

And so, my lords, traveling on Israel's highway of prophecies, a highway that is peppered and dotted with major and telling events, we now leave behind the old prophet Abraham and let the years roll down their slippery slope until we come upon another prophet 464 biblical years after Abraham [1856 BC to 1398 BC is 458 solar years, which is equivalent to 464 biblical years].

The doomed earth has now aged 464 years in its allocated short lifespan, my lords. And soon we shall arrive to some of you.

The name of the man we are to meet today on Israel's highway of prophecies, my lords, is Balaam. Balaam, himself, is not an Israelite, your majesties, but still he was a prophet of the God of all the nations and the peoples of the earth—the high and the low. And Balaam had a few prophecies to make, but with your permission, my lords, we shall select the one that is of particular interest to us living here today.

> [Edit: Balaam, 1398–1397 BC, was one of the earliest prophets of the Bible who spoke of events that reach to our own modern time. Once again, see EOOO volume 1 & 2.]

Now, my lords, this old prophet Balaam looked down from the top of the cliff Pisgah where he stood. He looked down and saw below him thousands of battered and homeless desert dwellers milling at the foot of the cliff. These battered people had forty years ago escaped slavery from Egypt and were just about to enter the homeland of their ancestor Abraham.

The godly man then, in a trance, we believe, my lords, prophesied that one day, this collection of twelve Israelite tribes of homeless refugees and ex-slaves, one day shall have a star of a king who shall rule the countries of the region of the Middle East. Is this a fantasy or a prophecy?

These, here below, battered and homeless twelve tribes milling by the foot of the cliff shall one day become an imperial empire, a strong nation, which shall rule other nations—a superpower.

Go ahead, please, prophet Moses. Tell their majesties what prophet Balaam has said of the star, which was promised to the homeless children of Israel.

> NUM 24:17 *I shall see him, but not now: I shall behold him, but not nigh [soon]:* <u>*there shall come a Star out of Jacob, and a Sceptre [royal insignia of a staff] shall rise out of Israel*</u>*, and shall smite the corners of Moab, and destroy all the children of Sheth.*
> NUM 24:18 *and Israel shall do valiantly.*
> NUM 24:19 <u>*Out of Jacob [Israel] shall come he that shall have dominion*</u>

But then, my lords, prophet Balaam went farther in the future beyond the time of this Star of Jacob.

Indeed, my lords, he did also prophecy of all the future superpowers that shall reach to our own time. And by this we mean, my lords, that he prophesied of all the superpowers that were to spring around Israel and fulfill its past and future prophecies.

Balaam, my lords, had prophesied of your empires more than five hundred years before you came, your majesties, and ruled the world. Balaam standing out there on the cliff, my lords, prophesied of the empires of Iraq, Iran, Greece, and Rome.

The name of the biblical prophet Balaam was found by archaeologists (see E0001). On March 17, 1967, Professor Henk J. Franken of the Dutch University of Leiden led an archeological dig in Jordan, where he unearthed the ancient ruins of a building destroyed by an earthquake about 750 BC (the earthquake is mentioned in the Bible as well). The plastered walls of the building had ancient writings on them, which begin with the following lines:

"Inscription of (Ba)laam (son of Beo)r, the man who was a seer of the gods. Lo, the gods came to him at night and (spoke to) him." (image source: unknown)

Prophet Balaam, listen to us here, sir. You prophesied of the Assyrian domination of the world over 500 years before its new empire made appearance. But yet, they, the dwellers of that ancient land of Shinar, came. The Assyrians came, the Iraqi empire rose, and so did that of Persia [Iran], and they dominated our world for nearly 585 long years between them, sir.

Prophet Balaam, you prophesied of the Greek domination of the world over a thousand years before the Greek armies chased off every superpower that dominated the world before it. We can tell you, sir, that Greece became the reigning superpower of the planet and ruled the people of the earth for nearly 185 years.

And you, sir, indeed prophesied of the Greek Empire's defeat nearly 1,300 years before it happened.

And the victor, who defeated the remnant of all previous empires of the planet—the Iraqis, Iranians, and Greeks—this victor, the Roman Empire of Europe, has lasted to the minute we woke up this morning, sir, just as you prophesied from the top of the cliff Pisgah.

But then sir, an Israeli prophet by the name of Daniel came 870 prophetical years after you [1398 BC to 539/538 BC is 859 solar years] and prophesied that dead Iraq and Iran, who were thrashed thoroughly by the Greeks, shall come alive once again in the days of the end. And as a result, Israel shall once again be in great trouble, sir; the prince of the planet shall aid her enemies, sir. This is happening now as we speak to you, sir.

At any rate, dear prophet Balaam, some of these great men who founded these empires that dominated this planet of ours are gathered here today to tell one another what they did to fulfill your ancient prophecy of God's timetable of the earth.

Go ahead, please, prophet Moses, tell their majesties of Balaam's prophecy.

> NUM 24:21 *And he [Balaam] looked on the Kenites, and took up his parable, and said, Strong is thy dwelling place, and thou puttest thy nest in a rock [the Kenites lived secure and well protected in the rocky highlands of Jordan].*
> NUM 24:22 *Nevertheless the Kenite shall be wasted, <u>until Asshur [Assyria, the Empire of Assyria] shall carry thee away captive.</u>*
> NUM 24:23 *And he took up his parable, and said, Alas, who shall live when God doeth this [brings about the Assyrian Empire]!*
> NUM 24:24 <u>*And ships shall come from the coast of Chittim [Greek ships], and shall afflict Asshur [Assyria], and shall afflict Eber [the Greeks were to defeat the Assyrian Iraqis and the Persian Iranians], and he [the Greek Empire] also shall perish for ever [the Roman leagues were to defeat the Greeks and establish the Roman European Empire, which survives to our day].*</u>

With your permission, my lords, we would like to call upon prophet Daniel to confirm to you the sweeping long range overview that prophet Balaam has seen of the superpowers, which were to checkmark the time on the calendar of this beautiful yet doomed planet.

Your majesties, one day long ago, prophet Daniel, had stood before His Babylonian Majesty King Nebuchadnezzar of Iraq, who presently sits in your company, and prophesied to him of the prophetical superpowers that would rise around Israel for the next thousands of years.

Go ahead please, prophet Daniel, tell their majesties what you had said nearly 2,500 years ago to His Babylonian Majesty King Nebuchadnezzar of Iraq.

> DAN 2:39 *after thee [King Nebuchadnezzar] shall arise another kingdom inferior to thee [the Persian Empire], and another third kingdom of brass [the Grecian Empire of Alexander the Great], which shall bear rule over all the earth.*

DAN 2:40 *And the fourth kingdom [the European Roman Empire] shall be strong as iron: forasmuch as iron breaketh in pieces and subdueth all things: and as iron that breaketh all these, shall it break in pieces and bruise.*

DAN 2:44 *And in the days of these kings [of the Roman Empire] shall the God of heaven set up a kingdom [Christ Jesus appeared in the flesh and established the kingdom of God, the nation of God], which shall never be destroyed: and the kingdom shall not be left to other people, but it shall break in pieces and consume all these kingdoms, and it shall stand for ever [the nation of God, the kingdom of God, shall last forever].*

The mysterious fourth kingdom, which has ten horns, the Walters Museum, Baltimore, Maryland, USA (image source: author).

We shall meet again and again with prophet Daniel, my lords, and by then your majesties, his enigmatic prophecies will become quite clear.

Having listened to Balaam and his prophesies, the twelve tribes of Israel were then encouraged, my lords, to move along and fight their way to their promised land of Israel.

## 1397–1004 BC
## Running from Slavery to Poverty

Unfortunately, my lords, right from the start, the twelve tribes of the children of Israel did not dwell securely in the Promised Land of their ancestor Abraham. They knew not peace.

They were steadily harassed by the neighbors, and were constantly raided year after year. Their harvests, cattle, staff of life, property, and even their wives and children were taken in raids after raids, your majesties. They were never safe or secure. Indeed, the twelve tribes were scattered all over the Promised Land. And so they were weak and helpless, my lords, and as a result they became destitute and impoverished.

What kind of a promised land is this? They wondered. And what kind of an imperial kingdom is this? Where is the star king?

He was nowhere in sight, my lords.

And the heavy years stumbled along so ever slowly over the worried and desperate families of Israel. There came the months when they hid in the caves of the mountains from before their enemies, my lords. And when they steeled themselves and ventured out of their dark hiding places, they found that their harvest was gone. Lean years of hunger lay ahead for them and for their children, your majesties.

With your permission, my lords, we shall now call on some of the scribes, writers of Israel, my lords, to detail you on the harshness of Israel's existence.

> JUDG 6:2 the hand of Midian [northern Saudi Arabia and parts of Jordan] prevailed against Israel: and because of the Midianites the children of Israel made them the dens [hid and lived in dens and caves] which are in the mountains, and caves, and strong holds.
> JUDG 6:3 And so it was, when Israel had sown [planted crops], that the Midianites came up, and the Amalekites, and the children of the east, even they came up against them;
> JUDG 6:4 And they encamped against them, and destroyed the increase [the harvest] of the earth, till thou come unto Gaza [near the borders of Egypt], <u>and left no sustenance for Israel, neither sheep, nor ox, nor ass</u>.
> JUDG 6:5 For they [the raiders and invaders] came up with their cattle [to feed their traveling fighters] and their tents, and they came as grasshoppers for multitude; for both they and their camels [to carry away the crop and the goods] were without number: and they entered into the land [of Israel] to destroy it.
> JUDG 6:6 And <u>Israel was greatly impoverished</u> because of the Midianites; and the children of Israel cried unto the LORD.

## 1004 BC
## A Reddish-Haired King and Musician

You were right, prophet Balaam, son of Beor. You managed indeed to see events 400 years [biblical years] in advance [1398/1397 BC to 1004 BC].

And no one can deny, sir, that your prophecy of imperial future for those refugees you saw from the top of Pisgah went against any rational possible outcome.

But today, sir, a youngster by the name of David became the darling of the battered, hopeless twelve tribes of Israel. These tribes, sir, were not only battered by the neighboring nations; they themselves were also fighting amongst themselves for survival.

Yet, sir, this good-looking, red-haired David managed to reconcile them and unite them into a kingdom, which, during his lifetime, became an empire.

And indeed, again, prophet Balaam, the imperial empire of King David and his famous son, the wise King Solomon, the wealthiest man ever lived, was one of the first empires in the region after Egypt and its mighty King Thutmose III.

You were right, prophet Balaam; you were right, sir.

Israel has now become a nation and a kingdom.

Go ahead, please, biblical scribes with your record.

*1 KINGS 4:25 Judah and Israel [the northern half and southern half] dwelt safely, every man under his vine and under his fig tree, from Dan [in the far north] even to Beersheba [in the south of Israel], all the days of Solomon.*

And this King David of theirs, my lords, was not only a good-looking and physically strong man, he was also a man of many talents, your majesties. He wrote songs and sang them, invented musical instruments, and trained a 4,000-men choir to sing his songs. They called him, my lords, the "sweet singer of Israel."

Carry on, please, scribes.

*2 SAM 23:1 David the son of Jesse said … the man who was raised up on high, the anointed of the God of Jacob, and <u>the sweet psalmist [singer] of Israel</u>*

The Good Shepherd, 4th century, Istanbul Archaeological Museum (image source: author).

Ps 23:1 The LORD is my shepherd; I shall not want (have no need).

Ps 23:2 He maketh me to lie down in green pastures: he leadeth me beside the still waters.

Ps 23:3 He restoreth my soul: he leadeth me in the paths of righteousness for his name's sake.

Ps 23:4 Yea, though I walk through the valley of the shadow of death, I will fear no evil: for thou art with me; thy rod and thy staff they comfort me.

Ps 23:5 my cup runneth over.

Ps 23:6 Surely goodness and mercy shall follow me all the days of my life: and I will dwell in the house of the LORD (in the vast heavens) for ever.

Here are some of his songs, my lords, which we still sing in our modern time, even though we do not know how His Majesty King David and his choir sang them.

> PS 139:23 Search me, O God, and know my heart: try [test] me, and know my thoughts:
> PS 139:24 And see if there be any wicked way in me, and <u>lead me in the way everlasting</u>.
> JOB 26:13 By his spirit he hath <u>garnished the heavens</u>
> PS 19:1 <u>The heavens declare the glory of God; and the firmament sheweth his handywork [skill]</u>.
> PS 19:2 Day unto day uttereth speech, and night unto night sheweth knowledge.
> PS 19:3 There is no speech nor language, where their voice is not heard [no words are needed for God's handiwork speaks for itself].
> PS 19:4 Their line [statement] is gone out through all the earth, and their words to the end of the world.

Ps 139:14 I will praise thee; for <u>I am fearfully (delicately) and wonderfully made</u>: marvellous are thy works; <u>and that my soul knoweth right well</u>.

Ps 90:2 "Before the mountains were brought forth, or ever thou hadst formed the earth and the world, <u>even from everlasting to everlasting, thou art God</u>", added the prophet Moses.

I am wonderfully made: Human flesh that can see (eyes), human flesh that can hear (ears), human flesh that is mostly water yet can taste (tongue), human flesh that can smell (nose), and human flesh that can imaging, analyze, think, remember and even heal itself (brain) – wonderfully made and I know that very well (image source: Wikipedia, Petr Novák).

Ps 107:23 They that go down to the sea in ships, that do business in great waters;

Ps 107:24 These see the works of the LORD, and his wonders in the deep.

Ps 104:25 So is this great and wide sea, wherein are things creeping <u>innumerable</u>, both small and great beasts.

BOTTOM RIGHT: Sea World, London (image source: author).

## Wonderful Are Thy Works

The Bible teaches that the creatures in the sea are so many that they are innumerable. Scientists believe that the number of spices in the world is in the millions. Many more are still being discovered in remote and previously inaccessible regions of the planet.

On the other hand, the Islamic prophet Muhammad of Arabia believes in a small and limited number.

> Al-Tirmidhi, 1452
>
> No locusts were seen in one of the years of Umar's caliphate, the year in which he died, and becoming very anxious on this account he sent a rider to the Yemen, another to Iraq and another to Syria to enquire whether any locusts had been seen. The rider who came from the Yemen brought him a handful and scattered it in front of him, and when Umar saw it he said, "Allah is Most Great," and told that he had heard Allah's Messenger (peace be upon him) say, "Allah who is great and glorious created a thousand species, six hundred in the sea and four hundred on the land. The first species to perish will be the locusts, and when they perish the species will follow one another like beads on a string."

The Natural History Museum of Vienna exhibits over 30 million species.

Naturhistorisches Museum Wien, Austria (images source: author).

# 931 BC Break Up

It did not last long, my lords.

Those days of prosperity and boom times, my lords, were short lived—only seventy years of a united kingdom [1004–931 BC].

And then, my lords, the rich and strong Israel began to lose something very, very important.

It so happened, my sovereigns, that after the death of H.M. King Solomon that the united kingdom of Israel split into two rival sisters, two kingdoms, a northern half and a southern half.

The southern half, my lords, was called the kingdom of Judah, and the northern and larger half, confusingly enough, my lords, was called the kingdom of Israel, and sometimes Ephraim, being its largest and most dominant tribe of the ten tribes who lived in the north [those are the ten tribes that are involved in the legend of the lost ten tribes of Israel].

The man who managed to accomplish this feat of breaking up Israel, my lords, was a governor by the name of Jeroboam.

This Jeroboam, your majesties, was an employee of H.M. King Solomon the wise. His majesty, my lords, promoted the energetic Jeroboam and made him the governor of the northern half of the kingdom and its ten tribes. Eventually, my lords, Jeroboam, taking advantage of the resentment between the northern and southern halves of Israel, managed to proclaim independence for the northern half following the death of H.M. King Solomon the wise.

And he was not challenged, my lords.

Indeed, the small army of Governor Jeroboam, my lords, was not challenged by the strong army of the kingdom because Governor Jeroboam was egged along and supported by the mighty army of H.M. King Shishak of Egypt. This, your majesties, is the Egyptian pharaoh who found the hiding place of the huge amount of gold of H.M. King Solomon. [See EOOO.1]

## A False Prophet of a Poor Copy

Nonetheless, my lords, his new majesty King Jeroboam of Israel north was scared that the ten tribes of Israel who occupied his budding kingdom would rebel against him in order to rejoin the motherland and return Israel to a united kingdom once more.

And so, my lords, in order to make the break between Judah and Israel a permanent one, H.M. King Jeroboam came up with a great idea, the most powerful deception of all times, my lords.

In short, he brought in a wolf dressed in a sheep's clothing. Nothing, my lords, could be more powerful because nothing could be more deceitful to the unwary and the unlearned.

His idea, my lords, was to proclaim that he is returning the "religion of the Holy One of Israel" to its original form.

His back-to-basics new religion was really nothing, my lords, but a poor copy of the first books of the Bible, plus his own teachings. And then, H.M. King Jeroboam, my lords, installed himself as the prophet, the high priest of his new religion, which included kissing stones. The stones in this case, my lords, were gilded stone statues of two calves placed at both northern and southern ends of Israel North.

Indeed, he may have added the worshipping of the two calves, my lords, in order to please his Egyptian benefactors who, themselves, worshipped the bull god Apies for generations.

Worshipping the Egyptian bull god Apies, c. 379–361 BC, the Louvre Museum, Paris (image source: author).

For details on King Shishak and fascinating archaeological discoveries that show where King Solomon hid his staggering amount of gold, refer to EOOO.1.

At any rate, over time, my lords, Israel went farther and farther astray along with its king and his successors. Israel north, my lords, forsook its mission to the world. It was no longer the preacher nation of the world. It was no longer, my lords, the spokesman for the plan of God for mankind. Israel north, my lords, was now the preacher of new teachings of a false religion of a false prophet.

And according to its new teachings, it was now enough to make a pilgrimage to the gilded stone statue and kiss it. This would please God. Just imagine!

Of course the true prophets, especially those from the still faithful southern kingdom of Judah, began to rain warnings on Israel north. No, pilgrimage and kissing a stone shall never be enough to inherit the new world. No, a pilgrimage to kiss a stone is far from enough to qualify for the eternal companionship of the Holy One.

Warn as they may, my lords, the situation got worse.

## Kissing Stones

The Christian apostle Paul caused major riots in the ancient Greek city of Ephesus when he preached that revering statues, stones, or metals were not sufficient to inherit eternal life and qualify for the company of the Holy One.

But the devoted and sincere worshippers of the goddess Diana believed wholeheartedly that their revered statue had definitely fallen down from heaven, specifically from the planet Jupiter.

Acts 19:35 *And when the townclerk [mayor] had appeased the people, he said, Ye men of Ephesus, what man is there that knoweth not how that the city of the Ephesians is a worshipper of the great goddess Diana, <u>and of the image which fell down from Jupiter</u>?*

The goddess Artemis of Ephesus (called Diana by the Romans), 2nd Century AD, Naples Archaeological Museum, Italy (image source: author).

# HAIL TO THE KING OF EGYPT—67

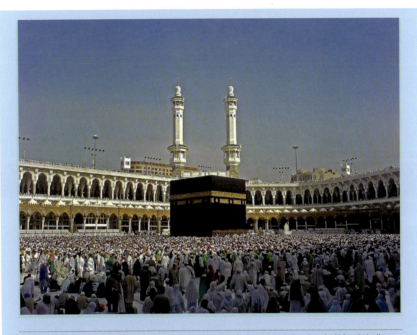

The Islamic Kaaba in Mecca/Saudi Arabia houses the black stone, which the devoted Islamic believers kiss in imitation of the Islamic prophet Muhammad and his successors. The black stone was revered by pagans and then by the Islamic prophet as a stone that had fallen from heaven. The Islamic prophet Muhammad began his career as a preacher of the Bible to the Arabs, but later added his own rules; see EOOO 1& 2 (image source: Muhammad Mahdi Karim, Wikipedia Commons).

## Big Trouble! I am Rich

And indeed, it got worse, my lords. Whereas Abraham lived in heaven and worked on earth, his children, the children of Israel, moved out of heaven altogether. The future meant nothing. The present meant everything.

Was this the general sentiment of the absorbed population, prophet Isaiah?

> ISA 22:13 *let us eat and drink; for to morrow we shall die.*

In the course of time, my lords, both sister kingdoms grew more and more prosperous and their armies became two of the strongest armies of the Middle East. Their prosperity and strength, my lords, made them self-sufficient and independent; they no longer needed the good shepherd of H.M. King David. Instead, they were very absorbed with their prosperity.

They were becoming very rich for the present, but very poor for the world to come, warned their prophets.

> REV 3:17 *Because thou sayest, I am rich, and increased with goods, and have need of nothing; and knowest not that thou art wretched, and miserable, and poor, and blind, and naked:*

They forgot their Holy One and along with Him they forgot their mission on earth. The preacher of the Savior of the world abandoned his mission and began to sink deeper and deeper in all the temporary pleasures of the present doomed planet.

What eternal life? There is no eternal life; there is no resurrection and there is no life after death. All we have is today.

> 1 Cor 15:32 *what advantageth it me, if the dead rise not? let us eat and drink; for to morrow we die.*

And so, my lords, the prophets kept on raining down warnings after warnings upon the proud and wealthy leaders of the ten tribes of Israel North.

Wealthy Israel, remember the prophet Balaam. Your days are numbered. The king of Assyria Iraq is on his way.

We do not care. If Assyria tears down our brick houses, we can afford to rebuild them with stones.

Carry on please, prophet Isaiah, tell their majesties how the leaders reacted to the warnings.

> ISA 7:17 *The LORD shall bring upon thee, and upon thy people, and upon thy father's house, days that have not come from the day that Ephraim [Israel] departed from Judah; even <u>the king of Assyria.</u>*
> ISA 7:8 <u>*within threescore and five years [65 years; it happened as foretold] shall Ephraim [Israel north] be broken.*</u>
> ISA 7:9 *If ye will not believe, surely ye shall not be established.*
> ISA 9:9 *And all the people shall know, even Ephraim [i.e., Israel] and the inhabitant of Samaria [the government seat of Israel north where its wealthy leaders lived], that say in the pride and stoutness of heart,*
> ISA 9:10 <u>*The bricks are fallen down, but we will build with hewn stones:*</u> *the sycamores are cut down, but we will change them into cedars.*

There was no remedy left to try, my lords, nothing. The people kicked back against the Lord and His prophets. As their scribes will now tell you.

DEUT 32:15 *Jeshurun [the upright—straight, meaning the "good" Israel] waxed [became] fat, and kicked: thou art waxen fat, thou art grown thick, thou art covered with fatness; then he forsook God which made him, and lightly esteemed the Rock of his salvation.*
2 CHR 36:16 *they [the children of Israel] mocked the messengers of God, and despised his words, and misused his prophets … <u>there was no remedy</u>.*

These arrogant Israeli leaders did not know what was coming their way, or perhaps more accurately, your majesties, they did not believe the prophets.

Yet in no time at all, my lords, they and we too shall meet up with the first leader from the land of 666.

Indeed, my sovereigns, the following sequent of events shall be repeated in our day according to the timekeepers of the plan of God. Israel shall be invaded from the north, and then Jerusalem shall be surrounded. The future events, my lords, shall be so much similar to the past ones that the people of our present day, your majesties, when they shall read all about these old events, shall presume that we are relating the events of our present time.

## *Heroes & Future Kings*

But if the majority of the population lived in the present and could not bother about the future, there were, nonetheless, those who had strong faith that sooner or later the future would come, and the door shall be shut.

And because of their strong faith of the promised future, and because of their strong faith of the life to come in the heavens, the city of God, they endured the unendurable.

Heb 11:35 *others were tortured, not accepting deliverance; that they might obtain a better resurrection:*
Heb 11:36 *And others had trial of cruel mockings and scourging [beatings], yea, moreover of bonds [chained] and imprisonment:*
Heb 11:37 *They were stoned, they were sawn asunder [quartered], were tempted, were slain with the sword: they wandered about in sheepskins and goatskins; being destitute, afflicted, tormented;*
Heb 11:38 *Of whom the world was not worthy: they wandered in deserts, and in mountains, and in dens and caves of the earth.*
Heb 11:13 *These all died in faith, not having received the promises, <u>but having seen them afar off, and were persuaded of them, and embraced them</u>, and confessed that they were strangers and pilgrims on the earth.*

> <sup>Heb 11:14</sup> For they that say such things declare plainly that they seek a country [they are looking forward for a heavenly residence].
> <sup>Heb 11:16</sup> But now they desire a better country, that is, <u>an heavenly</u>: wherefore God is not ashamed to be called their God: for he hath prepared for them a city.
> <sup>Heb 11:6</sup> But without faith it is impossible to please him: for he that cometh to God must believe that he is, and that he is a rewarder of them that diligently seek him.

## Chapter Three

# First 666 – Coming Alive

**746/745 BC**
**Assyria**

While Israel, my lords, was drifting away from its task, her designated enemy was growing into his task.

Assyria of Iraq, the northern half of Iraq to be exact, my lords, came alive indeed under H.M. King Adad-Nirari II [911 BC] after many years in a state of comatose.

Assyria, today home of the Sunni Muslims, a sect of a new religion, my lords, came alive when strong and violent rulers were born to their land—brutal and ruthless men, my lords, who eventually called themselves "rulers of the universe."

> And so the "crown having passed from head to head in the same family," my lords.[1]

Indeed, your majesties, gradually and over the span of a couple of hundred of years, Assyria of Iraq began to stretch out its borders and swallow the properties of its close neighbors—farmlands, towns and cities— until small Assyria grew to a large and strong country.

But then Assyria of northern Iraq stumbled and staggered for about forty years, your majesties, and began to lose its control of the small neighboring nations it had captured.

Civil wars broke out in northern Iraq, my lords.

And then out of the chaotic and confused civil war, a governor by the name of Pul, a man unrelated to the crown, made himself the one and undisputed ruler of old Assyria. The man came from nowhere to become the king of the world. And he is, my lords, the man who was to lay the foundation of the new empire of Assyria Iraq.

He came from nowhere, but yet he was also expected, my lords.

We look in the past and see the future your majesties.

---

[1] Ancient Iraq, 256.

This man, my lords, reorganized the chaotic government of northern Iraq, and out of its many fighters, he began to create a standing army—an army, my lords, which needed a steady supply of recruits. And the recruits, my lords, were to come from foreign fighters.

Shall we one more time, my lords, call on Balaam son of Boer!

Go ahead, prophet Balaam.

> NUM 24:21 *And he [Balaam] looked on the Kenites [a neighboring nation of Israel, today's Jordan], and took up his parable, and said, Strong is thy dwellingplace [well-protected homeland], and thou puttest thy nest in a rock [mountainous highlands hard for an invading army to scale].*
>
> NUM 24:22 *Nevertheless the Kenite shall be wasted, <u>until Asshur</u> [Assyria, the empire of the Assyrian Iraqis who will play a major role in bringing in the great tribulation in the last years of the earth, according to God's timetable] <u>shall carry thee away captive.</u>*
>
> NUM 24:23 *And he took up his parable, and said, Alas, who shall live [it is far in the future] when God doeth this [brings about the strong armies of the Assyrian Iraqis—the Assyrian Empire]!*

But Iraq, my lords, was also groomed by the maker of the calendar of the earth to become an earthly discipline rod in His hand, a rod, which He would use to clean and restore His errant preacher of the world.

And Iraq's work is not done yet, my sovereigns. Iraq has yet more work to do in our modern day.

Prophet Micah, please describe the task of Iraq to their majesties.

> MIC 6:9 *<u>the man of wisdom shall see thy name: hear ye the rod</u> [the Assyrian Iraqis], <u>and who hath appointed it</u>.*

## Remarkable! Land of Shinar—666

His Iraqi Majesty King Tiglathpileser III, the man who would begin the job of emptying Israel north of its people, my lords, appeared on the scene around 745 BC.

Prophet Balaam, son of Boer, my lords, spoke of the rise of the Iraqi destroyer about 1397 BC.

The number of years, my lords, between the prophecy and the crowning of his Iraqi majesty King Tiglathpileser III is 652 solar years [1397–745 BC], which is about 666 prophetical years, my lords.

My sovereigns, the turbulent age of the Iraqi Antichrist, whose number is 666, has begun.

Go ahead, please, biblical scribes.

The biblical prophetical year is 360 days, whereas the solar year of our modern calendar is about 365.25 days.

Thus, 652 solar years X 365.25 / 360 = 662 prophetical years.

If one is to allow for slight differentiation for the exact months the events took place, the number of leap years [366 days] included, then it is quite plausible that the difference between the two events is 666 years.

360 Days/ Prophetical Year

> Rev 11:2 it is given unto the Gentiles: and the holy city shall they tread under foot forty and two months [three and one half years].
> Rev 11:3 And I will give power unto my two witnesses, and they shall prophesy a thousand two hundred and threescore [60] days [1260 days / 3.5 years = 360 days/year] , clothed in sackcloth.

*1 CHR 5:25 And they [Israel] transgressed against the God of their fathers, and went a whoring after the gods of the people of the land [started worshiping the religions of the neighbors]*
*1 CHR 5:26 And the God of Israel stirred up the spirit of Pul king of Assyria, and the spirit of Tilgathpilneser king of Assyria*

Endless beheadings: Assyrian soldiers of northern Iraq beheading the enemies of the great god Assur, British Museum (image source: author).

My lords, we shall meet again with 666.

Moreover, my lords, we the living today, we shall meet him yet one last time.

May we, my lords, introduce the Christian apostle John who prophesied of this beast whose number is 666!

My lords, much of what the apostle John would say to you shortly shall sound very enigmatic at this point of time. But much of it shall become clear, my lords, as we travel up the highway of prophecy.

For now, my lords, would you please pay special attention to some of his imagery, such as the beast with two horns! He is a beast, my lords, who, on one hand, appears as peaceful as a lamb, yet he is nothing but as violent as a dragon—a wolf in sheep's clothing—my lords, a false prophet. This beast is Iran, my lords, which had its hay day in the past, but shall rise again, more powerful, in the last days of the earth.

As we have said already, my lords, we are travelling to the past in order to see the future.

Go ahead, please, apostle John.

> REV 13:11 *And I beheld another beast coming up out of the earth; and <u>he had two horns like a lamb, and he spake as a dragon</u>.*
> REV 13:12 *And he exerciseth all the power of the first beast before him, and causeth the earth and them which dwell therein to worship the first beast, <u>whose deadly wound was healed [Iran and Iraq]</u>.*
> REV 13:13 *And he doeth great wonders, so that he <u>maketh fire come down from heaven</u> on the earth [<u>nuclear explosion, which is designed to explode above the surface of the earth</u>] in the sight of men,*

A picture of an atomic bomb explosion. From FEMA (U.S. Federal Emergency Management Agency) publicity poster (image source: WC).

> REV 13:14 *And deceiveth them that dwell on the earth by the means of those miracles which he had power to do in the sight of the beast; saying to them that dwell on the earth, that they should make an image to the beast, which had the wound by a sword, and did live.*

REV 13:15 *And he had power to give life unto the image of the beast, that the image of the beast should both speak, and cause that as many as would not worship the image of the beast should be killed.*

REV 13:16 *And he causeth all, both small and great, rich and poor, free and bond, to receive a mark in their right hand, or in their foreheads:*

REV 13:17 *And that no man might buy or sell, save he that had the mark, or the name of the beast, or the number of his name.*

REV 13:18 <u>*Here is wisdom. Let him that hath understanding count the number of the beast: for it is the number of a man; and his number is Six hundred threescore and* six.</u>

# 745 BC
# By Armageddon

My lords, six years after his coronation, H.M. King Tiglathpileser III went on a rampage and ravaged northern Israel, the northern kingdom.

Please step up front, your majesty, King Tiglathpileser III, please step up, sir. Your fellow leaders wish to hear from you personally. Take the podium, sir, and read to their majesties some of your documents, which your scribes wrote on the clay tablets and on your monuments and on the walls of your palace in Nineveh, across from modern Mosul.

And above all, sir, tell their majesties what you have done to the kingdom of Israel north, specifically, the northern Israeli province of Galilee—the province where one day, the prophets say, sir, that a great light shall shine and beam out to the entire world an unshakable promise of unending celestial life.

Go ahead, please, sir.

> "(T)he cities ... which are on the border of Bit-Humria (House of Omri, Israel) ... <u>the wide land of Naphtali</u>, in its entirety, I brought within the border of Assyria. My official I set over them as governor
> 
> ...
> 
> <u>The land of Bit-Humria [Israel] ...... all of its people, together with their goods I carried off to Assyria</u>".[2]

Thank you, sir; this is good enough for now. Have a seat, sir. Have a throne, your majesty.

---

[2] *Ancient Records of Assyria and Babylonia,* Part one, Daniel David Luckenbill, Ch. XIV. 815, 816, P.P. 292

# 76—EARTH OUT OF ORBIT

ABOVE: Israel north was called Bit-Humria, House of Omri; Omri was one of the strongest and most famous kings of the kingdom of Israel north. Above is a limestone column capital from his palace of Samaria, capital of Israel north, 9th century B.C., The Jewish Museum, NY (image source: author).

Assyrian Iraqi King Tiglathpileser III, c. 728 BC, from Nimrud, Central Palace, London, British Museum (image source: author).

Tiglathpileser III is considered to be the founder of the Assyrian Empire of northern Iraq, which was to deport the children of Israel to Iraq. Mass deportation was unheard of until he made it a war routine in order to beef up his army with foreign fighters, as well as to build northern Iraq. Northern Iraq today is mainly inhabited by the Sunni Muslims.

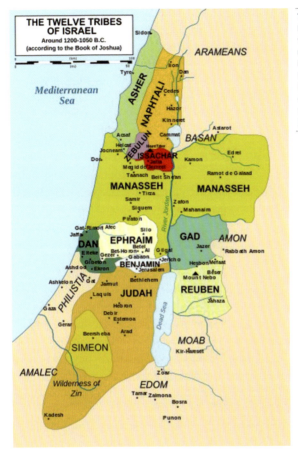

The Israeli province of Naphtali, situated in the wide region of Galilee of northern Israel, was invaded by the Assyrian Iraqi King Tiglathpileser III, as the Bible claims, and as the ancient Iraqi writings do confirm W.C, Richardprins

Now, your majesties, we would like to bring up the old biblical scribes to read out their record in support of the claim of His Iraqi Majesty King Tiglathpileser III in which he declares that he devastated the province of Naphtali of Galilee of northern Israel, a province close to his Iraq, my lords.

It is also the province that includes the valley of Megiddo, a future battlefield, my lords, known as Armageddon.

After introducing the ancient biblical scribes, my lords, we wish to introduce also prophet Isaiah who would tell you a bit more about the devastated land of Galilee in northern Israel.

Now, biblical scribes, could you please confirm the claim of his Iraqi majesty regarding what he has done in the province of Naphtali, home of Armageddon.

*2 KIN 15:29* In the days of Pekah king of Israel <u>came Tiglathpileser king of Assyria</u>, and took Ijon, and Abelbethmaachah, and Janoah, and Kedesh, and Hazor, and Gilead, <u>and Galilee, all the land of Naphtali</u> [this verse matches the ancient Assyrian documents "the wide land of Naphtali"]<u>, and carried them captive to Assyria</u> [another match].

## A Child Shall Be Born

As you have seen then, my sovereigns, H.M. King Tiglathpileser and the biblical scribes agree that the Iraqis began their invasion in the Israeli province of Galilee, where they also carried away its population.

Now may we, my lords, hear what the old prophet Isaiah had to say about this part of Israel north that was attacked by the Iraqis!

Thank you, my lords.

Over five hundred years in advance, prophet Daniel, my lords, gave us the exact year when the Savior of the world shall appear and invite the peoples of the world to the kingdom of heaven.

On the other hand, my lords, prophet Isaiah had prophesied to us where the Savior shall start his mission. Prophet Isaiah, my lords, prophesied that the savior shall begin His preaching from the same province, where the enemy of the nation of the Savior, the Iraqi Antichrist, began his invasion, the province of Galilee.

The invasion of grace was to begin where the invasion of darkness began.

A child shall be born in Israel, prophesied Isaiah, a child whose name … may we say His name your majesties?

His name is "The Mighty God, the Everlasting One … the Prince of Peace" is His name, my lords.

The Mighty God?

The Everlasting One?

Yes, my lords, His name is amazing—Wonderful.

It is impossible, my lords, that He can be anything else but the Eternal Himself.

The One my, sovereigns, who grants eternal life must be the Eternal Himself … the One, my lords, who grants the celestial heavens must be the One who owns the heavens, the One who pays for the faulty must be faultless and holy, Himself, and the One who shall be worshipped must be the Creator and not a creation. He came down to earth in order to bring man to the heavens.

And so now, my lords, we call upon the so-called beloved apostle John, along with apostle Paul and prophet Isaiah.

Please go ahead in your order, gentlemen.

> *1 JN 4:19* We love him, because he first loved us.
> *GAL 2:20* I am crucified with Christ: nevertheless I live; yet not I, but Christ liveth in me: and the life which I now live in the flesh <u>I live by the faith of the Son of God, who loved me, and gave himself for me</u>.

And so here, my lords, is what old prophet Isaiah had said nearly 700 years in advance.

Please go ahead, prophet Isaiah.

> *IS 9:1* Nevertheless the dimness [darkness of hopelessness] shall not be such as was in her vexation [depression], when at the first he [the Iraqis] lightly afflicted the land of Zebulun <u>and the land of Naphtali, and afterward [the Iraqi leaders came again and] did more grievously afflict her by the way of the sea [in the region of the east side of the Jordan River, near Iraq], beyond Jordan, in Galilee of the nations.</u>
> *IS 9:2* <u>The people that walked in darkness have seen a great light: they that dwell in the land of the shadow of death, upon them hath the light shined.</u>
> …
> *IS 9:6* <u>For unto us a child is born, unto us a son is given: and the government shall be upon his shoulder: and his name shall be called Wonderful, Counsellor, The mighty God, The everlasting Father, The Prince of Peace.</u>
> *IS 9:7* <u>Of the increase of his government and peace there shall be no end</u> … with judgment [fairness] and with justice from henceforth even for ever. The zeal of the LORD of hosts will perform this.

## Unto You and Unto Us

The cycles of time drifted along its predetermined course until the fullness of time arrived. And when the time became full and ready, the rock of ages, the Governor, the King of kings, the Great light came and shone brightly.

> *Rom 5:8* God commendeth [proved] his love toward us, in that, while we were yet sinners, Christ died for us.

And the invitation went out, the invitation to live an endless life in the heavens. And of course the invitation to live in the heavens went out by the owner of the heavens Himself.

> Mat 22:2 *The kingdom of heaven is like unto a certain king, which made a marriage for his son,*
> ...
> Mat 22:8 *Then saith he to his servants, The wedding is ready*
> ...
> Mat 22:9 *Go ye therefore into the highways, and as many as ye shall find, bid [invite] to the marriage.*

And the inhabitants of the region of Galilee, of northern Israel, were the first people to be invited. The poor, the lonely, the bruised, and the brokenhearted—whether rich or poor, high or low—were all invited by none less than the King of kings and the Lord of lords, and the holder of everything by His power.

And the masses came from everywhere to Galilee in the region of Naphtali to behold the gracious King and accept His unbelievable invitation to the celestial city of God.

And they came from the nations and cities all around Israel.

And the crowds and the masses were so numerous and great that He could not enter the cities, but had to preach in the wide open fields outside the towns and cities.

And He went around to explain and to invite the priest and the prostitute, the killer, and the kindhearted to inherit the bright future of mankind in the lands of heavens. And in hearing Him, some became winners, but, alas, there were also losers.

Alas, there were losers too.

> Mat 16:26 *For what is a man profited, if he shall gain the whole world, and lose his own soul? or what shall a man give in exchange for his soul?*

In His day, the prophecy of the first great event in the plan of God was fulfilled. *He* was the great event. The second, whose date is kept secret, is yet to come.

> Lk 23:5 *And they [the high priest of Israel and his attendants] were the more fierce, saying [to the Roman governor Pilate], He [Christ Jesus] stirreth up the people, teaching throughout all Jewry [Israel], <u>beginning from Galilee to this place</u> [Jerusalem, the capital city].*
> Lk 4:14 *And Jesus returned in the power of the Spirit <u>into Galilee: and there went out a fame of him through all the region round about.</u>*
> Lk 4:16 *And he came to Nazareth [in Galilee], <u>where he had been brought up</u>: and, as his custom was, he went into the synagogue on the sabbath day, and stood up for to read.*

FIRST 666 – COMING ALIVE—81

Lk 4:17 *And there was delivered unto him the book of the prophet Esaias [Isaiah]. And when he had opened the book [a scroll], he found the place where it was written,*
Lk 4:18 *<u>The Spirit of the Lord is upon me, because he hath anointed me to preach the gospel to the poor; he hath sent me to heal the brokenhearted, to preach deliverance [freedom] to the captives [prisoners of sin], and recovering of sight to the blind, to set at liberty them that are bruised,</u>*
Lk 4:19 *<u>To preach the acceptable year of the Lord [before the door to the kingdom of heaven is closed].</u>*
Lk 4:20 *And he closed the book, and he gave it again to the minister, and sat down. And the eyes of all them that were in the synagogue were fastened on him.*
Lk 4:21 *And he began to say unto them, <u>This day is this scripture [this prophecy] fulfilled in your ears</u>.*
Lk 4:22 *And all bare him witness, and wondered at the gracious words which proceeded out of his mouth.*

*Amazing grace! How sweet the sound*
*That saved a wretch like me!*
*I once was lost, but now am found;*
*Was blind, but now I see.*

**RIGHT:** One of the pottery jars with lids in which the scrolls of the book of Isaiah were stored in the caves of Qumran, prior to 70 AD, i.e., shortly after the resurrection of Christ Jesus, University of Chicago Oriental Museum (image source: author).

"Photographic reproduction of the Great Isaiah Scroll, the best preserved of the biblical scrolls found at Qumran (caves in the west bank territory of Israel). It contains the entire Book of Isaiah in Hebrew, apart from some small damaged parts." (Image source: Website of The Israel Museum, Jerusalem, WC).

And so, your majesties, starting in Galilee, the Assyrian rod, the Iraqi rulers began their assigned job of plucking and hauling away Israel, the fallen preacher of the nations.

With your permission, your majesties, we now ask the biblical scribes to fill in the details.

> *2 KIN 10:32* In those days the LORD began to cut Israel short

At any rate, my lords, first came H.M. King Tiglathpileser III and devastated the Israeli region of Galilee. And then he finished off his invasion by carrying away two and a half tribes out of the ten tribes who inhabited the northern half of Israel. Two and a half fingers of Israel's ten fingers have now been amputated, my lords.

Soon the rest shall be amputated—soon.

> *1 CHR 5:26* And the God of Israel stirred up the spirit of Pul king of Assyria, and the spirit of <u>Tilgathpilneser king of Assyria, and he carried them away [two and one half tribes]</u>, even the Reubenites, and the Gadites, and the half tribe of Manasseh, and brought them unto Halah, and Habor, and Hara, and to the river Gozan, unto this day.

Six years after his coronation, H.M. King Tiglathpileser III of northern Iraq, home of the Sunni Muslims of today, my lords, invaded the province of Galilee, home of Armageddon.

And then after another six years, my lords, he went on and invaded Syria and assassinated its leader.

> *2 KIN 16:9* the king of Assyria went up against Damascus, and took it, and carried the people of it captive to Kir, and slew Rezin [the ruler of Syria].

And then three years after, my lords, his Iraqi majesty King Tiglathpileser III went on to capture southern Iraq, Babylonia, home of the Shiite Muslims of today, my lords, and invaded Arabia.

Go ahead, please, Your Majesty.

> "The wide land of Karduniash (Babylonia), to its farthest border, I brought under my sway and exercised sovereignty over it."[3]

---

[3] *Ancient Records of Assyria and Babylonia* – Part One, Daniel David Luckenbill, 1989, 788, 283.

> "Samsi, queen of Arabia .... I imposed upon her .... Submitted at my feet."[4]

So far the Sunnis of the time, so to speak, my lords, had the upper hand over the Shiites of the time. But things will change for Syria, Iraq, Iran, Israel, and even Saudi Arabia of the time, my lords.

His majesty led the Sunnis of the time for about seventeen or eighteen years from the throne of Assyria of northern Iraq [745/744–727 BC] and then bid the eye of the sun farewell.

But the Iraqi invasions were only begun by him, my lords. And shall continue until the landmark of Israel is destroyed and the date checked on God's calendar.

Almost every year, usually in the springtime, as was common with most of you, my lords, one successor Iraqi leader after another kept on invading the cities of the neighboring nations around them. This time they invaded five small neighboring countries and nine major cities. Next time they will invade more countries and more cities and haul away more goods. And so it went with Assyria Iraq of today's Sunnis, my lords.

And each of these successive ambitious kings and dictators, my lords, kept bragging and competing amongst themselves for a reputation of brutality. They kept inventing all forms of brutality, thinkable and unthinkable, including flaying and skinning people alive. And their brutality worked well for them, your majesties. Their reputation of ruthlessness scared their neighbors to submission. And they became heroes and champions in their own eyes and in the eyes of their adoring and enriched Iraqi population.

May we, with your permission, my lords, call now and then on some of the Assyrian kings sitting amongst you today to read us a bit out of their ancient writings!

Your majesty King Sargon, would you wish to say what you have done in order to please your god "Adad, the violent, the powerful"!

> "I made their blood run down the ravines and precipices like a river, dyeing plain, countryside and highlands red like a royal robe ... I cut off their heads ... like ants in distress, made their way over most difficult trails. In the heat of my terrible weapons I went after them,

---

[4] *Ancient Records of Assyria and Babylonia* – Part One, Daniel David Luckenbill, 1989, 778, 279.

filling the ascents and descents with the corpses of (their) warriors ... from Mount Uaush to Mount Zimur ... totally annihilated them."[5]

## 727–722 BC King Shalmaneser V —Samaria

And so, my lords, following the death of His Iraqi Majesty King Tiglathpileser III, his successor H.M. King Shalmaneser V went on to build on his success.

Alas, my lords, for those in Israel north did not believe the prophecies. Yet, the words of the prophets were hurrying home fast.

H.M. King Shalmaneser V, my lords, brought the Iraqi army and besieged Samaria city itself, the capital of Israel [724 BC, three years after the death of King Tiglathpileser III].

But proud Samaria, my lords, was a strong and well-defended city. The Iraqis, my lords, could not breach it quickly.

A year passed, my lords, and then a second one, and now came the third, but still Samaria, the proud fortress of Israel north, stood fast against the Iraqis.

And then, unexpectedly, my lords, the news reached the Iraqi army besieging Samaria city that H.M. King Shalmaneser V had died all of a sudden.

Rejoice not, besieged Samaria; break not out in singing or dancing yet.

And how indeed, my lords, could Samaria rejoice? The famine was taking hold inside the surrounded city, my lords. The city's defenders were weakened after three years of a siege. The fortress of Israel was ripe for the taking.

## 722 BC King Sargon II & the Lost Ten Tribes

The succession took place quite smoothly, my lords.

The new Iraqi warlord H.M. King Sargon II [722-705] moved quickly, my lords, and stormed the famished Samaria city.

Samaria, capital of the kingdom of Israel north, home of the Israeli army, which defends the ten tribes of Israel, had been breached and sacked by the Iraqis, my lords.

---

[5] *Ancient Records of Assyria and Babylonia* – Part Two, Daniel David Luckenbill, 1989, 155, PP.82, 83

Israel, children of Abraham, get ready to travel. Get ready to leave your happy home for a one-way trip on the sad highways leading to the foreign streets, homes, and fields of Iranian, Iraqi, and Syrian cities.

Where are those Israeli leaders who boasted that if the brick houses gave in, they would have built new ones with stones? Where are those proud Israeli leaders who said that if the wooden beams of the houses made of sycamore could not hold up, then they would build new houses with cedar beams? Where are they today, my lords?

Go ahead, please, prophet Amos.

> AM 5:16 *Therefore the LORD, the God of hosts, the Lord, saith thus; Wailing shall be in all streets; and they shall say in all the highways, Alas! alas! and they shall call the husbandman [farmers] to mourning [for their lost fields], and such as are skilful of lamentation to wailing [professional mourners].*
> AM 5:27 *Therefore will I cause you to go <u>into captivity beyond Damascus [to Assyria Iraq]</u>, saith the LORD, whose name is The God of hosts.*

The largest part of the family of the preacher of the world is now homeless, my lords.

King Sargon II hauled away the inhabitants of Samaria, which was sacked by his predecessor King Shalmaneser V, the Louvre (image source: author).

Their Iraqi majesty King Shalmaneser V and then Sargon II, sitting today amongst you, my lords, are the two men who destroyed Samaria, and hauled away the largest part of the family of Israel, its ten tribes. And thus, my lords, these two men started the legend of the lost ten tribes of Israel.

But we can tell you today, my lords, that the ten tribes of the nation of Israel were not lost. They were not, my lords, for indeed their children came back home in due time.

May we now, my lords, call on H.M. King Sargon II to read out a few lines of his ancient records!

No, let us this time call on the biblical scribes first.

Certainly, your majesties!

Go ahead, please, biblical scribes and give their majesties your account of what happened to the ten tribes of northern Israel, and what happened to its capital city, fortress Samaria.

> *2 KIN 18:9* it came to pass in the … the seventh year of Hoshea son of Elah king of Israel [the northern Israeli kingdom], that <u>Shalmaneser king of Assyria came up against Samaria, and besieged it.</u>
> *2 KIN 18:10* <u>And at the end of three years they took it … Samaria was taken.</u>
> *2 KIN 18:11* <u>And the king of Assyria did carry away Israel unto Assyria [Iraq], and put them in Halah and in Habor by the river of Gozan, and in the cities of the Medes [northwestern Iran]</u>:

Your majesties, we are now calling on His Assyrian majesty King Sargon II himself to verify the biblical record.

But did the biblical scribes ever mention H.M. King Sargon?

Yes, my sovereigns, the prophet Isaiah did. He had in a later occasion mentioned his name when King Sargon's general, Tartan, came to attack the neighboring Philistine city of Ashdod, my lords, [711 BC].

Prophet Isaiah, go ahead, please.

> *ISA 20:1* In the year that Tartan came unto Ashdod, <u>when Sargon the king of Assyria sent him</u>, and fought against Ashdod and took it.

All right then. Let H.M. King Sargon read out his own record regarding the fall of Samaria.

Go ahead, sir.

> [At the beginning of my rule, in my first year of reign] … <u>Samerinai (the people of Samaria)</u> … [27,290 people, who lived therein] <u>I carried away</u>; 50 chariots for my royal equipment, I selected from [among them]"[6]

"I plundered the city of Shinuhtu, <u>Samirina (Samaria) and the whole land of Bit-Humria (Israel)</u>."[7]

"[D]evastated the wide land of Bit-Humria,"[8]

---

[6] *ARAB* – Part Two, 4, P. 2.
[7] ARAB – Part Two, 80, P 40.
[8] ARAB – Part Two, 118, P.61.

## Bit-Humria

As a reminder, the kingdom of Israel north, where the ten tribes, or family branches, of Israel lived, was called *Bit Humria* by the Assyrians. It means House [Bit] of Omri [Humria], Omri being one of the most famous kings of Israel at the time.

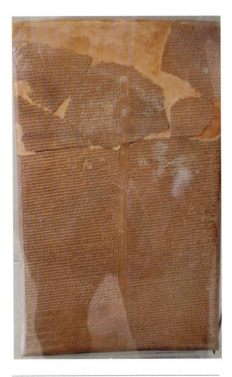

ABOVE LEFT: A letter from King Sargon II to the god Assur describing his war campaigns, the Louvre Museum, Paris (image source: author).

RIGHT: King Sargon II, whose record, in agreement with the biblical account, claims that he completed the destruction of Samaria and deported Israel's ten tribes to Iran and Iraq, British Museum (image source: author).

The records of King Sargon of Assyria are inscripted between the legs of a guardian bull monument, Oriental Institute, Chicago (image source: author).

King Sargon II documented on this brass, gold, and silver tablet the construction of his capital city, the Louvre Museum (image source: author).

And so, your majesties, as you can well see from the biblical and the Assyrian accounts, the Iraqis did indeed manage to destroy the northern half of Israel and deport its population to the enemy cities of Iraq and Iran.

Yet this was not all the damage they did to Israel, my lords. They did more. It is all in the plan, say the prophets. In a minute, we shall report to you, my lords, what more they did.

But at this moment in time, as you can imagine, my lords, the Israeli population and its families, its ten tribes, are in deep morning. They are in shock that such a disaster could happen to them. It is unreal. Where is God? Where is the Eternal One? Does He really care? Could He really help? Does He really have a plan?

And should you wish to know your majesties, soon the people of Israel will ask this same searing question in the future days of our present time—where is the God of Israel?

Meanwhile, my lords, the important date of the total exile of all of Israel, north and south, the date of the locking up of the preacher of the world, was fast approaching.

But the first attempt to fulfill this prophecy failed. It failed because it was the wrong time.

And indeed, my lords, it would take the two regions of Iraq, Assyria, and Babylon, the northern half and the southern half, the Sunnis and the Shiites halves, to chase the preacher of the world from his home and take him captive, a prisoner.

## 705–681 BC
## King Sennacherib

And so, my sovereigns, the territory of the northern half of Israel is now under the authority of an Iraqi governor. Iraq, my sovereigns, now owns the northern half of Israel, the half which includes the valley of Armageddon.

And according to the timetable of the Holy One of Israel, they shall in the future do the same, my lords, own part of northern Israel for a predetermined number of years.

And so what does this, your majesties, leave us of the old united kingdom of Israel?

Well, it leaves us, my lords, with the two tribes that live in the southern half of the kingdom, the Israeli kingdom of Judah or Judea, my lords.

And as you may very well have expected, your majesties, the Assyrian Iraqi kings did indeed turn their attention to the wealthy but strong half of the old empire of Israel.

May we, my lords, address his Roman majesty Emperor Titus, sitting amongst you, for a short minute!

Your majesty Emperor Titus, we shall soon, sir, call upon your colleague his Iraqi majesty King Sennacherib, son of King Sargon II.

King Sargon II, to the left, facing his son King Sennacherib, British Museum, London (image source: author).

He came upon the southern half of Israel [701 BC] a bit over 770 solar years before you did, sir, [70 AD], but he too has done what you yourself have done, sir.

His Iraqi majesty King Sennacherib, sir, went around from town to town wrecking havoc in the Israeli kingdom of Judea. But most importantly, sir, we remember him for what happened to him at the foot of the walls of Jerusalem.

Indeed, sir, what happened to H.M. King Sennacherib at the foot of Jerusalem is very important to us today, your majesty Emperor Titus. Because the prophets say that a similar event such as the one that happened to him by the walls of Jerusalem city of Israel shall happen again, presumably in our present time, sir.

The Roman Emperor Titus (79-81AD), Louvre Museum, Paris (image source: author).

Emperor Titus played a major part in the fulfillment of a biblical prophecy.

Mat 24:1 And Jesus went out, and departed from the temple: and his disciples came to him for to shew him the buildings of the temple.
Mat 24:2 And Jesus said unto them, See ye not all these things? verily I say unto you, There shall not be left here one stone upon another, that shall not be thrown down (Nearly forty years after this prophecy, the Roman legions of commander Titus, later emperor Titus, surrounded Jerusalem and dismantled the stones of the temple, stone by stone).

Go ahead, your majesty King Sennacherib, and read out of your ancient Iraqi records, sir. Tell their majesties what you have done in the southern Israeli kingdom of Judah and what happened to you at the walls of Jerusalem.

"I destroyed, I devastated, I turned into ruins … the houses … I set on fire and turned them into (a mass) of flames."

"I swept like a hurricane. The people, great and small, males and female … I carried off."[9]

Will he continue to boast?

He will, sir.

In that case, let us give him sometime to cool off while we hear the biblical scribes tell us what exactly he did at the walls of Jerusalem.

Biblical King Sennacherib, praying in front of divine symbols. The inscription on the limestone slab above reads in part: "Sennacherib, the great king, mighty king, king of the universe, king of Assyria, king of the four regions (of the world), favorite of the great gods … Trusting in their great might, I led my armies from one end of the earth to the other and brought in submission at my feet all princes, dwelling in palaces, of the four quarters (of the world)." Istanbul Museum (image source: author).

The biblical scribes say, my lords, that his Iraqian majesty had first attacked and sacked the second most important city of Israel, the populated and well-fortified city of Lachish.

And does his Iraqian majesty say the same thing as the biblical scribes about sacking Lachish city?

Yes, sir, his Iraqian majesty lined up the walls of his palace at Nineveh, across from Mosul, with the scenes of attacking and sacking Lachish city and deporting its residents. Indeed, Lachish city, my lords, is the greatest jewel of his crown.

---

[9] *Ancient Records of Assyria and Babylonia* – Part Two, Daniel David Luckenbill, Histories & Mysteries of Man LTD., London, England, 1989, 236 & 237, P. 117

And incidentally, my lords, should you wish to know, H.M. King Sennacherib named his palace in Nineveh "the palace without rival."

The Iraqi Assyrian armies of biblical King Sennacherib, who besieged Jerusalem, storms a walled city, British Museum (image source: author).

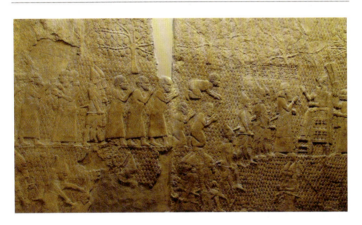

A panel from the palace of Nineveh shows biblical King Sennacherib, sitting on a throne, to the right of the panel, reviewing the Israeli prisoners taken from the city of Lachish, the second most important Israeli city after the capital Jerusalem.

Following the sack of Lachish, King Sennacherib moved on to surround Jerusalem.

Bottom left, an Iraqi soldier beheading an Israel captive, British Museum (image source: author).

Good enough. What else did the biblical scribes say, besides the sack of Lachish?

So now, my lords, seeing that Lachish fell, it became painfully obvious to his Israeli majesty King Hezekiah of Judah, sitting amongst you today, that his rich city of Jerusalem was the next target on the list of the Assyrian Iraqi invader.

94—EARTH OUT OF ORBIT

The size of Jerusalem and the number of its population and its strong fortifications did not seem to discourage H.M. King Sennacherib, who had indeed by then gathered a lot of soldiers and ammunitions from the sacked cities of Israel.

Go ahead, please, biblical scribes.

> *2 CHR 32:1 After these things, and the establishment thereof, <u>Sennacherib king of Assyria came</u>, and entered into Judah, and <u>encamped against the fenced cities, and thought to win them for himself</u> [Sennacherib's records say that he sacked 46 Israeli towns and cities].*
> *2 CHR 32:2 Hezekiah [king of Judaea] saw that Sennacherib was come, and that he was purposed to fight against Jerusalem.*

At the end, my lords, the city of Jerusalem did not fall in the hands of the Iraqis. However, we would ask your permission, your majesties, to relate the details of the Iraqi invasion because we are told that a similar event shall take place in our time.

Meanwhile, my lords, we are getting closer and closer to the destruction of the landmark of God's calendar.

(L) A handle in the form of four nude females was found in the center of the throne room of biblical King Sennacherib of Assyria Iraq, Brooklyn Museum, New York (image source: author).

(R) A relief fragment of three decapitated heads found in the palace of biblical King Sennacherib of Assyria Iraq, Brooklyn Museum, New York (image source: author).

## *What Is in a Name?*

The name of King Sennacherib, who besieged Jerusalem but failed to take it, is made up of the name of the moon god Sin, Sennacherib.

It may be interesting to note that the symbol of the moon god Sin was the crescent moon.

And it is common knowledge today that the last religion to adopt this symbol, the crescent moon, is the religion of Islam. Indeed, the crescent moon crowns all the mosques of Islam.

And as happened in the past, in the days of King Sennacherib, so shall happen in the coming days as the mobs and armies of the east shall once again come and surround Jerusalem city.

**The crescent moon crowns all the minarets of the Blue Mosque of Istanbul, Turkey (image source: author).**

*ARAB* – Part Two, 133, P.69

"the double-hour god (Beru, i.e., Sin), ... the exalted(?) (lord), who has no mercy upon humankind, whose wrath is great."

*ARAB* – 154, P.82

"I cut off their heads."

*ARAB* – Part Two, 172, P.95

"cups incrusted with silver, siprate, crescents."

96—EARTH OUT OF ORBIT

An Elamite, Iranian, stele (slab) showing the symbols of the three great divinities: the star of Ishtar, the sun of Shamash, and the crescent moon of Sin, the Louvre Museum, Paris (image source: author).

## The Black King of Egypt

And so now, my lord, Emperor Titus and your majesties, the biblical scribes say that in the face of the overwhelming Assyrian power surrounding Jerusalem, the Judean king, H.M. King Hezekiah, had no choice but to seek the help of the king of mighty Egypt and its armed forces.

And furthermore, sir, the biblical scribes say that the king of Egypt at that time was an African black man. He sits quite a distance away from you, sir.

Some would think that this is impossible, your majesty. The biblical account must be wrong. How could mighty Egypt be ruled by a foreigner? And they may also ask, sir, whether King Sennacherib's records agree with this strange biblical claim?

And yes indeed, your majesty, the ancient Assyrian Iraqi records do agree with the biblical scribes and their strange claim.

At any rate, sir, this African king of Egypt had hailed from the Sudan or Nubia, which in their time, sir, was summed up with the larger region around it and was called "Ethiopia" or "Kush."

And so, with your permission, sir, we will let the biblical scribes pepper our comments with their records.

And we can also tell you, sir, in advance, that this biblical King Tirhakah will inadvertently bring a total disaster not only on his Egypt, my lord, but also on his own Ethiopian people, as well as upon the Lebanese people of Tyre. The island kingdom of Tyre, as you may know, your majesty Emperor Titus, was before your time one of the wealthiest kingdoms of the entire region, if not the world.

## *From Peak to Abyss*

The army of Assyria, under its last great kings, will defeat Assyria's two main competitors, the two countries with enough fortifications and armies able to resist them—Tyre of Lebanon and Egypt.

With the destruction of Tyre and Egypt, it would become abundantly clear to all the peoples of the world that there is no force on earth that could bring the Assyrian Iraqis down to their knees.

Yet in the face of overwhelming odds, Israeli prophets, such as Nahum, went on to prophecy of an imminent destruction of Assyria.

And then the prophets went so far as to name the destroyer of the Assyrian Empire and even how the destruction was to take place. Who is left to accomplish this?

From the very peak of its power, Iraq was to tumble down to a deep abyss in no time at all.

But once again, both Iraq and Iran shall, according to the prophets, rise one last time in the years of the end to fulfill another task assigned to them.

ABOVE: A Phoenician necklace with pendants, 5th-4th century B.C. Phoenicia, present day Lebanon, included the wealthy city of Tyre. Tyre was one of the most important trading cities of the ancient world with its busy shipping port, Brooklyn Museum, N.Y (image source: author).

Ezek 28:5 By thy great wisdom (king of Tyrus, or Tyre) and by thy traffick hast thou increased thy riches, and thine heart is lifted up because of thy riches:

It is a country that can afford to pay high taxes to Assyria

A Phoenician strap with pendants, 5th-4th century B.C. Brooklyn Museum, N.Y (image source: author).

Ezek 28:7 Behold, therefore I will bring strangers upon thee (king of Tyre), the terrible of the nations (the violent northern Iraqis of Assyria): and they shall draw their swords against the beauty of thy wisdom, and they shall defile thy brightness.

The Egyptian god Amun (a ram) protecting King Taharqa, the Ethiopian king of Egypt who was mentioned in the Bible and who was to come to assist King Hezekiah of Israel against the Iraqi King Sennacherib (690–664 BC), British Museum (image source: author).

Another statue of the Ethiopian king of Egypt, King Taharqa or Tirhakah of the Bible, British Museum (image source: author).

King Taharkah presents wine to the god Hemen, Louvre Museum, Paris (images source: author)

## Jerusalem All Alone

Tirhakah or not, your majesty, Emperor Titus, H.M. King Sennacherib dispatched a large segment of his troops, overwhelming troops, sir, and besieged Jerusalem, as you yourself did nearly 770 solar years later. And as the mobs and Islamic armies of the east shall yet do, sir.

Meanwhile, sir, H.M. King Sennacherib himself and the main force of the army went on from sacking Lachish to sack another city, Libnah.

Carry on, please, biblical scribes.

> 2 CHR 32:9 *After this did Sennacherib king of Assyria send his servants to Jerusalem, but he himself laid <u>siege against Lachish</u>, and all his power with him*

The two mural slabs above lined the walls of King Sennacherib's palace and show the deportation of the Israeli population of the city of Lachish of Judea, British Museum (image source: author).

My lord Emperor Titus, the Iraqi generals of H.M. King Sennacherib, according to the orders of their master, made threatening speeches to the besieged and terrified leaders and residents of Jerusalem.

Standing by the walls of the city, their speeches, your majesty, were aimed at encouraging the besieged Israelites to open the gates and surrender their city, and not to think that God could save them because no other god has so far managed to save his people from the Iraqi army of armies. And accordingly, why will the God of Israel be any different and more capable than the other gods to help His city of Jerusalem?

And indeed, your majesties, no city in the region had managed to hold up against his Iraqi majesty, and therefore Jerusalem, too, had in fact no chance to hold up either.

Go ahead, please, prophet Isaiah, with your report.

> *Isa 37:9* he [King Sennacherib] heard say [rumor] concerning <u>Tirhakah king of Ethiopia</u>, He is come forth to make war with thee. And when he [King Sennacherib] heard it, he sent messengers to Hezekiah [King of Judah],
>
> *Is 37:10* Thus [King Sennacherib ordered his generals] shall ye speak to Hezekiah king of Judah, saying, <u>Let not thy God, in whom thou trustest, deceive thee</u>, saying, Jerusalem shall not be given into the hand of the king of Assyria.
>
> *Isa 37:11* <u>Behold, thou hast heard what the kings of Assyria have done to all lands</u> by destroying them utterly; and shalt thou be delivered?
>
> *Isa 37:12* Have the gods of the nations delivered them which my fathers have destroyed, as Gozan, and Haran, and Rezeph, and the children of Eden which were in Telassar?
>
> *Isa 37:13* Where is the king of Hamath, and the king of Arphad [north of the modern Syrian city of Aleppo], and the king of the city of Sepharvaim, Hena, and Ivah?

## No, Not All Alone —Nature Came

And then, my lord, Emperor Titus, it all happened. It all happened, sir.

This great event did not happen when you besieged Jerusalem, sir, but it happened when the armies of the east, under the command of his Iraqi majesty King Sennacherib, besieged the city.

Jerusalem, as we mentioned, sir, was as good as finished. But that very night, sir, that very night, and before the dawn's assault of the Iraqi and easterners' troops, nature, sir—yes, nature—broke down in pieces.

Hopeless Jerusalem was saved, sir.

H.M. King Sennacherib could not run fast enough to get away from the walls of frightful Jerusalem.

Do the Assyrian records say the same thing?

In a roundabout way, yes, they do your majesty, but not quite in a straightforward admission of unexplainable setback or defeat.

Indeed, your majesty, the records of H.M. King Sennacherib do add more details to the statements of the biblical scribes, sir.

Go ahead, your majesty, King Sennacherib, read to my lords from your own ancient and unalterable account against Jerusalem.

"The officials, nobles and people of Ekron [a philistine city], who had thrown Padi, their king [this deposed king of the city of Ekron was a puppet and ally of King Sennacherib], bound by (treaty to) Assyria, into fetters of iron and had given him over to Hezekiah, the Jew (Iaudai), he kept him in confinement like an enemy, they (Lit., their heart) became afraid <u>and called upon the Egyptian kings</u>, the bowmen, chariots and horses of <u>the king of Meluhha (Ethiopia)</u>, a countless host ... As for Hezekiah, the Jew, who did not submit to my yoke, <u>46 of his strong, walled cities</u>, as well as the small cities in their neighborhood, which were without number, by escalade [ladders] and by bringing up siege engines(?), by attacking and storming on foot, by mines [digging in and under the wall], tunnels and breaches(?) I besieged and took (those cities)"[10]

King Sennacherib described his miltary campaigns on the above hardened clay prism, which also relates his third campaign against King Hezekiah and Jerusalem, Chicago Oriental Institute (image source: author).

Would you like to add any more claims, your majesty King Sennacherib?

---

[10] *ARA*- Part Two, 240, P.119

"I devastated the wide province of Judah; the strong, proud Hezekiah, its king, I brought in submission to my feet"[11]

"As for Hezekiah, the Jew, who had not submitted to my yoke ... Him, like a caged bird, in Jerusalem, his royal city, I shut up".[12]

Correct me if I am wrong, your majesty King Sennacherib, and all boasting aside, if you do not mind, sir, but it seems to me that you caged him in, but yet you did not manage to lay hands on him or on his city. Why is this, sir?

### A Future Repeat

In addition to the ancient Assyrian Chicago prism, featured earlier, the Sennacherib's prism (or Taylor prism), featured above, also records the siege of Jerusalem by the Assyrian King Sennacherib, British Museum (image source: author).

The biblical prophets went on to announce that there shall come a time in the future, their future, our day, when the children of Israel shall return from a worldwide exile to their ancient land of Israel.

This second return of the children of Israel did indeed take place after World War II.

The children of Israel were practically annihilated, but against all odds, and facing the most powerful enemy ever, they came back alive from their dug-up grave, so to speak.

And then the biblical prophets spoke of a time, following their return, when armies from the east shall gather around Jerusalem city and besiege it, such as what happened in the days of Iraqi King Sennacherib. We look to the past to see the future outcome.

---

[11] *ARAB* – Part Two, 327, P.148.
[12] *ARAB* – Part Two, 312, P.143.

If our understanding is correct, then soon the situation for Israel shall be a dire one. But then Jerusalem shall, one more time, be saved in a similar fashion as it was saved in the day back then when the Iraqi King Sennacherib and his assorted soldiers from many parts of the east besieged it.

Following the future siege of Jerusalem, then comes the event much anticipated and yearned for, the return of the One who out of sheer love gave mankind the chance for a never-ending life in a new celestial body in a vast universe without end.

We shall return from death new. We shall return better. We shall return glorious.

> Ps 102:13 <u>the set time, is come</u>.
> ...
> Ps 102:16 When the LORD shall build up Zion, <u>he shall appear in his glory</u> [the second coming of Christ following the future siege of Jerusalem].
> ...
> Ps 102:18 <u>This shall be written for the generation to come</u>: and the people which shall be created shall praise the LORD.

In the days of King Sennacherib, Jerusalem was saved by the strikes of nature and not by the Egyptian Ethiopian ruler, King Taharqa, who in fact did not show up at all at Jerusalem.

Jerusalem and Israel were left all alone then, and they shall be all alone in the strike to come.

This was not the first time that nature—the heavens, literally—came for help.

There was a similar dire situation in the old days of the Israeli judge Deborah, who sang of the deliverance of Israel against assorted armies of the east [again, armies from the east] under the command of Sisera, in the following words:

> Judg 5:19 The kings [of the easterner armies] came and fought, then fought the [local neighbors of Israel] kings of Canaan in Taanach [a town] by the waters of Megiddo [Armageddon]; they took no gain of money [the armies of the east attacked Israel first then they were joined by the immediate local neighbors of Israel and the battle took place in the valley of Armageddon. They, the easterners and the local neighbors, were defeated and took no gains].
> Judg 5:20 They [the stars] fought from heaven; <u>the stars in their courses [orbits] fought against Sisera [and his assorted armies from the east]</u>.

The same strikes of nature—the stars in their orbits, the meteors, the asteroids—shall also save Jerusalem and Israel in the days soon to come.

It happened in Deborah and Sisera's days. It happened in Hezekiah and Sennacherib's days. It shall happen again in our days.

> *1 Cor 10:11* Now all these things happened unto them for ensamples [examples/patterns]: and they are written for our admonition [education and encouragement], <u>upon whom the ends of the world are come</u>.

Nature shall break apart. The earth shall be bombarded by heavenly bodies—meteors and asteroids.

The usual routine of the earth shall be interrupted.

This news is indeed rather unbelievable because it has never happened before in our life time. We have no experience with an oscillating earth or major meteorite bombardment and an unprecedented earthquake and volcanoes.

At any rate, the prophets then continue to say that when you see these events happen, know that the time of your transformation to a new body—celestial and eternal body—is near, i.e., the second coming of Christ and the transformation of those who love Him is near.

But to back up a bit, one may question whether the armies of the east shall also aid nature with a nuclear disaster, which would trigger the unprecedented earthquake, the oscillation of the earth, and the coalition with meteors and asteroids.

> *2 Pet 3:7* But the heavens and the earth, which are now ... are ... <u>reserved unto fire</u> against the day of judgment and perdition of ungodly men.
>
> *2 Pet 3:8* beloved, be not ignorant of this one thing, that <u>one day is with the Lord as a thousand years, and a thousand years as one day</u>.
>
> *2 Pet 3:9* The Lord is not slack concerning his promise [the second coming of Christ Jesus], as some men count slackness; but [the Lord] is longsuffering [patient] to us-ward, <u>not willing that any should perish</u>, but that <u>all</u> should come to repentance [and receive God's promise of eternal life in the eternal heavens].
>
> *2 Pet 3:10* But the day of the Lord will come as a thief in the night [unpredictable]; <u>in the which the heavens shall pass away with a great noise, and the elements [splitting of the atoms, or nuclear fission] shall melt with fervent [high] heat, the earth also and the works that are therein shall be burned up [great noise, heat and fire]</u>.
>
> *2 Pet 3:11* Seeing then that all these things shall be <u>dissolved</u>, what manner of persons ought ye to be
>
> *2 Pet 3:12* Looking for and hasting unto the coming of the day of God, wherein <u>the heavens being on fire shall be dissolved, and the elements shall melt with fervent heat?</u>

But following the meltdown of the heavens and the fiery holocaust end of the earth, there shall be a new beginning, a new eternal heaven, and a new eternal earth. And humans, the selected family of God, transformed into a new celestial and eternal creature, will never again look the same as in our present form of flesh and bones. Today, we look nothing like our eternal body.

Today, we are earthbound. Tomorrow, we shall sail the heavens. We shall come back from death new. This has been God's desire from day one when He created man, that at last man would take God's own image and likeness, the eternal companions of God—His eternal family—chosen, tested, and justified in their selection.

> Ps 102:25 Of old hast thou laid the foundation of the earth: and the heavens are the work of thy hands.
> Ps 102:26 They shall perish [come to an end], but thou shalt endure: yea, all of them shall wax old [grow old] like a garment; as a vesture [a piece of cloth] shalt thou change them, and they shall be changed [the universe shall be changed]:
> Ps 102:27 But thou art the same, and thy years shall have no end.

And as the prophets say: this earth is a temporary home. This temporary earth was designed to fulfill a certain task, which is producing and testing the children of God, the royal family of God—the future rulers and governors of a new and lasting universe without end.

> 2 Pet 3:13 Nevertheless we, according to his promise, look for new heavens and a new earth, wherein dwelleth righteousness.

## Fiery and Noisy Nuclear Holocaust?

Here are then some of the words the prophets used to describe the fallout that shall follow the future siege of Jerusalem. One may note that the words describe what may appear to be nuclear fallout, such as how a government official marks a "contaminated" body and touches it not until a specialized team of officials come after him and carefully remove the body.

All said and done, the prophesies shall guide us and tell us how close we are to these events.

We watch Israel. We watch what happens to Israel. It is the clock that indicates how near the hour is.

And along with Israel, we watch Syria, Iran, and Russia as the prophets shortly shall show why. Not to mention the United Emirates and Saudi Arabia. Saudi Arabia shall worry that Iran and Russia are coming for its wealth, says the prophecy. And the United Emirates shall ally with the enemy.

> Zech 14:12 And this shall be the plague wherewith the LORD will smite all the people that have fought against Jerusalem; Their flesh shall consume away while they stand upon their feet, and their eyes shall consume away in their holes, and their tongue shall consume away in their mouth.
> Ez 39:12 And seven months shall the house of Israel be burying of them, that they may cleanse the land.

> Ez 39:14 And they shall sever out [set aside] men of continual employment [full-time job], passing through the land to bury with the passengers [travelling teams to search for dead bodies of the armies of the east] those that remain upon the face of the earth [scattered upon the fields], to cleanse it: after the end of seven months shall they search.
> Ez 39:15 And the passengers [the travelling teams] that pass through the land, when any seeth a man's bone, <u>then shall he set up a sign by it</u>, till the buriers have buried it in the valley of Hamongog.
> Ez 39:16 And also the name of the city shall be Hamonah. Thus shall they cleanse the land.

The danger is coming—and nothing can be done to avert it. Jerusalem shall be surrounded by the Islamic armies of the east, it shall fall, and it shall be occupied for a determined period of time.

> Mk 13:14 But when ye shall see the abomination of desolation, spoken of by Daniel the prophet, standing where it ought not, let him that readeth understand, then let them that be in Judaea flee to the mountains:
> Mk 13:15 And let him that is on the housetop not go down into the house, neither enter therein, to take any thing out of his house:
> Mk 13:16 And let him that is in the field not turn back again for to take up his garment.
> Mk 13:17 But woe to them that are with child, and to them that give suck in those days!
> Mk 13:18 And pray ye that your flight be not in the winter.
> Mk 13:19 For in those days <u>shall be affliction, such as was not from the beginning of the creation which God created unto this time, neither shall be</u>.
> Mk 13:20 And except that the Lord had shortened those days, no flesh should be saved: but for the elect's sake, whom he hath chosen, he hath shortened the days.
> Mk 13:21 And then if any man shall say to you, Lo, here is Christ; or, lo, he is there; believe him not:
> Mk 13:22 For false Christs and false prophets shall rise, and shall shew signs and wonders, to seduce, if it were possible, even the elect.
> Mk 13:23 But take ye heed: behold, I have foretold you all things.
> Mk 13:24 But in those days, <u>after that tribulation</u>, the sun shall be darkened, and the moon shall not give her light,
> Mk 13:25 <u>And the stars of heaven shall fall, and the powers that are in heaven shall be shaken</u>.
> Mk 13:26 And then shall they see the Son of man [Christ Jesus] coming in the clouds with great power and glory.
> Mk 13:27 And then shall he send his angels, and shall gather together his elect from the four winds, from the uttermost part of the earth to the uttermost part of heaven.

Emperor Titus and your majesties, it should be mentioned, my lords, that after H.M. King Sennacherib had rushed away from the walls of Jerusalem and back to his land, he never again tried to besiege Jerusalem or even get near it.

In fact, according to the biblical scribes, H.M. King Sennacherib was assassinated by his two elder sons.

And indeed, history, my lords, and the archaeological records do in fact confirm this biblical prophecy, which was made by the prophet Isaiah.

It is suggested, your majesty, that his assassination was because of his failure to take Jerusalem as well as of his devastation of Babylon.

Prophet Isaiah, and Babylonian scribes, present your report gentleman please.

> ISA 37:37 *So Sennacherib king of Assyria departed, and went and returned, and dwelt at Nineveh.*
> ISA 37:38 *And it came to pass, as he was worshipping in the house of Nisroch his god, that Adrammelech and Sharezer his sons smote him with the sword; and they escaped into the land of Armenia [northern enemies of Assyria]: and Esarhaddon his son reigned in his stead.*
>
> "On the 10th day of the month Tebet [Dec/Jan 681 BC], Sennacherib king of Assyria by his own son was murdered in an insurrection."[13]

Note, my lords, that the Bible says two sons were involved in the plot. Indeed, Sennacherib had two sons older than Prince Esarhaddon who succeeded him, but perhaps only one did the actual killing.

---

[13] The ancient *Babylonian Chronicles*, Column III: 34, 35. http://www.sacred-texts.com/ane/rp/rp201/rp20109.htm

110—EARTH OUT OF ORBIT

Biblical King Sargon II (right) and his crown prince Sennacherib (left) on a relief from Khorsabad, Louvre, Paris (image source: http://www.livius.org/men-mh/mesopotamia/kings.html).

## Forty-Seven Years in Advance

Your majesties, may we now travel faster in time to reach the peak and then the fall of the greatest nation on earth at the time, Assyria Iraq, which emptied Israel of its ten tribes and held them fast in Iranian and Iraqi cities!

Once we reach the end of the Assyrian dominion of the world, my lords, then we will come face to face with the next superpower. The one that shall empty Israel of its last two tribes, destroy the house of prayer, the temple of the Lord, and the parliament of God—and nearly exterminate and totally obliterate the nation of Israel off the face of the earth. The earth would then have no preacher from the Holy One, nor a calendar.

And so, my lords, in the face of the nonstop invasions and increasing power of Assyria Iraq, the other strongest and wealthiest three leaders of the ancient Middle East decided to unite their efforts and face off the Assyrians. These leaders, my lords, were the wealthy king Ba"lu of Tyre of Lebanon, King Hezekiah of Judah Israel, and King Tirhakah of Egypt, whom King Hezekiah of Judah had asked for help against H.M. King Sennacherib.

A Phoenician (Phoenicia, with its wealthy kingdom of Tyre, was part of present-day Lebanon) pair of bracelets, 5th–4th century BC, Brooklyn Museum, N.Y (image source: author).

This alliance, my lords, was the opening move in a series of events that shall eventually fulfill an old prophecy by the prophet Isaiah, the timekeeper of the plan of God for our bright future.

The prophet Isaiah, my lords, had documented his prophecy in the year when his Assyrian majesty King Sargon came and attacked the Philistine city of Ashdod [711 BC, as archaeologically dated].

Isaiah, my lords, prophesied that the Assyrian Iraqis shall attack and invade Tyre of Lebanon, Egypt, and its ally Ethiopia. And the outcome of the invasion would be a disaster for the two defendants.

Forty years after Isaiah foretold it, my lords; Tyre, Egypt, and the Ethiopians were indeed caught in the prophecy.

Within this forty years, my lords, King Sargon II had come and gone; his successor King Sennacherib had also come and gone as well. But the prophecy was not fulfilled in their days.

Was then the prophet Isaiah wrong? No, my lords!

Sometimes, it takes a sequel of several years and rulers to complete a biblical prophecy. The completion may start with one king, continues with another ruler, and then finishes with yet a third one. We keep this in mind, my lords, when we think of the prophecies of our own present day.

Indeed, my lords, the odds against fulfilling Isaiah's prophecy were quite high. For Isaiah did not have a large window of opportunity, that is to say he did not have the luxury of a long time for his prophecy to be fulfilled, my lords. The reason is that this great Assyrian empire of their majesties King Tiglathpileser III, King Shalmaneser V, King Sargon II, and King Sennacherib—the northern Iraqi rulers of the universe—would come crumbling down, my lords, within 86 years [711–625 BC] of Isaiah's prophecy. And so, your majesties, the prophecy of a great Assyrian victory over the strong and mighty Egypt of King Tirhakah and his native and far away Ethiopia, in addition to the well-fortified and wealthy Tyre of King Ba"lu, did not have the luxury to wait a long time for fulfillment.

But Isaiah's prophecy was fulfilled, your majesties. And this Isaiah, your majesties, is the very same man who had also prophesied that our earth will oscillate out of orbit, presumably in our generation, if we understand him correctly, my lords.

Go ahead with your record please, prophet Isaiah.

> *ISA 20:1* *In the year that Tartan [an Assyrian general] came unto Ashdod [711 BC, Ashdod is a Philistine city], when Sargon the king of Assyria sent him, and fought against Ashdod, and took it;* *ISA 20:2* *At the same time spake the LORD by Isaiah the son of Amoz, saying*
> ...
> *ISA 20:4* *So shall the king of Assyria <u>lead away the Egyptians prisoners, and the Ethiopians captives</u> [Esarhaddon and the Assyrian Iraqis invaded Egypt starting 671 BC], young and old, naked and barefoot, even with their buttocks uncovered, to the shame of Egypt.*

"Young and old, naked and barefoot, even with their buttocks uncovered, to the shame of Egypt," prophesied Isaiah.

The above panel of the bronze gates of Balawat (Shalmaneser III) shows naked captives being hauled away by the Assyrians, The British Museum (image source: author).

It seems that the Middle East never sleeps, never rests, my lords. Its poor people were and are always having nightmares of being butchered as sheep.

But if the Middle East could afford one night of rest, my lords, Israel in the middle of it could not.

First came H.M. King Tiglathpileser III [745–727 BC] and emptied Israel north of two and one half of its tribes [732 BC]. Then after him came their majesties King Shalmaneser V [727–722 BC] and King Sargon II [722–705 BC], who besieged Samaria and emptied Israel north of the rest of its ten tribes [722 BC]. Israel north, my lords, became an Assyrian Iraqi property.

And then, my lords, H.M. King Sennacherib came to the remaining southern half of Israel and destroyed over forty Israeli towns and cities, and then besieged Jerusalem city but failed to take it.

## Revolt in Transition Time

Following the assassination of H.M. King Sennacherib by his eldest two sons, he was then followed, my lords, by his younger son, H.M. King Esarhaddon [681–669 BC].

The transition time between two kings, my lords, as you may very well know, is an opportune time for an enemy of a state to cause problems. And if the transition time is a critical time in ordinary circumstance, it was much the more so, my lords, at this time in Assyria following the assassination of H.M. King Sennacherib, which was carried out by his two princes, who were in line for the crown.

## 114—EARTH OUT OF ORBIT

This, then, my lords, was the time when H.M. King Ba"lu of Tyre of Lebanon decided to revolt against Assyria Iraq. And he did so, my lords, encouraged By King Tirhakah of Egypt and King Hezekiah of Judah Israel. Accordingly, my lords, H. M. King Ba"lu refused to pay his annual tribute to the new and untested king of Assyria Iraq H. M. King Esarhaddon.

This revolt, my lords, will bring the prophecies home.

How, my lords, could prophet Isaiah have seen the twists of forty years in advance [711–671 BC]?

His Assyrian majesty King Esarhaddon had no option now, my lords, but to attack Tyre of Lebanon and its allies before all the countries under his dominion copycat King Ba"lu and stop making their annual tributes.

And so, my lords, as soon as his majesty settled his affairs at home, he took the great Assyrian army and marched out for Lebanon. We shall follow him for a short while, my lords, because during these marches of his and of his successor, the face of Israel shall be changed. And out of this change, they shall give us the background for the Good Samaritan. Yet these marches shall also be the funeral marches of the great Assyrian empire. The giant shall fall backward and crash.

At any rate, as mentioned before, my lords, forty years before this attack took place, Isaiah prophesied [711 BC] that it would happen and that the wealthy, strong and well-fortified Tyre shall fall into the hands of the Iraqi Assyrians.

Carry on, please, prophet Isaiah.

> *ISA 23:5* *As at the report concerning Egypt, so shall they be sorely pained [Egypt shall be afraid]* <u>*at the report of Tyre*</u> *[King Esarhaddon left part of his army behind to besiege the city of Tyre while he, himself, led the rest of the army against Egypt. The city of Tyre, of present Lebanon, was on the highway that stretched from Assyria Iraq to Egypt].*

Would you please, your majesty King Esarhaddon, read to their majesties a few lines of your ancient and unalterable records regarding your invasion of Tyre of Lebanon, Egypt, and Ethiopia [671 BC]!

> "In my tenth campaign ... I took [the road to ... (and) [turned] my face toward the land of ... which in the language of the people of Ethiopia (Kush) and Egypt [is called ...], I mobilized the numerous hosts of Assur which were in ... In the month of *Nisanu*, the first month, I departed from my city Assur. The Tigris (and) Euphrates I crossed at their flood; over mighty (difficult) mountains I advanced, like a wild-ox.

> In the course of my <u>campaign I threw up earthworks against Ba"lu, king of Tyre, who had put his trust in his friend Tirhakah (Tarku), king of Ethiopia, had thrown off my royal yoke and had sent me insolent (messages)</u>. Food and drink (water) (which would) keep them alive, I withheld (i.e., cut off) [Tyre city is besieged].
>
> ...
>
> <u>I butchered like sheep.</u>"[14]

Carry on please, your majesty King Esarhaddon.

> "Of Tirhakah, king of Egypt and Ethiopia (Kush), the accursed of their great godhead, from Ishhupri to Memphis [present day Cairo, capital of Egypt], his royal city, 15 day's march (was) the ground (covered) daily, without cessation I saw multitudes of his men, and him I smote five times with the point of my javelin, with wounds (from which there was) no recovery. Memphis, his royal city, in half a day, with mines, tunnels, assaults, I besieged, I captured, I destroyed, I devastated, I burned with fire. His queen (lit., woman of his palace), his harem, Ushanahuru [the crown prince], his heir (lit., son of his begetting), and the rest of his sons and daughters, his property and his gods, his horses, his cattle, his sheep, in countless numbers, I carried off to Assyria
>
> ...
>
> "Over all of Egypt I appointed anew kings, viceroys, governors, commandants, overseers (and) scribes. Offerings and fixed dues I established for Assur and the great gods for all time. <u>I made a stele</u> [monument] made with my name inscribed (thereon) and on <u>it I caused to be written the glory of the valor of Assur, my lord</u>, my mighty deeds, how I went to and fro under the protection of Assur, my lord, and the might of my conquering hand. <u>For the gaze of all my foes, to the end of days</u>, I set it up".[15]

> "Amidst gladness and rejoicing I entered Memphis, the royal city [of Tirhakah].... which was covered with gold, I sat down amidst jubilation."[16]

---

[14] *ARAB* – Part Two, 554-556, 564, P.219, 220.
[15] *ARAB* – Part Two, 580, P.226, 227.
[16] *ARAB*, 583, P.228

Biblical Assyrian King Esarhaddon capturing King Taharqa's crown prince as well as King Ba"lu of Tyre. Both figures are tied with a rope that passes through their lips and into the left hand of King Esarhaddon.

The small kingdom of Tyre, situated on the shores of the Mediterranean Sea, was in its heyday the business hub of the world with loaded ships coming and going nonstop to its harbor, similar to such harbors as modern-day Hong Kong, Alts Museum, Berlin (image source: author).

"I am powerful, I am all powerful, I am a hero, I am gigantic, I am colossal, I am honored, I am magnified, I am without an equal among all kings, the chosen one of Assur," wrote King Esarhaddon on his monuments.[17]

---

[17] *ARAB* – Part Two, 577, P. 226.

King Esarhaddon indeed documented his campaign against Egypt and Ethiopia (present-day Sudan/Nubia) on the monument, stele, above. The stele shows him capturing Taharqa's crown prince, Prince Ushanahuru (the smallest figure at Esarhaddon's feet with Negroid features), Alts Museum, Berlin (image source: author).

## The Summit of Power

Assyria of northern Iraq, my lords, home of today's Sunni Muslims, is reaching its highest peak, having now owned the entire Middle East, including the mighty Egypt.

But then, my lords, H.M. King Esarhaddon died and the Egyptians, encouraged by his death and the transition time in Assyria Iraq, revolted against their Assyrian governors.

Now, my lords, biblical King Tirhakah who had managed to run away to his native land of Kush ahead of H.M. King Esarhaddon, did then return once again to Egypt to see if he could reclaim his throne.

It was not to be.

And so, my lords, following the death of H.M. King Esarhaddon, his new successor King Assurbanipal [669–631/627 BC] marched for Egypt to rescue and restore the Assyrian governors to their positions and capture biblical Tirhakah once and for all.

That, too, did not happen, my lords.

Yet, Isaiah's prophecy was on its way for fulfillment. It took two kings and forty-seven years of gradual fulfillment [Edit: Isaiah prophesied in 711 BC, King Esarhaddon invaded Egypt in 671 BC, and then King Assurbanipal sacked the holy city of Thebes, today's Luxor, in 664 BC, forty-seven years after Isaiah had prophesied].

Your majesty King Assurbanipal, please recite your 2,700-year-old record regarding your invasion of Egypt.

> "In my first campaign I marched against Magan and Meluhha. <u>Tarku (Tirhakah), king of Egypt and Ethiopia (Kush), whom Esarhaddon, king of Assyria, the father who begot me, had defeated</u>, and whose land he had brought under his sway, that Tarku forgot the power of Assur, Ishtar and the great gods, my lords, and trusted in his own strength.
> 
> <u>Against th kings, the governors, whom my father had installed in Egypt, he marched</u>, (intent) on slaying, plundering and seizing Egypt. He broke upon them and established himself (lit., sat down) in Memphis, the city which my father had captured and added to the territory of Assyria. A swift courier came to Nineveh and reported to me.
> 
> ...
> 
> I directed the march.
> 
> ...
> 
> Tarku, king of Egypt and Ethiopia, heard of the advance of my army, in Memphis, and mustered his fighting men against me, offering armed resistenceand battle... I defeated his army in a battle on the open (lit., wide) plain.
> 
> Tarku heard of the defeat of his armies, while in Memphis.
> 
> ...
> 
> <u>He forsook Memphis [capital city of northern Egypt] and fled to save his life, to Ni' (Thebes) [Luxor, the relegious and capital city of southern Egypt]. That city I seized; I had my troops eneter and occupy it.</u>
> 
> ...

With much plunder and heavy spoil I returned in safety to Nineveh."[18]

"In my second campaign I made straight for Egypt and Ethiopia."[19]

"That city (i.e., Ni') [Luxor] my hands captured in its entirety, with the aid of Assur and Ishtar. Silver, gold, precious stones, the goods of his palace, all there was, brightly colored and linen garments, great horses, the people, male and female, two tall obelisks, made of shining electrum (ahale), whose weight was 2,500 talents, (and) which stood by the gate of the temple, I removed from their positions and carried them off to Assyria. Heavy plunder, and countless, I carried away from Ni'. Against Egypt and Ethiopia I waged warfare and established my might. With a full hand I returned in safety to Nineveh, my royal city."[20]

Queen Hatshepsut's temple, Deir el-Bahri, in the holy city of Luxor, the temple, which was most likely built by biblical Moses; see *Earth out of Orbit, Volume One – The Past and Future Prophecies of the World*. (Image source: Roland Unger, WC).

---

[18] *ARAB Part Two*, 770, 771, P.292-294.
[19] *ARAB*, 776, 777, P.295.
[20] *ARAB*, 778, P.296

120—EARTH OUT OF ORBIT

King Assurbanipal, the destroyer of the Egyptian holy city of Luxor, being one of the two men who fulfilled Isaiah's 47-year-old prophecy, is depicted hunting lions on a mural from his palace in Nineveh, British Museum of London (image source: author).

The army of King Assurbanipal, limestone wall mural from his palace in Nineveh, London's British Museum (image source: author).

FIRST 666 – COMING ALIVE—121

King Assurbanipal recorded his invasion of Egypt inscribed on part of this prism, which is housed in the Louvre Museum of France (image source: author).

Archaeologists have discovered 30,000 clay tablets belonging to Assurbanipal's library.

## 715 & 711 BC
## The Changing Face of Israel—Immigrants

And so, my lords, these were the five rulers who came from Assyria Iraq and who were responsible for destroying and stripping away the northern half of Israel. And as we have shown you, your majesties, they began their destruction in the province of Galilee until at last they hauled away the entire ten tribes of Israel, as both biblical and Assyrian scribes agreed in their ancient records.

But the last two or three of these five Iraqi rulers, my lords, did more harm to Israel than deporting away the ten tribes. They did also, my lords, bring foreigners to inhabit the sparsely populated, lonely, and empty towns and cities of the northern half of Israel, including its sad and desolate capital Samaria.

Now your majesties, both parties, the Assyrian and the biblical scribes, once again are in agreement that H.M. King Assurbanipal, whom the biblical scribes call "Asnappar," like his predecessor King Sargon II, had brought foreigners to inherit the gutted Samaria.

And, thus, my lords, the northern half of Israel became no longer the home of Israelites. Israel, my lords, became a country of mixed races of Arabs, Iraqis, Iranians, and many other nationalities.

And if we may digress for a minute here, my lords, in later times the children of Israel would call all these mixed foreigners of Israel "Samaritans," and they would despise them. Yet, the savior of the world, the gift of all gifts, the blessed son of God, Christ the Lord, used a Samaritan, the Good Samaritan example to teach a lawyer to love his fellow man whatever his race is.

May we now call on the biblical scribes, my lords, to speak to this forced immigration to Israel!

Go ahead, please, gentlemen.

> EZ 4:10 <u>And the rest of the nations whom the great and noble Asnappar [Assyrian King Assurbanipal] brought over, and set in the cities of Samaria</u>

> 2 KIN 17:24 <u>And the king of Assyria brought men</u> from Babylon, and from Cuthah, and from Ava, and from Hamath, and from Sepharvaim, <u>and placed them in the cities of Samaria instead of the children of Israel: and they possessed Samaria, and dwelt in the cities thereof.</u>

Biblical King Assurbanipal defeated the Arabs, burned their tents, deported them, and brought some of them to Samaria, the capital of the northern half of Israel, as the biblical Scriptures state. The Vatican Museum (image source: author).

Monument of biblical King Ashurbanipal, found in Nabu Temple, Bosippa, British Museum (image source: author).

And so now, my lords, we call on his Assyrian majesty King Sargon II to verify the biblical scribes!

Go ahead, your majesty, and read out your old record, sir, regarding the different races you brought to Israel.

> "I caused others to take their (the deported inhabitants') portion; I set my officers over them and imposed upon them the tribute of the former king."[21]

> "[At the beginning of my rule, in my first year of reign] ... <u>Samerinai (the people of Samaria)</u> ... [27,290 people, who lived therein] <u>I carried away</u>; 50 chariots for my royal equipment, I selected from [among them] ... [<u>The city I rebuilt], I made it greater than it was before; people of the lands (my hand had conquered, I settled therein</u>. My official I placed over them as governor). Tribute, tax, I imposed upon them ... I mixed together."[22]

> "The tribes of Tamud, Ibadid, Marsimanu and Haiapa, <u>distant Arabs, who inhabit the desert</u>, who knew neither high nor low official (governors nor superintendents) ... I struck them down, the remnant of them <u>I deported and settled them in Samaria</u>"[23]

> devastated the wide land of Bit-Humria (Israel) ... conqueror of the people of Tamud, Ibadidi, Marsimani, Haiapa, whose remnant was driven out and settled in the midst of Bit-Humria [Israel].[24]

## I Will Make Your Grave

One half of Israel, my lords, its largest half, has been sent to foreign rivers to be washed and cleansed in tears. The preacher of the world, the preacher of the plan, and the savior of the world needed to be washed in sweat and tears in enemies' land. The preacher of holiness needed to be renewed in mind and spirit—needed to be born again.

As for you, Assyria of Iraq, you have finished your assigned task. You have completed your job. You have fished Israel north out of the cesspool. But Assyria Iraq, home of the Sunni Muslims, you yourself you have grown vile and ruthless. And it is time now for you to go. The nations have suffered enough of your brutality and vileness. You commit fornications

---

[21] *ARAB* – Part Two, 55, P.26
[22] *ARAB* – Part Two, 4, P. 2
[23] *ARAB* – Part Two, 17, P.7
[24] *ARAB* – Part Two, 117, P.61

in the name of God, and in the name of God you destroy and burn. It is time for you to go. You shall no more go marching through the cities of the nations with your ruthless fighters to cut throats, and skin people alive, and throw them from higher grounds, and stuff them in pillars while yet breathing. There is no end to your brutality. The Babylonians, the Shiites of southern Iraq, are after you.

> ### Everyone Hates Us
>
> A Babylonian civil servant from Nippur once dared write to King Esarhaddon: "The king knows that all lands hate us on account of Assyria."[25]

Go ahead, please, prophet Nahum, and recite your prophecy regarding the fate of Assyria to their majesties.

> NAH 1:14 the LORD hath given a commandment concerning thee [Assyria Iraq], that no more of thy name be sown ... <u>I will make thy grave; for thou art vile</u>.
> NAH 1:15 Behold upon the mountains the feet of him that bringeth good tidings, that publisheth peace! O Judah [of Israel], keep thy solemn feasts, perform thy vows: for <u>the wicked shall no more pass through thee; he is utterly cut off</u>.
> NAH 3:7 And it shall come to pass, that all they that look upon thee shall flee from thee, and say, Nineveh [the capital of Assyria Iraq at the time] <u>is laid waste: who will bemoan her</u>?

The prophet Nahum, who uttered this prophecy, my lords, went further to prophesy that the Assyrian empire shall rise again no more—ever. It never did, to our present time, my lords.

That said, we now, my lords, steadily approach the field of Armageddon.

## Do You See Any Difference?

But, prophet Nahum, if we may ask you sir, who do you suggest would be able to put the mighty Assyria in its grave? Who can loosen its iron chokehold off the throat of the

---

[25] *Ancient Iraq*, Georges Roux, Penguin Books, 1966, P.278

nations? Who can dare tell the kings of the universe to abandon their monopoly and make room for a new royal family on earth?

Well, my lords, we shall call upon the ones sitting amongst you who put northern Iraq, home of the Sunni Muslims, into its grave. And they are none, my lords, but its own relatives from the south and their relatives' allies from the East—the Shiite and the Iranians of today, my lords.

## Same Ally Then and Now

Since time immortal, the northern half of Iraq, which is called Assyria, fought endless wars with the southern half of Iraq, which is called Babylonia. Babylonia's capital is Babylon city. The wars had religious bases to it—much the same as today.

Today, the northern half of Iraq is Sunni Muslims, whereas the southern half is Shiite Muslims.

And the bombings and the fights between these two sects of Islam are bloody and deadly.

This bloody feud began immediately upon the death of the Islamic prophet Muhammad, which triggered bloody fights between two branches of his family, each branch vying to rule after him. The prophet's family was considered to be the top believers.

Shiite Muslims whip their bloodied backs in an annual ceremony to commemorate the bloody massacre of the first Shiite Muslim ruler who was killed by his rivals, the Sunni Muslim rulers of early Islam, Wikipedia, Muhammadhani

However, back then in the endless wars between Assyria, of northern Iraq, and Babylonia, of southern Iraq, Assyria had the upper hand. Yet through the efforts of one man—and his stamina and vision— Babylonia did manage twice to free itself from the Assyrians, albeit for short durations.

The first Babylonian liberation lasted slightly over ten years. And indeed the name of this Babylonian freedom fighter is recorded in both the Bible and archaeology. His name is Merodach-baladan II.

As a matter of fact, it was this Babylonian freedom fighter, the man from the south, home of the Shiite Muslims, who led the way to the final destruction of the great and mighty Assyrian empire. But he did not do it all alone. His ally then was the same ally of the Shiite Muslims of today: Iran.

Merodach-baladan II made his first attempt to liberate Babylonia from its Assyrian masters in the days, which followed the death of the Assyrian King Shalmaneser V in 722 BC.

And indeed, with the help of his Iranian neighbors, where he was sheltered for a time, he fought the Assyrians and succeeded to take Babylon city from them. He consequently reigned over Babylonia of southern Iraq for ten years until the successor of Shalmaneser V, King Sargon II, returned from his other wars and fought him and defeated him.

However, the defeated Merodach-baladan II managed at that time to escape and run away across the borders to take shelter once again with his Iranian allies.

One may recall that King Sargon II was the Assyrian monarch who destroyed Samaria city of Israel and deported its ten tribes to exile. He also had a few unkind words to describe the Babylonian rebel Merodach-baladan II.

*ARAB* – Part Two, 66, P.P. 33

"Merodach-baladan, son of Iakin, king of Chaldea, seed of a murderer (lit., murder), prop of a wicked devil".

## *A Great Marvel*

But freedom fighter Merodach-baladan II was not a man to quit easily.

Now, upon the death of King Sargon II in 705 BC, Merodach-baladan II, seventeen years after his first attempt, came once again with his Iranian supporters, attacked, and defeated the Assyrian forces stationed in Babylon in 703 BC, and installed himself as the king of Babylonia.

The successor of King Sargon II was King Sennacherib, who mutilated Judah and besieged Jerusalem but failed to take it.

Now Merodach-baladan II, residing in Babylon, wasted no time to try and recruit more international allies, in addition to his Iranian friends.

One of these potential new allies was King Hezekiah of Judah Israel.

At that time King Hezekiah was certain that the Assyrian King Sennacherib intended to attack Israel and the surrounding region. Thus, he began to dig an underground tunnel to bring in waters inside the walls of Jerusalem from a natural spring located outside the city's walls. In doing so, King Hezekiah intended on one hand to make it hard for the Assyrian soldiers of King Sennacherib to get water for themselves, their horses, and the cattle that they brought with them for food; and on the other hand, he would enable the population of Jerusalem to withstand a long siege by King Sennacherib and his Assyrian army.

King Hezekiah's tunnel, which he built before Assyrian King Sennacherib, came and invaded Israel, Wikipedia, Tamar Hayardeni

Now, this tunnel winding many feet underground was an engineering feat.

Since the rush to dig and finish the tunnel was on, two crews began on both ends, one by the fountain outside the wall of Jerusalem, and the other far inside the city by a pool. The two crews began to dig feverishly.

It remains a mystery how the two crews were directed under the ground in order to line up properly and join the two halves of the tunnel.

Tunnel aside, it also happened that the Israeli King Hezekiah had fallen ill but later did recover from his fatal illness. Now upon hearing this, the newly installed, King Merodach-baladan II of Babylon, the thorn in Assyria's side, sent his son as a head of a Babylonian delegation to Jerusalem, ostensibly to congratulate the Israeli King Hezekiah for his recovery.

> Isa 39:1 At that time Merodachbaladan, the son of Baladan, king of Babylon, sent letters <u>and a present</u> to Hezekiah: for he had heard that he had been sick, and was recovered.

King Hezekiah gladly received the Babylonian Iraqi delegation. But being completely unguarded and unsuspecting, he revealed to them his wealth and showed them his entire army's equipment and ammunitions.

> 2 Kin 20:13 And Hezekiah hearkened [listened] unto them [the Babylonian delegation of King Berodachbaladan], and showed them <u>all the house of his precious things, the silver, and the gold, and the spices, and the precious ointment</u>, <u>and all the house of his armour</u>, <u>and all that was found in his treasures</u>: there was nothing in his house, nor in all his dominion, that Hezekiah showed them not.

It was at that time that prophet Isaiah went to see King Hezekiah and prophesied of a major event to come.

Now the visit of the Babylonian delegation took place around 703/702 BC. At which time, King Merodach-baladan II had only managed to remain as king of Babylon for nine months, starting in 703 BC. Thus, Isaiah's prophecy, which was made at that time, was fulfilled one hundred and fifteen years later in 587 BC.

And it was a prophecy against all odds.

Superpower Assyria was gaining strength steadily, conquering even Egypt and wealthy Tyre, while trodden Babylon, home of today's Shiite Muslims, was weakening just as fast.

And yet Isaiah prophesied that Babylon, the new friends of King Hezekiah, and not Assyria, the deadly enemies of King Hezekiah, shall one day come and devastate Israel—Judah to be exact—and carry the remainder of the Israelite population away to exile.

Babylon, the new friends of Israel, shall devastate what is left of Israel, prophesied the prophet 115 years in advance and against any natural or logical outcome.

> Isa 39:6 Behold, the days come, that all that is in thine house [King Hezekiah's palace], and that which thy fathers have laid up in store until this day, <u>shall be carried to Babylon: nothing shall be left</u>, saith the LORD.

*Isa 39:7* *And of thy sons that shall issue from thee, which thou shalt beget, shall they [the Babylonians] take away; and they shall be* <u>*eunuchs in the palace of the king of Babylon*</u> *[indeed one of these eunuchs shall prophecy for events, which shall take place in our own time - his name is Daniel]."*

The irony is that this Babylon of which Isaiah spoke was in fact in line to be razed to the ground in a few months.

Biblical Merodach-baladan (L), king of Babylon, Altes Museum, Berlin (image source: author).

Biblical King Merodach-baladan II of Babylon, details, Altes Museum, Berlin (image source: author).

As mentioned, King Merodach-baladan did not reign long over Babylon in his second attempt to free it from Assyria. Indeed, King Sennacherib, upon leaving Jerusalem city in a hurry, went to Babylon, and in a fit of unprecedented and boundless rage attacked and destroyed the holy city, which was revered by the Babylonians and the Assyrians alike. Babylon was the Mecca of its day.

And it is presumed that Sennacherib's sons assassinated him because of his failure at Jerusalem, as well as because of erasing sacred Babylon to the ground and hauling away all its gods into the temples of his own capital city.

*ARAB* –Part Two, 257, P.128

"At the beginning of my reign, when I solemnly took my seat on the throne, and ruled the inhabitants of Assyria with mercy and grace, <u>Merodach-baladan, king of Babylon, (whose heart is wicked)</u>, an instigator of revolt, plotter of rebellion ... doer of evil, whose guilt is heavy, <u>brought over to his side Shutur-Nahundu, the Elamite [Iranians]</u>, and gave him gold, silver and precious stones, and so secured him as an ally."

*ARAB* – Part Two, 260, P.P 130

"I raged like a lion, I stormed like a tempest, with my merciless warriors I set my face against Merodach-baladan, (who was) in Kish. And that worker of inequity saw my advance from afar; terror fell upon him, he forsook all of his troops, and fled to the land of Guzummanu.

...

In joy of heart and with a radiant face I hastened to Babylon and entered the palace of Merodach-baladan

...

his wife, his harem, his slave girls(?), his officials, his nobles, his courtiers, the male and female musicians, the palace slaves, who gladdened his princely mind, all of the artisans, as many as they were, his palace menials(?), - (these) I brought forth and counted as spoil. I hurried after him, sent my warriors to Guzummanu, into the midst of the swamps and marshes and they searched for him for five days, but his (hiding)- place was not found."

**Ancient Babylonian (?) harpist, Louvre Museum, Paris (image source: author).**

*ARAB* – Part Two, 234, P.P 116

"In the midst of that battle he forsook his camp, and made his escape alone, (so) he saved his life.
The chariots, horses, wagons, mules, which he left behind at the onset of the battle, my hands seized.
Into his palace, which is in Babylon, joyfully I entered.
I opened his treasure-house: -gold, silver ... precious stones of every kind (name), goods and property without limit (number) ... his harem, (his) courtiers and officials, singers, male and female, all of his artisans, as many as there were, the servants of his palace, I brought out, I counted as spoil."

*ARAB* – Part Two, 345, P.P 153

"Merodach-baladan ...That one fled alone to the sea-land and the gods of his whole land, with the bones of his fathers, (who lived) before (him), (which) he gathered from their coffins, and his people, he loaded on ships and crossed over to Nagitu, which is on the other side of the Bitter Sea (Persian Gulf); and in that place he died."

Merodach-baladdan died but not the Babylonian rebellion. The Babylonian rebellion continued as his son and his grandson, whose name is Nabu-bel-shumate, took up the fight to free southern Iraq from the chains of its northern half.
In due time, Babylon, home of the Shiite, in alliance with Shiite Iran next door, would indeed succeed to destroy Assyria, home of the Sunni Muslims of today.
And in future time, the Shiite of southern Iraq, old Babylon, shall ally themselves with Shiite Iran against Israel. And the armies of the east shall march across the dried-up marshes of southern Iraq heading for Jerusalem.

Babylon, Iraq, 1932, WC, Library of Congress Prints and Photographs Division Washington DC.

Your majesties, seeing that you come from different eras, we would need a little pause from interviewing your royal colleagues in order to introduce to you, my lords, one of the most important events that struck Israel. Indeed, the prophecies, which deal with our present and future events, are calculated and dated back to the day this particular disastrous event hit Israel.

## The House of the Lions

Over three hundred years, your majesties, Assyria of northern Iraq ruled supreme over the world of the Middle East, including the mighty Egypt. Over the years, it gave birth to great although brutal men, if you may allow us to say so, my lords, of your colleagues. These brutal men were the builders, the founding fathers of the Assyrian superpower. Men, my lords, such as King Tiglathpileser III, who invaded the Galilee region of Israel; King Shalmaneser V, who besieged Samaria, capital of Israel North; King Sargon II, who finished the job of capturing Samaria and deporting the ten tribes of Israel; King Sennacherib, who ravaged the southern half of Israel, the kingdom of Judah, and its great city of Lachish but failed to sack the capital Jerusalem; King Esarhaddon, who invaded Egypt and sacked the wealthy kingdom of Tyre of Lebanon; and, lastly, the great one King Assurbanipal, who firmed up Assyria's hold over Egypt.

And until his last day of breathing, my lords, everything in the world, and the Middle East seemed normal, routine, and predictable.

And yet, your majesties, fifteen short years after the death of the great King Assurbanipal, Assyria suddenly crumbled and ended forever.

Can you believe it, your majesties? Within fifteen years of the peak of its power, and the widest swath of its borders, the greatest and most powerful nation on earth, with the strongest army around, Assyria Iraq was snuffed cold and for good. Assyria Iraq, my lords, went from the world champion to suffering a massive heart attack. It died within fifteen years from its sunniest days. Who would have thought this possible?

But wait, my lords, although the empire of Assyria and its hold on the neighboring countries would be dead forever, according to the prophets, the same cannot be said for its mother country, Iraq. Our present Iraq, as we said several times, my lords, has yet an important act to fulfill in the coming months when Jerusalem of Israel would be surrounded and taken.

Here is then what transpired, my lords, in those fifteen short years.

Following the death of H.M. King Assurbanipal, the last of the great Assyrian lions, a slew of weak and spoiled offspring and siblings came along. They fought amongst themselves, each eyeing the throne, the luxury of the palace, the use of the harem, and the lackeys.

As an example, my lords: one inheritor of the great empire never personally ventured anywhere out of Iraq to join the army. In fact, if we are to believe it, my lords, he hardly left the palace and was a feminine cross-dresser who wore a makeup.

We would like at this time, my lords, to introduce to you the Greek historian Diodorus Siculus, who lived nearly 550 years after the final stroke of the great empire!

The ancient historian Diodorus Siculus, my lords, described a number of the last slew of the kings of Assyria. But we do not think his report is correct regarding the very last king, my lords. The report may be true for one of the last descendants all right, but definitely not for the very last one. At any rate, my lords, here is how he described the last of the kings of mighty Assyria.

Go ahead, please, historian Diodorus.

> "Sardanapallus, the thirtieth in succession from Ninus, who founded the empire, and the last king of the Assyrians, <u>outdid all his predecessors in luxury and sluggishness</u>. For not to mention the fact that he was not seen by any man residing outside the palace, he lived the life of a woman, and spending his days in the company of his concubines and spinning purple garments and working the softest of wool, he had assumed the feminine garb and so covered his face and indeed his entire body with <u>whitening cosmetics</u> and the other unguents used by courtesans, that he rendered it more delicate than that of any luxury-loving woman. He also took care to make even his voice to be like a woman's, and at his carousals not only to indulge regularly in those drinks and viands which could offer the greatest pleasure, but also to pursue the delights of love with men as well as women; for he practiced sexual indulgence of both kinds without restraint, showing not the least concern for the disgrace attending such conduct.
>
> To such an excess did he go of luxury and of the most shameless sensual pleasure and in temperance, that he composed a funeral dirge for himself and commanded his successors upon the throne to inscribe it upon his tomb after his death; it was composed by him in a foreign language but was afterwards translated by a Greek as follows:
>
> > "Knowing full well that thou wert mortal born,
> > Thy heart lift up, take thy delight in feast;
> > When dead no pleasure more is thine. Thus I,
> > Who once o'er mighty Ninus ruled, am naught

> But dust. Yet these are mine which gave me joy
> In life — the food I ate, my wantonness,
> And love's delights. But all those other things
> Men deem felicities are left behind.
>
> "Because he was a man of this character, not only did he end his own life in a disgraceful manner, but he caused the total destruction of the Assyrian Empire, which had endured longer than any other known to history."[26]

We know this is out of order, my lords, but we do not know if we can agree with his majesty's conclusion about life.

We are on earth but for a passing moment. Mummy of a young priest, the 22nd Egyptian dynasty – Toledo Museum (image source: author). Was this God's purpose of creating man--death? Man, lives, works like a donkey, and then dies—perishes forever?

Death Defeated – The Graves Opened – The Gift of God

Heb 9:27 it is appointed unto men once to die, <u>but after this the judgment</u>:
Rom 6:23 For the wages of sin is death; but <u>the gift of God is eternal life</u> through Jesus Christ our Lord.
1 Cor 15:52 In a moment, in the twinkling of an eye, at the last trump: for the trumpet shall sound, and the dead shall be raised incorruptible (never to die again), <u>and we shall be changed</u>.
1 Cor 15:53 For this ... mortal must put on immortality (a new and a celestial body that is able to live and last forever).
1 Cor 15:54 So when ... this mortal shall have put on immortality, then shall be brought to pass the saying that is written, Death is swallowed up in victory.
1 Cor 15:55 O death, where is thy sting? <u>O grave, where is thy victory?</u>

But if this epitaph of the Assyrian monarch King Sardanapallus is not enough of a dirge your majesties, then the prophet Nahum who had seen all

---

[26] *The Library of History of Diodorus Siculus*, Book 2, 23: 1-4. http://penelope.uchicago.edu/Thayer/E/Roman/Texts/Diodorus_Siculus/2A*.html#23

of these in advance proposed his own as he prophesied of Nineveh, the capital city of the great and mighty Assyria.

The war chariots shall fill your streets O' Nineveh.

The shields of your mighty soldiers shall be covered in crimson blood.

And the gates of your river shall be open.

Well, this is a remarkable prophecy of its own, my lords, regarding the river. Indeed, your majesties, the waters of the river provided the remarkable strategy, which the invaders used to penetrate the impenetrable solid walls of Nineveh, capital of the world.

Who will cry for you Nineveh? None. No one will, said the Israeli prophet. Your brutality made you much-hated everywhere. Nineveh, den of the lions, the fortress of the masters of the world, you shall be penetrated.

Go ahead, please, prophet Nahum, speak to their majesties in your own words.

> NAH 2:3 *The shield of his mighty men is made red, the valiant men are in scarlet [covered in blood]: the chariots shall be with flaming torches in the day of his preparation, and the fir trees shall be terribly shaken.*
>
> NAH 2:4 *The chariots shall rage in the streets, they shall justle one against another in the broad ways: they shall seem like torches, they shall run like the lightnings.*
>
> NAH 2:5 *He [the king of Assyria] shall recount his worthies [his elite soldiers]: they shall stumble in their walk; they shall make haste to the wall thereof, and the defence shall be prepared.*
>
> NAH 2:6 <u>*The gates of the rivers shall be opened*</u>, *and the palace shall be dissolved.*
>
> NAH 2:11 *Where is the dwelling of the lions, and the feedingplace of the young lions, where the lion, even the old lion, walked, and the lion's whelp [cub], and none made them afraid?*
>
> Nah 2:12 *The lion did tear in pieces enough for his whelps, and strangled for his lionesses, and filled his holes with prey, and his dens with ravin.*
>
> NAH 3:7 *And it shall come to pass, that all they that look upon thee shall flee from thee, and say,* <u>*Nineveh is laid waste: who will bemoan her? whence shall I seek comforters for thee*</u>*?*
>
> NAH 3:18 *Thy shepherds [leaders] slumber, O king of Assyria: thy nobles shall dwell in the dust: thy people is scattered upon the mountains, and no man gathereth them.*
>
> NAH 3:19 *There is no healing of thy bruise; thy wound is grievous: all that hear the bruit of thee shall clap the hands over thee: for upon whom hath not thy wickedness passed continually?*

# Chapter Four

# Babylon the Golden

Here, my lords, is the start of what happened to the world champion. We begin seven short years after the death of the great king, H.M. King Assurbanipal.

And here too, my lords, are the next kings of the world. They, too, shall rise and they shall fall. But they shall rise again at the time of the end.

For now, my lords, a rising star, a Babylonian governor, from the land of the Shiites, a man who was appointed by his Assyrian majesty himself, and whose name is Governor Nabopolassar.

Following the death of H.M. King Assurbanipal, Governor Nabopolassar revolted against his Assyrian masters and managed to take control of Babylonia.

Rebel Nabopolassar, my lords, managed to do so nearly eighty years after his fellow countryman Merodach-Baladan II was run out of Babylon by H.M. King Sennacherib of Jerusalem fame.

On a side note, my lords, Governor Nabopolassar is the father of the famous Babylonian King Nebuchadnezzar.

And then four years after his revolt against his Assyrian masters, the rebel Babylonian Governor Nabopolassar was joined by another rising star––a man who came from nowhere, the new Iranian Mede King Cyaxares.

Iran and southern Iraq decided to join their armies against northern Iraq.

It was the right combination at the right time to take down the unstoppable vicious Assyrian men of northern Iraq. The same shall happen in our modern time, my lords.

After fierce four years of fighting, Iranian King Cyaxares and Babylonian Governor Nabopolassar managed to sack the mistress city of the world, the one and only great city of Nineveh, home of the great kings of Assyria—the lions of the world.

## The Land of Shinar

Shinar, the land of southern Iraq, home of the Shiite Muslims, the allies of Iran, is a land where the two rivers, Euphrates and Tigris, empty their waters into the Persian Gulf.

The most southern part of southern Iraq is a wetland, a land full of muskegs and marshes, which are called the Mesopotamian Marshes. These Mesopotamian Marshes of southern Iraq extend all the way to southern Iran, Iraq's next door neighbor.

It is there, in the land of Shinar, by these marshes that the Zagros Mountains, which separate Iraq from Iran, leave an opening—a gate, so to speak—for the traffic between the friendly Shiite Muslims of Iraq and Iran.

The marshlands of southern Iraq and Iran (image source: Wikipedia, U.S. Army Corps of Engineers).

It is estimated that ninety percent of the marshlands are now drained because of the war between Iran and Iraq during the time of the late Iraqi President Saddam Hussein. President Hussein drained the marshes of Babylon, southern Iraq, in order to prevent Iranian Shiite fighters from hiding in them before they could slip into Iraq.

The marshes have been also drained as a result of the persistent draught of the last few years.

> The Iranian Shiites, accompanied by the armies of the East, shall march through the mountain gates into Shiite southern Iraq on their way to besiege Jerusalem and answer the call of the Dome of the Rock.
>
> *Rev 16:12* And the sixth angel poured out his vial upon the great river Euphrates; <u>and the water thereof was dried up, that the way of the kings of the east might be prepared</u>.
>
> *Zech 5:8* wickedness
> ...
> *Zech 5:10* Then said I to the angel that talked with me, Whither do these bear the ephah [where are they taking wickedness]?
> *Zech 5:11* And he said unto me, <u>To build it an house in the land of Shinar</u>: and it shall be established, and set there upon her own base.

**612 BC** But the last Assyrian king, my lords, managed to escape from Nineveh. He and the remnant of his Assyrian army fled to a fortress city nearby whose name is "Haran."

And it was there in Haran where they dug in for their last stand. The champion of the world was cornered, my lords.

But it was not all doom and gloom. Indeed, his Assyrian majesty, my lords, he too gained a surprising ally. Help, help from an unexpected source was on the way.

And so let us, my lords, go back for a minute to where this help came from. And then find out what it was going to lead to, my lords. Indeed, one giant, one champion shall chase the other champion. And the chaser shall stumble on Jerusalem city. And Jerusalem shall die.

The tablet fragment above is a letter written by the last Assyrian king, King Sin-sharr-ishkun, to the rebel Babylonian Governor Nabopolassar, of southern Iraq, who became the king of Babylon, requesting a truce, Brooklyn Museum, New York (image source: author).

The Babylonian Chronicle (615–609 BC) recorded the fall of Nineveh, capital of Assyria of northern Iraq, to the allied forces of Iran and Babylon of southern Iraq, British Museum (image source: author).

## The Valley of Megiddo

As you may recall, my lords, the Assyrian Iraqis had invaded Egypt and appointed local Egyptian governors, twenty of them in fact, to rule the country on their behalf. These Egyptian governors were to answer directly to his Assyrian majesty King Esarhaddon.

However, later on these Egyptian governors conspired along with the deposed Ethiopian ruler, King Tirhakah, and revolted against Assyria.

The plot was discovered in time, my lords, and the Assyrian army marched back to Egypt, captured all of the Egyptian governors, and took them prisoners in chains to Assyria for punishment.

However, King Esarhaddon's son, now the new king of Assyria, H.M. King Assurbanipal, pardoned one of them, a governor by the name of "Necho I."

Bad move, my lords. Because later on, your majesties, Governor Necho I's son would, in his turn, revolt against the Assyrians. Except that he did better than his father and allied himself with the Greeks and indeed succeeded to rid Egypt from its Assyrian masters and crown himself King Psamtik I, king of free Egypt.

The biblical King Necho of Egypt; it is not quite certain, however, whether this statuette belongs to King Necho I or II. Brooklyn Museum, New York (image source: author).

But the irony of it all though, my lords, is that in the course of time, it was King Psamtik I's son, King Necho II, who came in a great rush to help the cornered Assyrians in fortress Haran.

His Egyptian majesty rushed to the Euphrates River in order to help the dying empire—the same Assyrians whose father, King Psamtik I, had, with the help of the Greeks, booted out of Egypt.

Why?

We do not know exactly why, your majesties.

It is possible, my lords, that H.M. King Necho may have indeed wanted his own share of the world pie before everything was taken by the Iranians and Babylonian allies.

At any rate, my lords, the helper came in a great rush. But his great rush was halted because an unexpected obstacle had sprung out from nowhere on his road to Carchemish city. It was in Carchemish by the Euphrates River that the battle between the Assyrians and the Babylonians was to take place, my lords.

The blockage, your majesties, took place at Megiddo. This is the plain where Armageddon's battle is to take place in the future years, my lords.

The army, your majesties, of King Josiah of Judah Israel came out of its barracks, barricaded the highway, and blocked the advance of H.M. King Necho II of Egypt. The Israeli army, my lords, blocked the way of a man in a great rush to Carchemish, where the two halves of Iraq were in a deadly fight of their life.

Biblical scribes, please go ahead: Tell their majesties what happened at Megiddo, according to you.

> *2 CHR 35:20* *Necho king of Egypt came up to fight against Carchemish [city] by Euphrates [River]: and Josiah [king of Israel] went out against him.*
> *2 CHR 35:22* *Josiah would not turn his face from him [King Necho II], but disguised himself [went into the battle as a common soldier so that he would not become an obvious target for the Egyptians], that he might fight with him, and hearkened not unto the words of Necho … and came to fight in the valley of Megiddo.*

A statuette of either King Necho I or his son, the biblical King Necho II, Brooklyn Museum, New York (image source: author).

May we also, your majesties, call upon the ancient historian Herodotus to verify the account of the biblical scribes!

Go ahead, sir.

> "King Necos … turned his attention to war; he had triremes [navy ships] built, some on the Mediterranean coast, others on the Arabian gulf, where the docks are still to be seen, and made use of his new fleets as occasion arose; and in addition <u>he attacked the Syrians [Israel and Gaza were all lump summed as the region of Syria] by land and defeated them at Magdolus</u>, afterwards taking Gaza, a large town in Syria. The clothes he happened to wear on this occasion he sent as an offering to Apollo at Branchidae in Milesia."[1]

---

[1] Herodotus, *The Histories*, by Aubrey de Selincourt, Penguin Books, 2:159, P.P 193

Ancient statues of the Greek historian, Herodotus, (R) Napoli Archaeological Museum, (L) National Archaeological Museum of Rome, Italy (images source: author).

## Rage Ye War Chariots

The obstacle was removed, my lords. His Egyptian majesty King Necho II succeeded to beat King Josiah of Israel and indeed kill him. Israel was beaten in the valley of Armageddon, my lords. This was the same valley where nature came to its aid in the days of the old Judge Deborah, as we have mentioned previously, my lords.

But unfortunately, my sovereigns, this is a hollow victory for the Egyptians, according to the prophet Jeremiah.

This Jeremiah, my lords, prophesied that H.M. King Necho II of Egypt will get the worst in his battles with the Babylonian general Nebuchadnezzar. According to the prophet, his royal highness Crown Prince Nebuchadnezzar shall end up victorious because he was a man assigned an important job to fulfill. The man from the Shiite lands was assigned the job of destroying the landmark of the calendar.

May we now hear the prophet, my lords!

> JER 46:1 *The word of the LORD which came to Jeremiah the prophet against the Gentiles;*

*JER 46:2* *Against Egypt, <u>against the army of Pharaoh necho king of Egypt, which was by the river Euphrates in Carchemish, which Nebuchadrezzar king of Babylon smote</u> in the fourth year of Jehoiakim the son of Josiah king of Judah [who was killed in the battle against King Necho II].*

*JER 46:3* *Order ye the buckler and shield, and draw near to battle.*

*JER 46:4* *Harness the horses; and get up, ye horsemen, and stand forth with your helmets; furbish the spears, and put on the brigandines [leg protection].*

King Necho II, Philadelphia Archaeological Museum (image source: author). A special thank you to the museum for the private showing

JER 46:5 *Wherefore have I seen them dismayed and turned away back? and their mighty ones are beaten down, and are fled apace [scattered], and look not back: for fear was round about, saith the LORD.*

JER 46:6 *Let not the swift flee away, nor the mighty man escape; they shall stumble, and fall toward the north <u>by the river Euphrates</u>.*

JER 46:7 *Who is this that cometh up as a flood, whose waters are moved as the rivers?*

JER 46:8 *Egypt riseth up like a flood, and his waters are moved like the rivers; and he saith, I will go up, and will cover the earth [with many soldiers]; I will destroy the city [Carchemish by the Euphrates River] and the inhabitants thereof.*

JER 46:9 *Come up, ye horses; and rage, ye chariots; and let the mighty men come forth; the Ethiopians and the Libyans [the allied soldiers of Egypt], that handle the shield; and the Lydians [it is historically recorded that indeed the Greeks, Lydians, were recruited in the Egyptian/Ethiopian army by the dynasty of Necho II] that handle and bend the bow.*

JER 46:10 *For this is the day of the Lord GOD of hosts, a day of vengeance, that he may avenge him of his adversaries: and the sword shall devour, and it shall be satiate and made drunk with their blood: for the Lord GOD of hosts hath a sacrifice in the north country by the river Euphrates.*

JER 46:11 *Go up into Gilead, and take balm [ancient medicine for wounds], O virgin, the daughter of Egypt: in vain shalt thou use many medicines; for <u>thou shalt not be cured</u>.*

JER 46:12 *The nations have heard of thy shame [the defeat], and thy cry hath filled the land: for the mighty man hath stumbled against the mighty [the mighty Egyptians against the mighty Babylonian army of Nebuchadnezzar], and they are fallen both together [indeed the battle was more or less a draw with the Egyptians getting the worst of it].*

And now, my lords, we wish to call upon the Babylonian scribes to read from the ancient Babylonian tablets in order to verify the biblical account regarding the clash between the Egyptians and the Iraqis for the domination of the world!

Go ahead, please gentlemen.

1. "In the twenty-first year (605/604 BC) the king of <u>Akkad (Nabopolassar)</u> stayed in his own land, <u>Nebuchadnezzar</u> his eldest son, the crown-prince,
2. mustered the <u>Babylonian</u> army and took command of his troops; <u>he marched to Karchemiš which is on the bank of the Euphrates</u>,
3. and crossed the river to go against the Egyptian army which lay in Karchemiš.

4. They fought with each other and the Egyptian army withdrew before him.

5. He accomplished their defeat and beat them to non-existence. As for the rest of the Egyptian army

6. which had escaped from the defeat so quickly that no weapon had reached them, in the district of Hamath

7. the Babylonian troops overtook and defeated them so that not a single man escaped to his own country."[2]

The observe side of the ancient Jerusalem tablet of Nebuchadnezzar, image courtesy of the trustees of the British Museum

---

[2] *The Babylonian Chronicle*, (ABC) 5, http://www.livius.org/cg-cm/chronicles/abc5/jerusalem.html, obverse, 1-7

BABYLON THE GOLDEN—149

A brick with a stamped inscriptions that reads: "Nebuchadnezzar, king of Babylon, Guardian of ther temples Esaglla and Ezida, firstborn son of Nabopolassar, king of Babylon," Brooklyn Museum, New York (image source: author).

Ishtar Gate. It was constructed in about 575 BC by the order of biblical King Nebuchadnezzar II, Pergamum Museum, Berlin (image source: author).

# Jerusalem! Jerusalem!

Allow us to backup a bit, my lords!

When his Egyptian majesty King Necho II killed his counterpart, his Israeli majesty King Josiah in the battlefield of Megiddo, the leaders of Israel, for whatever reason it may be, my lords, chose King Josiah's younger son, instead of the oldest, as their new king. His name, your majesties, was Prince Jehoahaz.

Go ahead scribes: Please pepper our comments with your records.

> 2 KIN 23:29 *In his days [King Josiah's] Pharaoh nechoh king of Egypt went up against the king of Assyria [Nabopolassar and his son Nebuchadnezzar] to the river Euphrates: and king Josiah went against him; and he [King Necho II] slew him at Megiddo, when he had seen him.*
>
> 2 CHR 36:1 *Then the people of the land <u>took Jehoahaz the son of Josiah, and made him king in his father's stead in Jerusalem</u>.*

And then again, your majesties, for whatever reason it may be, this choice of the people did not very much please the new master of Israel, His Egyptian Majesty King Necho II. Indeed, his majesty arrested young King Jehoahaz and replaced him with his older brother Jehoiakim as the new king of Judah Israel.

King Jehoiakim's main job now, my lords, was to collect a heavy annual payment from his people and send it to His Egyptian Majesty King Necho II, the assassin of his father.

And so now, your majesties, at this point of time Israel lies flat under the Egyptian heel as its wealth of gold and silver is hauled away to Egypt.

We can tell you, my lords, that this situation would change in due time. It was destined to change, my lords.

> 2 KIN 23:33 *And Pharaoh nechoh put him [Jehoahaz, the choice of the people of Israel] in bands [chains] at Riblah in the land of Hamath, that he might not reign in Jerusalem [capital city of Israel]; <u>and put the land to a tribute of an hundred talents of silver, and a talent of gold</u> [a huge annual payment].*
>
> 2 KIN 23:34 *And <u>Pharaoh nechoh made Eliakim the son of Josiah king in the room of Josiah his father, and turned his name to Jehoiakim</u>, and took Jehoahaz away: and he came to Egypt, and [Jehoahaz] died there.*
>
> 2 KIN 23:35 *And Jehoiakim gave the silver and the gold to Pharaoh; but he taxed the land to give the money according to the commandment of Pharaoh: he exacted the silver and the gold of the people of the land, of every one according to his taxation, to give it unto Pharaoh nechoh.*

> *2 KIN 23:36 Jehoiakim was twenty and five years old when he began to reign; and he reigned eleven years in Jerusalem*

And so as we said, my lords, the Babylonian General Nebuchadnezzar, son of Nabopolassar ,the destroyer of the Assyrian Empire beat his Egyptian majesty King Necho II at the battlefield of Carchemish by the Euphrates River but did not stop at that.

Crown prince Nebuchadnezzar, my lords, when he finally had the chance to leave the battlefields against the Assyrians, he then turned his attention to Egypt, where he took the Babylonian army to fight Pharaoh Necho II.

In his way to Egypt, the future King Nebuchadnezzar, my lords, went through Jerusalem city of Israel, the servant nation of Egypt. And we can tell you, my lords, that it was a sad day for Jerusalem, the capital of Israel.

It is your turn, prophet Daniel.

> *DAN 1:1 In the third year of the reign of Jehoiakim king of Judah came Nebuchadnezzar king of Babylon unto Jerusalem, and besieged it.*
> *DAN 1:2 And the Lord gave Jehoiakim king of Judah into his hand [into Nebuchadnezzar's hand], with part of the vessels of the house of God: which he carried into the land of Shinar [southern Iraq] to the house of his god; and he [Nebuchadnezzar] brought the vessels into the treasure house of his god [the treasury of the temple].*

And so now, my lords, as a result of its defeat by General Nebuchadnezzar, the annual tribute of Judah of Israel, its wealth of gold and silver, started to travel north east to Babylon instead of southwest to Egypt.

But this, too, was not to last your majesties.

## *A Prince and a Prophet*

It was during this siege and sack of Jerusalem city that the Babylonians deported many Israelite royalty and elites to Iraq. Later on, some of them were selected to serve in the royal palace of King Nebuchadnezzar of Babylon.

Now one of these selected Israeli royals was a godly young man by the name of Daniel. This Daniel, 2,700 years ago prophesied of events that were fulfilled as recently as forty years ago.

> *Dan 1:3* And the king [King Nebuchadnezzar] spake unto Ashpenaz the master of his eunuchs, that he should bring certain [a number] of the children of Israel, and of the king's seed [royal house of Israel], and of the princes;
> *Dan 1:6* Now among these were ... Daniel, Hananiah, Mishael, and Azariah:
> *Dan 1:7* Unto whom the prince of the eunuchs gave names: for he gave unto Daniel the name of Belteshazzar; and to Hananiah, of Shadrach; and to Mishael, of Meshach; and to Azariah, of Abednego.

Meanwhile, my lords, in Babylon the rebel Nabopolassar, who conquered Assyria and sacked Nineveh with the help of the Iranians, had died and then his son General Nebuchadnezzar became the new king of Babylon.

Long live the king!

For three years, my lords, H.M. King Jehoiakim of Israel made his annual payment of silver and gold to pharaoh Necho II of Egypt. And then for another three years, he was forced to change landlords and make his annual rent, so to speak, my lords, to his Babylonian majesty King Nabopolassar and then his son H.M. King Nebuchadnezzar.

But then, my lords, with the encouragement of the Egyptians, H.M. King Jehoiakim of Israel switched sides and sent his huge annual payment to Egypt.

As you may expect, my lords, in due time his Babylonian majesty King Nebuchadnezzar was to respond in full force to King Jehoiakim's rebellion and return once more to besiege Jerusalem.

Meanwhile, and until he is free to do so, his Babylonian majesty sent smaller units to harass King Jehoiakim and Israel. This is then just the start, my lord, the first steps.

Go ahead, please, biblical scribes and prophet Jeremiah.

> *2 KIN 24:1* In his days Nebuchadnezzar king of Babylon came up, and Jehoiakim became his servant three years: <u>then he turned and rebelled against him.</u>
> *2 KIN 24:2* And the LORD sent against him bands [gangs] of the Chaldees [of southern Iraq], and bands of the Syrians, and bands of the Moabites, and bands of the children of Ammon, and sent them against Judah to destroy it, according to the word of the LORD, which he spake by his servants the prophets.

The time has ripened, and the day has arrived, my lords.
And it was over for both Egypt and Israel.

The armies of his Babylonian majesty King Nebuchadnezzar came and besieged Jerusalem.

The population of Jerusalem threw their ruler, King Jehoiakim, like a dead donkey over the wall in order to appease H.M. King Nebuchadnezzar. The Israeli king was buried outside the city, where the city dump is located. His majesty was not buried in the grounds of the royal palace.

Nevertheless, his Babylonian majesty did not left off the siege of the doomed city.

The date is racing home.

The date?

The date of the temple and the number of the beast—666!

> JER 22:18 *Therefore thus saith the LORD concerning Jehoiakim the son of Josiah king of Judah; They shall not lament for him, saying, Ah my brother! or, Ah sister![they shall not cry for the princes and princesses] they shall not lament for him, saying, Ah lord! or, Ah his glory [his majesty]!*
>
> JER 22:19 <u>*He shall be buried with the burial of an ass, drawn [hauled] and cast forth beyond the gates of Jerusalem.*</u>

## 597 BC

And so, my lords, the people of Israel at this point of time had to crown a new king to replace the one they threw over the wall. The new king, my lords, is H.M. King Jehoiachin.

Meanwhile, Jerusalem city, capital of Israel, was still besieged by the armies of H.M. King Nebuchadnezzar of Babylon Iraq, home of the Shiite Muslims of our modern day.

The countdown now, my lords, has come down to three months.

Biblical Scribes, please gentlemen, interrupt the comments when appropriate.

> 2 KIN 24:6 *So Jehoiakim slept with his fathers [died]: and Jehoiachin his son reigned in his stead.*
>
> 2 KIN 24:7 *And the king of Egypt came not again any more out of his land: for the king of Babylon had taken from the river of Egypt unto the river Euphrates all that pertained to the king of Egypt.*

His majesty King Jehoiachin, my lords, did not manage to hang on too long to the throne of Israel. Indeed, the city fell within three months to the hands of the Babylonian armies of H.M. King Nebuchadnezzar.

Jerusalem city fell, my lords, the Israeli king and the royalty and the professionals and tradesmen of Israel, along with the Israeli soldiers and men of war—all these very valuable individuals were taken captives and deported to Babylon.

The city, for a second time, my lords, was emptied of its finest men of skills along with its valuables.

The end is near your majesties.

But not everyone at the time believed so, my lords.

What not to believe?

Important men, good thinkers, stood up to say, no, the end is not near. Things will sort themselves out.

But they did not have the entire field for themselves. Opposite to them, came another prophet warning; say what you may but the end is near. We shall meet this prophet in a minute, my lords.

> *2 Kin 24:8* Jehoiachin was eighteen years old when he began to reign, and he reigned in Jerusalem three months
> …
> *2 Kin 24:11* And Nebuchadnezzar king of Babylon came against the city, and <u>his servants did besiege it</u>.
> *2 KIN 24:12* And Jehoiachin the king of Judah went out [surrendered] to the king of Babylon, he, and his mother, and his servants, and his princes, and his officers: and the king of Babylon took him in the eighth year of his [Nebuchadnezzar's] reign [the Jewish calendar documents the years differently – the Babylonian scribes say the seventh year].
> *2 KIN 24:13* And he carried out thence all <u>the treasures of the house of the LORD [temple of Solomon], and the treasures of the king's house [the royal palace], and cut in pieces all the vessels of gold</u> which Solomon king of Israel had made in the temple of the LORD, as the LORD had said [would happen].
> *2 KIN 24:14* And he carried away all Jerusalem, and <u>all the princes, and all the mighty men of valour [soldiers]</u>, even ten thousand captives, and <u>all the craftsmen and smiths</u>: none remained, save the poorest sort of the people of the land.

So then, my lords, was this bad enough news to convince the doubters that the end was near?

No, the end was not near. The craftsmen and the royalty of Israel, everyone and everything of value, shall come back to Jerusalem, said the sober thinkers of Israel.

As you wish, gentlemen!

> *2 KIN 24:15* <u>And he [King Nebuchadnezzar of Babylon] carried away Jehoiachin to Babylon</u>, and the king's mother, and the king's wives, and his officers, and the mighty of the land, those carried he into captivity from Jerusalem to Babylon.

2 KIN 24:16 *And all the men of might, even seven thousand, and craftsmen and smiths a thousand, all that were strong and apt for war, even them the king of Babylon brought captive to Babylon.*

My lords, may we now call on the ancient Babylonian scribes to verify the account of the siege and the fall of Jerusalem!

Go ahead, gentlemen, and read from your ancient baked clay tablet, which we today call the "Babylonian Chronicle," and which is at the present time housed in the British Museum of London, should you wish to know! Some of you, my lords, such as his majesty Emperor Hadrian, know where London is.

> "Seventh year [598/597]: In the month of Kislimu, the king of Akkad [the ancient name of Babylonia] called up his army, marched against Syria [the general region around Israel] (lit. Hattu-land),
> Encamped against the city of Judah (URU la-a-hu-du) [i.e. the capital city; Jerusalem] and seized the town on the second day of the month of Adar. He captured the king [Jehoiachin] ... He took much booty from it and sent (it) to Babylon."[3]

And while we are with the Babylonian scribes, your majesties, may we interrupt the events line for a minute and jump ahead to King Nebuchadnezzar's son before we return once again to the action of H.M. King Nebuchadnezzar?

Thank you, my lords. We wish to mention here that King Nebuchadnezzar's son, H.M. King Evilmerodach, would in the course of time release the Israeli King Jehoiachin from jail. Nonetheless, he would keep him in Babylon and provide him and his sons with daily meal rations.

Go ahead, please, Babylonian scribes, for your take on this development!

## *Jehoiachin's Rations Tablets*

Archaeologists unearthed Jehoiachin's rations tablets in a royal archive room belonging to King Nebuchadnezzar near the Ishtar gate. Four tablets list the rations given to Israeli King Jehoiachin.
The tablets also show that his ration was more than anyone else.

---

[3] *The Ancient Near East, An Anthology of Texts and Pictures* (ANT), James B. Pritchard, Princeton University Press, P. 203

Jehoiachin's Ration Tablets, http://www.livius.org/ne-nn/nebuchadnezzar/anet308.html. These tablets are now in Berlin, Germany.

Text Babylon 28122, obverse 29-33:

"...t[o?] Ia-'-u-kin, king... [to King Jehoiachin]"

Text Babylon 28178, obverse ii 38-40:

"10 (sila of oil) to ... [Ia]-'-kin, king of Ia[...]
2½ sila (oil) to [...so]ns of the king of Judah (Ia-a-hu-du)
4 sila to 8 men from Judah (amella-a-hu-du)"

Text Babylon 28186, reverse ii 13-18:

"10 (sila) to Ia-ku-u-ki-nu, the son of the king of Ia-ku-du, 2½ sila for the 5 sons of the king of Ia-ku-du"
"1½ sila (oil) for 3 carpenters from Arvad, 1/2 sila each,
11½ sila for 8 ditto from Byblos, 1 sila each. . .
3½ sila for 7 ditto, Greeks 1/2 sila each
1/2 sila to Nabu-etir the carpenter
10 (sila) to Ia-ku-u-ki-nu, the son of the king of Ia-ku-du (i.e. Judah)
2½ sila for the 5 sons of the king of Judah (Ia-ku-du)"[4]

And now, my lords, we would like to turn the floor to prophet Jeremiah in order to read out his record regarding freeing King Jehoiachin, so that you may judge for yourselves, my lords, whether he is in agreement with the ancient Babylonian records.

Go ahead, please, prophet Jeremiah.

---

[4] *ANT*, P.P 205

JER 52:31 *And it came to pass in the seven and thirtieth year of the captivity of Jehoiachin king of Judah, in the twelfth month, in the five and twentieth day of the month, that Evilmerodach king of Babylon in the first year of his reign* <u>lifted up the head of Jehoiachin king of Judah [honored him], and brought him forth out of prison,</u>
JER 52:32 *And spake kindly unto him, and set his throne above the throne of the kings that were with him in Babylon,*
JER 52:33 *And changed his prison garments: and he did continually eat bread before him [had his meals with the Babylonian king] all the days of his life.*
JER 52:34 *And* <u>for his diet, there was a continual diet given him of the king of Babylon, every day a portion</u> *until the day of his death, all the days of his life.*

A prayer, possibly by biblical King Amel-Marduk (Evilmerodach), to the Babylonian god Marduk, British Museum (image source: author).

Turning back to where we left off, my lords, H.M. King Nebuchadnezzar deported King Jehoiachin and jailed him in Babylon, and in his place installed his uncle, whose name was Zedekiah, as the new king of Judah Israel. This is another step to bring us closer to the date on God's calendar, my lords.

And now, if we may, your majesties, we would like to ask the Babylonians scribes to read out the full account on their clay tablet "The Babylonian Chronicle," as it speaks of King Nebuchadnezzar deportation of King Jehoiachin and the appointment of his uncle.

Gentlemen, please!

"In the month of Kislīmu, the king of Akkad [King Nebuchadnezzar] called up his army, marched against Syria,

Encamped against the city of Judah (URU la-a-hu-du) [Jerusalem] and seized the town on the second day of the month of Adar.

He captured the king [Jehoiachin] ... <u>He appointed there a king of his own choice [Zedekiah]</u>. He took much booty from it and sent (it) to Babylon."[5]

The reverse side of the Babylonian Chronicle tablet, image courtesy of the trustees of the British Museum. The following quote is taken from the British Museum: "Nebuchadnezzar marched to Syria in 599 BC. He marched westwards again, in December 598 BC, as Jehoiakim, the king of Judah, had ceased to pay tribute. Nebuchadnezzar's army besieged Jerusalem and captured it on <u>15/16th March 597 BC</u>. The new king of Judah, Jehoiachin, was captured and carried off to Babylon."

---

[5] *ANT*, P.P 203

Besides the Jerusalem tablet, shown above, there is other historical and archaeological evidence of the exile of the Israelites to Babylon. There are indeed hundreds of other ancient tablets, such as those known as Murashu tablets (5th century BC), which were found in Nippur, Babylonia.

The above tablet is a photo of the exhibit at the Diaspora Museum, Tel Aviv. The text on the tablets records transactions between a large Babylonian family banking firm and many Israelites living in 28 settlements in the Nippur region of Babylon. http://www.cojs.org/pdf/exile_return.pdf (image source: WC, Sodabottle).

And now, my lords, our biblical scribes shall also read out their own lengthy account of the gradual destruction of Jerusalem, the capital city of Israel. And they will be accompanied by prophet Jeremiah.

> 2 KIN 24:17 *And the king of Babylon [Nebuchadnezzar] made Mattaniah his father's brother [Jehoiachin's uncle] king in his stead, and changed his name to Zedekiah.*
> 2 KIN 24:18 *Zedekiah was twenty and one years old when he began to reign, <u>and he reigned eleven years</u> in Jerusalem*

Here we go.

My lords, King Zedekiah of Israel, who swore fidelity to his Babylonian majesty King Nebuchadnezzar, made a huge mistake—the end is near, my lords. Now, why did he deliberately commit such a mistake, my lords? Perhaps because of the false prophets, such as the man Hananiah, who proclaimed prophesies in the fourth year of King Zedekiah's reign. Perhaps! But we truthfully do not know for certain, my lords, why King Zedekiah made such a great and disastrous blunder.

> *JER 28:1 And it came to pass the same year, in the beginning of the reign of Zedekiah king of Judah, <u>in the fourth year, and in the fifth month</u>, that Hananiah the son of Azur the prophet [a false prophet], which was of Gibeon, spake unto me in the house of the LORD, in the presence of the priests and of all the people, saying,*
>
> *JER 28:2 Thus speaketh the LORD of hosts, the God of Israel, saying, <u>I have broken the yoke [the burden] of the king of Babylon [Babylon is finished]</u>.*
>
> *JER 28:3 <u>Within two full years will I bring again into this place all the vessels of the LORD'S house, that Nebuchadnezzar king of Babylon took away from this place, and carried them to Babylon:</u>*
>
> *JER 28:4 <u>And I will bring again to this place Jeconiah the son of Jehoiakim king of Judah, with all the captives of Judah, that went into Babylon, saith the LORD: for I will break the yoke of the king of Babylon.</u>*
>
> …
>
> *JER 28:11 And Hananiah spake in the presence of all the people, saying, Thus saith the LORD; Even so will <u>I break the yoke of Nebuchadnezzar king of Babylon from the neck of all nations within the space of two full years</u>*

What can one say, my lords! The people were more inclined to wish their fears away and believe the good news of the false prophets, and doubt the fearful news of the true prophets who proved their calling. And so they heaped scorn and insults upon their prophets of doom and gloom. And there was no remedy left, my lords.

> *2 CHR 36:16 But they mocked the messengers of God, and despised his words, and misused [abused] his prophets, until the wrath of the LORD arose against his people, till there was no remedy.*

# 596 BC
# First Punch in the Twilight

And so, my lords, in the ninth year of his reign, King Zedekiah of Israel rebelled against his landlord his Babylonian majesty King Nebuchadnezzar and did not make his obligatory annual payment.

> *2 CHR 36:13 And he [King Zedekiah of Israel] also rebelled against king Nebuchadnezzar, who had made him swear by God [to keep the alliance with Babylon and make the annual payment]*

# BABYLON THE GOLDEN—161

*2 KIN 25:1 And it came to pass in the ninth year of his reign [Zedekiah's], in the tenth month, in the tenth day of the month, that <u>Nebuchadnezzar king of Babylon came, he, and all his host, against Jerusalem, and pitched against it; and they built forts against it round about [Jerusalem city was put under siege]</u>.*

The Assyrian Iraqis brought mobile towers against the walls of the besieged Israeli city of Lachish in order to be on level with the defenders on the wall. The ancient busy mural shows torches flying, attackers climbing ladders and escalades, as well as deportees carrying their sacks on their shoulders (middle bottom), British Museum (image source: author).

The Babylonian Iraqi army and its thousands of soldiers came to Jerusalem city and stayed, my lords. They besieged the strong and walled-up Jerusalem city for nearly three years.

The food inside the city began to run out. Severe shortage of food and depleting famine began to take hold on the hungry and starving population. The defenders and guards, who were tasked to keep the Babylonians on the outside, ran out of energy and hope.

You, your majesties, understand all of these, of course. It was now every man for himself. Escape from the doomed city if you can and run as fast as your weak legs can carry you—king and all.

Escape, your majesty, the king in the dark of the night and let us hope that the Babylonian night guards will not spot you.

But they spotted him, and they captured him, and a puzzling prophecy by the man of God, the prophet Ezekiel, was fulfilled, as now the biblical scribes and the prophet shall explain your majesties.

*2 KIN 25:2* And the city was besieged unto the eleventh year of king Zedekiah.

*2 KIN 25:3* And on the ninth day of the fourth <u>month the famine prevailed in the city, and there was no bread for the people of the land</u>.

*2 KIN 25:4* <u>And the city was broken up, and all the men of war fled by night by the way of the gate between two walls</u>, which is by the king's garden: now the Chaldees [Babylonians] were against the city round about: and the king went the way toward the plain.

*2 KIN 25:5* And the army of the Chaldees pursued after the king [Zedekiah], and overtook him in the plains of Jericho: and all his army [his armed guards] were scattered from him.

*2 KIN 25:6* So they took the king, and brought him up to the king of Babylon to Riblah; and they gave judgment upon him.

The Babylonian soldiers caught him, my lords, and the somewhat puzzling prophecy of Ezekiel was made clear.

*EZEK 12:12* And the prince [King Hezekiah] that is among them shall bear upon his shoulder [carry his belongings in a sack on his shoulders] in the twilight, and shall go forth: they shall dig through the wall to carry out thereby: he shall cover his face, that he see not the ground with his eyes.

*EZEK 12:13* My net also will I spread upon him, and he shall be taken in my snare: and <u>I will bring him to Babylon to the land of the Chaldeans; yet shall he not see it, though he shall die there [how is it he comes to Babylon but not see it?]</u>.

Indeed, the last thing the prince, King Hezekiah of Israel, would see and would remember till his dying day, my lords, was the sight of his sons being slaughtered in agony.

*2 KIN 25:7* <u>And they slew the sons of Zedekiah before his eyes, and put out the eyes of Zedekiah [gouged out his eyes and blinded him], and bound him with fetters of brass, and carried him to Babylon</u>.

A city wall being attacked by archers and a battering ram while it was defended by its soldiers stationed on top of the city wall, British Museum (image source: author).

The gate, walls, and towers of an ancient city, British Museum (image source: author).

## A Second and a Third Punch

Where are the false prophets who proclaimed the good news that Babylon would be destroyed in two years? Where are they, my lords?

Go ahead please, prophet Jeremiah, and your fellows, the biblical scribes.

> JER 8:15 *We looked for peace, but no good came; and for a time of health, and behold trouble!*

# 164—EARTH OUT OF ORBIT

No, my lords, there was no remedy left for Israel. The people did not care about the warning of doom and gloom. The end is near meant nothing to them—it was rather a laughable sentence.

> *2 CHR 36:17 Therefore he [the Lord] brought upon them the king of the Chaldees, who slew their young men with the sword in the house of their sanctuary [the temple, home of safety, home of prayers], and had no compassion upon young man or maiden, old man, or him that stooped for age: he gave them all into his hand. 2 CHR 36:20 And them that had escaped from the sword carried he away to Babylon; where they were servants to him [Babylonian King Nebuchadnezzar] and his sons until the reign of the kingdom of Persia:*

One captive's head is being cut off, another his feet and left hand are amputated, and now his right hand is to be cut off. Next to him is a third, whose hands and feet are cut off, is impaled alive on a spear, and next to him is a number of decapitated heads. It is the viciousness of war, in this case the Assyrian Iraqis wars, British Museum (image source: author).

Zech 9:9 Rejoice greatly ... shout, O daughter of Jerusalem: behold, thy King (the Lord's second coming) cometh unto thee: he is just, and having salvation
Zech 9:10  (He) will cut off the (war) chariot from Ephraim (Israel), and the (war) horse from Jerusalem, and the battle bow shall be cut off: and he shall speak peace unto the heathen (the nations): and his dominion shall be from sea even to sea, and from the river even to the ends of the earth.
Jer 31:26 Upon this I awaked, and beheld; and my sleep was sweet unto me.

## 586 BC A Year for the Count

The Babylonians, my lords, came on the seventh year, and then on the eighteenth/nineteenth year, as well as on the twenty fifth year of King Nebuchadnezzar. They came three times to Jerusalem city in order to strip it completely, burn it down to the ground, and haul away all its skillful and able-bodied men and women. They destroyed the landmark of God's calendar and broke down the walls of the city.

And the fact that they came on three main occasions, my lords, is important, as you shall soon when we count 666.

> 2 KIN 25:8 And in the fifth month, on the seventh day of the month, which is the nineteenth year of king Nebuchadnezzar king of Babylon [586 BC], came Nebuzaradan, captain of the guard, a servant of the king of Babylon, unto Jerusalem:
> 2 KIN 25:9 And he burnt the house of the LORD, and the king's house [the royal palace], and all the houses of Jerusalem, and every great man's house burnt he with fire.
> 2 KIN 25:10 And all the army of the Chaldees, that were with the captain of the guard, brake down the walls of Jerusalem round about [the city is now exposed and vulnerable to any and all of its local enemies].
> ...
> 2 KIN 25:21 So Judah [the last half of Israel] was carried away out of their land.

> JER 52:30 In the three and twentieth year of Nebuchadrezzar [582 BC] Nebuzaradan the captain of the guard carried away captive of the Jews seven hundred forty and five persons: all the [surviving and deported] persons were four thousand and six hundred.

Now, my lords, we wish to jump ahead in time and make a quick observation.

The number of years, which passed from the destruction of the temple by Babylonian King Nebuchadnezzar to the destruction of the temple by Roman Emperor Titus is 666 prophetic years, my lords.

The temple was destroyed by his Babylonian King Nebuchadnezzar in 586 BC. And then the second temple was destroyed by his majesty Emperor Titus, a general at the time, in the year 70 AD.

Thus, my lords, 586 BC + 70 AD = 656 solar years, which are equivalent to 666 prophetical years [656 X 365.25 / 360 = 666 prophetic years].

This goes to show you, your majesties, the importance of these temple dates in God's calendar for the earth. Indeed, my lords, these temple dates help us living here today date future prophecies.

## Missing Smoke Signals

There are twenty baked-clay tablets that speak of the Babylonian invasion of Israel. These ancient tablets, called the "Lachish" tablets, speak of Israeli army officers, along with ordinary citizens fleeing Israel to Egypt ahead of the Babylonian invaders.

> "And to your servant it has been reported saying: <u>The commander of the army Konyahu son of Elnatan, has gone down to go to Egypt</u> and he [while he was] sent to commandeer Hodawyahu son of Ahiyahu and his men from here [he was assigned to commandeer these group of soldiers before running away to Egypt]."[6]

The above are two out of the twenty one letters known as "The Lachish letters". They are "potsherds inscribed in black ink ...date to ... when the Babylonians under Nebuchadnezzar had invaded Judah and were laying siege to Jerusalem ... The letters were sent from outposts of Lachish to the city's military commander ... and represents field reports monitoring the situation". The preceding quote is taken from the British museum, London where the ostraca, potsherds, are housed (image source: author).

The Bible also states that there were a few walled cities remaining in Israel after the first Babylonian invasions.

> Jer 34:7 *When the king of Babylon's army fought <u>against Jerusalem</u>, and against all the cities of Judah that were left, <u>against Lachish [thirty miles from Jerusalem], and against Azekah [18 miles south west of Jerusalem]</u>: for these defenced cities[walled cities] remained of the cities of Judah.*

The ancient clay tablets of Lachish verify the biblical account and indicate that these remaining walled cities sent smoke signals to other cities in order to coordinate their defenses against the Babylonians.

---

[6] https://en.wikipedia.org/wiki/Lachish_letters

> "Let him also know that we are watching for the beacons of Lachish, in accordance with all the fire-signals that my lord has given, but we do not see Azekah."[7]

## Another Man of Mystery

Catastrophe!

This was an end, my lords. This was a countdown date on God's calendar. Future events have their dates calculated from this date, your majesties.

The entire kingdom of Israel was demolished and carried away to its first exile—the Babylonian exile.

The nation of the savior is no more.

There, the children of Israel would naturally die away. The children of Israel would become a nation no more.

The nation of the prophecies and prophets of the earth at this time is destined to melt away into bits and pieces scattered in Iranian and Iraqi enemy cities. The nation, which was employed to mark and tell what time it is on earth, according to God's plan, is dead.

Who can bring them back from the grave and make them a nation again?

Their enemies can, your majesties. Their own enemies can, my lords.

Jerusalem, my lords, was totally demolished nearly one hundred and forty solar years after Samaria of the north was destroyed [722 BC and 582 BC].

But we can tell you today, my lords, that they will come back. They will build the temple. They will build the wall. And the savior will grace the earth with His presence.

And then … and then, my lords, the rebuilt temple, the second temple, will also be demolished. And the time from destruction of temple to destruction of temple is 666 prophetic years, my sovereigns.

The temple, my lords, has a great meaning, according to the prophets. The temple, my lords, is a symbol of the body of the son of God.

We wish now, my lords, to allow the apostle Matthew to tell you of his record of the destruction of the second temple.

> LK 19:43 *[Jerusalem] the days shall come upon thee, that thine enemies shall cast a trench about thee, and compass thee round, and keep thee in on every side [besiege the city],*

---

[7] http://Cojs.org

*MAT 24:1 And Jesus went out, and departed from the temple: and his disciples came to him for to shew him the buildings of the temple. MAT 24:2 And Jesus said unto them, See ye not all these things? verily I say unto you, <u>There shall not be left here one stone upon another, that shall not be thrown down</u>.*

The Arch of Titus celebrating the siege of Jerusalem and the destruction of the temple, 70 AD. The arch was constructed c. 82 AD by the Roman Emperor Domitian in honor of his older brother Emperor Titus. The Jewish menorah could be seen in the panel above, Rome, Italy (image source: author).

In the year 70 AD, the nation of Israel was destroyed. The children of Israel were scattered worldwide. The land of Israel was deserted of them. Israel as a nation was finished by the Romans. But over 700 years before the Romans destroyed Israel, the prophets prophesied that the children of Israel shall come back from all over the world at the time of the end. They shall come back from near extermination and become a nation again--a strong nation. This indeed happened in our lifetime at the end of the Second World War

Isa 11:11 And it shall come to pass in that day, that the Lord shall set his hand again <u>the second time</u> to recover the remnant of his people, which shall be left, from Assyria, and from Egypt, and from Pathros, and from Cush, and from Elam, and from Shinar, and from Hamath, and from the islands of the sea.
Isa 11:12 And he shall set up an ensign for the nations, and shall assemble the outcasts of Israel, and gather together the dispersed of Judah from the four corners of the earth.

It happened, my lords. And the man who finished this job of destroying the temple is the man we were talking with not long ago, H.M. Roman Emperor Titus.

And it happened, my lords, 666 prophetical years after the first destruction.

The final destruction by his Iraqi majesty King Nebuchadnezzar took place in the year 586 BC.

And the destruction by the Roman legions under H.M. Emperor Titus, at the time a general, took place 70 AD.

The number of years between the Babylonian destruction and the Roman destruction of the house of the lord, your majesties, is 586 BC plus 70 AD, which gives us 656 solar years, which in turn, my lords, is equivalent to 662. Again with yearly discrepancy, this number, my lords, may amount to 666 prophetical years [656 X 365.25/360].

But yet there are other important dates besides this one, my lords.

## 582 BC How Can We Sing the Lord's Song?

At this point of time, my lords, the nation of the prophets is broken into a number of groups and incarcerated in far enemy cities. No reasonable man, your majesties, can see why any master, especially an enemy, would volunteer to release those much-needed servants and slaves.

Day shall follow day and night shall follow night, my lords, and the family of the prophets would sooner and later die off in the cities, towns, and villages where they are held captives. Their children, my lords, would naturally assimilate with the Iraqi and Iranian children, and would grow up knowing nothing of their world mission. Nothing would be the same anymore.

Has God forgotten His plan for the peoples of the earth? Who shall preach His amazing plan if not the nation of the prophets? Shall He abandon the idea of giving the world a clock to measure time with? And who shall be the nation of the savior of the world?

The prophets answered the troubling questions, my lords, and then repeated their answers.

Yes, the clock of the world shall be hauled away but it shall not stop keeping time. After 70 years, these enslaved men and women of the mighty Iraqi Assyrians shall rise off the floor, throw away their shackles, and take the highway for home—renewed.

Israel shall rise of the ashes in seventy years.

Hope?

No

A Promise?

Yes

But how?

You shall see after seventy years.

Go ahead, prophet Jeremiah.

> *JER 25:9* **Behold, I will send and take all the families of the north** [Iranian and Iraqi soldiers of the army of King Nebuchadnezzar], **saith the LORD, and Nebuchadrezzar the king of Babylon, my servant, and will bring them against this land** [invade Israel], **and against the inhabitants thereof, and against all these nations round about**
>
> *JER 25:11* **And this whole land shall be a desolation** [sparsely populated], **and an astonishment; and these <u>nations shall serve the king of Babylon seventy years</u>.**
>
> *JER 25:12* **And it shall come to pass, when seventy years are accomplished, that I will punish the king of Babylon, and that nation, saith the LORD, for their iniquity, and the land of the Chaldeans** [Babylonia], **and will make it perpetual desolations.**
>
> *JER 25:13* **And I will bring upon that land all my words which I have pronounced against it, even all that is written in this book, which Jeremiah hath prophesied against all the nations.**
>
> *JER 25:14* **For many nations and great kings shall serve themselves of them** [of the Babylonians] **also: and I will recompense them according to their deeds, and according to the works of their own hands.**
>
> *JER 29:10* <u>**For thus saith the LORD, That after seventy years be accomplished at Babylon I will visit you, and perform my good word toward you, in causing you to return to this place** [the land of Israel]**.**</u>

Do not ignore the prophets of Israel, my lords. Do you remember Isaiah, and his prophecy?

We hope you have not forgotten, my lords.

## One Hundred Years in Advance

Archaeologists give us the year. It was in the year 703 BC that the Babylonian rebel Merodach-baladan took advantage of the death of the mighty Assyrian king, King Sargon II, and rebelled against Assyria.

He declared himself the king of independent Babylonia, the southern half of Iraq, and lasted for only nine months 703/702 BC.

It was during this short reign of his that he sent a delegation to congratulate King Hezekiah of Israel for his recent recovery from a fatal illness.

> *Isa 39:1* At that time Merodachbaladan, the son of Baladan, king of Babylon, sent letters and a present to Hezekiah: for he had heard that he had been sick, and was recovered.

The prophet Isaiah, upon the departure of the Babylonian delegation, prophesied that Babylon and not the powerful Assyria, the masters of the universe as they called themselves, will sack Jerusalem and send the population to its first exile.

This, of course, took place under King Nebuchadnezzar in 587–582 BC according to archaeology.

Thus, Isaiah's prophecy was fulfilled after he was dead and buried, indeed, nearly one hundred and twenty years after he stated it [703–582 BC].

> Isa 39:5 *Then said Isaiah to Hezekiah, Hear the word of the LORD of hosts:*
> Isa 39:6 *Behold, the days come, that all that is in thine house [royal palace], and that which thy fathers have laid up in store until this day, <u>shall be carried to Babylon</u>: nothing shall be left, saith the LORD.*
> Isa 39:7 *And of thy sons that shall issue from thee, which thou shalt beget, shall they take away; and they shall be eunuchs in the palace of the king of Babylon.*

But Isaiah's prophecies did not only deal with past and historical events. They also deal with events, which indeed took place recently in our modern days and some, very drastic ones, are yet to take place in the days and years to come. One of the prophecies he made deals with the earth oscillating out of orbit.

An example of a destroyed ancient city; the above is the destroyed ancient city of Herculaneum (97 BC) (image source: author).

172—EARTH OUT OF ORBIT

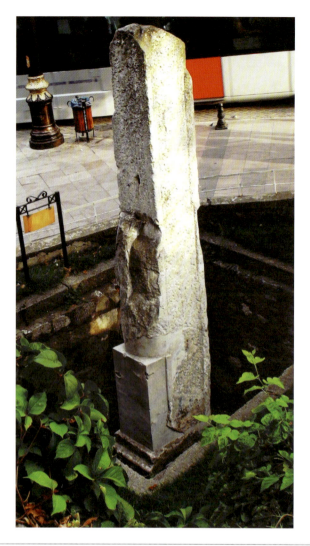

"This stone pillar is all that remains of a Byzantine (eastern Roman Empire) triumphal arch from which road distances to all corners of the empire were measured." Istanbul, Turkey (image source: author).

The year in which the house of the Lord was destroyed, 586 BC, is a year that calculates the dates of future important events; one of them is 666

Meanwhile, my lords, the deportees of Israel sat in Babylon and cried. Their cries were lamentation for the charred Jerusalem and the pile of rubbish that once was the house of the Lord.

*PS 137:1* *By the rivers of Babylon, there we sat down, yea, we wept, when we remembered Zion [Jerusalem].*
*PS 137:2* *We hanged our harps upon the willows in the midst thereof.*
*PS 137:3* *For there they that carried us away captive required of us a song; and they that wasted us required of us mirth, saying, Sing us one of the songs of Zion.*
*PS 137:4* *How shall we sing the LORD'S song in a strange land?*
*PS 137:5* *If I forget thee, O Jerusalem, let my right hand forget her cunning.*

Lyre player, 2000-1900 BC, ancient Iraq, Royal Ontario Museum, Canada (image source: author).

## By the Rivers of Babylon

Following are the abbreviated lyrics of the modern pop song that commemorates the exile to Babylon. The song could be heard on the Internet.

> "By the rivers of Babylon, there we sat down
> Ye-eah we wept, when we remembered Zion.
>
> When the wicked
> Carried us away in captivity
> Required from us a song
> Now how shall we sing the lord's song in a strange land
>
> Let the words of our mouth and the meditations of our heart
> Be acceptable in thy sight here tonight
>
> By the rivers of Babylon, there we sat down
> Ye-eah we wept, when we remembered Zion.
>
> By the rivers of Babylon (dark tears of Babylon)
> There we sat down (You got to sing a song)
> Ye-eah we wept, (Sing a song of love)"

## Remarkable—1290 & 666

It is remarkable and it defies logic. It challenges any rational thinking.

The man Daniel was a prince of the royal house of Israel. But this fact is immaterial. More to the point: the man Daniel was a prince and a royal in God's eyes, and it is this fact that matters.

The young Daniel and the elder Daniel was a man who proved his love for God when he faced the severest of persecutions. He would not deny the God he loved even in the face of death—a death ordered by the king no less.

And as such, Daniel gained a higher stature with the owner of heaven and earth, the God who can tell the future and can convey it in visions of dreams to His heroes, and giants of faith. And He did so when He singled out men such as Daniel, and John the beloved.

And yet prophecies challenge the human mind.

And the only rationalization one can accept is that they must have been written after the fact.

Yet, this answer does not stand very long.

Daniel's book, most likely, has been in the ancient Library of Alexandria since approximately 300 BC, where it was translated to Greek, the language of the Greek Empire, by the order of Greek King Ptolemy II.

And even if this is debatable, still, the logical answer that the prophecies were written after the fact does face strong challenges in more than one front. However, the strongest challenge is that some of Daniel's prophecies and many of John's prophecies happened within the last sixty years of our modern day.

It is without much controversy that the book of Daniel and the book of Revelations of the apostle John have been in existence for over sixty years.

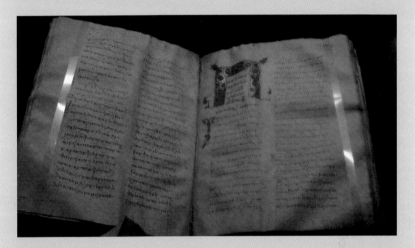

The Bible has been in publication for more than sixty years. The above-shown parchment of the gospels was produced in a Constantinopolitan workshop 11th Century. Benaki Museum, Athens, Greece (image source: author).

## Events Leading to the Dome of the Rock

The Children of Israel, against all odds, returned from Babylon alive. And then they built the second temple.

> Dan 9:25 Know therefore and understand, that *from the going forth of the commandment to restore and to build Jerusalem [city] unto the Messiah the Prince [Christ Jesus] shall be seven weeks, and threescore and two weeks [69 weeks]*: the street shall be built again, and the wall [of Jerusalem city, which was destroyed by King Nebuchadnezzar of Babylon, was to be rebuilt again], even in troublous times [The Israelites were indeed harassed by their local neighbors when they attempted to rebuild the temple and the wall of the city of Jerusalem, as shall be seen].

*Dan 9:26* And after threescore and two weeks [62 weeks] <u>shall Messiah be cut off</u> [crucified], but not for himself [not for His sins]: and the people of the prince that shall come [the Romans, under Emperors Titus and Hadrian, over six hundred years after Daniel wrote his prophecies] shall destroy the city [Jerusalem] and the sanctuary [House of the Lord – the temple]; and the end thereof shall be with a flood [the children of Israel scattered everywhere like the spreading of a flood], and unto the end of the war desolations [the land of Israel shall be empty, desolate of its children who would be sent to exile – a worldwide exile, which would last many years as Daniel will say later on].

*Deut 28:64* And the LORD shall scatter thee among all people, from the one end of the earth even unto the other

And from there, from the second destruction of the House of the Lord, and the second exile of Israel by the Roman legions of Titus and Hadrian, Daniel carried on to our own modern time and our future days.

For example, Daniel prophesied that an "abomination" shall be set up, built, on the site of the temple. And as long as this "abomination" sits there, there shall be no temple. This "abomination" was to be built by the followers of one man—the Antichrist. Note: he is not anti-God; he is anti-Christ.

This prophecy of Daniel was then later confirmed by the Lord Himself.

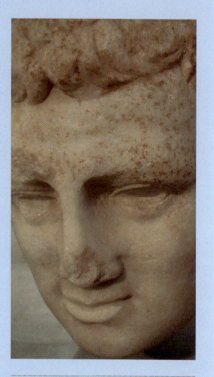

Roman General Titus, later emperor, destroyed the temple and began the worldwide scattering of the children of Israel (Their second and last return to their ancient homeland took place in the last sixty years), The National Archaeological Museum of Athens, Greece (image source: author).

*Dan 12:11* And <u>from the time that the daily sacrifice shall be taken away, and the abomination that maketh desolate set up</u>, there shall be a thousand two hundred and ninety days [note: 1,290, prophetical years].

## The Dome of the Rock

The Babylonian armies of King Nebuchadnezzar had destroyed the temple in 586 BC. Thus, the year 586 BC of our solar calendar was the year the daily sacrifice in the temple came to a stop.

> *Dan 12:11* And <u>from the time that the daily sacrifice shall be taken away [582 BC]</u>
> *2 Kin 25:8* And in the fifth month, on the seventh day of the month, which <u>is the nineteenth year of king Nebuchadnezzar king of Babylon</u> [586 BC], came Nebuzaradan, captain of the guard, a servant of the king of Babylon, unto Jerusalem:
> *2 Kin 25:9* <u>And he burnt the house of the LORD, and the king's house [the royal palace]</u>, and all the houses of Jerusalem, and every great man's house burnt he with fire.

Now Daniel goes on to say that there shall pass 1290 prophetical years [360 day/year] from the year 582 BC to the setting up of an abomination on the site of the temple.

Therefore, if one is to add 1,290 prophetical years, approximately 1,272 years of our solar calendar, to that date of 586 BC, one would then reach the year the abomination was to be set up on the site of the temple.

586 BC plus 1,272 solar years will bring us to 690 AD [582 BC + 1272 = 690 AD].

It is believed that the construction of the Dome of the Rock, which sits on the site of the house of the Lord, the temple, began around 687-689 AD.

Thus, a very small adjustment, and a plausible one, of the conversion between the prophetical year and the solar year would make the calculated date of the prophecy and the historical date of building the Dome of the Rock identical.

> *Dan 12:11* And from the time that the daily sacrifice shall be taken away [by Babylonian King Nebuchadnezzar – 586 BC], and the abomination that maketh desolate [prevents re-building the temple on its site] set up, there shall be a thousand two hundred and ninety days [1290 prophetical years X 360 / 365.25 = 1272 solar years. The solar year, approximately 365.25 days, is longer than prophetical year, which is 360 days].

Now, once again it is quite remarkable that Daniel makes such a prophecy, which indeed took place over 1,200 years after his day. And once again, his book was in the hands of many people and in thousands of homes of many nations, including Arabia, prior to the fulfillment of the prophecy in the year 687–689 AD of our era.

It is remarkable.

## *Confirming the Date of the Dome of the Rock – 1290 & 666*

## *First Date*

The prophet Daniel prophesied in advance that a building, the Dome of the Rock, shall occupy the site of the temple 1,290 prophetical years after King Nebuchadnezzar destroyed the temple.

And his date proved correct.

## *Second Date & Confirmation*

However, the prophet Daniel was not the only one to provide the date of the construction of the Dome of the Rock on the site of the temple.

Indeed, the Lord Himself told His disciples that the site of the temple shall be occupied by an abomination that shall prevent the rebuilding of the temple.

> Mat 24:15 When ye therefore shall see <u>the abomination of desolation</u> [the building, which causes the desolation], spoken of by Daniel the prophet, stand in the holy place, whoso readeth, let him understand:

The blessed Son of God, made His confirmation of Daniel's prophecy a few days before He was crucified.

The date of His crucifixion and resurrection is calculated to be April 1, 31 AD, based on biblical accounts. Indeed, the year 31 AD is the Year of Jubilee when all slaves are set free. This was a symbol of the sacrifice of the Lord in order to set all men free from sin and guilt.

> Lev 25:9 Then shalt thou cause the trumpet of the jubile to sound ... in the day of atonement [pardon of sins] shall ye make the trumpet sound throughout all your land.
> Lev 25:10 And ye shall hallow the fiftieth year, and <u>proclaim liberty throughout all the land unto all the inhabitants thereof</u>

However, archaeologists conclude that the date of the crucifixion is either April.1 31 AD or April.1 33AD. However they are more inclined to support the later.

Now, six hundred sixty-six [666] prophetical years is equivalent to 656–657 of our modern calendar years, which are solar years.

If one is to add 666 Hebrew years [656-657 solar years] to the date the Lord made His prophecy to His disciples [31 AD], one would then end with 31 + 656-657 = 687-688 AD.

The date of the construction of the Dome of the Rock is presumed to be 687- 689 AD.

Thus, whether one is to use Daniel's prophecy of the date of the abomination, being 1,290 years after the destruction of the temple by Nebuchadnezzar, or the Lord's 666 years after His crucifixion, Himself being the temple of God, one would still reach 687–689 AD, the year of the Dome of the Rock.

The crucifixion of the Lord mounts to the destruction of the temple of God.

Indeed, the Lord is the real temple of God, in that the spirit of the Holy One, His father, dwelt in Him bodily. Thus, the temple on earth was nothing but a figure of Him who is the actual temple.

Indeed, the Bible goes on to say that the children of God are also His temple, the living temple in which His spirit dwells and purifies. God is in you.

> Jn 2:19 *Jesus answered and said unto them, <u>Destroy this temple, and in three days I will raise it up</u>.*
> Jn 2:20 *Then said the Jews, Forty and six years was this temple in building, and wilt thou rear it up in three days?*
> Jn 2:21 *But he spake of <u>the temple of his body</u>.*
> Jn 2:22 *When therefore he was risen from the dead [in three days], his disciples remembered that he had said this unto them; and they believed the scripture, and the word which Jesus had said.*
>
> Col 2:9 *For in him dwelleth all the fulness of the Godhead bodily.*

## *And So It Is Today*

The children of Israel have returned to their land for a second and last time, according to the prophecy. But they cannot rebuild the temple. The Dome of the Rock sits on its site.

The prophecy is intact and the schedule of God remains on track towards the deadline of God's invitation for eternal life in the celestial heavens.

And the Dome of the Rock shall occupy the site, and will continue to do so to the time of the end and of the great tribulation. 1353 [1334 + [687-689] = [2021-2023] – 7.

## *Wait No More! It Is Certainly Him - April 3, 31/33 AD*

The following article was published in several publications including the *Huffington Post*.

> "Geologists from Germany and the US claim that they've finally found scientific proof of the date of Jesus Christ's crucifixion.

> "And when Jesus had cried out again in a loud voice, he gave up his spirit. At that moment the curtain of the temple was torn in two from top to bottom. The earth shook, the rocks split and the tombs broke open," the Gospel of Mathew says.
>
> The year of Christ's crucifixion has been widely debated. biblical scholars had hitherto agreed that Jesus was crucified on a Friday near Passover, under Pontius Pilate (26 – 36 AD). The most often suggested date was Friday April 3, 33 AD.
>
> The Gospel of Matthew mentions that the crucifixion took place during an earthquake.
>
> Researchers have tried to establish whether this was historical fact, or biblical allegory.
>
> In their latest study published in the International Geology Review, geologist Jefferson Williams of Supersonic Geophysical and his colleagues Markus Schwab and Achim Brauer of the German Research Center for Geosciences looked at seismic activity by the Dead Sea, just 20 kilometers away from Jerusalem.
>
> Their research revealed that at least two earthquakes took place in the region: <u>a strong jolt in 31 BC</u>, and another seismic event sometime between 26 AD and 36 AD.
>
> Having analyzed Jewish calendar data, seismic activity in the region and astronomical calculations, after correlating the data with the information from all four canonical Gospels, the scientists determined that the best match for the date of the crucifixion would be <u>Friday, April 3, 33 AD.</u>
>
> Geologist Jefferson Williams says he also hopes to uncover the mystery of darkness associated with the crucifixion, as three of the four canonical Gospels report on this phenomenon having taken place on crucifixion day.
>
> The scientist suggests the darkness might have been the consequence of a dust storm."[8]

## *666 and Gold*

It seems that the measurements and weights of gold in the Bible, or in biblical times, were associated with the number six and its multiples such as sixty and one hundred and twenty, etc.

Babylonian King Nebuchadnezzar built a huge statue of gold, and he commanded his subjects to fall before the golden statue in worship. The measurements of this golden statue are made in the multiples of the number six. It should be noted that a "score" in the Bible equals the number twenty.

---

[8] http://www.huffingtonpost.com/2012/05/25/jesus-crucifixion-date-possible_n_1546351.html

*Dan 3:1* Nebuchadnezzar the king made an image [a statue] of gold, whose height was threescore [60] cubits, and the breadth thereof six cubits [6]: he set it up in the plain of Dura, in the province of Babylon.
...
*Dan 3:4* Then an herald cried aloud, To you it is commanded, O people, nations, and languages,
*Dan 3:5* That at what time ye hear the sound of the cornet, flute, harp, sackbut, psaltery, dulcimer, and all kinds of musick, ye <u>fall down and worship the golden image</u> that Nebuchadnezzar the king hath set up:

The ancient historian Herodotus does indeed mention a statue that may be that of which the biblical prophet Daniel wrote above.

"In the temple of Babylon … In the time of Cyrus there was also in this sacred building <u>a solid golden statue of a man some fifteen feet high</u> – I have this on the authority of the Chaldaeans [Babylonians of the south of Iraq], though I never saw it myself."[9]

There are other times as well where the Bible associates gold with the number six and its multiples.

*1 Kin 9:14* And Hiram [king of Tyre of Lebanon, neighbor of Israel] sent to the king [Solomon, king of Israel] sixscore [120] talents of gold.

*1 Kin 10:10* And she [Queen of Sheba of Yemen, who came to visit King Solomon of Israel] gave the king <u>an hundred and twenty talents of gold</u>, and of spices very great store, and precious stones: there came no more such abundance of spices as these which the queen of Sheba gave to king Solomon.

The same connection is mentioned for the total weight of gold, which King Solomon had received in one year.

*1 Kin 10:14* Now the weight of gold that came to Solomon in one year was <u>six hundred threescore and six</u> [666] talents of gold,

The Bible does also prophesy that in the last days of the earth, a beast shall arise, and shall deceive many of the population of the earth.
Who is this beast? What nation or peoples this beast represents?
Soon the prophecies will point him out.

*Rev 13:11* And I beheld another beast coming up out of the earth; and he had two horns like a lamb [this statement is very important, as shall be seen], and he spake as a dragon.

---

[9] Herodotus, *The Histories*, Book One, 181, P.P 114

...
*Rev 13:13 And he doeth great wonders, so that he maketh fire come down from heaven on the earth in the sight of men [nuclear explosion?],*
*Rev 13:14 And deceiveth them that dwell on the earth by the means of those miracles which he had power to do in the sight of the beast; saying to them that dwell on the earth, that they should make an image to the beast, which had the wound by a sword, and did live.*
...
*Rev 13:18 Here is wisdom. Let him that hath understanding count <u>the number of the beast</u>: for it is the number of a man; and <u>his number is Six hundred threescore and six</u> [666].*

The golden Dome of the Rock, which sits on the site of the temple of the Lord, and which fulfilled Daniel's prophecy, as it was built 1,290 years after the first temple was destroyed, or 666 after the Lord foretold His disciples (image source: Wikipedia, Godot13).

## It Shall Come to Pass

And so, your majesties, Babylon of southern Iraq ruled supreme. Iraq and its golden ruler, King Nebuchadnezzar, and his army killed, captured, and brought various ethnic groups to its cities and towns, including the clock of the world—the children of Israel.

Most of these foreigners, my lords, were brought in as cheap workers. They toiled away in fields, in digging irrigation canals, in building temples, in staffing palaces, and in constructing new cities.

Babylon of H.M. King Nebuchadnezzar, my lords, became the mistress of the world, the one and only lady of the planet. And she ruled unchallenged, and there was none that could disturb her. She was the golden city, the beauty of the Chaldeans.

But the golden city shall be destroyed, said the prophet one hundred and seventy-two years ahead of time [711–539 BC].

Prophet Isaiah, would you please, sir, tell their majesties who precisely shall destroy the golden city? And who can free Israel from the den of the lion and bring it back to its base so that it can once more tell us the time on earth?

> ISA 13:19 *Babylon, the glory of kingdoms, the beauty of the Chaldees' excellency [Chaldees are the peoples of southern Iraq], shall be [destroyed] as when God overthrew Sodom and Gomorrah.*
> ISA 13:20 *It shall never be inhabited, neither shall it be dwelt in from generation to generation:*
> ISA 14:4 *Babylon ... How hath the oppressor ceased! the golden city ceased [finished]!*

## Servants Defeat Masters

The quick answer to who shall defeat the Babylonian/Iraqi Empire and free the children of Israel is none else but the servants of the Babylonians, as the prophet Zechariah of Israel had prophesied.

> Zech 2:9 *For, behold, I will shake mine hand upon them [the Babylonian Iraqis], and <u>they shall be a spoil to their servants</u>: and ye shall know that the LORD of hosts hath sent me [you shall know at that time that I prophesied the truth].*

Glazed lion, palace of biblical king Nebuchadnezzar, who wrote: "Babylon, the exalted city, the city of the god Marduk ... its foundation I laid in the heart of the underworld, its summit I built as high as a mountain." New York Metropolitan Museum, NY (image source: author).

> Dan 4:28 king Nebuchadnezzar.
> Dan 4:29 At the end of twelve months he walked in the palace of the kingdom of Babylon.
> Dan 4:30 The king spake, and said, **Is not this great Babylon, that I have built for the house of the kingdom by the might of my power, and for the honour of my majesty?**

My lords, where is the noble young Israeli prisoner groomed to work in the palace of H.M. King Nebuchadnezzar, who sits amongst you?

Here you are, sir.

Would you, sir, prophet Daniel, tell their majesties what will happen next to our world. Would you please sir, repeat to the rest of their majesties what you had told his Babylonian majesty King Nebuchadnezzar—your master and the conqueror of your people of Israel!

I told H.M. King Nebuchadnezzar that after the fall of his Babylonian empire, there shall arise three more empires around Israel. And that the fourth empire shall be a very dreadful empire. And that out of it shall arise ten notable kingdoms that shall remain to the very last days of the earth.

And I also had told H.M. King Nebuchadnezzar that at the start, in the early days of this fourth empire, a new and a totally different type of a kingdom shall be born.

And that contrary to the four empires, the reign of the princes and princesses of this unusual kingdom shall never come to an end. Its princes and princesses shall rule forever.

And the reason their rule shall never end is that their kingdom is a kingdom that shall be established by the owner of heaven and earth Himself.

Thank you, prophet Daniel, for this brief overview, which covers the future of the earth to its last days.

And we will now proceed to have you repeat your exact words to their majesties.

However, we would ask you to please give us further details on the three empires that were to come after the Iraqi Babylonian empire of H.M. King Nebuchadnezzar, so that we can relate your prophecy to our present time.

My lords, we caution you that much of his prophecy would be difficult for, your majesties, to comprehend at this time. But, nonetheless, please do allow him, my lords, to recite his exact words for your consideration.

> DAN 2:37 *Thou, O king, art a king of kings [Iraqi Babylonian King Nebuchadnezzar]: for the God of heaven hath given thee a kingdom, power, and strength, and glory [a very rich kingdom with much gold].*

BABYLON THE GOLDEN—185

DAN 2:38 *And wheresoever the children of men dwell, the beasts of the field and the fowls of the heaven hath he given into thine hand, and hath made thee ruler over them all.* <u>*Thou art this head of gold*</u>.

DAN 2:39 *And after thee shall arise another kingdom inferior to thee [Persian Empire], and another third kingdom of brass [Grecian Empire], which shall bear rule over all the earth.*

DAN 2:40 <u>*And the fourth kingdom [European Empire] shall be strong as iron*</u>*: forasmuch as iron breaketh in pieces and subdueth all things: and as iron that breaketh all these, shall it break in pieces and bruise.*

DAN 2:41 *And whereas thou sawest the feet and toes, part of potters' clay, and part of iron, the kingdom shall be divided; but there shall be in it of the strength of the iron, forasmuch as thou sawest the iron mixed with miry clay.*

DAN 2:42 *And as the toes of the feet were part of iron, and part of clay, so the kingdom shall be partly strong, and partly broken.*

DAN 2:43 *And whereas thou sawest iron mixed with miry clay, they shall mingle themselves with the seed of men: but they shall not cleave one to another, even as iron is not mixed with clay.*

DAN 2:44 <u>*And in the days of these kings [the Romans] shall the God of heaven set up a kingdom [the family of God], which shall never be destroyed*</u>*: and the kingdom shall not be left to other people, but it shall break in pieces and consume all these kingdoms,* <u>*and it shall stand for ever*</u>*.*

DAN 2:45 *Forasmuch as thou sawest that the stone was cut out of the mountain without hands [a kingdom established by God not by man], and that it brake in pieces the iron, the brass, the clay, the silver, and the gold; the great God hath made known to the king [King Nebuchadnezzar]* <u>*what shall come to pass*</u> *hereafter: and the dream is certain, and the interpretation thereof sure.*

Were these your exact words to his Babylonian majesty King Nebuchadnezzar?

Yes.

May we now ask you, sir, to give their majesties, who had ruled before your time, more details as to what was in store for the world after the Iraqi Babylonian Empire? And, particularly, what was in store for the nation of the prophets—the timekeepers of the plan of God—your nation of Israel?

# Chapter Five

# The Unequal Two Horns of Iran

And to begin, would you please, sir, tell their majesties your prophecy about the ram that had two unequal horns?

> DAN 8:1 *In the third year of the reign of king Belshazzar [c. 547 BC] a vision appeared unto me, even unto me Daniel*
> DAN 8:3 *I lifted up mine eyes, and saw, and, behold, there stood before the <u>river a ram which had two horns</u>: and the two horns were high; <u>but one was higher than the other</u>, <u>and the higher came up last</u>.*

And then what did this ram with unequal two horns do sir?

> DAN 8:4 *<u>I saw the ram pushing westward, and northward, and southward</u>; so that no beasts might stand before him, neither was there any that could deliver out of his hand; but he did according to his will, <u>and became great</u>.*

We understand, sir, that an enemy sprung up against this mighty ram of unequal two horns, correct?

> DAN 8:5 *as I was considering, behold, <u>an he goat came from the west on the face of the whole earth, and touched not the ground [moving very fast]: and the goat had a notable horn between his eyes [considered the greatest general ever lived]</u>.*
> DAN 8:6 *And he [the fast goat] came to the ram that had two horns …<u>and ran unto him in the fury of his power</u>.*
> DAN 8:7 *And I saw him [the fast goat] come close unto the ram, and he was moved with choler [fierce anger] against him, and <u>smote the ram, and brake his two horns: and there was no power in the ram to stand before him</u>, but he cast him down to the ground [the goat with the notable horn destroyed the ram], and stamped upon him: and there was none that could deliver the ram out of his hand.*

Vessel terminating in the head of a ram, northwestern Iran, 8th–7th century BC, Metropolitan Museum, New York (image source: author).

An ancient Iranian (Persian) drinking vessel, 5th century BC, terminating in a head of a ram, Metropolitan Museum of Art New York (image source: author).

And then, sir, what happened to this fast he goat with the great horn?

> DAN 8:8 Therefore the he goat [who came from the west] waxed very great: and when he was strong, the great horn [the greatest general ever lived] was broken; <u>and for it came up four notable ones [four notable kingdoms] toward the four winds of heaven [ruling in the north, south, east and west]</u>.

With your permission, prophet Daniel, we would wish to leave the prophecy about the fast he goat for the time being. We are more interested, sir, at this point of time to let their majesties understand your prophecy regarding the ram with two unequal horns.

My lords, we are very interested to know as much as we can about this ram with two unequal horns because we understand that he would come alive in the last days of the earth to frighten the world and threaten the reborn nation of Israel, which arose a second time from its grave.

> REV 13:11 And I beheld another beast coming up out of the earth; and <u>he had two horns like a lamb, and he spake as a dragon</u> [a wolf in sheep's clothing].
> REV 13:13 And he doeth great wonders, so that <u>he maketh fire come down from heaven on the earth in the sight of men</u> [nuclear bomb?],

## A Grandson Against A Grandfather

Your majesties, this was the prophecy.

And now we wish, my lords, to call upon a few ancient historians to recount to you the major events that took place around Israel in the days that came after some of you had passed on. These events, my lords, would in due time form the beginnings and set the base for future prophecies.

The fast he goat who came from the west against the ram with two unequal horns, the National Museum of Denmark, Copenhagen (image source: author).

Strange beginnings, my lords!

A nation, which was destined to rule the world, began with a small incident of a grandson revolting against his grandfather, nothing more and nothing less.

But we need to go further back in time, my lords, in order to reach this rebellious grandson.

There once, my lords, was a man by the name of Deioces. Deioces obviously did not know it, but he was, my lords, one of the men who prepared the way of the great man who was to fulfill an important prophecy in God's schedule for the earth.

In ancient Iran, my lords, there were half a dozen major tribes, which were loosely connected and vulnerable. As a result, my lords, they were steadily hounded and hunted down by the bloody and ferocious Assyrians of Iraq, the rulers of the universe.

How things will change at the times of the end when Iran and Iraq would become allies against Israel!

At any rate, historian Herodotus, where are you, sir? Please go ahead and tell their majesties how Iran was governed in the past.

In Iran there "was no sort of organized government whatever."[1]

Thank you, sir! But do standby if you do not mind.

Ancient Greek historian Herodotus, Metropolitan Museum, New York (image source: author).

Now this Iranian Deioces, my lords, was the man who came up with the idea of setting up a kingdom for the suffering Iranian tribes.

And, indeed, it took a skilful man and troublesome times, my lords, to unite together the scattered tribes. And now, a new nation, Iran was born, my lords.

But unbeknown to him, your majesties, he was preparing the way for the ram and the goat.

His Iran will in due time expand and become the greatest friend of Israel and its deadliest enemy.

Indeed, my lords, the great Iranian leader, whom the world was waiting for, was born one hundred and fifty years after Deioces. Deioces did not even know his name, but the prophet Isaiah, of the nations of the prophets, Israel, announced his name that far ahead in time.

---

[1] Herodotus, *The Histories*, P.81

Now building a new kingdom, my lords, need more than pleasant words and good will. It also needs stones and a man of silk and steel.

Carry on, please, historian Herodotus.

> "Deioces put pressure on the Medes [the northern tribes of Iran] to build a single great city ... and the city now known as Ecbatana [i.e., a meeting place of many ways, or a hub] was built, a place of great size and strength fortified by concentric walls, these so planned that each successive circle was higher than the one below it ... the circles are seven in number, and the innermost contains the royal palace and the treasury."[2]

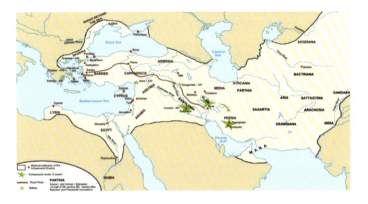

Ancient Iran, Iraq's neighbor, was made up of Media in the north, Elam in the center, and Persia in the south, Wikipedia

No Iranian chief, my lords, until Deioces' time had a palace. But now your majesties, Deioces, the first founding father of the up and coming superpower of the world, built himself a well-fortified palace in the center of the strongly fortified new city of Ecbatana.

And then, my lords, the visionary man turned into a fierce dictator.

It does not matter, my lords. He was there to prepare the way for the man in-waiting.

Carry on, historian Herodotus, please, and tell their majesties about Deioces' secret service.

> "[h]is [Deioces'] spies were busy watching and listening in every corner of his dominions"

---

[2] Herodotus, *The Histories*, P.82

> Nonetheless "The achievement of Deioces, who reigned for fifty-three years, was to unite under his rule the people of Media."³

Deioces' secret service, my lords, kept a close eye on his newly born nation.

And then H.M. King Deioces wrapped up his book of life and went the way of all the earth.

Naturally, my lords, his successor, the second founding father, wanted to build on what he has inherited.

Now Iran, my lords, more precisely western Iran, back then was made up of Media in the far north, Elam in the middle, and Persia in the south.

Please carry on, historian Herodotus

> "His [Deioces'] son Phraortes …was not content to be king only of Media; he carried his military operations further afield, and the first country he attacked and brought into subjection was Persia."⁴

No stopping now, my lords.

Unbelievable as it may sound, H.M. King Phraortes, son of Deioces, wants at this point of time, my lords, to try the impossible. He wants to go to war against the old tormenters and masters of his people—the masters of the universe themselves.

A great mistake is looming, my lords!

> "and finally attacked the Assyrians – the Assyrians of Nineveh, that is, who were formerly masters of all Asia … in the campaign against them Phraortes and most of his army were killed. Phraortes reigned for twenty-two years and was succeeded by his son Cyaxares."⁵

Ah, well, it did not work for the second founder of Iran, my lords. But time is not stopping; neither is the schedule of God.

And so now, my lords, we come to the third Iranian founder, whose name is Cyaxares, son of Phraortes, son of Deioces. My lords, a pair of two large feet is looming on the horizon of the world.

But let us keep in mind, your majesties, that all of these great men were from Media of northern Iran; they were not from Elam or Persia. This is a very important point, my lords: they were all from Media.

---

[3] Herodotus, *The Histories*, P.83
[4] Herodotus, *The Histories*, P.83
[5] Herodotus, *The Histories*, P. 83

"This prince [Cyaxares] had a far greater reputation than his father or grandfather. It was he who first organized the Asiatic armies by dividing them into separate units–spearmen, archers, and cavalry.

Previously the different arms had all been mixed up in a mob. It was Cyaxares who fought the battle with the Lydians on the occasion when the day was darkened [sun eclipse], and it was he who united all Asia beyond the Halys [near Greece] under his rule.

The first act of his reign was to march against Nineveh at the head of all his subject nations ... then Cyaxares died, after a reign – including the period of the Scythian domination–of forty years. He was succeeded by his son Astyages."[6]

Now, my lords, let us stop here for a minute to catch our breath.

Cyaxares, you said?

Yes, we did, my lords.

Is he not the Iranian king who allied himself with the Babylonian Governor Nabopolassar, father of the biblical Nebuchadnezzar, and together sacked Nineveh city and defeated the mighty Assyrian Iraqis?

Indeed, he is, my lords.

In fact, his Iranian majesty King Cyaxares lived for twenty seven years after his victory and long savored his great achievement of putting an end to the uncontested, one and only champion of the world.

## *Iran Against Iraq*

In our modern times, Iran, under its late leader Ayatollah Khomeini, and Iraq, under its late leader Saddam Hussein, fought a devastating war that lasted more than eight years [1980–1988] and presumably resulted in the death of one million soldiers and civilians.

Things have changed since then. And the change shall cause grief for Israel and the world.

Indeed, history shall repeat itself.

In the past, as has already been seen, King Cyaxares of Iran joined Nabopolassar of Babylon, the southern half of Iraq, and together defeated the Assyrians of the northern half of Iraq.

In due time, Shiite Iran shall join the Shiite Muslim population of southern Iraq in order to defeat the Sunni Muslim population of the northern half of Iraq.

---

[6] Herodotus, *The Histories*, PP. 83, 84

194—EARTH OUT OF ORBIT

President Saddam Hussein, when captured by American forces during the Gulf War (image source: Wikipedia).

Grand Ayatollah Khomeini, of Iran who fought against President Saddam Hussein (Image source: Wikipedia).

It was unbeknown to his Iranian majesty King Cyaxares, my lords. But he was one of the Iranian leaders who was assigned to clear the way for the man with the rendezvous with destiny. The Iranian man of destiny, my lords, was to be born nearly thirty years after H.M. King Cyaxares' death.

And so, my lords, after the death of the third founding fathers of Iran, H.M. King Cyaxares, came his successor, the fourth man, whose name was Astyages.

Now this Median Iranian King Astyages, my lords, married off his daughter Mandane "to a Persian named Cambyses, a man he knew to be of good family and quiet habits—though he considered him much below a Mede even of middle rank,"

Here you can see how Iranians of different regions view each other, my lords. This feeling of inferiority for some regions and superiority of other regions shall play an important role in the rise of the man of destiny your majesties.

Iran, my lords, had become one nation all right. Media and Persia were forged together, but the Medians of the north and the Persians of the south did not consider themselves equal, not at all, my lords.

Yes, even a high class Persian of the despised south was not even considered equal to a middle class Median of the north.

And if the Medians looked down and despised the Persians, the Persians hated and resented the rule of the Medians over them and looked for the day they could be free. This sentiment, my lords, was the spark that shall light the fire.

Is this true, historian Herodotus?

"The Persians had long resented their subjection t the Medes."[7]

But one must ask now, my lords, how can the despised Persians squeeze themselves out from under the Median boot? And the answer, my lords, is, the Median elite, the Median high class would help them.

Why would the Median upper class, the elite of the north, help the despised lowly Persians of the south?

The prophet Daniel of Israel, of the nation of the prophets, had prophesied it, my lords.

---

[7] Herodotus, *The Histories*, 126, P .94

196—EARTH OUT OF ORBIT

At any rate your majesties, King Astyages' daughter, now married to a Persian, gave birth to a son who was, of course, half Median and half Persian. And the new baby, my lords, was named Cyrus.

The Median empire about 600 B.C (questioned). Wikipedia, the Historical Atlas

Media and Persia (Persis) make up the modern nation of Shiite Iran. To the west of Iran is ancient Babylonia, the Shiite southern half of modern Iraq.

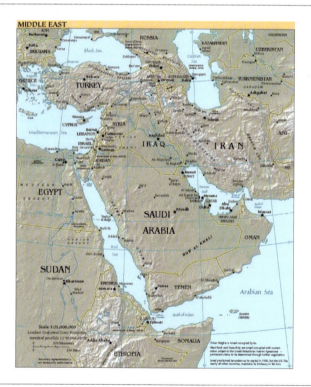

Northern Iraq and Iran, hostile neighbors in ancient and in modern times; Iraq and Iran, WC, CIA.

They shall soon ally themselves to fulfill their future task, according to the plan and schedule of God.

And so, my lords, in the course of time, His Median Iranian majesty King Astyages saw it fit to appoint his grandson Cyrus, who is half Persian, as the governor of the southern Iranian region of Persia.

This, my lords, was the first stage for fulfilling Daniel's prophecy.

Meanwhile, his aging Iranian majesty King Astyages continued to treat his citizens harshly. Indeed, his majesty was a divisive man, even a cranky man. So much so, my lords, that the elite and the aristocrats of Media hated him. And these were the people, my lords, you do not want to hate you at best of times.

On the other hand, your majesties, Governor Cyrus, the ruler of the southern region of Persia, being half Median and half Persian, did his best to be friendly to all. Indeed, he was by nature, my lords, a man who wanted to reconcile differences and unite fighting factions.

And so we can tell you, my lords, that this is why after his death they ended up calling him the father of the nation. But the father of which nation did he become, Media or Persia?

My lords, the prophet Daniel had seen it and prophesied it before it happened, unlikely as it may have sounded to the ears of those who have heard it.

Prophet Daniel, please read the paragraph we are referring to.

DAN 8:1 *In the third year [c. 547 BC] of the reign of [Babylonian] king Belshazzar a vision appeared unto me, even unto me Daniel* DAN 8:3 *Then I lifted up mine eyes, and saw, and, behold, there stood before the river <u>a ram which had two horns [Media and Persia]: and the two horns were high; but one was higher than the other, and the higher came up last [Persia]</u>.*

My lords, one fateful day, Cyrus, governor of the region of Persia of southern Iran invited his Persian army brass and all of his soldiers to an open-air banquet. The governor, my lords, went all out to entertain the army brass with the best food and wine money could buy. Then he stood up to make a speech.

The schedule of God was moving along according to plan, my lords. Please, historian Herodotus, cut in whenever I wave to you.

"<u>Men of Persia</u>," he said, "listen to me; obey my orders, and you will be able to enjoy a thousand pleasures as good as this without ever turning your hands to menial labor ... take my advice and <u>win your freedom</u>. I am the man destined to undertake your liberation, and it <u>is my belief that you are a match for the Medes in war as in everything else</u>. It is the truth I tell you. Do not delay, but fling off the yoke of Astyages [his own grandfather] at once."

"When news of these events reached Astyages, he summoned Cyrus to appear before him; but Cyrus' answer was to send the messenger back with the threat that he would be there a good deal sooner than Astyages liked."[8]

The Nabonidus Chronicle, British Museum (image source: author).

This tablet records Cyrus' revolt against his Median grandfather (550 BC) and Persia conquering Media. It also documents the attack on Lydia and the capture of Sardis (547 BC), as is related below.

My lords, H.M. King Astyages of the mother Median kingdom could not put down the Persian revolt. War broke out between his majesty and his grandson Cyrus.

After a long four years of fighting, my lords, Cyrus finally succeeded to sack the fortified Median city of Ecbatana and arrest his grandfather.

And so, suddenly, my lords, the governor of humble and despised Persia became the great king of all of Iran and its colonies everywhere [550 BC].

---

[8] Herodotus, *The Histories*, PP. 94, 95

## THE UNEQUAL TWO HORNS OF IRAN—199

And this was only the start for the humble and despised Persia, my lords—today Media, tomorrow Europe.

> "(the) <u>Medes have become slaves instead of masters, and the Persians masters of the Medes though they were once their slaves</u> … (the) Medes, who had been masters of Asia beyond the Halys for a hundred and twenty-eight years except for the period of Scythian domination, were forced to bow before the power of Persia."[9]

> "Thou foundest the Persians a race of slaves, thou hast made them free men:
>
> Thou foundest them subject to others, thou hast made them lords of all,"* said general Hystaspes to his king, Cyrus, the man of destiny. The man who was to build the greatest empire the world has known, but only to see it burn down to ashes by a young fellow who came along two hundred years later.
>
> Yet, at the moment, my lords, he had not yet performed the task allotted to him. The fulfillment time was not ripe yet, my lords. The date according to God's timetable of the earth was eleven years away.[10]

And if you allow us here, my lords, to jump forward to the future for a minute, King Cambyses who was the son and later the inheritor of H.M. King Cyrus, upon his deathbed had a few final words to entrust to his subordinates:

> "do not allow the dominion to pass again into the hands of the Medes."[11]

Incidentally, my lords, historian Herodotus was born approximately 46 years after King Cyrus' death

Now, my lords, we do wish to ask the prophet Daniel to repeat his prophecy concerning the future of Media and Persia.

Please go ahead, sir.

*DAN 8:1* *In the third year [c. 547 BC] of the reign of king Belshazzar a vision appeared unto me, even unto me Daniel*

---

[9] Herodotus, *The Histories*, Book One, P.95
[10] *Herodotus, *The Histories*, Book 1, P. 95
[11] Herodotus, *The Histories*, 3:65, P. 231

*DAN 8:3* I lifted up mine eyes, and saw, and, behold, there stood before the <u>river a ram which had two horns</u> [Media and Persia]: and the two horns were high; <u>but one was higher than the other, and the higher came up last</u> [Persia of Astyages' grandson Cyrus].

*DAN 8:4* <u>I saw the ram [the powerful Persian Empire] pushing westward, and northward, and southward</u>; so that no beasts might stand before him, neither was there any that could deliver out of his hand; but he did according to his will, and became great [indeed the Persian Empire is one of the greatest empires the world has ever known to this date].

Media and Persia of Iran unite; a Median (L) and a Persian (R), British museum (images source: author)

# As Rich as Croesus

*DAN 8:4* "I saw the ram pushing westward", prophesied the prophet Daniel, my lords.

Now, your majesties, the richest man in the world, his majesty Greek King Croesus of Lydia at the eastern borders of Europe began to worry about the rising power and the ambitions of H.M. King Cyrus of Persia [Iran].

THE UNEQUAL TWO HORNS OF IRAN—201

And if the Median Iranians of the north, my lords, despised and looked down upon the Persian Iranians of the south, the Greeks of Lydia despised all Iranians—Medians and Persians alike.

And so his Greek majesty King Croesus decided not to wait but to go to war against his Persian majesty King Cyrus immediately. The wealthy Greek monarch, my lords, did not heed the words of a wise man who advised him against it.

All of these events, my lords, shall with time merge into a river streaming along towards the roaring ocean of the future prophecies of our modern time.

The brown and red colors are the possible territory of the kingdom of Lydia at the time of King Croesus. Lydia today is part of modern Turkey, Greece's neighbor to the east (image source: Wikimedia, WillemBK).

This is possibly a gold coin of the fabulously wealthy King Croesus, 560–547 BC. Greek King Croesus was the first to mint gold and silver coins (image courtesy of the trustees of the British Museum, London).

Go ahead, please, historian Herodotus, tell their majesties what the backward and poor Iranian people would do once they tasted the luxuries of the wealthy west.

> "But while the preparations [for the war] were going on, he [Croesus] received a piece of advice from a Lydian named Sandanis, who was already known for his good sense, and by the opinion he then expressed greatly increased his reputation amongst the Lydians.
>
> "My lord," he said, "you are preparing to fight against men who dress in leather – both breeches and everything else. So rough is their country that they eat as much as they have, never as much as they want. They drink no wine but only water. They have no good things at all, not even figs for desert.
>
> Now if you conquer this people, what will you get from them, seeing <u>they have nothing for you to take</u>? And if they conquer you, think how many good things you will lose; <u>for once they taste the luxuries of Lydia they will hold on to them so tightly that nothing will make them let go</u>.
>
> I am thankful myself that the gods have never put it into the Persians' heads to attack the Lydians."
>
> "Croesus did not take this advice though Sandanis was right: the Persians before their conquest of Lydia had no luxuries of any kind."[12]

> And yes, my lords, the richest man of the world had the same opinion as well regarding the Persian Iranians; "<u>The Persians are violent men; and they are poor</u>," said Croesus.[13]

Be that as it may, my lords, the war was now on.

His Persian majesty King Cyprus began his determined march towards Europe in order to stem the invasion of Greek King Croesus.

And it was over in two weeks.

The city of Sardis, my lords, the prosperous and wealthy royal capital of Greek King Croesus, after a siege of fourteen days, fell to the Iranians. Indeed, King Croesus himself was captured alive, my lords.

Iran now, your majesties, had tasted the western luxuries and sat at the doorstep of Europe.

Once again, prophet Daniel, please continue with your prophecy.

---

[12] Herodotus, *The Histories*, 1:70, 71, P. 68
[13] Herodotus, The Histories, 1.89, P. 77

> DAN 8:1 *In the third year of the reign of king Belshazzar [of Babylon] a vision appeared unto me, even unto me Daniel*
>
> DAN 8:3 *Then I lifted up mine eyes, and saw, and, behold, there stood before the river a ram [the Iranian Empire of Persia and Media] which had two horns: and the two horns were high [Media and Persia]; but one was higher than the other [Persia], and the higher came up last [Media of Astyages was conquered by Persian Cyrus].*
>
> DAN 8:4 *I saw the ram pushing westward [towards Europe], and northward, and southward [beginning by Cyrus and continued by his successors]; so that no beasts might stand before him [the Persian Empire of Iran was the largest the world ever known], neither was there any that could deliver out of his [the ram's] hand; but he did according to his will, and became great.*
>
> ...
>
> DAN 8:15 *And it came to pass, when I, even I Daniel, had seen the vision, and sought for the meaning, then, behold, there stood before me as the appearance of a man.*
>
> DAN 8:16 *And I heard a man's voice between the banks of [the River] Ulai, which called, and said,* <u>Gabriel, make this man to understand the vision.</u>
>
> DAN 8:17 *So he came near where I stood: and when he came, I was afraid, and fell upon my face: but he said unto me, Understand, O son of man: for at the time of the end shall be the vision.*
>
> DAN 8:19 *And he said, Behold, I will make thee know what shall be in the last end of the indignation [the end of the Babylonian Exile of the Children of Israel]: for at the time appointed the end shall be.*
>
> DAN 8:20 <u>*The ram which thou sawest having two horns are the kings of Media and Persia.*</u>

His Persian Iranian majesty King Cyrus is not done yet, my lords. Greek Lydia at the gates of Europe is just the start.

There is another shining jewel to be pocketed—the mistress of the world herself, and nothing less.

And to be honest with you, my lords, the lady has been on King Cyrus' mind all along.

The plan of God marches along just fine, my sovereigns. The savior is coming to the jail in order to free the prisoners.

> "for his mind was on Babylon ... and the Egyptians [southward], against whom he intended to lead an expedition in person."[14]

---

[14] Herodotus, *The Histories*, 1:154, P. 103

## Total Indifference

But the lady, the golden Babylon city of the successor of H.M. King Nebuchadnezzar, the master of the world, was well fortified, lords—a fortress within fortresses.

> Babylon at this time, my lords, was "a vast city in the form of a square with sides nearly fourteen miles long and a circuit of some fifty-six miles, and in addition to its enormous size ... it is surrounded by a broad deep moat full of water, and within the moat there is a wall fifty cubits wide and two hundred high ... on the top of the wall ... a four-horse chariot [can] pass."[15]

Unfortunately, my lords, the enormous size of the city of Babylon worked against it.

Carry on please, historian Herodotus, and please do not mind our interjections here and there as you speak.

> "The Euphrates, a broad deep, swift river ... runs through the middle of the city and divides it in two."
>
> Now this river shall be the downfall of Babylon, my lords.
>
> "There is a fortress in the middle of each half of the city: in one the royal palace surrounded by a wall of great strength, in the other the temple of Bel."[16]

And, unfortunately, again, my lords, the great wall, which protected the temple of Bel, failed to protect the idol statue of the god of Babylon of southern Iraq. The prophet Jeremiah of Israel, the prophet from the nation of the prophets of the Holy One, had seen it all before it happened, my lords.

Go ahead please, prophet Jeremiah.

> JER 50:1 *The word that the LORD spake against Babylon and against the land of the Chaldeans [ancient name of southern Babylonia, also the name of the priests of the god Bel,* Herodotus, the Histories 1:180, P.114*] by Jeremiah the prophet.*
>
> JER 50:2 *Declare ye among the nations, and publish, and set up a standard; publish, and conceal not: say, Babylon is taken, Bel is confounded [Bel has been put to shame], Merodach [another important god] is broken in pieces; her idols are confounded, her images [statues of idol gods] are broken in pieces.*

---

[15] Herodotus, *The Histories*, 1:80, P. 113
[16] Herodotus, *The Histories*, 1:113, P. 181

JER 50:3 _For out of the north [Cyprus and his servant nations] there cometh up a nation against her, which shall make her land desolate_, and none shall dwell therein: they shall remove, they shall depart, both man and beast.

The day of reckoning of golden Babylon, which destroyed Judah of Israel and whose King Nebuchadnezzar deported them to Babylonia, is come.

Sir!

"In the temple of Babylon there is a second shrine lower down, in which is a great sitting figure of Bel, all of gold on a golden throne, supported on a base of gold, with a golden table standing beside it."[17]

His Persian majesty King Cyrus, my lords, made his preparations to put the well-fortified Babylon city, the capital of the world, under siege. But what can his Iranian majesty do to a city surrounded by a mote and huge walls after huge walls?

On the other hand, as you may expect, my lords, the Babylonian leaders and the population of the city had for quite a while already made their preparations to withstand a long siege. No worries! Dance the night away.

Sir!

"The Babylonians ... they already knew of Cyrus' restless ambition ... had taken the precaution of accumulating in Babylon a stock of provisions sufficient to last many years, _they were able to regard the prospect of a siege with indifference_.

The siege dragged on, no progress was made, and Cyrus was beginning to despair of success."[18]

Do not despair your majesty King Cyrus. The year and the day of destiny are racing in for home.

## Dance the Night Away

My lords, here cometh the hour!
The schedule of God is on track.

H.M. King Cyrus is taking a major gamble. It is not advisable.

---

[17] Herodotus, *The Histories*, 1:181, P. 114
[18] Herodotus, *The Histories*, 1.192, P. 117

His Iranian majesty, my lords, approved of a bold and a very dangerous plan to overrun the great city of Babylon, the lady, the mistress of the world, who holds many prisoners of many nationalities in its iron grip.

You may recall, your majesties, that the Euphrates River ran through the middle of the great city. Now there was also a shallow lake near the bottom end of the river.

And so now, your majesties, you have the layout of the city so that you may go ahead and ponder how you, yourselves, would have sacked this well-fortified golden Babylon, and what advice you would have given His Iranian majesty King Cyrus to penetrate it.

Well, somebody did, my lords, give his majesty an advice. And, indeed, his majesty managed with a thousand hands under his command to do the impossible that night.

What night, you may ask, my lords?

It is the night of the banquet, my lords.

It was the night of the banquet, which the prophet Daniel wrote about years before.

Do you remember, your majesties, what the old historian Herodotus had said about the attitude of the population and the leaders of the well-stocked golden Babylon?

Go ahead, historian Herodotus, open up your ancient scrolls and repeat your words, sir.

> "The Babylonians ... they already knew of Cyrus' restless ambition ... had taken the precaution of accumulating in Babylon a stock of provisions sufficient to last many years, <u>they were able to regard the prospect of a siege with indifference</u>. The siege dragged on, no progress was made, and Cyrus was beginning to despair of success."[19]

In such a situation, my lords, can there be any greater danger than indifference?

Now would you please, prophet Daniel, carry on and tell their majesties what happened?

> DAN 5:1 Belshazzar [coregent king of Babylon at this time] the king <u>made a great feast</u> to a thousand of his lords, and drank wine before the thousand.

---

[19] Herodotus, *The Histories*, 1.192, P. 117

*DAN 5:2* Belshazzar, whiles he tasted the wine, commanded to bring the golden and silver vessels which his father [i.e. ancestor] Nebuchadnezzar had taken out of the temple which was in Jerusalem; that the king, and his princes, his wives, and his concubines, might drink therein.

*DAN 5:4* They drank wine, <u>and praised the gods</u> of gold, and of silver, of brass, of iron, of wood, and of stone [it was a religious feast].

*DAN 5:5* In the same hour came forth fingers of a man's hand, and wrote over against the candlestick upon the plaister [plaster] of the wall of the king's palace: and the king saw the part of the hand that wrote.

*DAN 5:7* The king cried aloud to bring in the astrologers, the Chaldeans [priests of Bel], and the soothsayers. And the king spake, and said to the wise men of Babylon [the educated priests and astrologers], Whosoever shall read this writing, and shew me the interpretation thereof, shall be clothed with scarlet, and have a chain of gold about his neck, and shall be <u>the third ruler in the kingdom</u> [why third ruler? Who are the first two kings of Babylon, and why did Babylon have two kings at that time?].

*DAN 5:8* Then came in all the king's wise men: but they could not read the writing, nor make known to the king the interpretation thereof.

## *Why the Third? Why Not Second?*

The king of Babylon at the time was a man by the name of Nabonidus.

In the third year of his rule, Nabonidus entrusted the army and the kingdom to his firstborn son, and then departed Babylon to Tema in the Arabian desert in order to worship his newly adopted god, the moon god, whose symbol is the moon crescent.

Thus, Babylon at that time had indeed two kings.

And this is why co-regent, joint ruler King Belshazzar spoke of awarding the interpreter of the writing on the wall the position of the third ruler of Babylon.

There are in fact several archaeological monuments that record the acts of King Nabonidus and his firstborn son Belshazzar. One of these ancient inscription, 6$^{th}$ or early 5$^{th}$ century BC, speaks of Nabonidus' temporary abdication to his son Belshazzar.

"[w]hen the third year was about to begin - he entrusted the army (?) to his oldest son, his first born, the troops in the country he ordered under his command.
He let everything go, entrusted the kingship to him, and, himself, he started out for a long journey. The military forces of Akkad marching with him, he turned to Temâ deep in the west."

*The verse account of Nabonidus*, http://www.livius.org/ct-cz/cyrus_I/babylon03.html

Babylonian King Nabonidus, father of biblical King Belshazzar, accompanied by symbols of gods including the crescent moon, British Museum (image source: Wikipedia, Jona lendering).

On the stele above, King Nabonidus, father of biblical King Belshazzar, recorded his religious activities and the external harassment Babylonia was facing at the time. Istanbul Museum (image source: author).

Two cylinders belonging to Babylonian King Nabonidus. On the immediate one, above, Nabonidus inscribed a prayer for his son, the biblical King Belshazzar, saying: "As for me, Nabonidus, king of Babylon, save me from sinning against your great godhead and grant me as a present a life long of days, and as for Belshazzar, the eldest son–my offspring – instill reverence for your great godhead in his heart and may he not commit any cultic mistake, may he be sated with a life of plenitude."*British Museum (image source: author).

*The quotation is copied from http://www.livius.org/cg-cm/chronicles/cm/nabonidus.html

Your majesties, the royal astrologers failed to interpret the writings on the wall.

But do not despair, your majesty King Belshazzar.

# THE UNEQUAL TWO HORNS OF IRAN—211

Her majesty the queen has recalled the now-aging wise man who was brought as a captive from Israel by His great majesty King Nebuchadnezzar.

Carry on, please, prophet Daniel, with the record.

> DAN 5:13 *Then was Daniel brought in before the king. And the king spake and said unto Daniel, Art thou that Daniel, which art of the children of the captivity of Judah, whom the king my father brought out of Jewry?*
>
> DAN 5:14 *I have even heard of thee, that the spirit of the gods is in thee, and that light and understanding and excellent wisdom is found in thee.*
>
> DAN 5:15 *And now the wise men, the astrologers, have been brought in before me, that they should read this writing [on the wall], and make known unto me the interpretation thereof: but they could not shew the interpretation of the thing:*
>
> DAN 5:16 *And I have heard of thee, that thou canst make interpretations, and dissolve doubts: now if thou canst read the writing, and make known to me the interpretation thereof, thou shalt be clothed with scarlet, and have a chain of gold about thy neck, <u>and shalt be the third</u> [again the third] <u>ruler in the kingdom</u>.*
>
> DAN 5:17 *Then Daniel answered and said before the king, Let thy gifts be to thyself, and give thy rewards to another; yet I will read the writing unto the king, and make known to him the interpretation.*
>
> DAN 5:25 *And this is the writing that was written, MENE, MENE, TEKEL, UPHARSIN.*
>
> DAN 5:26 *This is the interpretation of the thing: MENE; God hath numbered thy kingdom [of Babylon], and finished it.*
>
> DAN 5:27 *TEKEL; Thou art weighed in the balances, and art found wanting [came short].*
>
> DAN 5:28 <u>*PERES; Thy kingdom is divided, and given to the Medes and Persians.*</u>
>
> DAN 5:29 *Then commanded Belshazzar, and they clothed Daniel with scarlet, and put a chain of gold about his neck, and made a proclamation concerning him, that he should be the third ruler in the kingdom.*
>
> DAN 5:30 *In that night [the night of the banquet] was Belshazzar the king of the Chaldeans [Babylonians] slain.*

And if Daniel's record is not enough, your majesties, then you may as well listen to the words of Jeremiah, another prophet from Israel, the nations of the prophets.

> *JER 50:8 Remove out [get out] of the midst of Babylon, and go forth out of the land of the Chaldeans*
> *JER 50:9 For, lo, <u>I will raise and cause to come up against Babylon an assembly of great nations from the north country [Media and Persia and all their conquered nations]</u>: and they shall set themselves in array against her [besiege Babylon]; from thence she shall be taken: their arrows shall be as of a mighty expert man; none shall return in vain [the arrows will find their targets].*
> *JER 50:10 And Chaldea shall be a spoil: all that spoil her shall be satisfied [shall find good spoils in her], saith the LORD.*

All said and done, your majesties, it may have been this banquet that brought an end to the one and great Babylon—the golden city of His majesty King Nebuchadnezzar. How ironic! A feast that ended all feasts!

But let us return, your majesties, to the actual details of the sack of Babylon city.

The victorious king who defeated Greek Lydia at the eastern gate of Europe was so discouraged and frustrated to the point that he was willing to approve of a daring plan to breach and penetrate Babylon.

Your majesties, another date on God's calendar is running very fast towards us. Another task, which He had assigned to one more king, is about to be faithfully carried out.

Where is historian Herodotus? Go ahead, sir, with your record. Tell their majesties about the dangerous plot that was suggested to His Iranian Majesty King Cyrus.

And again, if you do not mind, sir, allow us to interject here and there for the benefit of their majesties.

> "The siege dragged on, no progress was made, and Cyrus was beginning to despair of success. Then somebody suggested or he himself thought up the following plan: he stationed part of his force at the point where the Euphrates flows into the city and another contingent at the opposite end where it flows out."[20]

And then, my lords, hundred thousand hands of a multitude of soldiers diverted the river to the shallow lake. And the water level of the river dropped.

> "by means of cutting he diverted the river into the lake (which was then marsh) and in this way so greatly reduced the depth of water

---

[20] Ancient historian Herodotus, *The Histories*, 1:191, P. 118

in the actual bed of the river that it became fordable, and the Persian army ... entered the river, now deep enough to reach about the middle of a man's thigh, and, making their way along it, got into the town."[21]

And now is the looming danger of such a reckless plot becomes clear, my lords.

"If the Babylonians had learnt what Cyrus was doing or had seen it for themselves in time, they could have let the Persians enter and then, by shutting all the gates which led to the waterside and manning the walls on either side of the river, they could have caught them in a trap and wiped them out"[22]

Yes. That night, this would have been the end of what one day was to become the largest empire ever existed—the Persian empire. Can you imagine what a different world we would have had today? Who can tell?

But that night was the right night for such a dangerous and risky plot of the frustrated Iranian, the man of destiny, the man who was to fulfill a task slated on God's timetable for the temporary earth. That night!

A bronze statue of Herodotus, first half of 4th century BC, was found in Benha, Egypt. Cicero, one of the greatest Roman philosophers and politicians (106 BC), called Herodotus "the father of history." Brooklyn Museum, New York (image source: author).

"[t]hey could have wiped them out. But as it was <u>they were taken by surprise</u>. The Babylonian themselves say that owing to the great size of the city the outskirts were captured without the people in the center knowing anything about it; <u>there was a festival going on, and they continued to dance and enjoy themselves, until they learned the news the hard way</u>. That, then, is the story of the first capture of Babylon."[23]

---

[21] Ancient historian Herodotus, *The Histories*, 1:191, P. 118
[22] Ancient historian Herodotus, *The Histories*, 1:191, P. 118
[23] Ancient historian Herodotus, *The Histories*, 1:191, P. 118

Yes, indeed your majesties! The prophet Jeremiah of Israel had seen this in advance and foretold of it.

> JER 50:24 *I have laid a snare for thee, and thou art also taken, O Babylon, and thou wast not aware ["they were taken by surprise", says ancient historian Herodotus]: thou art found, and also caught, because thou hast striven against the LORD.*

Now, your majesty King Cyrus, now you are beginning to faithfully carry out the task that the Holy One of Israel, the Ancient of Days, the Maker of heavens and earth, has assigned you, as His prophets say.

Now, sir, that you have put an end to the power of golden Babylon, and have gathered much authority in your hands, you may then, sir, proceed to undertake your major task.

## 539 BC In Writing

It was an incredible decree, my lords, which his Iranian majesty King Cyrus issued following his victory over Babylon.

We shall always ask: why did he do it? Why did he issue such a decree?

We do not know exactly why, your majesties, because there may have been a combination of a number of reasons. But he did it. And not only for the Israelites, but he did it for others besides.

One thing is for sure, my lords: it is a new policy. And it is in writing. And it is not written in many pages; it is written in a few short lines.

But these few lines proved to the world, my lords, that the date on the timetable of God has arrived.

Wake up, silent and empty land of Israel, wake up! You have been asleep for many years now. Wake up! They are coming—get ready. Get ready to greet them.

Your children, the nation of the prophets, the nation of the gift of God, your children were not busy with their assigned task of preaching the incredible plan of God. Instead, most of them were toiling away as slaves and labors for the Babylonian Iraqis, their masters. They lost all hope to see you again—a hill on a high mountain. Babylon of Iraq became their new home and grave. There was none who could free them from the jaws of the Babylonian lion. And you, land of Israel, you went to sleep all alone, empty and deserted in the silent dark nights of one night after another.

Go ahead, please, prophet Jeremiah, remind their majesties of your prophecy.

> *JER 50:17* *Israel is a scattered sheep; the lions have driven him away: first the king of Assyria hath devoured him [beginning by Assyrian King Tiglathpileser III who devastated the Galilee region]; and last this Nebuchadrezzar king of Babylon hath broken his [Israel's] bones.*
> *JER 50:18* *Therefore thus saith the LORD of hosts, the God of Israel; Behold, I will punish the king of Babylon and his land, as I have punished the king of Assyria.*
> *JER 50:19* *And <u>I will bring Israel again to his habitation</u>, and he shall feed on [Mounts] Carmel and Bashan, and his soul shall be satisfied upon mount Ephraim and Gilead.*

My lords, his Iranian majesty King Cyrus had made a declaration upon becoming the new owner of the best real estate of the world—the golden Babylon. And the strange declaration was written on the standard barrel-like cylinder of baked clay.

We have it here, my lords.

His Iranian majesty, the comprising man, has forthwith granted permission to the captives of Babylon, the war prisoners, to return to their homelands and take away with them their sacred objects.

There it is, my lords. There is the cylinder. Get close, your majesties, and read line thirty two.

What do you think now, my lords?

> "I [King Cyrus] returned the images [the idol status] of the gods, who had resided there [i.e., in the temples of Babylon], to their places [native temples] and I let them dwell in eternal abodes [to remain there for good]. I gathered all their inhabitants [nationals] and returned to them their dwellings [homelands]."[24]

Why would any king, my lords, deprive himself the manpower he needs for a strong and large army? Why would any king deprive himself the manpower he needs for the construction of his new temples, palaces, and cities?

Why would any king, without anyone forcing him, volunteer to deprive himself the manpower he needs to work his huge farms, ranches and canals––to raise his crops and cattle, to enrich himself, and feed and please his people? Why would he let the silver and gold and the protective gods slip away between his fingers while he already had them in his grip?

Why? Who knows which reason or which reasons, my lords?

---

[24] http://www.livius.org/ct-cz/cyrus_I/cyrus_cylinder2.html

Assyrian soldiers of King Tiglathpileser III carrying away gods captured from a defeated enemy, about 728 BC, British Museum (image source: author).

## *The Wisdom of Compromising*

Several great rulers found it wiser to show great tolerance towards the religions and national customs of the nations and the peoples they conquered.

Indeed, the powerful Greek King Alexander the Great went as far as to order his generals and soldiers to assimilate to the customs of the defeated peoples of Persia and Babylonia.

These great rulers were by nature tolerant people, yet very strong and determined in character, which perhaps was the reason they could afford to be tolerant.

The same was also said of the Iranian King Cyrus the Great, as recorded by the ancient Greek historian Herodotus.

> "The Persians have a saying that Darius [a successor] was a tradesman [businessman], Cambyses [another successor] a tyrant, and Cyrus a father – the first being out to profit whenever he could get it, the second harsh and carless of his subjects' interests, and the third, Cyrus, in the kindness of his heart always occupied with the plans for their well-being."[25]

Indeed, King Cyrus the Great was so revered by his Iranian subjects that the kings who followed him had to be initiated through a ritual that was

---

[25] Herodotus, *The Histories*, book three: 90, P. 243

designed to honor him and keep his legacy alive. In fact, this tradition of honoring him lasted for many generations of Iranian kings after him.

The ancient Greek historian Plutarch [b. 46 AD] recorded the initiation of the Iranian king Artaxerxes II, the ninth successor of King Cyprus, in his book *Parallel Lives* as following:

> "Into this sanctuary the candidate for initiation must pass, and after laying aside his own proper robe, must put on that which Cyrus the Elder used to wear before he became king; then he must eat of a cake of figs, chew some turpentine-wood, and drink a cup of sour milk."[26]

Wake up, land of Israel! It has been so far fifty prophetical years of lonely sleep ... wake up! The Iranian man of destiny has put his decree down in writing. This means we are only twenty years away from the major marker on God's calendar. Stir up and rise children of Israel. Time to go home!

Go ahead, please, gentlemen.

> 2 CHR 36:20 *And them [the surviving Israelites] that had escaped from the sword [of King Nebuchadnezzar] carried he away to Babylon; where <u>they were servants to him and his sons until the reign of the kingdom of Persia</u> [under King Cyrus the great]:*
> 2 CHR 36:21 *To fulfil the word of the LORD by the mouth of Jeremiah ... <u>threescore and ten years</u> [70 years].*
> 2 CHR 36:22 *Now <u>in the first year of Cyrus king of Persia, that the word of the LORD spoken by the mouth of Jeremiah might be accomplished, the LORD stirred up the spirit of Cyrus king of Persia, that he made a proclamation throughout all his kingdom, and put it also in writing</u>, saying,*
> 2 CHR 36:23 *<u>Thus saith Cyrus king of Persia, All the kingdoms of the earth hath the LORD God of heaven given me; and he hath charged me to build him an house in Jerusalem, which is in Judah. Who is there among you of all his people? The LORD his God be with him, and let him go up</u> [to Jerusalem].*

> JER 50:4 *<u>In those days, and in that time, saith the LORD, the children of Israel shall come,</u> they and the children of Judah together [This statement shows that the legend of the lost ten tribes is indeed what it is: a legend], going and weeping: they shall go, and seek the LORD their God.*

---

[26] Plutarch, *Parallel Lives, the Life of Artaxerxes*, 3:1.2, penelope.uchicago.edu

218—EARTH OUT OF ORBIT

The famous 2,500-year-old Cyrus cylinder preserved in the British Museum and photographed by the author. It documents the capture of Babylon in 539 BC and the repatriation of the displaced nations

In 1971, the United Nations and its general secretary at the time, Mr. U Thant, had declared the cylinder to be an ancient declaration of human rights (debatable). A copy of the cylinder hangs next to the security chamber of the United Nations headquarters in New York City.

Isa 44:28 "Cyrus, He is my shepherd, and shall perform all my pleasure: even saying to Jerusalem, Thou shalt be built; and to the temple, Thy foundation shall be laid," read the ancient words of the biblical prophecy.

Extract from the Cyrus Cylinder (lines 15-21), giving the genealogy of Cyrus the Great and an account of his capture of Babylon in 539 BC, Wikipedia, Babylonian Life and History, P. 86. Religious Tract Society, London

## *The Cylinder*

The cylinder, which dates to 539 BC, was discovered in 1879 in the ruins of Babylon.

King Cyrus' decree allowed the Israelites to return to their homeland and rebuild Jerusalem city and the temple. However, the returning Israelis faced militant opposition from the local neighboring nations as they began to rebuild. The local neighbors claimed that the Israelites were revolting against Persia, and that no one had given them the authority to rebuild the city, the walls, or the temple.

In response, the leaders of the returning Israelites sent a letter requesting the Persian kings who succeeded King Cyrus to search for Cyrus' decree, which was documented on the official cylinder.

> Ezra 6:1 Then Darius the king made a decree, and search was <u>made in the house of the rolls [archives], where the treasures were laid up in Babylon</u>.
> Ezra 6:2 And there was found at Achmetha, in the palace that is in the province of the Medes, a roll, and therein was a record thus written:

My lords, in addition to his decree of freedom for all prisoners of war, H.M. King Cyrus gave instructions to his treasurer to return the golden and silver vessels, which Babylonian King Nebuchadnezzar had carried away from Jerusalem's temple nearly fifty prophetic years before. These were the vessels, which Babylonian King Belshazzar drank of in his fateful banquet—the vessels of the Lord caused his demise.

Go ahead, please, scribe Ezra.

> EZRA 1:8 *Even those [gold vessels of the temple] did Cyrus king of Persia bring forth by the hand of Mithredath the treasurer, and numbered them unto Sheshbazzar, the prince of Judah [one of the royal descendants who now was entrusted by King Cyrus to take the Children of Israel back to their homeland].*

The year 539 BC, my lords, the year of the decree, is an important year. But it is not the important year, which we are chasing after. The important date, which we are after, my lords, is the date the temple, the parliament of God, was rebuilt once again. This date, my lords, would be a solid date, which would tell us what time it is on earth, according to God's calendar for our planet.

This statue, in Sydney/Australia Olympic Park, is a replica of a bas relief, of King Cyrus the Great, discovered in Pasargadae, the capital city of Persia. The statue purported to depict King Cyrus the Great in a Babylonian costume, Jewish helmet, and with two wings and a short Persian beard (Image source: Wikipedia).

At this point of time, my lords, and following the decree of his Iranian majesty King Cyrus, many of the Israelite captives began to stir up their dreams and their longings and saddle their belongings on beasts of burden to begin the trek that would lead them to the lonely land of their fathers.

And the crowds of them have gathered, my lords, and are now moving along [539/538 BC] under the leadership of Israeli Prince Sheshbazzar, whom H.M. King Cyprus had appointed as the governor of Judah of Israel.

## *Unimaginable Today*

The edict of the Persian Iranian King Cyrus the Great was only a start. Indeed, his heirs and successors, the Iranian kings who came after him, did go as far as financing the return of the children of Israel to their homeland. And this was not all. They went even farther still and financed the rebuilding of the walls of Jerusalem city and its temple—the house of prayers for all peoples.

Today, it is unimaginable that Iran would finance Israel to rebuild its ancient temple. It is simply unimaginable because, as mentioned before, the Islamic Dome of the Rock, an Islamic mosque, sits right on top of the site of Israel's old temple—the temple of the Holy One.

And so, obviously, Iran will not, under any circumstances whatsoever, allow the destruction of the Dome of the Rock in order to allow Israel to rebuild the temple of the Holy One.

The Islamic Dome of the Rock (Image source: Wikipedia commons, briony from San Francisco).

The Dome of the Rock, the war cry of the armies of the East, sits on the ancient site of the temple.

The Babylonian grave has now been opened, my lords. The dead is rising and travelling. It took them months of travelling to arrive to their motherland, the tower from which they were to proclaim the good news of an amazing future to all mankind—Persians and Arabs alike—a pardon and eternal life in the celestial heavens of heavens.

> *JN 3:16 For God so loved the world, that he gave his only begotten Son, that whosoever believeth in him should not perish, but have everlasting life.*
> *ROM 5:8 But God commendeth [shows] his love toward us, in that, while we were yet sinners, Christ died for us.*

And today, my lords, at this junction of time, the once hopeless but now resurrected children of Israel decided to express their gratitude to the One who never sleeps but watches over them day and night.

You can see, my lords, that this here is a different generation from their fathers. Their fathers had lost interest in anything but the present—and God was not on their mind.

And so in order to express their gratitude, they built an altar to lay upon it the best of the best of what they had, the most precious of all.

Blessed God, they prayed, "From Your hands we received much, and to You in gratitude, we give back the most precious of all You gave us.

Their God, they say, is not a cheap God or stingy, and He gave them a lot.

> *1 TIM 6:17 the living God, who giveth us richly all things to enjoy;*
> *JAS 1:5 ask of God, that giveth to all men liberally [generously]*

We will, blessed God, slaughter to You the most precious of what You gave us—a price for the life of our souls. We shall slaughter to you today the most precious, which You, Yourself, gave us.

But this sacrifice, my lord, was exactly what Israel, the preacher of the world, was all about. They were to proclaim that Christ, the gift of the Father, shall come and shall open the doors of heaven to man.

Their sacrifice, my lords, is a symbol. It is a symbol, my lords, for the future slaughtering, crucifying of the gift of all gifts, which God gave the world.

Scribe Ezra and prophet Isaiah, please, gentlemen, give your account to their majesties.

> *EZRA 3:1 And when the seventh month was come, and the children of Israel were in the cities, the people gathered themselves together as one man to Jerusalem.*

> *EZRA 3:2 Then stood up [priest] Jeshua the son of [Priest] Jozadak, and his brethren the priests, and [Prince and Governor] Zerubbabel the son of Shealtiel, and his brethren, and <u>builded the altar of the God of Israel</u>, to offer burnt offerings thereon, as it is written in the law of Moses the man of God.*
>
> *EZRA 3:6 From the first day of the seventh month began they to offer burnt offerings unto the LORD. <u>But the foundation of the temple of the LORD was not yet laid.</u>*

And so, my lords, the returning children of Israel carried on with offering their sacrifice—the symbol of the Savior, which they and the entire world were waiting for. The Lamb of God, of whom their prophet Isaiah spoke of over a century before, the sacrifice that was to bear man's sorrows and women's grief, and with whose beatings, and sufferings, and humbleness, all were to be healed.

Heaven is not cheap, my lords. It is bought with the most precious sacrifice of all—the Lamb of God, as prophet Isaiah and his fellow Israelite prophets proclaim. And it is unbelievable; it is unbelievable "what the Lord has done for you."

> *ISA 53:1 Who hath believed our report [who can believe what we say]? and to whom is the arm of the LORD revealed [the strength of the Lord, who can raise the dead]?*
>
> *ISA 53:4 Surely he [Christ the Lord] hath borne our griefs, and carried our sorrows*
>
> *ISA 53:5 he was wounded for our transgressions, he was bruised for our iniquities: the chastisement [payment] of our peace was upon him; <u>and with his stripes we are healed.</u>*
>
> *ISA 53:6 All we like sheep have gone astray; we have turned every one to his own way; <u>and the LORD hath laid on him [His only begotten son] the iniquity of us all</u>.*
>
> *ISA 53:10 thou shalt make his soul an offering [payment] for sin*

But the long-held dream for the dead who are now alive did not stop in building an altar, my lords. It was not the altar they dreamt of building—the altar was only a temporary first step.

And so, today, on the second month of the second year of their arrival, they did what they yearned to do all along. Today, my lords, they laid the foundation of the temple, the landmark, the symbol of the body of Christ, and in whom God and man meet.

Go ahead, scribe Ezra.

*EZRA 3:8* <u>Now in the second year</u> *of their coming unto the house of God at Jerusalem, in the second month, began ... all they that were come out of the captivity unto Jerusalem ... to set forward the work of the house of the LORD.*

*EZRA 3:10 And ...* <u>the builders laid the foundation of the temple of the LORD</u>

*EZRA 3:12 But many of the priests and Levites and chief of the fathers, who were ancient men, that had seen the first house [temple of Solomon, which Babylonian King Nebuchadnezzar had destroyed], when the foundation of this house was laid before their eyes, wept with a loud voice; and many shouted aloud for joy:*

The son who went astray, the Prodigal Son, has come back home.

> *1 JN 1:3 and truly our fellowship [relationship] is with the Father, and with his Son Jesus Christ.*
> *1 JN 1:4 And these things write we unto you, that your joy may be full.*

Unfortunately, my lords, it was not going to be easy for the returning nation of the prophets to do much more than laying the foundation of the house of joy.

And the first weapon the longtime enemies of Israel planned to use against it, my lords, was a relentless letter campaign.

Go ahead, scribe Ezra, finish your report, please.

*EZRA 4:5 And [their local neighboring nations] hired counsellors [lobbyists] against them, to frustrate their purpose, all the days of Cyrus king of Persia*

## Little Earth Covers My Body

One day, my lords, a youngster sitting amongst you today did come to pay a visit to the resting place, the tomb of his Iranian majesty King Cyrus the Great. The visit came almost exactly two hundred years after the great one died. A living great came to visit a dead great.

And the genius youngster, and you know who you are, sir, wanted to have the ancient Iranian inscription on the tomb read to him. And "The text was as follows. 'O man, whoever you are and wherever you come from, for I know you will come, I am Cyrus who won the Persians their empire. Do not therefore grudge me this little earth that covers my body.'*

"These words made a deep impression"* on the youngster, a future king of the world, "since they reminded him of the uncertainty and mutability of mortal life"* and therefore the youngster, my lords, ordered that the text to be re-inscribed below the original in the youngster's own language.[27]

However, sympathetic or not, my lords, this youngster sitting amongst you today did come to the region with one purpose in mind; he came to destroy the great Persian empire, which his Iranian majesty King Cyrus had created.

Tomb of King Cyrus the Great of Persia at Pasargadae, photo taken in July 2001 by fr:Utilisateur:Mbenoist.

"O MAN, I AM CYRUS; I ESTABLISHED THE PERSIAN EMPIRE AND WAS KING OF ASIA. GRUDGE ME NOT THEREFORE THIS MONUMENT."[28]

---

[27] ancient historian *Plutarch. The Age Of Alexander*, translated and annotated by Ian Scott-Kilvert, Penguin Books 1973, P.326

[28] [ancient historian] *Strabo's Geography*, Book Fifteen, Chapter.3:7, http://rbedrosian.com/Classic/strabo15f.htm

Ps 90:12 So teach us to number our days
Heb 9:27 it is appointed unto men once to die, but after this the judgment:
Heb 6:2 Of the doctrine of ... resurrection of the dead, and of eternal judgment.
Isa 26:19 Thy dead men shall live, together with my dead body shall they arise. Awake and sing, ye that dwell in dust.

Egyptian mummy, 3,400 BC, British Museum (image source: Author).

And so, my lords, H.M. King Cyrus the great died. He was the founder of the Persian Empire, but he was not its richest king. A richer successor of his shall turn his face west towards Europe. And we shall soon, my lords, meet him at his station on the highway of prophecy.

Go ahead, prophet Daniel.

> DAN 11:2 *And now will I shew thee the truth. Behold, there shall stand up yet three kings in Persia [Cyrus, Cambyses, Darius I, and Xerxes]; and the fourth shall be far richer than they all: and by his strength through his riches he shall stir up all against the realm of Grecia [Greece, the gateway of Europe].*

## THE PERSIAN EMPIRE SPREAD ITS WINGS

### Cambyses II
### 530–522 BC

H.M. King Cyrus the great bid the eye of the sun farewell and went to his rest so that one day, my lords, he may rise again from his sleep to face the final evaluation of the life he was granted on planet earth.

Shall now his kingdom—which includes Iran, Iraq, and Turkey—disintegrate after his death?

Not according to the prophet Daniel, my lords.

Today, at this point of time, your majesties, King Cyrus' son, his Iranian majesty King Cambyses II, is the commander in chief of the greatest power on planet earth. And he knows it very well, my lords.

But what he may or may not know, my lords, is that there is a prophecy waiting to be fulfilled. And he may be part of it. And this prophecy, which is dated years before he or even his father King Cyrus were born, is the same prophecy that foretold of the rise of the Persians when they were but nothing.

And that prophecy, my lords, went on to say that the Persians, who were despised even by their Iranian cousins, the Medians, shall go on and stretch their borders far and wide even to deluge the mighty superpower Egypt, home of the great pharaohs. The nobodies, my lords, shall, according to the prophecy, swallow the nobles.

And who would have believed such a prophecy, my lords, that the despised Persians could one day govern and possess the mighty land of the Nile and all of the pharaohs' riches? He would have to be a mad man to believe such a prophecy.

Iran of King Cyrus, the savior of Israel, was destined, my lords, to become great in the reward given to it by the shepherded of Israel.

Prophet Daniel!

> DAN 8:4 *I saw the ram [Media and Persia – today's Iran] pushing <u>westward</u> [towards Europe – has begun by defeating King Cruses], and <u>northward</u> [Armenia], and <u>southward</u> [Egypt and Ethiopia]; so that no beasts [other kingdoms] might stand before him, neither was there any that could deliver out of his hand; but he did according to his will, and became great*
>
> DAN 8:20 *The ram which thou sawest having two horns are the kings of Media and Persia.*

Indeed, my lords, their invasion of Egypt shall leave behind a mystery that will last to our modern day as we shall relate to you, your majesties.

But we must also admit, my lords, that H.M. King Cambyses II, son of King Cyrus, is not our main interest. Nevertheless, my lords, we must introduce him to you because he leads us to the one-ear king, who is indeed our main interest.

# 525 BC
# Lashing with Whips

My lords, on this day back then, his Iranian majesty King Cambyses II, had received a pledge of safe conduct from the Arabs along the highway to Egypt. And they say, your majesties, that the Arabs had gathered a great number of sewed camel skins, which they filled with water. These water bottles of camel skins were then strung together, my lords, in order to form a long water pipe that lined up the desert route, which the army of His Iranian majesty King Cambyses II was to take to one of the finest paradises on earth.

And we can tell you, my lords, that the Egyptians have been routed out. Paradise was captured.

The Egyptian king, H.M. King Amasis, was fortunate enough to die before the lowly, unheard of Persian Iranians invaded his ancient land of many majesties.

But if King Amasis escaped the humiliation, his corpse did not, my lords.

Please go ahead, historian Herodotus, with your ancient record of that time.

> "Cambyses ... no sooner had he entered the palace of Amasis [king of Egypt, who died before the Persian Iranian invasion had begun, 525 BC] than he gave orders for his body to be taken from the tomb where it lay. This done, he proceeded to have it treated with every possible indignity, such as lashing with whips, pricking with goads, and the plucking of its hairs ... and at last Cambyses ordered it to be burnt ... the Persians believe that fire is a god."[29]

Iran takes control of Egypt, as the biblical prophet Daniel had prophesied.

Above, King Cambyses II of Persia, the first successor of King Cyrus the Great, is seen capturing pharaoh Psamtik III of Egypt. Behind him, four prisoners are tied at the necks. Image is engraved on a Persian seal, VI century BC (image source: WC).

---

[29] Herodotus, *The Histories*, 3:16, P. 209

Some say, my lords, that H.M. King Cambyses II, son of the great King Cyrus, is an unhinged madman. Indeed, those holding this opinion, my lords, say that he is a madman because he has sent his army to the secluded desert shrine of the most important and most revered Egyptian god, with an order to crush the statue of the god to pieces. Imagine such a thing, my lords! Imagine how would the Egyptians feel?

## A Bridge Over Hell

The Iranian kings were the followers and believers of the early version of the Zoroastrian religion.

This Iranian religion predated the Arabs' religion of Islam by more than one thousand and two hundred years. However, the teachings of the Zoroastrian religion traveled with the caravans' crews, who plowed the busy highway from Iran, home of Zoroastrian, to Iraq and down south to Saudi Arabia.

It is, therefore, no surprise that the new startup religion of Islam borrowed some of its teachings from the older Zoroastrian religion, in addition, of course, to its core base of Arabian-flavored Judaism.

One of the teachings of the Zoroastrian religion is that the soul of the dead must first pass over a bridge, called the "Chinawad Bridge," before it reaches paradise. This bridge is stretched above hell, and railed up along its sides with sharp hooks. The spirit of good men would be met at the bridge by good-looking, large-breasted, teenage virgins.

> 9. "In that wind there comes to meet him his own law in the figure of a maiden, one beautiful, shining, with shining arms; one powerful, well-grown, slender, with large breasts, praiseworthy body; one noble, with brilliant face, one of fifteen years, as fair in her growth as the fairest creatures.

*Dadestan*, Chapter 21, http://www.sacred-texts.com/zor/toz/toz05.htm

The Arabian prophet Muhammad appreciated and borrowed the idea of the dangerous passage on a bridge over hell and expanded on it, as he did with the Old Testament's Scriptures [Edit: see EOOO 1 & 2].

Following his borrowing of the bridge idea, he then added his own take on the teenage virgins with large breasts.

The quotes below come from the sacred Islamic books of Hadith. And the bracketed comments in the quotes are those made by Muslim scholars only.

## 230—EARTH OUT OF ORBIT

### *Bukhari*, 009, 093, 532A

"Then a Bridge will be laid across Hell (Fire)' I and my followers will be the first ones to go across it … In Hell (or over The Bridge) there will be hooks like the thorns of As-Sa'dan (thorny plant).
Have you seen As-Sa'dan?
"They replied, ""Yes, O Allah's Apostle!""
He said, ""So those hooks look like the thorns of As-Sa'dan, but none knows how big they are except Allah. Those hooks will snap the people away according to their deeds.
Some of the people will stay in Hell (be destroyed) because of their (evil) deeds, and some will be cut or torn by the hooks (and fall into Hell) and some will be punished and then relieved.
When Allah has finished His Judgments among the people, He will take whomever He will out of Hell through His Mercy.
He will then order the angels to take out of the Fire all those who used to worship none but Allah from among those whom Allah wanted to be merciful to and those who testified (in the world) that none has the right to be worshipped but Allah.
<u>The angels will recognize them in the Fire by the marks of prostration (on their foreheads), for the Fire will eat up all the human body except the mark caused by prostration as Allah has forbidden the Fire to eat the mark of prostration.</u>

Muslims prostrating in the prayer ritual (image source: WC, Cpl. Bryan Nygaard).

# THE UNEQUAL TWO HORNS OF IRAN—231

The face of late Egyptian president, Anwar Sadat, a practicing Moslem, shows the dark mark of prayer prostration on his forehead.

Next to President Sadat stands the Israeli minister Ezer Weizman during the Camp David Summit in the USA, source of image: W.C, Jimmy Carter Library (NLJC), 441 Freedom Parkway, Atlanta, GA, 30307-1498.

They will come out of the (Hell) Fire, completely burnt and then the water of life will be poured over them and they will grow under it as does a seed that comes in the mud of the torrent.
Then Allah will finish the judgments among the people, and there will remain one man facing the (Hell) Fire and he will be the last person among the people of Hell to enter Paradise.
He will say, 'O my Lord! Please turn my face away from the fire because its air has hurt me and its severe heat has burnt me.' So he will invoke Allah in the way Allah will wish him to invoke, and then Allah will say to him, 'If I grant you that, will you then ask for anything else?'
He will reply, 'No, by Your Power, (Honor) I will not ask You for anything else.'
He will give his Lord whatever promises and covenants Allah will demand. So Allah will turn his face away from Hell (Fire).
When he will face Paradise and will see it, he will remain quiet for as long as Allah will wish him to remain quiet, then he will say, 'O my Lord! Bring me near to the gate of Paradise.'
Allah will say to him, 'Didn't you give your promises and covenants that you would never ask for anything more than what you had been given? Woe on you, O Adam's son! How treacherous you are!'
He will say, 'O my lord,' and will keep on invoking Allah till He says to him, 'If I give what you are asking, will you then ask for anything else?'
He will reply, 'No, by Your (Honor) Power, I will not ask for anything else.' Then he will give covenants and promises to Allah and then Allah will bring him near to the gate of Paradise.

> When he stands at the gate of Paradise, Paradise will be opened and spread before him, and he will see its splendor and pleasures whereupon he will remain quiet as long as Allah will wish him to remain quiet, and then he will say, O my Lord! Admit me into Paradise.'
> Allah will say, 'Didn't you give your covenants and promises that you would not ask for anything more than what you had been given?' Allah will say, 'Woe on you, O Adam's son! How treacherous you are! '
> The man will say, 'O my Lord! Do not make me the most miserable of Your creation,' and he will keep on invoking Allah till Allah will laugh because of his sayings, and when Allah will laugh because of him, He will say to him, 'Enter Paradise,' and when he will enter it, Allah will say to him, 'Wish for anything.' So he will ask his Lord, and he will wish for a great number of things, for Allah Himself will remind him to wish for certain things by saying, '(Wish for) so-and-so.'"

The Arabian prophet Muhammad of Islam repeated these teachings about the bridge several times with minor variations here and there.

### *Bukhari*, 009, 093, 532B

> "Then the Bridge will be laid across Hell."
> We, the companions of the Prophet said, "O Allah's Apostle! What is the Bridge?'
> He said, "It is a slippery (Bridge) on which there are clamps and (Hooks like) a thorny seed that is wide at one side and narrow at the other and has thorns with bent ends. Such a thorny seed is found in Najd and is called As-Sa'dan.
> Some of the believers will cross the Bridge as quickly as the wink of an eye, some others as quick as lightning, a strong wind, fast horses or she-camels. So some will be safe without any harm; some will be safe after receiving some scratches, and some will fall down into Hell (Fire).
> The last person will cross by being dragged (over the Bridge)."
> ...
> Allah will say, 'Go and take out (of Hell) anyone in whose heart you find faith equal to the weight of one (gold) Dinar.' ... They will go to them and find some of them in Hell (Fire) up to their feet, and some up to the middle of their legs.
> So they will take out those whom they will recognize and then they will return, and Allah will say (to them), 'Go and take out (of Hell) anyone in whose heart you find faith equal to the weight of one half Dinar.'
> They will take out whomever they will recognize and return, and then Allah will say, 'Go and take out (of Hell) anyone in whose heart you find faith equal to the weight of an atom (or a smallest ant), and so they will take out all those whom they will recognize ... the Almighty (Allah) ... will then hold a handful of the Fire from which He will take out some people whose bodies have been burnt, and they will be thrown into a river at the entrance of Paradise, called the water of life. They will grow on its banks, as a seed carried by the torrent grows. You have noticed how it grows beside a rock or beside a tree, and how the side facing the sun is usually green while the side facing the shade is white. Those people will come out (of the River of Life) like pearls, and they will have (golden) necklaces, and then they will enter Paradise whereupon the people of Paradise will say, 'These are the

people emancipated by the Beneficent. He has admitted them into Paradise without them having done any good deeds and without sending forth any good (for themselves).'"

As for the virgins, the Koran, the sacred book of the Arabian religion of Islam, states the following:

*The Koran*, Surah 78, The News, Verse 31-33
"But, for the God-fearing is a blissful abode,
Enclosed gardens and vineyards;
And damsels with swelling breasts."

The Arabian prophet went on to describe an unusual type of virgins, paradise virgins, which he called the "Houris." The Houris, according to him, are a unique kind of virgins in that they become virgins over and over again after each intercourse. Their virginity is a reward from Allah for the enjoyment and pleasure of the followers of Muhammad.

Furthermore, all of these young women, whom Allah will give as a reward to Muhammad's followers, are all white women.

And besides the reward of the "ever-virgins," the paradise virgins, the followers of the Islamic prophet would also enjoy a fair number of additional numbers of white women.

*Al-Tirmidhi*, 1494
Allah's Messenger (pbuh) said, "The lowliest of the inhabitants of Paradise will be he who has eighty thousand servants, seventy-two wives ... "Those who are to go to Paradise, who die whether young or old, will come into Paradise aged thirty and never grow older. The same applies to those who will go to Hell." ... "When a believer in Paradise wishes for a child, its conception, delivery and growth to full age will be accomplished in a moment as he wishes."

But rest assured, your majesties, that the Iranian army of H.M King Cambyses, the Zoroastrian king, could not succeed to smash to pieces the statue of the god of gods of Egypt. Indeed, the entire 50,000 soldiers of his majesty could not do it, my lords. The reason is that the regiment and all its huge number of soldiers were lost in the trackless desert, where they all perished and no one could find where their corpses lay—even in our modern days, my lords. It is a mystery—the mystery of the Island of the Blessed.

Go ahead, please, historian Herodotus.

Cambyses "Arrived at Thebes [the ancient capital city of southern Egypt], he detached a body of 50,000 men with orders to ... burn the oracle of Zeus

...

The force ... started from Thebes [today's Luxor] with guides, and can be traced as far as the town of Oasis ... the place is known in Greek as the Island of the Blessed. General report has it that the army got as far as this, but of its subsequent fate there is no news whatever. It never reached the Ammonians and it never returned to Egypt ... a southerly wind [a sandstorm] of extreme violence drove the sand over them in heaps as they were taking their midday meal, so that they disappeared for ever."[30]

> ## *Mystery Solved?*
>
>
>
> **Professor Kaper says that the disappearance of a Persian army in 524 BC has been solved, thanks to deciphering ancient temple blocks (pictured) (image source: British *Daily Mail* newspaper).**
>
> A report in the British paper, the Daily Mail, written by Jonathan O'Callaghan and published in the paper's edition of June 27, 2014, claims that the old mystery of the lost army of King Cambyses II in Egypt may have been solved.
>
> > "In 524 BC, a Persian army of 50,000 men sent by King Cambyses II marched into the Egyptian desert from Thebes-now known as Luxor. But, after entering the desert, they were never heard from again.

---

[30] Herodotus, *The Histories* 3:25, 26

For centuries, it has been presumed they were swallowed by a sandstorm, but now a researcher claims that wasn't the case-and instead they must have been defeated in battle.

In the 5th century BC, Greek historian Herodotus wrote that the disappearance of the army could be attributed to an unfortunate end involving sand dunes.

University of Leiden Egyptologist Professor Olaf Kaper, however, disagrees.

"'Since the 19th century, people have been looking for this army: amateurs, as well as professional archaeologists,'" he said.

"'Some expect to find, somewhere under the ground, an entire army, fully equipped.

'However, experience has long shown that you can't die from a sandstorm, let alone have an entire army disappear.'"

Professor Kaper is now putting forward an entirely different explanation.

He argues that the army did not disappear, but was instead, defeated.

"'My research shows that the army was not simply passing through the desert; its final destination was the Dachla Oasis,'" he said.

'This was the location of the troops of the Egyptian rebel leader Petubastis III.

'He ultimately ambushed the army of Cambyses, and in this way managed from his base in the oasis to reconquer a large part of Egypt, after which he had himself crowned Pharaoh in the capital, Memphis.'

Kaper said he made the discovery accidentally.

In collaboration with New York University and the University of Lecce, he was involved for the last ten years in excavations in Amheida, in the Dachla Oasis.

And earlier this year, he deciphered the full list of titles of Petubastis III on ancient temple blocks.

'That's when the puzzle pieces fell into place', said the Egyptologist.

'The temple blocks indicate that this must have been a stronghold at the start of the Persian period.

'Once we combined this with the limited information we had about Petubastis III, the excavation site and the story of Herodotus, we were able to reconstruct what happened.'

The fact that the fate of the army of Cambyses remained unclear for such a long time is probably due to the Persian King Darius I, who ended the Egyptian revolt with much bloodshed two years after Cambyses' defeat.

He attributed the shameful defeat of his predecessor to natural elements, and 75 years after the events, all Herodotus could do was take note of the sandstorm story.

But now this new research sheds light on one of the greatest archaeological mysteries of all time."

And the lost army was not the only mystery, my lords, of this Iranian campaign into the mighty land of Egypt. There was also another one. The second mystery, my lords, was how his Iranian majesty King Cambyses II died. Was he assassinated in Egypt, or did he commit suicide, or did he simply die in a riding accident, as some say? Who knows, my lords? who knows?

And what is this we hear, your Majesty king Cambyses? We hear, sir, that someone back home in Iran has rebelled against you and declared himself king in your absence.

How could this happen, your majesty? Did you know who he was who dared to do such a thing against you, sir? Did you find out how was it possible that this rebel could gather so many followers so fast and take over your Iranian throne in your absence?

We have some answers for you, your majesty.

They say that the powerful rebel was a religious fanatic—a priest.

And to boot, your majesty, he managed to convince the population that he was your dead young brother, Smerdis. And indeed, sir, he looked very much like your dead young brother.

As for his name, sir, well, you take your pick. Some, your majesty, call him "Bardiya"; others call him "Gaumata," and yet, sir, he is also known as "Tanooxares," or "Tonyoaxarces." And we wonder, sir, if he is the biblical King Artaxerxes.

At any rate, my lords, after three years in Egypt, his majesty is at this point of time rushing home to deal with the serious revolt of Tonyoaxarces.

Hurry up, sir.

## 522 BC Tonyoaxarces —The King Has no Ears

One more time, your majesty King Cyrus the Great, one more time, sir; please tell us what did your Persian Iranian folks say about you? We ask you this again, sir, because we believe that you, kind as you may have been, you may also have made a grave mistake, sir—you cut a man's ears.

And the man, to boot, sir, is a priest and a Median. Today, this man is pretending to be your son and the inheritor of your throne.

But, sir, it is not all your fault. Perhaps nothing would have happened, sir, had your son H.M King Cambyses II not stayed away too long in Egypt. But he did, sir, and things do happen when the king is away for too long. And things are prone to happen more readily, sir, when many people consider their ruler to be a spoiled tyrant and a madman.

Historian Herodotus, please, sir, tell their majesties once again what the leading men of Persia thought of H.M King Cyrus.

> "Thou foundest the Persians a race of slaves, thou hast made them free men: Thou foundest them subject to others; thou hast made them lords of all,"* said General Hystaspes to his king, Cyrus, the founder and father of the Persian Empire. [31]

How true, sir! You indeed found the lowly Persians of southern Iran slaves to the powerful Medians of northern Iran—the small horn that came out first in Daniel's prophecy.

Please, prophet Daniel, remind their majesties.

> DAN 8:3 *I lifted up mine eyes, and saw, and, behold, there stood before the <u>river a ram which had two horns</u> [Media and Persia]: and the two horns were high; <u>but one was higher than the other</u> [Persia], <u>and the higher came up last</u>.*

And you, sir, turned the table around and made the Persians the masters––the taller horn that came up after. But watch out, sir. You cut the Median priest's ears and, today, eight years after your death, the table is about to turn around again against your legacy, sir. The arrogant Media, contrary to the prophecy of Daniel, is in its way, sir, to reduce Persia to slavery once more.

Did your prophecy fail, prophet Daniel? We know the answer, sir. It did not. Although for a short time, it seemed that it would indeed fail. In fact, this short time was all that was needed in order to fulfill your prophecy.

As for you, your majesty King Cyrus the Great, after three years in Egypt [525 to 522 BC], your son, H.M. King Cambyses II, is rushing home to deal with the Median rebel Priest Tonyoaxarces, the Median magus [Edit: magi is the plural of magus].

Unfortunately, sir, we have to deliver bad news to you. And you may as well brace yourself, sir, for worse ones yet to come. Your dear son, sir, King Cambyses II, has died before he could dislodge the Median imposter, which at this point of time sits on your dearly purchased throne.

But, sir, your son, in his last breath implored the mighty ones of his inner circle to make sure and restore your mighty throne back to your royal Achaemenian family of Persia.

---

[31] *Herodotus, *The Histories*, Book.1:211

Would you please confirm this, historian Herodotus, and comfort H.M King Cyrus the Great!

> Cambyses "sent for the leading Persians ... and addressed them in the following words: ... I must ... tell you with my last breath what I would wish you to do.
> In the name of the gods who watch over our royal house, the commandment I lay upon all of you, and especially upon those of the Achaemenidae who are here present, is this: <u>do not allow the dominion to pass again into the hands of the Medes.</u>"[32]

Inscription in Old Persian, Elamite and Akkadian languages carved on a column in Pasargadae, it reads: "I am Cyrus, an Achaemenid king" (image source: Wikipedia, <u>Truth Seeker (fawiki)</u>).

May we, your majesty, King Cyrus, read from the rock inscription in Behistun, which was carved by the order of one of your successors!

> "(11) there was a certain man, a <u>Magian</u>, Gaumâta [or Tonyoaxarces] by name, who raised a rebellion in <u>Paišiyâuvâdâ</u>, in a mountain called Arakadriš. On the fourteenth day of the month Viyaxana [11 March 522] did he rebel.
> He lied to the people, saying: 'I am Smerdis, <u>the son of Cyrus, the brother of Cambyses.</u>'
> Then were all the people in revolt, and from Cambyses they went over unto him, both Persia and Media, and the other provinces.

---

[32] Herodotus, *The Histories*, 3:65, P. 231

## THE UNEQUAL TWO HORNS OF IRAN—239

He seized the kingdom; on the ninth day of the month Garmapada [1 July 522] he seized the kingdom. Afterwards, Cambyses died of natural causes."[33]

The *Behistun Inscription* documented the rebellion of Gaumata and was carved in Old Persian, Elamite, and Babylonian languages. These reliefs and texts, as could be seen above, are engraved on the surface of a cliff on Mount Behistun (present Kermanshah Province, Iran) (image source: Wikipedia, Hara1603).

A close-up of the *Behistun Inscription* from, WC by KendallKDown

---

[33] The *Behistun Inscription,* http://www.livius.org/be-bm/behistun/behistun-t05.html#1.36-43

The Median imposter who seized your throne, your majesty King Cyrus, is a good politician. He is not reducing the burden of taxes on your subjects, sir, no; he is giving them a reprieve from taxes for a full three years. And, sir, the imposter is becoming more and more popular.

Where is ancient Roman historian Marcus Junianus Justinus? There you are, sir. Go ahead please, historian Justinus, [Latin historian Justin, 2nd–3rd century AD] and tell H.M. King Cyprus what transpired after his death.

> "The Magi, to gain the favour of the people, granted a remission of the taxes, and immunity from military service, for three years, that they might secure by indulgence and bounties the kingdom which they had gained by fraud."[34]

Historian Herodotus, please confirm the claims of historian Justinus, even though you might run ahead of the events.

> "the Magus, after assuming the name of Smerdis, son of Cyrus, found himself securely on the throne, and continued there for seven months ... During this time his subjects received great benefits from him, and he was regretted after his death by all the Asians under his rule, except by the Persians themselves, for to every nation within his dominion he proclaimed, directly he came to the throne, a three years' remission of taxes and military services."[35]

But today, your majesty King Cyrus, the imposter; His new Majesty, the Median fanatic priest, King Tonyoaxarces, who grabbed your great Persian throne, is showing his true colors.

The fanatic priest has gone on a tearing rage persecuting the followers of all other religions and even demolishing their temples and shrines and sacred places – he is nothing but a religious fanatic, sir.

This man Your Majesty is doing the very opposite to what you, yourself, had ordered, sir. You were tolerant sir, but he is a fanatic extremist.

Instead of allowing different religions to build temples and worship their gods as they inherited from their fathers, he is, sir, destroying the temples of all religions other than his.

Listen, sir, to what one of your successors wrote.

---

[34] Justin, Epitome of the Philippic History of Pompeius Trogus, Book 1:9
[35] Herodotus, *The Histories*, 3:66, P.232

"(14) King Darius says: The kingdom that had been wrested from our line I brought back and I reestablished it on its foundation. The temples which Gaumâta, the Magian, had destroyed, I restored to the people, and the pasture lands, and the herds and the dwelling places, and the houses which Gaumâta, the Magian, had taken away. I settled the people in their place, the people of Persia, and Media, and the other provinces. I restored that which had been taken away, as is was in the days of old. This did I by the grace of Ahuramazda, I labored until I had established our dynasty in its place, as in the days of old; I labored, by the grace of Ahuramazda, so that Gaumâta, the Magian, did not dispossess our house."[36]

This imposter, who is pretending to be your son, sir, is defying your own edicts—eternal edicts that no man is allowed or permitted to change.

How could he be so disrespectful of your wishes sir?

He is disrespectful of your edicts, sir, because he is a Median, and because he has a personal vendetta against you, as we reminded you, your majesty.

Look what he has done in Israel, sir.

The neighboring enemies of Israel seized the opportunity of his revolt to reverse your edict. It is the only way and the only chance for them to rescind your edict. And so they sent him letters, sir, aiming at stopping the children of Israel from rebuilding their temple—reversing the permission that you yourself, sir, have given them in writing. The Median priest is reversing your own orders, sir. And who can stop him now?

We will tell who can and would, sir.

## 530–525 BC Meanwhile, in Jerusalem

My lords, the madman of Iran, H.M. King Cambyses II, died after fulfilling the "south" portion of Daniel's prophecy. The race of slaves, the Persians, has now stretched its wings to cast its wide shadow on the masters of Egypt.

Go ahead, prophet Daniel.

DANIEL 8:4 *I saw the ram [Media and Persia–Iran] pushing <u>westward</u> [towards Europe], and <u>northward</u> [Armenia], and <u>southward</u> [Egypt]; so that no beasts [other kingdoms] might*

---

[36] *Behistun Inscription*, Livius.org.

> *stand before him, neither was there any that could deliver out of his hand; but he did according to his will, and became great*

As for you, Your deceased Majesty King Cyrus the Great, today your once-lowly two million Persians[37] are on their way to rule over forty million of the inhabitants of God's earth.

Yet, as you see, my lords, your Persian throne is very shaky at this moment. And the one who rocks it is a Median.

Meanwhile in Jerusalem city, my lords, a small altar was built, and the work on the city's wall continues.

Furthermore, the survivors of the Babylonian exile have also laid the foundation, just the foundation, of the temple—the parliament of God.

## *The Golden Opportunity*

The children of Israel, who were deported to Babylon by the Iraqi King Nebuchadnezzar, were then allowed to return to Israel by the Iranian King Cyrus the great.

Their country and especially Jerusalem was in ruins. The first task of these founding fathers of the reborn Israel was to build the protective walls of the city in order to keep the population safe and secure.

However, the most important project, which they desired to achieve, was a spiritual one—the rebuilding of the house of the Lord—the most important marker in God's calendar for the earth.

But against them, and their wishes, came the neighboring nations who were united in their determination of preventing the reconstruction of Jerusalem's walls. And they were just as much united on preventing the rebuilding of the house of the Lord.

Their best chance to prevent the reconstruction of the walls and the house of the Lord was to set the Iranian kings against the two projects. But this was impossible. It was impossible for a legitimate Persian successor of King Cyprus the great to reverse his orders and edicts.

Did the local neighbors find their golden chance at last?

Did they now have their best chance with a religious fanatic, Tonyoaxarces, who was against all other religions, and who was also a Median imposter willing to reverse Persian King Cyrus' edicts and decrees? Is

---

[37] The numbers are taken from *The Story of Civilization, Our Oriental Heritage,* Will Durant, Simon and Schuster, P.P. 355, 356.

he then the Artaxerxes of the Bible who sided with the local enemies of Israel and reversed Cyrus' decree?

Tonyoaxarces managed to hold to the throne of Iran for a mere seven months. A short period of time, yet, it was long enough to fulfill God's plan and timetable.

The circle in the middle of this earring "encloses a half figure probably represents Ahura Mazda, the supreme god of Zoroastrism, the official religion of the Achaemenid Empire.", this quote is taken from the Metropolitan Museum of Art, NY where the earring is housed (image source: author)

The leaders, my lords, of the enemy nations surrounding Israel have once more sent a letter to Iran in another attempt to stop the Israeli survivors from carrying on with their work.

Scribe Ezra, please read your account to their majesties.

> EZRA 4:5 *[the enemies of Israel] hired counsellors [delegations, lobbyists] against them [Children of Israel], to frustrate their purpose, all the days of Cyrus king of Persia, even until the reign of Darius king of Persia.*

EZRA 4:6 And in the reign of Ahasuerus, in the beginning of his reign, wrote they unto him an accusation against the inhabitants of Judah and Jerusalem.

EZRA 4:7 And in the days of [the imposter Tonyoaxarces?] Artaxerxes wrote [the enemies of Israel, the leaders of several local neighboring nations] Bishlam, Mithredath, Tabeel, and the rest of their companions, unto Artaxerxes king of Persia; and the writing of the letter was written in the Syrian tongue, and interpreted in the Syrian tongue.

EZRA 4:9 Then wrote Rehum the chancellor, and Shimshai the scribe, and the rest of their companions; the Dinaites, the Apharsathchites, the Tarpelites, the Apharsites, the Archevites, the Babylonians [Iraqis], the Susanchites, the Dehavites, and the Elamites [Iranians].

EZRA 4:10 And the rest of the nations whom the great and noble Asnappar [Assyrian King Assurbanipal] brought over, and set in the cities of Samaria, and the rest that are on this side the river, and at such a time.

EZRA 4:11 This is the copy of the letter that they sent unto him [the imposter King Tonyoaxarces?], even unto Artaxerxes the king; Thy servants the men on this side the river, and at such a time.

EZRA 4:12 Be it known unto the king, that the Jews which came up from thee to us are come unto Jerusalem, building the rebellious and the bad city, and have set up the walls thereof, and joined the foundations.

EZRA 4:13 Be it known now unto the king, that, if this city be builded, and the walls set up again, then will they not pay toll, tribute, and custom, and so thou shalt endamage the revenue of the kings.

EZRA 4:14 Now because we have maintenance from the king's palace, and it was not meet for us to see the king's dishonour, therefore have we sent and certified the king;

EZRA 4:15 That search may be made in the book of the records of thy fathers: so shalt thou find in the book of the records, and know that this city is a rebellious city, and hurtful unto kings and provinces, and that they have moved sedition within the same of old time: for which cause was this city destroyed.

EZRA 4:16 We certify the king that, if this city be builded again, and the walls thereof set up, by this means thou shalt have no portion on this side the river.

## The Good Samaritan

Allow us once again, my lords, to digress for a minute or two.

It was nearly two hundred years prior to where we are now, your majesties, that Israel north and its capital city, Samaria, were sacked by the Assyrians of northern Iraq. The Israeli population was then exiled to Iranian and Iraqi cities, which gave rise to the legend of the lost ten tribes, my lords, if you recall.

But the Assyrians, my lords, needed to repopulate Israel north and Samaria and their fields and shops so that the Assyrian Empire could receive an income from them.

And so, my lords, your colleagues, their Assyrian Iraqi majesties King Sargon II, and particularly King Assurbanipal, had replaced the exiled population of Samaria and Israel north with foreigners from many nationalities, Iraqis, Iranians, and Arabs—all of whom they brought to live and work in Samaria, the capital of empty Israel [Samaria fell to the Assyrian Iraqis in 722/721 BC].

Over time, my lords, the children of Israel would call all these despised foreigners "Samaritans."

However, the savior of the world used these hated and despised Samaritans for an example to love as God loves—for all are His and He is Love.

Go ahead, please, apostle Luke.

> LK 10:25 *And, behold, a certain lawyer stood up, and tempted him [Christ the Lord], saying, Master, <u>what shall I do to inherit eternal life?</u>*
>
> LK 10:26 *He said unto him, What is written in the law [of Moses]? how readest thou?*
>
> LK 10:27 *And he answering said, <u>Thou shalt love the Lord thy God with all thy heart, and with all thy soul, and with all thy strength, and with all thy mind; and thy neighbour as thyself.</u>*
>
> LK 10:28 *And he said unto him, Thou hast answered right: <u>this do, and thou shalt live.</u>*
>
> LK 10:29 *But he [the Israeli Lawyer], willing to justify himself, said unto Jesus, And who is my neighbour?*
>
> LK 10:30 *And Jesus answering said, A certain man [an Israelite] went down from Jerusalem to Jericho, and fell among thieves, which stripped him of his raiment, and wounded him, and departed, leaving him half dead.*
>
> LK 10:31 *And by chance there came down a certain priest that way: and when he saw him, he passed by on the other side.*
>
> LK 10:32 *And likewise a Levite [a priest's assistance, so to speak], when he was at the place, came and looked on him, and passed by on the other side.*
>
> LK 10:33 *But a certain Samaritan, as he journeyed, came where he was: and when he saw him, he had compassion on him,*
>
> LK 10:34 *And went to him, and bound up his wounds, pouring in oil and wine, and set him on his own beast, and brought him to an inn, and took care of him.*

> LK 10:35 *And on the morrow when he departed, he took out two pence, and gave them to the host, and said unto him, Take care of him; and whatsoever thou spendest more, when I come again, I will repay thee.*
> LK 10:36 *Which now of these three, thinkest thou, was neighbour unto him [the Israelite] that fell among the thieves?*
> LK 10:37 *And he said, He that shewed mercy on him. Then said Jesus unto him,* <u>Go, and do thou likewise</u> *[become a Good Samaritan even unto those who despise and hate you – one love to all].*
>
> LK 3:11 *He that hath two coats, let him impart [give] to him that hath none; and he that hath meat [extra food], let him do likewise.*

At any rate, my lords, the local neighbors and the mixed foreigners of Samaria have now sent a letter to H.M. King Artaxerxes, trying to persuade the Median religious fanatic to stop the children of Israel from building the walls and re-building the house of the Lord, the parliament of God.

The answer of the fanatic Iranian king, the Median Iranian, my lords, came quickly and was very clear.

Go ahead, please, scribe Ezra.

> EZRA 4:17 *Then sent the king an answer unto Rehum the chancellor, and to Shimshai the scribe, and to the rest of their companions that dwell in Samaria, and unto the rest beyond the river [the River Jordan], Peace, and at such a time.*
> EZRA 4:18 *The letter which ye sent unto us hath been plainly read before me.*
> EZRA 4:19 *And I commanded, and search hath been made, and it is found that this city of old time hath made insurrection against kings, and that rebellion and sedition have been made therein [nothing about the edict of King Cyrus, all search is about how rebellious was Jerusalem city].*
> EZRA 4:20 *There have been mighty kings also over Jerusalem, which have ruled over all countries beyond the river; and toll, tribute, and custom, was paid unto them.*
> EZRA 4:21 <u>*Give ye now commandment to cause these men to cease, and that this city be not builded, until another commandment shall be given from me*</u> *[thus he reversed the order and the promise of King Cyrus the Great].*
> EZRA 4:22 *Take heed now that ye fail not to do this: why should damage grow to the hurt of the kings?*
> EZRA 4:23 *Now when the copy of king Artaxerxes' letter was read before [the leaders of the local enemy nations of Israel] Rehum, and Shimshai the scribe, and their companions,* <u>they went up in haste to Jerusalem unto the Jews, and made them to cease by force and power.</u>

*EZRA 4:24* <u>Then ceased the work of the house of God which is at Jerusalem. So it ceased unto the second year of the reign of Darius king of Persia</u> *[who succeeded the fanatic Iranian imposter and re-established the order and promise of King Cyrus the Great].*

Amazing!
This man reversed the eternal edict of H.M. King Cyrus the great.
Go ahead, please, historian Herodotus.

"Now when Cyrus was on the throne he had punished Smerdis [Tonyoaxarces] the Magus for some serious crime by having his ears cut off."[38]

At any rate, my lords, the work in Jerusalem has now completely ceased.

And today in our modern time, my lords, the same conflict continues. The children of Israel can only dream of building the parliament of God on its original site. They can dream but they cannot build. The Moslems would not allow it, my lords, because of their Dome of the Rock. And one day, my lords, the dead image of the Dome of the Rock, the battle cry, would become alive on a device you never heard off, my lords, or even could imagine. And fire would rain down from heaven, my lords, and from weapons we dare not attempt to explain to you—they are far beyond your imaginations your majesties.

Until this point of time, my lords, the Median fanatic, King Tonyoaxarces, is still the man on the throne of H.M. King Cyrus the great. Furthermore, he is indeed very popular with some, while of course very hated and feared by others as a murderer and a killer.

But here, my lords, here comes the unexpected man who should fulfill another part of the prophecy of Daniel and hammer at the gates of Europe. Here he comes, the unexpected man who would lead to one of the most important dates on God's calendar for the earth—a date, my lords, that shall become the baseline for other dates—a date to count to and from.

No one in Iran, especially Media, of course, wants the present good times of no taxes to end, my lords, regardless whether these good times come

---

[38] Herodotus, *The Histories*, 3:70, P. 233

on the hands of an imposter or indeed a legitimate son of H.M. King Cyrus the great. And so, the imposter King Tonyoaxarces carries on unchecked.

But be on your guard, your majesty, because a fast moving conspiracy and a coup is brewing.

What coup? And what man can take down such a popular king when there is no legitimate heir left for the Persian throne?

The answer, my lords, is that no one man can topple him, but how about seven men, my sovereigns?

Ancient historian Justin, please, give the details to their majesties.

> "<u>To this conspiracy seven only were privy</u>, who at once (lest if time were allowed for change of mind, the affair should be made public by anyone) proceeded to the palace with swords hidden under their garments"[39]

At this moment, my lords, these seven men are in a hurry before the conspiracy becomes known. And they are not only in a hurry, they are also indignant. Come close, my lords, and listen to what one of them is saying.

> "'Friends,' said Gobryas, 'will there ever be a better moment than now to save the throne – or, if we fail, to die in the attempt? <u>Are Persians to be ruled by a Mede – a Magus – a fellow who has had his ears chopped off</u>? Those of you who stood by the deathbed of Cambyses are not likely to forget his dying curse upon the Persians who should make no effort to save the throne.'"[40]

And so, my lords, they proceeded without delay to the palace with their swords hidden in their garbs.

Fair enough. It is one thing to proceed to the palace, but it is altogether another thing to gain entry.

Who are these brash seven, you may ask your majesties?

We can tell you, my lords, that they did not fail. They succeeded. And indeed one of them, the son of a commander and a governor, was chosen as the new king of united Media and Persia—Iran.

And now watch what he will do, my lords, although he will have to waste two years fighting fires.

The prophecy of Daniel stood the test of a popular religious extremist. The horn, which came up second, Persia, remains still the high horn of power above Media.

---

[39] Justin, 1:9
[40] Herodotus, *The Histories*, 3:75, P. 235

## THE UNEQUAL TWO HORNS OF IRAN—249

Ancient historians Josephus and Justin, you have the floor, gentlemen.

> "After the slaughter of the magi, who, upon the death of Cambyses, attained the government of the Persians for a year, those families who were called the seven families of the Persians, appointed Darius, the son of Hystaspes, to be their king."[41]

> "Thus the kingdom of the Persians, recovered by the valour of seven of its noblest men."[42]

Allow us, my lords, to add a bit more details from the carved record of the *Behistun Inscriptions*.

> (13) "King Darius says: There was no man, either Persian or Mede or of our own dynasty, who took the kingdom from Gaumâta, the Magian.
>
> <u>The people feared him exceedingly</u>, for he slew many who had known the real Smerdis. For this reason did he slay them, 'that they may not know that I am not Smerdis, the son of Cyrus.' There was none who dared to act against Gaumâta, the Magian, until I came.
>
> Then I prayed to Ahuramazda; Ahuramazda brought me help.
>
> On the tenth day of the month <u>Bâgayâdiš</u> [29 September 522] I, with a few men, slew that Gaumâta, the Magian, and the chief men who were his followers. At the stronghold called Sikayauvatiš, in the district called <u>Nisaia</u> in Media, I slew him; I dispossessed him of the kingdom. By the grace of Ahuramazda I became king; Ahuramazda granted me the kingdom."[43]

Riots, my lords, street riots are breaking out in many cities. A number of governors are refusing to accept the conspirator Darius, the unexpected man, as the new king of Persia.

And at the moment, your majesty, King Cyrus, it seems that it would be a struggle for the brave Darius to hold to the throne he purchased with his courage. It is going to be a bloody struggle for him to enforce his authority, especially that he is not a son of yours, sir. Mind you, sir, he is putting out claims that he is more closely related to you than anyone else. And, that above all things—please note this, your majesty— the unexpected man wants to restore everything back to the way everything was in your days, sir.

This could also mean, my lord, that he may indeed reinstate your famous edict of allowing the nation of prophecy and prophets, Israel, to get

---

[41] Josephus, *Antiquities of the Jews*, Book XI, Chapter III: 1
[42] Latin historian Justin, 9:10
[43] *Behistun Inscription*, Livius.org

back to the task of rebuilding the temple—the parliament of God for all the peoples of the earth.

## 522–520 BC
## Two Years

And so, your majesty, King Cyrus, the enemies of your successor King Darius are piling up against him.

One of them, sir, is a fellow by the name of Phraortes. We mention him, sir, because H.M. King Darius I threatens that, by the grace of the god Ahuramazda, what befell Phraortes shall also fall upon all of those who are rebelling against him. By the grace of the god Ahuramazda, ruthlessness, sir, and bloodshed shall rule supreme in the kingdom of man.

> (32) "King Darius says: Thereupon that Phraortes fled thence with a few horsemen to a district in Media called Rhagae. Then I sent an army in pursuit. Phraortes was taken and brought unto me. <u>I cut off his nose, his ears, and his tongue, and I put out one eye, and he was kept in fetters at my palace entrance, and all the people beheld him</u>. Then did I crucify him in Ecbatana; and the men who were his foremost followers, those at Ecbatana within the fortress, <u>I flayed [alive] and hung out their hides, stuffed with straw</u>."[44]

And so, your majesty, King Cyrus the great, for two years, for two awful long years, sir, your successor, the unexpected man H.M. King Darius I has fought a total of nineteen battles, sir, before he could at last breathe and become the one and only king of your Persia. What an awful two bloody long years they were sir!

Allow us once again, your majesties, to read to you a bit more of the *Behistun Inscription*!

> (52) "King Darius says: This is what I have done. By the grace of Ahuramazda have I always acted. After I became king, I fought nineteen battles in a single year and by the grace of Ahuramazda I overthrew nine kings and I made them captive.[45]
>
> (63) King Darius says: On this account Ahuramazda brought me help, and all the other gods, all that there are, because I was not wicked, nor was I a liar, nor was I a despot, neither I nor any of my family. I have ruled according to righteousness. Neither to the weak

---

[44] Behistun Inscription, Livius.org
[45] Behistun Inscription, Livius.org

nor to the powerful did I do wrong. <u>Whosoever helped my house, him I favored; he who was hostile, him I destroyed</u>."[46]

All quotes above are taken from *Behistun Inscription*, Livius.org

**Relief of King Darius I , the third successor of King Cyrus the Great, at his tomb in Naqsh-e Rostam, Iran, note the script on the left, WC, <u>Erich Schmidt</u>**

## 520 BC Reinstating

As we have mentioned, my lord, the religious extremist, the Magian Tonyoaxarces, went out of his way to dishonor you, your majesty, King Cyrus, and rescinded your royal edicts. But now rest assured, sir, that H.M. King Darius

---

[46] Behistun Inscription, Livius.org

shall, on the other hand, do his very best, sir, to let everyone know that he is reversing everything Tonyoaxarces has done in order to show respect for your legacy. His majesty, sir, like a good Persian, shall indeed do just that.

He is even, and you may wish to know this, sir, is marrying one of your daughters in order to add your royal Persian name to his authority and show that he shall follow your ways to the letter.

Persia, sir, the high horn, shall not be the servants of Media.

> (14) "King Darius says: The kingdom that had been wrested from our line I brought back and I reestablished it on its foundation.
>
> <u>The temples which Gaumâta, the Magian, had destroyed, I restored to the people</u>, and the pasture lands, and the herds and the dwelling places, and the houses which Gaumâta, the Magian, had taken away. I settled the people in their place, the people of Persia, and Media, <u>and the other provinces</u>.
>
> I restored that which had been taken away, as is was in the days of old. This did I by the grace of Ahuramazda, I labored until I had established our dynasty in its place, as in the days of old; I labored, by the grace of Ahuramazda, so that Gaumâta, the Magian, did not dispossess our house."[47]

You may also go ahead now, historian Justin.

> "Darius was related to the preceding kings; and, in the beginning of his reign, he took to wife the daughter of Cyrus, in order to strengthen his kingdom by a royal marriage, so that it might not so much seem transferred to a stranger, as to be restored to Cyrus's family."[48]

---

[47] Behistun Inscription, Livius.org
[48] Latin historian Justin, 1:10

# THE UNEQUAL TWO HORNS OF IRAN—253

The *Behistun Inscription* is documenting for future generations the conquests of King Darius I, the second successor of King Cyrus the great. Note the inscriptions scattered around the images. These reliefs and texts are engraved on a cliff on Mount Behistun (present Kermanshah Province, Iran). Wikipedia, Hara1603

King Darius I, British Museum, London (image source: author)

## 520 BC
## Troublous Times

And so now, my lords, the dust has at last settled down after two long years of fighting nineteen battles.

Today H.M. King Darius I, the unexpected man, is the one and only ruler of the Persian Empire of Iran. He is also a candidate for the position of the ruler of the world.

Everyone in the empire can now breathe again after what mounted to two years of a civil war in the master nation of the world.

One of the groups, which can breathe easily now, my lords, are the leaders of Israel. By all indications they should no longer worry about resuming the construction of the parliament of the world, which came to a full stop under the Iranian extremist King Tonyoaxarces.

Go ahead, please, biblical scribes Ezra and Haggai.

> EZRA 4:24 Then ceased the work of the house of God which is at Jerusalem. *So it ceased unto the second year of the reign of Darius king of Persia* [It took King Darius two years to end the civil war in Iran, as his carvings on the Behistun has shown]

But your majesties, at this point of time, the leaders of Israel are divided in their opinions about rebuilding the house. Most, if not all of the leaders, are full of hope that the new Iranian king, H.M. King Darius I, may not be against their precious project. And thus, as far as this group is concerned, the time has indeed come to reboot and begin again working on the temple—the landmark of God's calendar.

On the other hand, my lords, a good percentage of the population feel defeated and say that the time is not yet ripe to restart building the house.

Go ahead with your reports, prophet Haggai and scribe Ezra.

> HAG 1:1 *In the second year [again the second year] of Darius the king*, in the sixth month, in the first day of the month, came the word of the LORD by Haggai the prophet [in Israel] unto Zerubbabel the son of Shealtiel, governor of Judah [of Israel], and to Joshua the son of Josedech, the high priest, saying,
> HAG 1:2 Thus speaketh the LORD of hosts, saying, *This people say, The time is not come, the time that the LORD'S house should be built.*

The people, my lords, are afraid to stir the hornet's nest of the neighbors. Israel is not strong enough by a long shot to tackle so many determined **neighbors**.

And then, to this mix of opposing opinions, my lords—to build or not to build—we now have two more gentlemen, two witnesses, or if you wish, my lords, two prophets who have a straightforward message for the frightened population of Israel.

The names of the two witnesses, my lords, are prophet Haggai and prophet Zechariah, son of Iddo. These two men, my lords, are encouraging Governor Zerubbabel, the leader of Israel, and the high priest, Jeshua, to get going on building the temple.

> EZRA 5:1 Then the prophets, Haggai the prophet, and Zechariah the son of Iddo, prophesied unto the Jews that were in Judah and Jerusalem in the name of the God of Israel, even unto them.
> EZRA 5:2 Then rose up Zerubbabel the son of Shealtiel, and Jeshua the son of Jozadak, and <u>began to build the house of God which is at Jerusalem</u>: and with them were the prophets of God helping them.

## 516 BC
## Do the Math

And there is a good reason, my lords, why these two witnesses are firm in their conviction that the time has come to rebuild the parliament of God. They say, my lords, that the seventy, 70, years of Jeremiah's prophecy come due this year.

> JER 29:10 For thus saith the LORD, That <u>after seventy years</u> be accomplished at Babylon I will visit you, and perform my good word toward you, in causing you to return to this place.

But this prophecy of seventy years is not as clear as it appears at first glance, my lords.

The question, your majesties, is when did the countdown for seventy years start?

His Babylonian majesty King Nebuchadnezzar attacked Israel and Jerusalem city on three occasions [596, 586 and 582 BC], and in each occasion he took many Israelis captives to Babylon, so when does one begin calculating the seventy years?

His Babylonian majesty, or his generals, my lords, came on the seventh year of the reign of his Babylonian majesty [596 BC], and then eleven years later they came back on the eighteenth/nineteenth year of his reign [586 BC], and finally, my lords, eighteen years after the first invasion, they came a third time on the twenty-fifth year of the reign of his Babylonian majesty King Nebuchadnezzar [582 BC].

And so depending on the date one would like to use, my lords, one could be off by a range of eleven to eighteen years.

And this is why, my lords, there was a debate in Israel over which year is the right year to rebuild the temple of the lord.

May we quote to you the biblical scribes, my lords!

> *2 KIN 25:1 And it came to pass <u>in the ninth year of his reign</u>, in the tenth month, in the tenth day of the month, that Nebuchadnezzar king of Babylon came, he, and all his host [army], against Jerusalem, and pitched against it; and they built forts against it round about.*
>
> *2 KIN 25:2 <u>And the city was besieged unto the eleventh year of king Zedekiah</u> [of Israel].*
>
> *2 KIN 25:3 And on the ninth day of the fourth month the famine prevailed in the city, and there was no bread for the people of the land.*
>
> *2 KIN 25:4 And the city was broken up, and all the men of war fled by night by the way of the gate between two walls, which is by the king's garden: (now the Chaldees [Babylonians of southern Iraq] were against the city round about:) and the king [of Israel] went the way toward the plain.*
>
> *2 KIN 25:5 And the army of the Chaldees pursued after the king, and overtook him in the plains of Jericho: and all his army were scattered from him.*
>
> *2 KIN 25:6 So they took the king, and brought him up to the king of Babylon to Riblah; and they gave judgment upon him.*
>
> *2 KIN 25:7 And they slew the sons of Zedekiah before his eyes, and put out the eyes of Zedekiah, and bound him with fetters of brass, and carried him to Babylon.*
>
> *2 KIN 25:8 And in the fifth month, on the seventh day of the month, which <u>is the nineteenth year of king Nebuchadnezzar king of Babylon [586 BC according to the Jewish calendar, which calculates years differently from the Babylonian one]</u>, came <u>Nebuzaradan, captain of the guard</u>, a servant of the king of Babylon, unto Jerusalem:*
>
> *2 KIN 25:9 <u>And he burnt the house of the LORD, and the king's house [the royal palace]</u>, and all the houses of Jerusalem, and every great man's house burnt he with fire.*
>
> *2 KIN 25:10 And all the army of the Chaldees, that were with the captain of the guard, <u>brake down the walls of Jerusalem round about</u> [the city has now become defenseless and vulnerable to any and all of its local enemies].*
>
> *...*
>
> *2 KIN 25:21 So Judah [the last half of Israel] was carried away out of their land.*

*JER 52:30* **In the three and twentieth year of Nebuchadrezzar** Nebuzaradan the captain of the guard carried away captive of the Jews seven hundred forty and five persons: all the [surviving and deported] persons were four thousand and six hundred.

Which year then is the start year of the seventy-year prophecy?

We can tell you, my lords, that nearly forty-two, 42, years later, the prophet Daniel understood which year should be the start year.

Go ahead, please, prophet Daniel.

*DAN 9:1* In the first year of Darius the son of Ahasuerus , of the seed of the Medes [540 BC], which was made king[governor] over the realm of the Chaldeans [southern Iraq];
*DAN 9:2* In the first year of his reign [this was of course a different Darius from King Darius I] <u>I Daniel understood by books the number of the years</u>, whereof the word of the LORD came to Jeremiah the prophet, that he would accomplish seventy years in the desolations of Jerusalem.

And just as the prophet Daniel, my lords, understood that the year the temple was destroyed [586 BC] would be the start year of the seventy-year calculation, so did the two witnesses. The calendar of God relies heavily on the events of the temple, my lords.

And so, my lords, the two prophets kept encouraging the population not to be afraid of the conspiracies and intrigue, which the Arab, Iraqi, and Iranian neighbors were hatching against Israel.

It is the right year, they insisted. The seventy years of the prophet Jeremiah have at last tallied up.

We would like to introduce to you, your majesties, the prophet Zechariah, one of the two witnesses of the Lord, who encouraged the people to build the house of the Lord.

Go ahead, please, sir.

*ZECH 8:4* Thus saith the LORD of hosts; There shall yet <u>old men and old women</u> dwell in the streets of Jerusalem [live in peace to ripe old age and not having their life cut short by war], and every man with his staff in his hand for very age.
*ZECH 8:5* And the streets of the city [of Jerusalem] shall be full of boys and girls playing in the streets thereof.
*ZECH 8:6* Thus saith the LORD of hosts; If it be marvellous [impossible] in the eyes of the remnant of this people in these days, should it also be marvellous in mine eyes [that Jerusalem will come alive once more]? saith the LORD of hosts.

> ZECH 8:9 *Thus saith the LORD of hosts; Let your hands be strong, ye that hear in these days these words by the mouth of the prophets, which were in the day that the foundation of the house of the LORD of hosts was laid, <u>that the temple might be built</u>.*

We would like, your majesties, to take a minute here to verify the calculations of the two witnesses who believe that this year is the year when the 70-year prophecy comes of age.

His Babylonian majesty King Nebuchadnezzar destroyed the temple in 586 BC.

Seventy prophetical years after, which is equivalent to 69 Solar years [70 X 360 / 365.25 = 69 solar years] would bring us to 517 BC [586 BC – 69 = 517 BC].

And so the people understood, my lords, and went to work.

Nonetheless, the harassment by the surrounding nations began immediately, your majesties.

The Iranian governors of the province west of the Euphrates River, which includes Israel, have indeed, my lords, come to Jerusalem and demanded to know what exactly the leaders of Israel were up to.

And to no one's surprise, my lords, the governor and the local leaders have drafted a letter to H.M. King Darius I, hoping to convince him to put a stop to rebuilding the temple.

Carry on, please, scribe Ezra.

> EZRA 5:3 *At the same time came to them [the leaders of Israel] Tatnai, [the Iranian] governor on this side the river, and Shetharboznai, and their companions, and said thus unto them, Who hath commanded you to build this house, and to make up this wall [around the temple]?*
>
> EZRA 5:6 *The copy of the letter that Tatnai, governor on this side the river, and Shetharboznai, and his companions the Apharsachites, which were on this side the river, <u>sent unto Darius the king</u>.*
>
> EZRA 5:8 *Be it known unto the king, that we went into the province of Judea [of Israel, where Jerusalem city is located], to the house of the great God [the temple], which is builded with great stones, and timber is laid in the walls, and <u>this work goeth fast on, and prospereth in their hands</u>.*
>
> EZRA 5:9 *Then asked we those elders, and said unto them thus, <u>Who commanded you to build this house, and to make up these walls</u>?*
>
> EZRA 5:10 *We asked their names also, to certify thee, that we might write the names of the men that were the chief of them.*

## Past and Future Threats

In the past, as has been seen already, the neighboring nations appealed to Iran to stop Israel from rebuilding the house of the Lord. And so they shall do in the days to come.

In the past there were two witnesses, two prophets, who encouraged the population of Israel to rebuild the house of the Lord, even in the face of the unabated aggression by Israel's enemies.

And, similarly, in the coming days there shall also be two witnesses, two prophets, at the time of the end who shall outline to the world the events that shall take place during the closing days of the earth, or to be exact, before the opportunity to join the royal family of God comes to an end.

> Mat 25:10 <u>and the door was shut</u>.

> Rev 11:3 And I will [in the future] give power unto my <u>two witnesses</u>, and they shall prophesy a thousand two hundred and threescore days [three years and a half], clothed in sackcloth [rags of sadly burdened men].
> Rev 11:6 These [two witnesses] have power to shut heaven, that it rain not in the days of their prophecy: and have power over waters to turn them to blood, and to smite the earth with all plagues, as often as they will.
> Rev 11:7 And when they shall have finished their testimony, the beast that ascendeth out of the bottomless pit shall make war against them, and shall overcome them, and kill them.
> Rev 11:8 And their dead bodies shall lie in the street of the great city [Jerusalem city of Israel], which spiritually is called Sodom and Egypt, where also our Lord was crucified.
> Rev 11:9 And they of the people and kindreds and tongues and nations shall see their dead bodies three days and an half, and shall not suffer their dead bodies to be put in graves.
> Rev 11:10 And they that dwell upon the earth shall rejoice over them, and make merry, and shall send gifts one to another; because these two prophets tormented them that dwelt on the earth.
> Rev 11:11 And after three days and an half the Spirit of life from God entered into them, and they stood upon their feet; and great fear fell upon them which saw them.
> Rev 11:12 And they heard a great voice from heaven saying unto them, Come up hither. And they ascended up to heaven in a cloud; and their enemies beheld them.
> Rev 11:13 And the same hour was there a great earthquake, and the tenth part of the city fell, and in the earthquake were slain of men seven thousand: and the remnant were affrighted, and gave glory to the God of heaven.

My lords, the two witnesses, Haggai and Zechariah, continued with their prophecies and preaching. And their message continued to be the same: Do not be afraid. Rise and build.

Go up the mountains and bring lumber for the beams for the parliament of God.

> HAG 1:8 Go up to the mountain, and bring wood, and build the house; and I will take pleasure in it, and I will be glorified, saith the LORD.
>
> HAG 1:14 And the LORD stirred up the spirit of Zerubbabel the son of Shealtiel, governor of Judah [Israel], and the spirit of Joshua the son of Josedech, the high priest, and the spirit of all the remnant of the people [who returned from the Babylonian Exile]; and they came and did work in the house of the LORD of hosts, their God,

## 516 / 515 BC
## A Year for the Counting!

The letter, my lords, has at this point of time arrived to the court of his Iranian majesty King Darius.

Scribe Ezra, carry on but please allow for our interruption, sir.

> EZRA 6:1 Then Darius the king made a decree [gave an order], and search <u>was made in the house of the rolls</u> [the royal archives], where the treasures were laid up in Babylon.
>
> EZRA 6:2 And there was found at Achmetha, in the palace that is in the province of the Medes, a roll, and therein was a record thus written:
>
> EZRA 6:3 In the first year of Cyrus the king the same Cyrus the king made a decree concerning the house of God at Jerusalem, Let the house be builded, the place where they offered sacrifices, and let the foundations thereof be strongly laid

My lords, they have indeed found the royal command that H.M. King Cyrus the great had issued eighteen years earlier. And H.M. King Darius I, the unexpected man, is now about to issue his important ruling.

All parties at this point of time are waiting anxiously.

> EZRA 6:6 Now therefore, Tatnai, [Iranian] governor beyond the river, Shetharboznai, and your companions the Apharsachites, which are beyond the river, <u>be ye far from thence</u>.
>
> EZRA 6:7 <u>Let the work of this house of God alone</u>; let the governor of the Jews and the elders of the Jews build this house of God <u>in his place</u>.

## THE UNEQUAL TWO HORNS OF IRAN—261

*EZRA 6:8 Moreover I make a decree what ye shall do to the elders of these Jews for the building of this house of God: that of the king's goods, even <u>of the tribute beyond the river</u>, forthwith expenses be given unto these men, that they be not hindered.*

Now, my lords, this would really hurt. His Iranian majesty had ordered that the taxes, which are gathered from the sordid enemies of Israel, are to be allocated to building the Israeli temple in Jerusalem city.

*EZRA 6:12 And the God that hath caused his name to dwell there destroy all kings and people, that shall put to their hand to alter and to destroy this house of God which is at Jerusalem. <u>I Darius have made a decree; let it be done with speed.</u>*

King Darius I, British Museum, London (image source: author).

Your majesties, the day that shall start the countdown for the most important event in the history of mankind—this day has begun this year. This cornerstone date on God's calendar for the earth, my lords, has at last approached after encountering threatening, twists, delays, and reversals. It faced serious challenges, my lords, but it is approaching at last. It is a day to count to and from.

> EZRA 6:14 And the elders of the Jews builded, and they prospered through the prophesying of Haggai the prophet and Zechariah the son of Iddo. <u>And they builded, and finished it</u>, according to the commandment of the God of Israel, and according to the commandment of <u>Cyrus, and Darius, and Artaxerxes [a second one]</u> king of Persia.
>
> EZRA 6:15 And this house was finished on the third day of the month Adar, which was <u>in the sixth year of the reign of Darius the king</u> [reigned September 522 – October 486 BC].

My lords, the parliament of God, the temple was rebuilt and completed in the sixth year of H.M. King Darius I, the man who came from nowhere to inherit the throne of Iran. It was completed in the solar year 516/515 BC.

Prophet Daniel, would you please, sir, recite to their majesties your prophecy that outlined the events of the next five hundred years, counting from 516 BC, the sixth year of H.M. King Darius I!

But first the usual caution, my lords, that you may not at this time fully understand his prophecy, which he had made nearly twenty-five years before the children of Israel even returned from the Babylonian Exile; never mind having built the temple.

Go ahead, sir.

> Dan 9:24 <u>Seventy weeks</u> are determined upon thy people and upon thy holy city, to finish the transgression, and to make an end of sins, and to make reconciliation for iniquity, and to bring in everlasting righteousness, and <u>to seal up the vision and prophecy, and to anoint the most Holy</u>.
>
> Dan 9:25 Know therefore and understand, that <u>from the going forth of the commandment to restore and to build Jerusalem</u> [by King Darius I and not King Cyrus the Great] <u>unto the Messiah the Prince shall be seven weeks, and threescore and two weeks</u>: the street shall be built again, and the wall, <u>even in troublous times</u>.
>
> DAN 9:26 <u>And after threescore and two weeks shall Messiah be cut off</u>, but not for himself: and the people of the prince that shall come shall destroy the city and the sanctuary; and the end thereof shall be with a flood, and unto the end of the war desolations are determined.

DAN 9:27 *And he shall confirm the covenant with many for one week: and in the midst of the week he shall cause the sacrifice and the oblation to cease, and for the overspreading of abominations he shall make it desolate, even until the consummation, <u>and that determined shall be poured upon the desolate</u>.*

## Joy—Wait No More

An ending and a beginning, my lords!

Ending one prophecy, the 70-year prophecy [586–516 BC], and beginning a series of prophecies reaching over five hundred, 500, years in the future, your majesties!

It is simply astounding, my lords.

In the year 539 BC, my lords, this man Daniel prophesied of the greatest event: the giving away of the key to the heavens' door, which was to take place in the year 31 AD.

Daniel's prophecies then, my lords, spanned 570 solar years [539 BC + 31 AD]. How could he do so; how could he see 570 years into the future?

They would tell you, my lords, that He who knows the future saw a lot in Daniel to love, and so He instructed him.

How?

In vivid and clear dreams—live visions, my lords.

> DAN 9:23 *At the beginning of thy supplications [prayers] the commandment came forth, and I am [an angel, a celestial being] come to shew thee; for <u>thou art greatly beloved</u>: therefore understand the matter, and consider the vision.*

We would wish to deviate here, my lords, and jump ahead to the future for a minute or two.

Our reason for doing so, my lords, is to show you how many important prophecies and dates are calculated to and from this year 516 BC in which the temple was rebuilt.

As you have seen so far your majesties, the prophet Daniel uses imagery in order to make his prophecies easy to envision, such as the goat with two horns, one higher than the other, or the dreadful beast with ten horns etc.

He does also, my lords, use weeks for years, not only to simplify envisioning the numbers, but also to restrict the understanding of his prophecies to those who value the word of his Holy One. His prophecies are to be made clear to some, and remain mysterious to those who care nothing of his Holy One, my lords.

Allow us, therefore, my lords, once again to let the prophet Daniel recite the earlier portion of his far- reaching prophecy—indeed, my lords, a prophecy that reaches to our modern time.

Go ahead, please, prophet Daniel, and do not mind our interruption.

> DAN 9:24 <u>Seventy weeks</u> are determined upon thy people [Israel] and upon thy holy city [Jerusalem], to finish the transgression, and <u>to make an end of sins, and to make reconciliation</u> for iniquity [to forgive sins and reconcile man with God], and to bring in everlasting righteousness, and to seal up the vision and prophecy [to fulfill the prophecy of the crucifixion and resurrection of the Lord, the Savior], and to anoint [the Lord] the most Holy.
>
> DAN 9:25 Know therefore and understand, that <u>from the going forth of the commandment</u> [by King Darius I in 516 BC] to restore and to build Jerusalem unto the Messiah the Prince [Crucified 33 AD] shall be seven weeks, and threescore and two weeks: the street shall be built again, and the wall, <u>even in troublous times</u>.
>
> DAN 9:26 And after threescore and two weeks shall Messiah be cut off [crucified], but not for himself [not because of his sins]: and the people of the prince that shall come [the Romans] shall destroy the city [70 AD] and the sanctuary [the temple]; and the end thereof shall be with a flood [the children of Israel shall be scattered all over the world as carried away by a flood], and unto the end of the war desolations are determined.
>
> DAN 9:27 And he shall confirm the covenant with many for one week: and in the midst of the week he shall cause the sacrifice and the oblation to cease, and for the overspreading of abominations he shall make it desolate, even until the consummation, and <u>that determined shall be poured upon the desolate.</u>

You see, my lords, what we meant when we said it would be hard to glean much of this loaded and far in the future prophecy! Yet, my lords, in no time the meanings shall become sharp and crystal clear. But even at this point of time, my lords, we still can decipher a few lines of the prophecy if you wish.

In his first verse, my lords, the prophet Daniel tells us that the greatest event in God's plan for man was to take place five hundred forty-six, 546, solar years from this year, 516 BC, the year of the temple.

Five hundred forty-six years after 516 BC, the aim of all prophecies shall be fulfilled. The Holy One shall rip the heavens and come down, and open the door for man to reconcile with God and become justified and qualified for everlasting life in the heavens. The cross shall become the ladder to the throne of grace and the heavens of heavens, my lords. The nailed palms shall keep the welcoming arms of the Savior wide open to embrace whosoever comes for pardon your majesties.

> DAN 9:24 *Seventy weeks [547 solar years] are determined upon thy people and upon thy holy city, to finish the transgression, and to make an end of sins, and to make reconciliation for iniquity [forgiveness of sins and peace with God], and to bring in everlasting righteousness [pardon for ever], and to seal up the vision and prophecy [to fulfill the prophecy of the crucifixion and resurrection of the Lord], and to anoint [the Lord] the most Holy.* DAN 9:25 *Know therefore and understand, that from the going forth of the commandment [by King Darius I in 516 BC]* <u>to restore and to build Jerusalem</u> *[445 BC. An event remains in the future at this point of time] unto the Messiah the Prince [Crucified 31 AD, another future event at this point of time] shall be seven weeks, and threescore and two weeks [476 years]: the street shall be built again, and the wall, even in troublous times.*

And, indeed, all of this happened on time, my lords, as we shall see up the highway of prophecy.

My lords, the prophet Daniel continued to give details following the crucifixion and resurrection of the Holy One. He goes on, my lords, to say that the legions of a future prince shall destroy Jerusalem city and the temple, which indeed happened in the year 70 AD, your majesties, under the command of your colleague H.M. Emperor Titus, as we have mentioned earlier.

But we shall leave all of these details, my lords, until we reach their dates on the highway of prophecy.

## *The Wait Is Over – It Is Him*

Daniel, in the repeated language of prophecy, speaks of a series of events that should culminate by the end of seventy weeks starting from the year of the temple, 516 BC.

The prophet carefully divided the seventy weeks into two sums: the first is a sum of one week only and the second sum is the remaining sixty-nine weeks.

The first singled out week is seventy [70] prophetical years.
The sixty-nine weeks are sixty-nine times seven, which yields 483 prophetical years.

The total of the seventy weeks therefore is 70 + 483 = 553 prophetical years, which are shorter than the solar years. The prophetical year is 360 days only, whereas the solar year is about 365.25 days.

Thus, the 553 prophetical years are equivalent to 545 solar years [553 X 360 / 365.25 = 545].

All our present calendar dates, whether BC or AD, are of course solar dates. This is why one must convert the prophetic years to the solar years in order to determine in which BC or AD year an event took place.

Thus, the prophet Daniel is saying that the Holy One shall come and reconcile mankind with God, seventy weeks [one week and sixty nine weeks], or 545 solar years following the year of the temple, which is 516 BC.

Indeed, adding 545 solar years to 516 BC brings us to the year 31 AD.

Indeed, 31 AD is the year the Lord was crucified for the life of the world. We bring you good tidings; wait no more.

"For God so loved the world, that He gave His only begotten son, that whosoever believeth in Him (relies on Him, trusts on Him) should not perish, but have everlasting life." Jn 3:16

"I am the living bread which came down from heaven: if any man eat of this bread, he shall live for ever: and the bread that I will give is my flesh, which I will give for the life of the world." Jn 6:51

"I am the resurrection, and the life: he that believeth in me (relies on me), though he were dead, yet shall he live:" Jn 11:25

## *Hava Nagila, Wait No More*

Let us rejoice.

The prophet Daniel then goes on to further confirm the year 31 AD in which the blessed son of God was sacrificed for the life of the world.

This time, however, Daniel tells the world the number of the years, which shall pass from the year the walls of Jerusalem were built to the crucifixion and resurrection of the Holy One.

> *Dan 9:25* Know therefore and understand, that from the going forth of the commandment [by King Artaxerxe, as we shall see] <u>to restore and to build Jerusalem</u> [445 BC] unto the Messiah the Prince [Crucified 31 AD] shall be seven weeks, and threescore and two weeks [69 weeks or 476 solar years]: the street shall be built again, and the wall, even in troublous times.

This indeed came to pass.

Jerusalem's walls were completed in 445 BC by the command of the Iranian King Artaxerxes as shall be seen.

The breakdown is [69 weeks X 7] 483 prophetic years, which are equivalent to 476 solar years of our calendar [483 X 360 / 365.25 = 476 solar years].

Adding 476 solar years to 445 BC would yield 31 AD.

It is simply remarkable.

Whether from the year the temple was built, or the year the wall was built, one reaches the year 31 AD

Simply remarkable!

## *The Apple of God's Eye*

We are.

To begin, the blessed son of God appeared in the flesh about 4 BC in a manger in Bethlehem.

> *Jn 1:1* In the beginning was the Word [the breath of God], and the Word was with God, and the Word was God.
> *Jn 1:3* All things were made by him; and without him was not any thing made that was made.
> *Jn 1:4* In him was life; and the life was the light of men.
> *Jn 1:14* <u>And the Word was made flesh, and dwelt among us, and we beheld his glory, the glory as of the only begotten of the Father, full of grace and truth.</u>

And then He began preaching about the kingdom of God, the celestial life in the heavens, when He was about thirty years of age.

> *Lk 1:77* To give knowledge of salvation unto his people by the remission of their sins,
> *Lk 1:78* Through the tender mercy of our God; whereby the dayspring from on high hath visited us,

And they came by droves from everywhere to hear Him.

> <sup>Mat 4:24</sup> And <u>his fame went throughout all Syria</u> [Syria then included today's Syria, Lebanon, Jordan, Iraq, and Israel]
> <sup>Mat 4:25</sup> And there <u>followed him great multitudes of people</u>
> <sup>Mk 1:45</sup> <u>Jesus could no more openly enter into the city</u> [because of the huge crowds that followed Him], but was without [outside the cities, in the open places] in desert places: and they came to him from every quarter.
> <sup>Lk 6:19</sup> And <u>the whole multitude sought to touch him</u>: for there went virtue out of him, and healed them all.
> <sup>Mk 2:4</sup> And when they could not come nigh unto him [get near Him to touch Him] for the press [the crowds], <u>they uncovered the roof [of a house] where he was: and when they had broken it up</u>, they let down the bed wherein the sick of the palsy lay.
> <sup>Mk 3:9</sup> And he spake to his disciples, that a small ship should wait on him [he will talk to them from a ship] because of the multitude, lest they should throng [mob] him.
> <sup>Mk 3:10</sup> For he had healed many; insomuch that they pressed upon him for to touch him, as many as had plagues.
> <sup>Jn 12:19</sup> The Pharisees [the hypocritical religious teachers who fought Him] therefore said among themselves, Perceive ye how ye prevail nothing? <u>behold, the world is gone after him</u>.

And He had compassion on them all: the poor, the rich, the high and the low. For He did not come to judge them, nor just to seek after them, He came to give His life for them all, to bear their judgment and save them from condemnation and grant them eternal life.

> <sup>Lk 19:10</sup> For the Son of man is come <u>to seek and to save that which was lost</u>.
> <sup>Rom 5:6</sup> Christ died for the ungodly.
> <sup>Jn 14:2</sup> In my Father's house are many mansions [the heavens of heavens of the vast space]
> <sup>Jn 14:3</sup> I will come again, and receive you unto myself; that where I am, there ye may be also.

And no one was too much of a sinner to ignore or cast away. He would not put out even the smoking flame ready to die, nor would he discard a splintered useless cane, for He came to make the dying live and the splintered whole.

> <sup>Mat 12:20</sup> A bruised reed shall he not break, and smoking flax shall he not quench
> <sup>Rom 5:8</sup> God commendeth his love toward us [proved His love for us], in that, while we were yet sinners, Christ died for us.

They wanted to make him the king of Israel. But what title is the king of Israel to the one who is the King of kings and the Lord of lords every day of eternity!

> Jn 6:15 When Jesus therefore perceived that they would come and take him by force, to make him a king, he departed again into a mountain himself alone.

But yet, this King of kings and Lord of lords had in fact no place to lay down His head to sleep.

And yet He is the heavenly prince upon whom waited millions of angels, and millions of celestial beings stood at His beck and call.

> Dan 7:10 thousand thousands ministered unto him, and ten thousand times ten thousand stood before him

> 2 Cor 8:9 For ye know the grace of our Lord Jesus Christ, that, though he was rich, yet for your sakes he became poor, that ye through his poverty might be rich.
> Jn 1:14 And the Word [the breath of life, the breath of God] was made flesh [human], and dwelt among us, and we beheld his glory, the glory as of the only begotten of the Father, full of grace and truth.
> Jn 1:16 And of his fulness have all we received, and grace for grace.
> Jn 1:18 No man hath seen God at any time; the only begotten Son, which is in the bosom of the Father, he hath declared him.
> Heb 1:3 Who being the brightness of his [father's] glory, and the express image of his person, and upholding all things by the word of his power, when he had by himself purged our sins, sat down on the right hand of the Majesty on high;
> Heb 2:9 we see Jesus, who was made a little lower than the angels for the suffering of death [made human in order to die for every single person], crowned with glory and honour; that he by the grace of God should taste death for every man.
> Phil 2:7 made himself of no reputation, and took upon him the form of a servant, and was made in the likeness of men:
> Phil 2:8 And being found in fashion as a man, he humbled himself, and became obedient unto death, even the death of the cross.

This is the humble King of kings who had no place to lay down His head. And this is the Prince who rules over high-ranking angels and celestial masters invisible to the eye of men.

> Col 1:16 For by him [the Lord Jesus] were all things created, that are in heaven, and that are in earth, visible and invisible, whether they be thrones, or dominions, or principalities, or powers: all things were created by him, and for him:

> Lk 9:57 And it came to pass, that, as they went in the way, a certain man said unto him, Lord, I will follow thee whithersoever thou goest.

> Lk 9:58 And Jesus said unto him, <u>Foxes have holes, and birds of the air have nests; but the Son of man hath not where to lay his head</u>.

Yet the King who had no room or a bed to sleep had deep compassion for His subjects. Indeed, compassion went ways ahead of Him and grace followed closely behind Him. A cry from His subjects makes Him stand still. And then He calls your name. Be of good comfort, you are the only one in His world, and He is there for you even if you are a blind beggar worth little to anyone. And He makes you whole and gives you abundance of life. Love does no less. He does not take His eyes off you, even if you were a bigger. God is love.

> Mk 10:46 and as he went out of Jericho [city] with his disciples and a great number of people, blind Bartimaeus, the son of Timaeus, sat by the highway side begging.
> Mk 10:47 And when he [the blind beggar] heard that it was Jesus of Nazareth, he began to cry out, and say<u>, Jesus, thou Son of [King] David, have mercy on me</u>.
> Mk 10:48 And many charged him that he should hold his peace [ordered him to shut up]: but he cried the more a great deal, <u>Thou Son of David, have mercy on me</u>.
> Mk 10:49 <u>And Jesus stood still</u>, and commanded him to be called. And they call the blind man, saying unto him, Be of good comfort, rise; <u>he calleth thee</u> [He calls you].
> Mk 10:50 And he, <u>casting away his garment</u>, rose, and <u>came to Jesus</u>.
> Mk 10:51 And Jesus answered and said unto him, What wilt thou that I should do unto thee?
> The blind man said unto him, Lord, that I might receive my sight [I want to see].
> Mk 10:52 And Jesus said unto him, Go thy way; thy faith hath made thee whole. And immediately he received his sight, and followed Jesus in the way.
>
> Jn 10:10 I am come that they might have life, and that they might have it more abundantly.

The King of kings was crucified by the Romans and by the permission of their governor, Pontius Pilate. But death could not keep the Holy One in its hold. The Lord is risen. He is risen indeed.

## *The Spirit of God*

Saudi Arabia was in a major transformation in the 7th century. There were many Christian converts and Jews who were teaching and preaching the Bible to the Arabs. As a result, many Arabs in Saudi Arabia and Yemen were converting from idol worshipping to Judaism and Christianity.

Indeed, some have used this wave of conversion to sell translations of the Bible in Arabic for a good prophet.

The middle-aged man Muhammad also wanted to join the fray and become a preacher of the Bible. However, he was an illiterate man who could not read or write and thus was unknowledgeable in the Bible. Fortunately for him, a cousin of his first wife, Khadija, was a Christian convert and a literate man who was preaching the Bible to his fellow Arabs. And so Khadijah took her husband Muhammad to her cousin so that he may teach him from the Bible.

All the following quotes are pasted and copied from the sacred Islamic books of Hadith. Any bracketed comments are made by Islamic scholars, and they only.

The word "Allah" in Arabic is equivalent to the word "God" in English.

> *Bukhari*, 9, 87, 111
>
> Allah's Apostle returned with ... his neck muscles twitching with terror till he entered upon Khadija ... Khadija then accompanied him to (her cousin) Waraqa bin Naufal bin Asad bin 'Abdul 'Uzza bin Qusai. Waraqa was the son of her paternal uncle, i.e., her father's brother, who during the Pre-Islamic Period <u>became a Christian and used to write the Arabic writing and used to write of the Gospels in Arabic</u> ... But after a few days Waraqa died <u>and the Divine Inspiration was also paused</u> for a while and the Prophet became so sad as we have heard that he <u>intended several times to throw himself from the tops of high mountains</u> and every time he went up the top of a mountain in order to throw himself down, Gabriel would appear before him and say, "O Muhammad! You are indeed Allah's Apostle in truth" whereupon his heart would become quiet and he would calm down and would return home.
> And whenever the period of the coming of the inspiration used to become long, <u>he would do as before</u>, but when he used to reach the top of a mountain, Gabriel would appear before him and say to him what he had said before.

Indeed Muhammad, who intended to commit suicide several times, has later reserved major punishments for those who did.

> *Muslim*, 1, 199
>
> the Messenger of Allah (pbuh) observed: He who killed himself with steel (weapon) would be the eternal denizen of the Fire of Hell and he would have that weapon in his hand and would be thrusting that in his stomach for ever and ever, he who drank poison and killed himself would sip that in the Fire of Hell where he is doomed for ever and ever; <u>and he who killed himself by falling from (the top of) a mountain would constantly fall in the Fire of Hell and would live there for ever and ever</u>.

In the course of time, Muhammad began to teach the Bible to a few acquaintances of his; men who were also illiterate and in deep poverty. Later on they would do much better financially as their prophet began to ambush the loaded caravans travelling the Yemen-Syria highway passing by Mecca and Medina, where he lived. In time he would have hundreds of fighters who would help him gain more booty and converts by the edge of the sword.

> *Bukhari, 7, 65, 343*
>
> I used to accompany Allah's Apostle to fill my stomach
>
> *Bukhari, 8, 76, 459*
>
> Narrated Abu Huraira:
> By Allah ... I used to lay on the ground on my liver (abdomen) because of hunger, and I used to bind a stone over my belly because of hunger.
>
> *Bukhari, 5, 57, 57*
>
> Ja'far bin Abi Talib. He used to take us to his home and offer us what was available therein. He would even offer us an <u>empty folded leather container (of butter) which we would split and lick whatever was in it</u>.
>
> *Bukhari, 5, 59, 647*
>
> Allah's Apostle sent us who were <u>three-hundred riders under the command of Abu Ubaida bin Al-Jarrah in order to watch the caravan of the Quraish pagans</u>. We stayed at the seashore for half a month and were struck with such severe hunger that we ate even the Khabt (i.e. the leaves of the Salam, a thorny desert tree), and because of that, the army was known as Jaish-ul-Khabt.

And so Muhammad began his preaching by telling his listeners that Jews and Christians were special in God's, Allah's, eyes, and no one else was. Indeed, even after he turned on both Christians and Jews, his followers continued in their desire to learn what the Bible had to say rather than what the Koran had to say.

In fact, Muhammad, himself, kept on imitating the Jews in variety of ways, including how they style their hair.

It should be said however that following the death of his wife's Christian cousin, the Islamic prophet began to add his own teachings to what he learned from the Bible. These deviations and additions were one of the reasons he fell out with the Jews and Christians who deemed his teachings to be un-biblical. To this accusation Muhammad replied that he is now preaching a new religion.

The people of the book in the following quote means Christians and Jews, being the people of the Bible, or the book.

> *Muslim, 40, 6853*
>
> Allah's Messenger (pbuh), while delivering a sermon one day, said ... Allah looked towards the people of the world and <u>He showed hatred for the</u>

> Arabs and the non-Arabs, but with the exception of some remnants from the People of the Book.
>
> *Bukhari*, 9, 92, 461
> Ibn 'Abbas said, "Why do you ask the people of the scripture about anything while your Book (Quran) which has been revealed to Allah's Apostle is newer and the latest?
> ...
> Does not the knowledge which has come to you prevent you from asking them about anything? No, by Allah, we have never seen any man from them asking you regarding what has been revealed to you!"
>
> *Bukhari*, 5, 58,280
> The Prophet used to keep his hair falling loose while the pagans used to part their hair, and the People of the Scriptures used to keep their hair falling loose, and the Prophet liked to follow the People of the Scriptures in matters about which he had not been instructed differently, but later on the Prophet started parting his hair.

Furthermore, in his earlier preaching of the Bible, Muhammad taught his followers that Christ Jesus is the spirit of God. And that he was born from a virgin, the Virgin Mary, and thus had no earthly, human father. And that Christ, the word and spirit of God could not be touched by the devil.

## *Christian Teacher Dies*

Now, following the death of his Christian relative, the Arabian prophet said to his followers that the divine inspiration has stopped.

And this was the time when he began to add his own stories and opinions to his old teachings. So much so that his followers began to worry that the slightest incident they cause may trigger a new revelation, which may pick on them and harm them, and would also end up added to the Koran.

Khaybar in the following quote was a fortress where the Jews lived. It was attacked by the Islamic prophet who at the time was in debt and ran out of money and booty to give his fighters in order to feed them and keep them.

> *Dawud*, 19, 3044
> We alighted with the Prophet (pbuh) at Khaybar, and he had his companions with him.
> The chief of Khaybar was a defiant and abominable man. He came to the Prophet (pbuh) and said: Is it proper for you, Muhammad, that you slaughter our donkeys, eat our fruit, and beat our women?
> The Prophet (pbuh) became angry ... the Prophet (pbuh) led them in prayer, stood up and said: Does any of you, while reclining on his couch, imagine that Allah has prohibited only that which is to be found in this Qur'an?

<u>By Allah, I have preached, commanded and prohibited various matters as numerous as that which is found in the Qur'an, or more numerous.</u>

*Bukhari*, 9, 88, 199

Allah's Apostle addressed the people saying, "Don't you know what is the day today?"
They replied, "Allah and His Apostle know better."
<u>We thought that he might give that day another name.</u>
The Prophet said, "Isn't it the day of An-Nahr?"
We replied, "Yes. O Allah's Apostle."
He then said, "What town is this? Isn't it the forbidden (Sacred) Town (Mecca)?"
We replied, "Yes, O Allah's Apostle."

*Bukhari*, 9, 93, 539

The Prophet then asked us, "Which month is this?"
We said, "Allah and His Apostle know (it) better."
He kept quiet so long that <u>we thought he might call it by another name</u>.
Then he said, "Isn't it Dhul-Hijja?"
We said, "Yes."
He asked "What town is this?"
We said, "Allah and His Apostle know (it) better.'
Then he kept quiet so long that <u>we thought he might call it by another name</u>.
He then said, "Isn't it the (forbidden) town (Mecca)?"
We said, "Yes."
He asked, "What is the day today?"
We said, "Allah and His Apostle know (it) better.
Then he kept quiet so long that we thought that he might call it by another name.
Then he said, "Isn't it the Day of An-Nahr (slaughtering of sacrifices)?"
We said, "Yes."

*Bukhari*, 7, 62, 115

During the lifetime of the Prophet <u>we used to avoid chatting leisurely and freely with our wives lest some Divine inspiration might be revealed concerning us</u>. But when the Prophet had died, we started chatting leisurely and freely (with them).

*Malik*, 15.4.9

the Messenger of Allah, may Allah bless him and grant him peace, was on one of his journeys, and one night Umar ibn al-Khattab, who was travelling with him, asked him about something, but he did not answer him.
He asked him again, but he did not answer him. Then he asked him again, and again he did not answer him. Umar said, "May your mother be bereaved of you, Umar. Three times you have importuned the Messenger of Allah, may Allah bless him and grant him peace, with a question and he has not answered you at all."
Umar continued, "I got my camel moving until, when I was in front of the people, <u>I feared that a piece of Qur'an was being sent down about me</u>. It

was not long before I heard a crier calling for me, and I said that I feared that a piece of Qur'an had been sent down about me." He continued, "I came to the Messenger of Allah, may Allah bless him and grant him peace, and said, 'Peace be upon you' to him, and he said, <u>'A sura has been sent down to me this night</u> that is more beloved to me than anything on which the sun rises.' Then he recited al-Fath (Sura 48).

The Arabian prophet was not only an illiterate man; he was also a man of simple surroundings, unlike the Jews who lived among the Greeks and the Romans for over four hundred years.

*Dawud*, 19, 3074

Narrated Zaynab:
<u>She was picking lice from the head of the Apostle of Allah</u> (pbuh) while the wife of Uthman ibn Affan and the immigrant women were with him.

The Arabian prophet did not mind to work naked.

*Muslim*, 3, 671

The Messenger of Allah (pbuh) was carrying along with them (his people) stones for the Ka'ba and there was a waist wrapper around him. His uncle," Abbas, said to him: O son of my brother! if you take off the lower garment and place it on the shoulders underneath the stones, it would be better. He (the Holy Prophet) took it off and placed it on his shoulder and fell down unconscious. He (the narrator) said: Never was he seen naked after that day.

And so, now on his own, the Islamic prophet made many laws that dealt with a variety of subjects.

For example, he prohibited the believers from cleansing themselves with dung or bone because those two items are the food, which the devils eat [see EOOO 1 & 2].

*Muslim*, 2, 504

Salman reported that it was said to him: Your Apostle (pbuh) teaches you about everything, <u>even about excrement</u>. He replied: Yes, he has forbidden us to face the Qibla at the time of excretion or urination, <u>or cleansing with right hand or with less than three pebbles, or with dung or bone</u>.

*Bukhari*, 7, 69, 534

Allah's Apostle said, "When you drink (water), do not breath in the vessel; and when you urinate, do not touch your penis with your right hand. And when you cleanse yourself after defecation, do not use your right hand." One of the believers would have wished to oppose the prophet's opinions, which he did not consider as divine inspiration but was afraid to do so.

*Bukhari*, 9, 92, 411

I asked Abu Wail, "Did you witness the battle of Siffin between 'Ali and Muawiya?" He said, "Yes," and added, "Then I heard Sahl bin Hunaif saying, 'O people! Blame your personal opinions in your religion. No doubt, I remember myself on the day of Abi Jandal; <u>if I had the power to refuse the order of Allah's Apostle, I would have refused it</u>.

*Bukhari*, 5, 58, 199

"I asked Masruq, 'Who informed the Prophet about the Jinns at the night when they heard the Qur'an?' He said, 'Your father 'Abdullah informed me that <u>a tree informed the Prophet about them</u>.' "

*Sunan Abu-Dawud*, Book 28, Number 3852:

The Prophet (pbuh) said: If anyone has himself <u>cupped on the 17th, 19th and 21st it will be a remedy for every disease</u>.

*Sahih Bukhari*, 7, 62, 133

An Ansari woman gave her daughter in marriage and the hair of the latter started falling out. The Ansari women came to the Prophet and mentioned that to him and said, "Her (my daughter's) husband suggested that I should let her wear false hair." The Prophet said, "No, (don't do that) for <u>Allah sends His curses upon such ladies who lengthen their hair artificially</u>."

*Bukhari*, 3, 39, 514

Narrated Abu Umama al-Bahili:
<u>I saw some agricultural equipments</u> and said: "I heard the Prophet saying: "There is no house in which these equipment enters except that <u>Allah will cause humiliation to enter it</u>."

*Dawud*, 1, 28

The Apostle of Allah (pbuh) forbade that anyone amongst us should comb (his hair) every day

*Muslim*, 2, 504

Salman reported that it was said to him: Your Apostle (pbuh) <u>teaches you about everything, even about excrement</u>. He replied: Yes, he has forbidden us to face the Qibla at the time of excretion or urination, or cleansing with right hand or with less than three pebbles, or with dung or bone.

*Muslim*, 2, 516

Abu Huraira reported: The Messenger of Allah (pbuh) said: Be on your guard against two things which provoke cursing. They said: Messenger of Allah, what are those things which provoke cursing? He said: <u>Easing on the thoroughfares or under the shades</u>.

*Dawud*, 16, 2840

The Prophet of Allah (pbuh) ordered to kill dogs, and we were even killing a dog which a woman brought with her from the desert. Afterwards he forbade to kill them, saying: Confine yourselves to the type which is black.

*Dawud*, 26, 3708

The Prophet (pbuh) forbade that a man should drink while standing.

*Dawud*, 32, 4123

The Apostle of Allah (pbuh) forbade that a man should put on sandals while standing.

*Bukhari*, 7, 72, 746

Allah's Apostle said, "None of you should walk, wearing one shoe only"

*Bukhari*, 7, 72, 747

Allah's Apostle said, "If you want to put on your shoes, put on the right shoe first; and if you want to take them off, take the left one first. Let the right shoe be the first to be put on and the last to be taken off."

*Dawud*, 1, 42

The Prophet (pbuh) urinated and Umar was standing behind him with a jug of water. He said: What is this, Umar? He replied: Water for you to perform ablution with. He said: I have not been commanded to perform ablution every time I urinate.

*Muslim*, 1, 131

Jarir b. Abdullah reported it from the Holy Prophet: When the slave runs away from his master, his prayer is not accepted.

## Beautiful White

The Arabian prophet's relationship with the Jews and Christian continued to sour, particularly when he began to attack their homes and confiscate their wealth. He, nonetheless, could not but revere Christ Jesus and hold Him in the highest esteem, including His physical appearance, which was quite in contrast with Muhammad's own appearance.

*Bukhari*, 54, 506

The Prophet said, "When any human being is born. Satan touches him at both sides of the body with his two fingers, except Jesus, the son of Mary, whom Satan tried to touch but failed

> *Sahih Bukhari*, 9, 87,128
>
> Allah's Apostle said, "I saw myself (in a dream) near the Ka'ba last night, and I saw a man with <u>whitish red complexion, the best you may see amongst men of that complexion having long hair reaching his earlobes which was the best hair of its sort</u> ...I asked, 'Who is this man?' Somebody replied, '(He is) Messiah, son of Mary.'

White skin was very highly prized by Muhammad and his followers, whereas black skin, according to him was undesirable. Indeed, according to him, it is a bad omen to see a black person in a dream, and that the faces of black people resemble pigeons' droppings and that Allah had created the black people for the purpose of sending all of them to hell [see EOOO volume 1 & 2].

> *Muwatta*, 050, 001
>
> Sahl was a man with <u>beautiful white skin</u>. Amir said to him, 'I have never seen anything like what I have seen today, not even the skin of a virgin.' Sahl fell ill on the spot, and his condition grew worse.
> Somebody went to the Messenger of Allah, may Allah bless him and grant him peace, and told him that Sahl was ill, and could not go with him.
> The Messenger of Allah, may Allah bless him and grant him peace ... said ... The evil eye is true.

> *Bukhari*, 7, 63, 229
>
> The Prophet said, "If that lady delivers ... a child with black eyes and huge lips ... then she delivered it <u>in the shape one would dislike</u>.

As already mentioned, the Arabian prophet relegated a beautiful physical description to Christ Jesus, the spirit of God, which was indeed in sharp contrast to Muhammad's own appearance.

> *Dawud*, 40. 4731
>
> AbdusSalam ibn AbuHazim AbuTalut said ... When Ubaydullah saw him, he said: This Muhammad of yours is <u>a dwarf and fat</u>.

Indeed, the Arabian prophet had on occasions reminded his fast-walking followers to slow down because he had become fat on account of eating too much honey.

> *Muslim*, 30, 5776
>
> Allah's Messenger (pbuh) had <u>a broad face with reddish (wide) eyes</u>, and lean heels.

He had also lost a front tooth when he fell off a horse.

## *Divine*

> *Muslim*, 1, 380
> the Messenger of Allah (pbuh) said ... Jesus, <u>the Word of Allah and His Spirit</u>
>
> *Qudsi*, 36
> Jesus ... <u>Allah's word and spirit</u>.
>
> Christ therefore was not human. Who is he then?

## *A Daily Miracle!*

How could it be a miracle when it happens daily?
    It is a miracle.
    Can you possibly divide anything into two, and yet the first remains the same and the second is no less? Is this possible?
    Is it possible to divide anything to two, and the one you divided remains intact?
    It is a miracle.
    And it happens daily by the millions.

---

The Islamic prophet Muhammad has borrowed many of the biblical passages and embellished them with his own words.
    One of the passages he borrowed was that of the creation of Eve.
    The following Islamic quotes are cut and pasted as is, without any editing.

> *The Koran*, Surah 7. The Heights
>
> 189. It is He Who created you from a single person, and made his mate of like nature

Following is one of the embellished biblical texts:

> *Muslim*, 8, 3467
>
> Woman has been created from a rib and will in no way be straightened for you; so if you wish to benefit by her, benefit by her while crookedness remains in her. And if you attempt to straighten her, you will break her, and breaking her is divorcing her.

> *Bukhari, 7, 62, 114*
>
> The Prophet said … women … are created from a rib and the most crooked portion of the rib is its upper part; if you try to straighten it, it will break, and if you leave it, it will remain crooked.

## *One Becomes Two*

Adam was one single person.
  Eve was born of him, of his rib.
  Adam became no less.
  And Eve is no less human than Adam.
  The one became two, and yet Adam did not diminish or Eve was less than a full human.
  Adam is Eve's father, so to speak.
  And Eve can rightfully say:
  I was in Adam. And Adam was in me.
  I and Adam were one.
  I am the same as Adam.
  But Adam was before me.

## *A Daily Miracle*

And the miracle happens daily and by the millions in just about all of God's creation.
  Here stands before us a woman.
  She is a single person.
  She is pregnant.
  She gives birth, say, to a daughter.
  The woman is no less because she gave birth.
  The daughter is no less a human than her mother.
  And the daughter can rightfully say:
  I and my mother were one.
  My mother was in me, and I was in my mother.
  I am equal to my mother.

  Indeed, God created man in His own image.

## *The Son of Mary*

However, a question remains to be asked.

How could the son of Mary become alive when He did not receive life from an earthly father?
What gave Him life?
The father dwelt in Him.

> Col 2:9 *For in him dwelleth all the fulness of the Godhead bodily.*
> Jn 14:10 *Believest thou not that I am in the Father, and the Father in me? ... the Father that dwelleth in me, he doeth the works [the miracles, which make the blind see, and the dead come to life].*
> Jn 10:30 *I and my Father are one.*
> Jn 14:11 *I am in the Father, and the Father in me*
>
> Phil 2:5 *Christ Jesus:*
> Phil 2:6 *Who, being in the form of God, thought it not robbery [not a false claim] to be equal with God:*
> Phil 2:7 *But made himself of no reputation, and took upon him the form of a servant, and was made in the likeness of men:*
> Phil 2:8 *And being found in fashion as a man, he humbled himself, and became obedient unto death, even the death of the cross.*
>
> Heb 1:2 *his Son ... by whom also he made the worlds;*
> Heb 1:3 *Who being the brightness of his glory, and the express image of his person, and upholding all things by the word of his power*
> Mat 3:17 *This is my beloved Son, in whom I am well pleased.*
>
> Gal 2:20 *I am crucified with Christ: nevertheless I live; yet not I, but Christ liveth in me: and the life which I now live in the flesh I live by the faith of the <u>Son of God, who loved me, and gave himself for me</u>.*

## 585 BC
## Europe Ties the Knot with Iran

My lords, we wish now to return back to the highway station we had left off in order to travel along and contact other important dates on God's calendar.

We therefore return, my lords, to the Persian Empire, the ram with two horns, which was destined to invade Europe and set the stage for more prophecies.

Prophet Daniel, go ahead, please.

> DAN 8:1 *In the third year of the reign of king Belshazzar [547 BC] a vision appeared unto me, even unto me Daniel*
> DAN 8:3 *I lifted up mine eyes, and saw, and, behold, there stood before the river a ram which had two horns [today's Iran]: and the two horns were high [Media and Persia]; <u>but one was higher than the other, and the higher [Persia] came up last</u>.*

*DAN 8:4* <u>*I saw the ram pushing westward*</u> *[towards Europe], and northward, and southward; so that no beasts might stand before him, neither was there any that could deliver out of his hand; but he did according to his will, and became great.*

Your majesties, in order to understand prophet Daniel's prophecy and the following events of invading Europe, we must first go back in time to the day Iran made its first contact with Europeans.

We need to go back in time, my lords, nearly twenty-six years before H.M. King Cyrus the great had reigned [559–530 BC]. Thus, my lords, we shall begin our march in the year 585 BC, the year the Iranians came in contact with Europeans and fell in love with their territory.

Your majesties, some may blame or attribute the Iranian's first contact with Europe on the "gypsies." And yes, indeed, the gypsies played a part in bringing the Iranians towards Europe. Indeed, my lords, the Iranians came to the borders of Europe chasing after gypsies.

But one can also blame the Iranians' first contact with Europeans on nature, my lords, on a sun eclipse and on the following marriage between a European princess and an Iranian prince.

As you may recall, my lords, it was a fellow by the name of Deioces who built the capital city of the province of Media in Iran, and whose son Phraortes after him unified the Median tribes of Iran into one kingdom, the kingdom of Media—the small horn, which sprung first in Daniel's prophecy.

> *Dan 8:3* *I lifted up mine eyes, and saw, and, behold, there stood before the river a ram which had two horns_[today's Iran]: and the two horns were high [Media and Persia];* <u>*but one was higher than the other [Persia]*</u>*,* <u>*and the higher [Persia] came up last.*</u>

And then after Deioces and Phraortes, a third king of Media came, H.M. King Cyaxares I. He was the king, my lords, along with the Babylonian rebel King Nabopolassar, who together invaded Nineveh, the capital of the vicious Assyrians of northern Iraq, and put an end to the Assyrian Empire.

Now his Iranian majesty King Cyaxares I, the third founder of Iran and conqueror of Assyria, was bent, my lords, on punishing a group of horse-riding nomads stealing and robbing his people on the far northern borders of Iran.

But these nomads, the Scythians to be exact, my lords, managed to slip off his fingers and escape towards the eastern borders of Europe. There at the eastern gates of Europe, they took shelter with the Greek Lydian King Alyattes in Sardis, the capital of Lydia.

Sardis, today in Turkey, was inhabited by Greeks in ancient times, and is only a hop and a skip away from the continent of Europe, Wikipedia, Roke

Now disappointed and furious H.M. King Cyaxares I sent messengers demanding His Greek majesty King Alyattes of Lydia to hand in the fugitives. H. M. King Alyattes refused.

And now it was war, my lords, between Iranians and Greeks.

This, my lords, was the first Iranian step towards Europe. And when you see the goods of Europe, my lords, you would want to get closer and closer.

Historian Herodotus, please cut in, sir.

"after five years of indecisive warfare, a battle took place in which the armies had already engaged when day suddenly turned into night [this sun eclipse, has been scientifically dated to May 28, 585 BC] ... both Lydians [Greeks] and Medes [Iranians] broke off the engagement when they saw this darkening of the day: they were more anxious than they had been to conclude peace, and a reconciliation was brought about by Syennesis of Cilicia and Labynetus of Babylon, who were the men responsible both for the pact to keep the peace and for the exchange of marriage between the two kingdoms.

<u>They persuaded [Greek King] Alyattes to give his daughter Aryenis to [Iranian Prince] Astyages, son of Cyaxares</u> – knowing that treaties seldom remain intact without powerful sanctions."[49]

So now, my lords, the Iranian prince Astyages was married off to a Greek princess.

How far is Europe now? It is getting closer, my lords.

Almost thirty-three years after [553 BC], Governor Cyrus of Persia of southern Iran went to war with his grandfather Astyages, the sun eclipse prince who was married to a Greek princess and who was now the king of Media and Persia.

And after three years of warring against his grandfather, Persian Governor Cyrus emerged as the new king of Media and Persia of Iran [550 BC].

This change now, my lords, worried King Astyages' in-laws in Greece. They had for years maintained good relations and trade with their, now defeated, relative H.M. King Astyages, the prince of the sun eclipse.

## 547/546 BC
## As Rich as Croesus

My lords, now, nearly forty years after the marriage of the Greek princess to the Iranian prince, enters Greek King Croesus.

Fabulously rich King Croesus is the son of the now-deceased Greek King Alyattes who married off his daughter, Croesus' sister, to the Iranian Astyages. Are you following so far, my lords? Do not worry, your majesties, we are getting close to the end of this history. But yet this history, my lords, is what eventually leads us to Marathon, to the hot gates, to the heroic last stand and the burning down of Athens city.

At any rate, my lords, H.M. King Croesus, the wealthiest man on earth, wanted to get rid of Persian King Cyrus and add Media and Persia to the Greek dominion of Lydia.

But Greek King Croesus, my lords, did not know that he was clawing against the prophecy of Isaiah concerning the beloved great Iranian king. H.M. King Cyrus was not to be defeated, says the Lord.

Go ahead, please, prophet Isaiah.

---

[49] Herodotus, *The Histories*, 3:74, P. 70

> ISA 45:1 *Thus saith the LORD to his anointed, to Cyrus, whose right hand I have holden, to subdue nations before him ... to open before him the two leaved gates [the gates of walled and fortified cities]; and the gates shall not be shut;*
> ISA 45:2 *I will go before thee, and make the crooked places straight: I will break in pieces the gates of brass, and cut in sunder the bars of iron:*
> ISA 45:3 *And I will give thee the [hidden] treasures of darkness, and hidden riches of secret places, that thou mayest know that I, the LORD, which call thee by thy name, am the God of Israel.*

And so this was the time then, my lords, as we had mentioned to you earlier, when H.M. King Croesus received that old good advice but did not heed it.

Historian Herodotus, go ahead, please.

> While the [Greek] preparations were going on, he [Greek King Croesus] received a piece of advice from a Lydian named Sandanis, who was already known for his good sense, and by the opinion he then expressed greatly increased his reputation amongst the Lydians.
>
> "My lord," he said, "you are preparing to fight against men [the Iranians] who dress in leather – both breeches and everything else. So rough is their country that they eat as much as they have, never as much as they want. They drink no wine but only water. They have no good things at all, not even figs for desert.
>
> "Now if you conquer this people, what will you get from them, seeing they have nothing for you to take? And if they conquer you, think how many good things you will lose; for once they taste the luxuries of Lydia they will hold on to them so tightly that nothing will make them let go [Aha! Remember these weighty words, my lords].
>
> "I am thankful myself that the gods have never put it into the Persians' heads to attack the Lydians."[50]

Wait, my lords; the gods are prone to change their minds when they see the goods of Europe and the Europeans.

At any rate, my lords, his Greek majesty King "Croesus did not take this advice though Sandanis was right: the Persians before their conquest of Lydia had no luxuries of any kind."[51]

---

[50] Herodotus, *The Histories*, 1:70, 71, P.68
[51] Herodotus, *The Histories*, 1:70, 71, P.68

"Gold and silver staters of Croesus, king of Lydia: foreparts of a lion and bull. Croesus was the first to introduce coins made of pure gold and silver. About 550 BC," University of Cambridge Archaeological Museum, UK (image source: author).

H.M. King Cyrus the great, my sovereigns, marched one thousand five hundred miles to Sardis and won his battle against the Greeks. And now, look what is the result!

The Greek cities at the edge of Europe and their families, Greek men and women, boys and girls, have fallen into the hands of the Iranians. The Greek rulers of these Greek cities of Lydia were now getting their orders directly from Persepolis, the capital city of Iran. Iran rules supreme.

The Iranians became the masters, and the Greeks of Europe became the obedient servants and slaves. What a change of destiny and circumstances, my lords! The rich and cultured Greeks have become poor, and the poor and uncultured Iranians rule.

There is more yet, my lords.

Why stop here?!

It looks good on the other side of the water fence.

The Iranian armies stationed in Lydia, my lords, started to forage around and sack more Greek populated cities in the neighborhood of Lydia, the region that is called Ionia, along the eastern frontiers of Europe.

Europe, my lords, is now a spear's throw distance from the "uncultured soldiers of Iran," as the Greeks label them.

The Iranian expansion, my lords, is forging ahead in line with Daniel's prophecy.

Iran, my lords, has planted its feet across from Europe and the Europeans.

Flip the years, your majesties, and let us move along with the months of the earth so that we can return to H.M. King Darius I, the unexpected man who ordered the completion of the parliament of the world, the house of the Holy One and the Father of the fatherless.

History is repeating itself today. Just as H.M. King Cyaxares I came to the frontiers of Europe to chase the Scythian gypsies, so does today his successor H.M. King Darius I, son of Hystaspes.

But when his majesty came, he saw and wanted to firm up the Iranian holdings across from the European shore. Europe is beautiful, and one of its rivers is the most beautiful there is. Indeed, his majesty King Darius I says that just as the Tearus River is the most imposing river of all, so is he amongst all men everywhere. At least this was the description that his scribes engraved on the pillar he erected by the River Tearus, my lords.

Is this correct, historian Herodotus?

> "Darius was so greatly charmed with the Tearus, that he erected another pillar close to its source with this inscription""The springs of the Tearus, whose water is the finest in action and noblest in appearance of all rivers, <u>was visited in the course of his march against Scythia by Darius son of Hystaspes</u>, finest in action and noblest in appearance of all men, King of Persia and the whole continent."⁵²

King Darius I, Persepolis (image source: Wikipedia, درفش کاویانی)

Unfortunately, your majesty King Cyrus the great, the wanderings of your successor H.M. King Darius I in the eastern fringes of Europe, in chase of the Scythian gypsies, did not end up in finding them or defeating them. Indeed, his majesty has given up trying to find them, sir. Instead, he is retracing his steps back to regroup in your Iranian holdings of western Turkey—the defeated Greek cities of the region of Ionia, which you took away from the wealthy Croesus, sir.

However, this campaign did not end up in a total failure sir; in fact, his majesty's present instructions to his Iranian commanders are to snap as many Greek cities at the fringes of Europe as they possibly can. Meanwhile, sir, his majesty has gone home to Iran.

---

⁵² Herodotus, *The Histories*, 4:92, P 301

The "gypsies," the Scythians, were the bait, which in time shall bring Daniel's prophecy home, my lords. But who would have known it at the time?

Above is a "gold signet ring with intaglio representation of a kneeling archer stretching a Scythian bow," Benaki Museum, Athens, Greece (image source: author).

And so to cap it up your majesties, the chasing of the gypsies has failed to find them and engage them in a war. On the other hand, winning more cities ringing Europe continues as we speak. The prophecy of Daniel, my lords, is on track. And when it is fulfilled, the Greeks will rule the world and change the face of Israel and fulfill one of its major prophecies.

Please cut in when appropriate, historian Herodotus.

> "The Persians whom Darius had left in Europe under Megabazus' command began hostilities against the Greeks on the Hellespont by subduing the Perinthians, who refused to accept Persian dominion.
> ...
> Megabazus marched through Thrace, bringing every city and every people in the country under the control of the Persian king. All this was according to orders; for he had received instructions from Darius to conquer Thrace."[53]

---

[53] Herodotus, *The Histories*, 5:1, P. 341

Your majesty King Cyrus the great, we have very good news, sir; Greek families are now being uprooted from Ionia and are being carried off to Iran and Asia.

Mix the races. This is how our world is being shaped at this point of time, sir.

The days pass and everything is proceeding according to plan, sir. Gradually, the Iranian soldiers of your successor are securing "command of the whole coastal district of Asia [across the Hellespont from Europe], with a large army and navy."[54]

Your Iranian people, sir, can see Europe from where they are standing today across the street—the water street. How beautiful Europe is, how beautiful and full of incomparable Greek history!

The Hellespont, similar to the Bosporus, is a narrow sea strait that separates the Asian and European continents (image source: author).

## 499–494 BC Greek Uprisings Everywhere

The world has put on more years, my lords, since the sun eclipse peace treaty of May 28, 585 BC, and the following fall of Greek Lydia and its capital Sardis to the hands of the Iranians and H.M. King Cyrus [545 BC].

And the beautiful but temporary earth has aged, my lords, since King Darius I, the unexpected man of the temple, conspired with six nobles, took the throne of Iran, and then went

---

[54] Herodotus, *The Histories*, 5:27, P. 350

chasing after the horse-riding nomads, the Scythian gypsies, hiding at the borders of Europe [510 BC].

And today, your majesty King Cyrus the Great, we talk to you again, sir, because we have some bad news to deliver to you at this time. But do not be too anxious, sir; this bad news would in the long run drive your Iranians right to the heart of civilized Europe and straight to its greatest treasures.

Today, sir, and after forty-six years of living under the heels of the garrisons of your Iranian soldiers and puppet Greek governors, the Greek Ionians are revolting against your successor, H.M. King Darius I the great. One Ionian city, sir, after another and one Ionian region after another are rising in revolts, sir.

And perhaps we should not blame the Greek Ionians too much, sir. For it seems, sir, that your Persian Iranian governors have been abusing the local Greek and European women.

Can you confirm this, historian Herodotus, to his majesty?

> "It was here not long afterwards that the Greeks under Xanthippus the son of Ariphron took Artayctes the Persian governor of Sestos, and nailed him alive to a plank – he was the man who collected women in the temple of Protesilaus at Elaeus and committed various acts of sacrilege."[55]

The Ionian Greeks are now saying "no more," sir. Enough is enough. We had enough of the uncultured Iranians, or "barbarians," as they call your people, sir, if you excuse the insult.

And it is no secret, sir, that none of these Greek populated cities of Ionia would have dared to revolt against your garrisons without the backing up and help of the most ancient and perhaps the greatest city of the world, sir, which is none other than Athens itself.

Athens ... it is the most cultured and civilized city there is, sir. It is the home of democracy and philosophy and science, if we may say so without offence, your majesty. And it is an open secret today, sir, that the leaders of Athens had supplied their Ionian Greek relatives across the water strait with many troops as well as with twenty warships to rebel against your successor H.M. King Darius I.

---

[55] Herodotus, *The Histories*, 7:30, P. 456

Go right ahead, please, historian Herodotus, go right ahead and speak of the events that happened a few years before you wrote your manuscript.

> "the Athenians passed a decree for the dispatch of twenty warships to Ionia, under the command of Melanthius, a distinguished Athenian."[56]

Undeterred, sir, your great successor H.M. King Darius I, the finest in action and noblest of appearance of all men, is deploying his troops in order to crush the Ionian Greek rebels.

Unfortunately, sir, the uprisings and riots of the Greek streets and towns did not settle quickly.

The ebb and tide of the war carried on spring after spring, year after year, for nearly five years, sir, a win here, a loss there, and finally a stalemate for months on end.

But on the other hand, sir, your Iranian troops showed no mercy once a Greek Ionian town fell into their hands.

Good news, sir.

Today and at last, sir, we are pleased to report to you that the troops of your great successor, the noblest of appearance of all men, regrouped and made a final push against the center of the Ionian uprising of the Greeks, and won a decisive battle, the Battle of Lade, sir. And this Battle of Lade, sir, has indeed put an end to the uprising of the Greek Ionians inhabiting the shores opposite of continental Europe, home of the once and great city of Athens.

The goddess Athena, the patroness of the city of Athens, Roman copy (1st century BC) of a Greek original, 430 BC., the Louvre Museum, Paris (image source: author).

> "once the towns were in their [Persian Iranian] hands, the best-looking boys were chosen for castration and made into eunuchs; the handsomest girls were dragged from their homes and sent to Darius' court, and the towns themselves, <u>temples and all</u>, were burnt to the ground. In this year the Ionians were reduced ... to slavery."[57]

---

[56] *The Histories*, 5:96, PP. 379
[57] Herodotus, *The Histories*, 6:28, P 398

## 494 BC
## Master, Remember the Athenians

Now Your majesty King Cyrus, some fifty years after you had crushed the Greek King Croesus and his Lydian subjects, today, sir, the European Greeks living in Asia are once more under the boots of your dear Persian successor, the unexpected man of the temple, H.M. King Darius I.

And now, sir, the families of the Iranian commanders and chiefs stationed here in Greek Ionia can intermarry with the Greek aristocratic families. And life, sir, can go on with its renovated rhythm of mixing the races in Ionia of Turkey across the narrow waters from Europe.

But as we have mentioned to you, sir, this control over the Greek Ionians of Turkey is nothing but an opening move of your Iranian people. It is also, my lord, an opening move towards more prophecies.

This here is an unfinished business as far as your successor H.M. King Darius I is concerned, sir.

And you may ask, sir, why this is unfinished business?

It is unfinished business, sir, because H.M. King Darius I intends to punish those Athenian leaders who backed the Ionian rebels against him, sir. The Athenians must be taught a lesson, sir, not to ever again interfere with Iranian plans. A day of revenge must come, sir.

And so the question now is: who is this Athens that dared to back the Ionian rebels against H.M. King Darius I the great, the man who came to chase gypsies and ended up staying in Ionia?

"Who is Athens?" asked your successor King Darius, sir.

Ask the marble, sir. The marble would tell you who made it move and talk loud. The marble, sir, sat down in a deep conversation with man—a conversation that covers so many topics, sir.

Athens, sir, is "the mother and kindly nurse of many other arts," says the old historian Plutarch.

But whatever she be, the marathon is on, sir.

The marathon is on to Athens "to grind her pride and self-esteem into the dust."

And the marathon is also on, my lords, to fulfill the events outlined on the Holy One's timetable.

THE UNEQUAL TWO HORNS OF IRAN—293

The ancient statue of the goddess Athens, 430 BC, the Louvre Museum (image source: author).

Go ahead, historian Herodotus, you know the circumstances we are referring to.

> "news was brought to Darius that <u>Sardis</u> [the main city of Greek Ionia where the Iranian troops were stationed since the victory of King Cyrus the great over Croesus. This Iranian garrison in the city was the first target of the Greek Ionian rebellion against Iran.] <u>had been taken and burnt by the Athenians and Ionians</u> ... The story goes that when Darius learns of the disaster, he did not give a thought to the

Ionians, knowing perfectly well that the punishment for their revolt would come; <u>but he asked who the Athenians were</u>, and then, on being told, called for his bow.

He took it, set an arrow on the string, shot it up into the air and cried:""'Grant, O God, that I may punish the Athenians'"".

Then he commanded one of his servants to repeat to him the words, ""<u>Master, remember the Athenians</u>"", <u>three times, whenever he sat down to dinner</u>. "[58]

To Europe we go, sir.

A new turning point in history is underway, your majesty, King Cyrus.

My lord, your great successor King Darius I, the gypsies hunter and builder of the temple, is amassing enough troops in order to drown Greece and its great city of Athens, home of the European civilization.

Europe, sir, shall become inhabited, populated, and ruled by your Iranian people if H.M. King Darius' plans mature properly. Let us hope so, sir.

## 490 BC A Word for the Ages

Your majesty King Cyrus, two years after the end of the revolt of the Greek cities in Asia, H.M. King Darius I had amassed enough troops and shall soon set sail to punish Athens city and take possession of Europe and the Europeans.

Disaster, sir!
Disaster number one, sir!
The gods! the gods!
Twenty thousand men!
Go ahead, historian Herodotus, whenever we gesture to you, sir.

"Then, in the following spring, Darius superseded all his other generals and sent Mardonius, the son of Gobryas, down to the coast in command of a very large force, both military and naval. Mardonius was still a young man, and had recently married Darius' daughter Artozostra.

...

[Mardonius] ferried the troops across the straight [Hellespont] and began his march through Europe, with Eretria [another Greeks who took part in the Ionians revolt] and Athens as his objectives.

...

---

[58] *The Histories*, 5:105, P. 382

>    They were caught by a violent northerly gale, which proved to be too much for the ships to cope with. A great many of them were driven ashore and wrecked on Athos – indeed, report says that something like three hundred were lost with over twenty thousand men.
>    
>    ...
>    
>    While this disaster was overtaking the fleet, on land Mardonius and his army in Macedonia [northern Greece – home of the future Alexander the Great] were attacked in camp ... The Persian losses were heavy, and Mardonius himself was wounded.
>    
>    ...
>    
>    The whole force, therefore returned to Asia in disgrace."[59]

We are telling it to you as it happened, sir.

Nature, sir, nature and the gods conspired against the first attempt to set Iranian foot in Europe. But, your majesty, King Darius, the finest, if you fail, then try again, sir. Europe, with its wealth, beauty, and people is worth the pain of trying again, sir.

The left arm of the Greek god Zeus, 2nd half of 2nd C. BC, The National Archaeological Museum of Greece (image source: author).

And from what we hear, his majesty would probably have a good chance, sir. Why you may ask? Yes, sir! The Greeks are arguing fiercely amongst themselves as what to do, what strategy to use in order to defend Europe against the ambitions of your Iran, sir. And it is getting worse for them, sir: the Greeks have been and still are fighting tooth and nail against each other.

Let them wear themselves down.

---

[59] Herodotus, *The Histories*, 6:41, PP. 42, 43

This is true, sir, but they may also end up getting better at war as they learn from fighting amongst themselves. Time will tell sir, time will tell.

> "While Athens and Aegina were at each other's throat, the king of Persia continued to mature his plans. His servant never failed to repeat to him the word ""<u>Remember Athens</u>""
>
> ...
>
> In consequence of the ill success of his previous expedition, he relieved Mardonius of his command, and appointed other generals, whom he proposed to send against Eretria and Athens, Datis, a Mede, and his own nephew, Artaphernes ... and their orders were to <u>reduce Athens and Eretria to slavery</u> and to bring the slaves before the king."[60]

Goddess Athena, get ready to defend your city; the Iranian troops are on the way.

The National Museum of Greece, Athens, a 3rd century AD copy of an original dated to 438 BC, which precedes the Iranian invasion (image source: author).

Sir, hopping from Greek island to Greek island, the navy and the army of your successor H.M. King Darius I, the man of the temple, has reached its first destination––Eretria.

And there, sir, his generals found a good field to deploy their main land force division, the great Persian horse division.

The chosen battlefield, your majesty King Cyrus, is near a town by the name of Marathon.

Carry on please, historian Herodotus. Interrupt us whenever you feel appropriate to do so, sir.

> "The part of Attic territory nearest Eretria – and also <u>the best ground for cavalry to manoeuvre in</u> – was Marathon. To Marathon, therefore, Hippias directed the invading army, and the Athenians, as soon as the news arrived, hurried to meet it.
>
> The Athenian troops were commanded by ten generals, of whom the tenth was Miltiades."[61]

---

[60] Herodotus, *The Histories*, 6:94, P. 421
[61] Herodotus, *The Histories*, 6:100, P 424

Rest assured, your majesty King Cyrus, that the Greek soldiers of the Athenian army are hugely outnumbered, sir, by your Persian Iranian soldiers and their recruits from all over the empire.

On the other hand, sir, we alert you that the Greek Athenians are sending a messenger to their strong kinsmen, the Greek Spartans, asking for help against your great successor H.M. King Darius I.

> "the Athenian generals sent off a message to Sparta. The messenger was an Athenian named Pheidippides, a professional; long-distance runner."[62]

The messenger, sir, is a long-distance runner, by the name of Pheidippides—what a difficult name to remember!

It is a difficult name to remember indeed, sir, but athletes from all over the world will try year after year to duplicate his feat, and even up to our modern time.

A Greek warrior, a 1st century BC copy of a mid-5th Century BC statue, British Museum, London (image source: author).

Anyway, back to Sparta, sir.

Unfortunately, for the overwhelmed Athenian army, their powerful Spartan kin cannot come to their aide, sir; they are celebrating a holy feast.

The Spartans and the rest of the Greeks, sir, are particular in not fighting during such feasts, and more so, sir, during the Olympic festival. Indeed, during this very important feast of the Olympic festival, sir, they cease all their hostilities so that the games may be held in a time of peace—European customs, sir.

## *The Olympic Games*

Of ancient times, the Greeks celebrated the Olympic Games every four years beginning in 776 BC.

---

[62] Herodotus, *The Histories*, 6:105, P 425

298—EARTH OUT OF ORBIT

The festivities included sporting, musical, and singing competitions. A truce was held during the games, the Olympic Truce, so that as many competitors as possible could be encouraged to travel and participate during this period of peace.

This simple enjoyment of sports and musical feasts of the sacred Olympic Games are not appreciated by all gods.

In more modern times, for example, sporting and musical activities were forbidden and considered sins by the Islamic Prophet Muhammad of Saudi Arabia, who grew up in a more basic surrounding than those of the ancient Greeks.

And even at the present time, his faithful and most sincere followers continue to obey his wishes and desires, and forbid their families and children from all forms of sporting and musical activities.

The above "Olympic medal was probably struck in AD 242, to mark the Olympic games celebrated that year in Macedonia, in honor of Alexander the Great." Cambridge University Archaeological Museum, UK (image source: author).

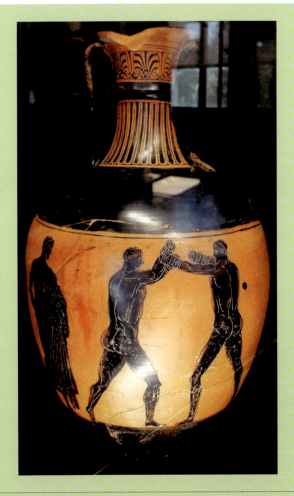

A judge and boxers, 340-339 BC, Louvre Museum, Paris, (image source: author).

The following quotes come from the sacred Islamic books of Hadith, which record the pronouncements of the Islamic Prophet Muhammad. They are copied verbatim without any editing. The abbreviation "pbuh" stands for "peace be upon him," a sentence that the devoted and sincere followers of the Islamic prophet pronounce each time his name is mentioned.

*Dawud*, 41, 4909

Salam ibn Miskin, quoting an old man who witnessed AbuWa'il in a wedding feast, said: They began to play, amuse and sing ... I heard the apostle of Allah (pbuh) say: <u>Singing produces hypocrisy in the heart</u>.

> *Dawud*, 41, 4920
>
> The Apostle of Allah (pbuh) said: <u>He who plays backgammon disobeys Allah and His Apostle</u>.
>
> *Dawud*, 26. 3677
>
> The Prophet (pbuh) forbade wine, game of chance, <u>drum</u>, and wine made from millet.
>
> *Malik*, 52, 52, 2.7
>
> Yahya related to me from Malik from Nafi from Abdullah ibn Umar that when he found one of his family <u>playing dice he beat him and destroyed the dice</u>. Yahya said that he heard Malik say, "<u>There is no good in chess</u>," and he disapproved of it." Yahya said, "I heard him disapprove of playing it and other worthless games. He recited this ayat, 'What is there after the truth except going the wrong way.'"
>
> *Malik*, 52, 52.2.6
>
> the Messenger of Allah, may Allah bless him and grant him peace, said, "Whoever plays games of dice has disobeyed Allah and His Messenger."
>
> *Muslim*, 28, 5612
>
> Allah's Apostle (pbuh) said: He who played <u>chess</u> is like one who dyed his hand with the flesh and blood of swine.

Great City of Athens, you, the gatekeeper of Europe and the European races, you are on your own. Live or die, swim or drown by yourself. Spartans or no Spartans—no one is available to help you against the invading Iranian armies of H.M. King Darius I.

Your majesty King Cyrus, the two armies, sir, are now facing each other on the battlefield of Marathon, and your great successor King Darius is today betting himself against several Greek generals, amongst whom is General Miltiades.

> "Among the Athenian commanders opinion was divided: some were against risking a battle on the ground that the Athenian force was too small to stand a chance of success; others – and amongst them Miltiades – urged it"[63]
>
> "At last the decision to fight was made.

---

[63] Herodotus, *The Histories*, 6:109, P 427

> ...
> The two [Athenian] wings were strong, but the line in the center was only a few ranks deep ...the word was given to move, and the Athenians advanced at a run towards the enemy, not less than a mile away."[64]

Your majesty King Cyrus, we do not know how to explain this to you, sir. But your huge numbers of Iranian soldiers and foreign recruits have been totally routed in Marathon. It must be the gods, sir. It must be the doings of god. The Spartans did not come, but the gods were there.

> "It was the Athenians who – after God – drove back the Persian king."[65]

But contain your anger sir; it is not over yet. There is yet hope.

## Joy. We Won. Now Die.

Ah, yes, your majesty. Those Iranians soldiers who managed to escape the carnage of the battlefield of Marathon took off on the run and rushed back to the ships. And there, your majesty, was their golden chance, sir.

Athens city is defenseless. It is empty of Greek defenders. All the Athenian soldiers are here in Marathon, sir, and there are hardly enough of them to begin with.

Is this statement correct, historian Herodotus?

In the ships, the Iranians rushed charting "a course round Sunium for Athens, which they hoped to reach in advance of the Athenian army."[66]

The ships, sir, of your successor H.M. King Darius I, are racing top speed to defenseless Athens city—the greatest of all European cities. The ships will get there, sir, full of soldiers and way before the Athenian soldiers could reach home.

In Athens, sir, the elders and the leaders of the city, thinking that their army was defeated in Marathon, would without any hesitation open the gates and surrender their beloved city to your Iranian soldiers.

---

[64] Herodotus, *The Histories*, 6:109, PP. 428, 429
[65] Herodotus, *The Histories*, 7:139, P. 487
[66] Herodotus, *The Histories*, 6:115, P 429

A reconstruction of beached Persian ships at Marathon, prior to the battle, WC, Tungsten

But we must also tell you, sir, that the ships of your successor are in a race against a runner. The runner, sir, has over forty miles on land to run, from Marathon to Athens. And he is running, sir. Ships against a runner! And he arrived ahead of the ships, sir. And the old historian Lucian [born circa 125 AD] commemorated the feat of this runner, sir. For this runner, sir, had managed to inform the Athenian leaders, in time, not to surrender the city.

We have won in Marathon. Our soldiers shall arrive soon. Do not open the gates! Do not surrender Athens.

Historian Lucian of Samosata, the floor is yours, sir.

> "Philippides the dispatch-runner. Bringing the news of Marathon, he found the archons [the leaders of Athens city] seated, in suspense regarding the issue[outcome] of the battle.
>
> "'Joy, we win!'" he said, and died upon his message, breathing his last in the word joy"[67]

But then, your majesty, King Cyrus the Great, the more ancient Greek historian Plutarch [b. circa 46 AD] relates it differently, sir, and even gave the famed runner another name.

Go ahead please, historian Plutarch.

> "most historians declare that it was Eucles who ran in full armour, hot from the battle, and, bursting in at the doors of the first men of the state, could only say, 'Hail! We are victorious!' and straightway expired."[68]

---

[67] *Pro Lapsu Inter Salutandum*, A Slip of the Tongue in Salutation, Lucian of Samosata, translated by Fowler, H W and F G Oxford, the Clarendon Press 1905, 3
[68] Plutarch, *On the Fame of Athens*, C

The Marathon race is celebrated around the world; the one above was held in Belfast, Northern Ireland, WC, Ardfern

## By the Memory!

From that day on, the ancient Greeks, sir, began to take the oath "by the memory of those of our ancestors who risked their lives for us at Marathon."[69]

Yes, sir, this is their national oath these days. They swear by the Greek Athenian soldiers who "had risked their lives at Marathon as though their souls were not their own," says Plutarch in his De Gloria, sir.

Let us face it, your majesty, King Cyrus the Great. Marathon took the wind off the sails of your Persia. But Marathon will not put an end to the hot and steamy rivalry that is now smoldering between Greece, the guardians of Europe, and your people of Persia [Iran], sir.

Another day shall arise, sir. In due time, it shall and Europe shall be yours.

But we can also tell you, sir, that there was another outcome of this invasion. Indeed, your majesty, this invasion and the following one, especially the following one, did, in the course of the years, weigh heavily on the mind of the youngster— the kid. And the kid, my lord, set his mind on invading your Iran in retaliation. And when he marched ahead to do so,

---

[69] Plutarch, *De Gloria*, C

my lord, he unknowingly marched to fulfill prophecies that spanned three hundred years.

> "When the news of the battle of Marathon reached Darius, son of Hystaspes and king of Persia, his anger against Athens, already great enough ... was even greater, and he was more than ever determined to make war on Greece. <u>Without loss of time he dispatched couriers to the various states under his dominion with orders to raise an army much larger than before</u>; and also warships, transports, horses, and grain. So the royal command went around; and <u>all Asia was in an uproar for three years</u>, with the best men being enrolled in the army for the invasion of Greece.
>
> ...
>
> Death, however, cut him off before his preparations were complete ... he died ... after a reign of thirty-six years [Sept 522-Oct 486 BC, secured throne in 520/519 BC]."[70]

---

[70] Herodotus, *The Histories*, 7:1&4, PP. 441, 442

The archers of King Darius I, as depicted on the walls of Darius' palace at Susa. Berlin Museum (image Source: author).

Tomb of King Darius I at Naqsh-e Rustam, Iran, WC, Pastaitaken

## 486–465 BC
## We Shall Own the Borders of God

Have you mentioned this to God?

Prophet Daniel, would you please, sir, repeat the statement you had made earlier regarding the four important kings of Iran!

DAN 11:2 *Behold, there shall stand up yet three kings in Persia; and the fourth shall be far richer than they all:* <u>*and by his strength through his riches he shall stir up all against the realm of Grecia.*</u>

Here comes the fourth, my lords. Here he is.

Your Majesty King Cyrus, the successor of deceased King Darius I, the man who shall now sit on your Persian throne, is H.M. King Xerxes I.

We would wish, sir, to inform your colleagues that Daniel's prophecy took place in the year 540 BC, several years before the reigns of your successors, H.M. King Cambyses, and H.M. King Darius I, and fifty-four years before the reign of H.M King Xerxes I.

And we wish to inform you, sir, that H.M. King Xerxes I, the new king of your Iran, is not interested at all in following the footsteps of his father, H.M. King Darius I, to invade Greece and Europe.

In which case, your majesty, the prophecy of Daniel is in jeopardy "and by his strength through his riches he shall stir up all against the realm of Grecia." And accordingly, sir, the youngster who was ordained to fulfill prophesies for three hundred years may not in fact come at all to Iran.

Go ahead, historian Herodotus, whenever we look your direction, sir.

"Xerxes first was not at all interested in invading Greece."[71]

Instead, my lord, H.M. King Xerxes I, was rather keen on recovering his revenue from the revolting Egypt.

Egypt, sir, is a good and productive farm.

True enough!

But Europe, on the other hand, insisted his general, is "a very beautiful place."[1]

It did not take long, your majesty, King Cyrus.

The general, who hoped that one day he would become the governor of Greece, did not need, neither he nor his friends, to try too hard to convince his majesty to head for Europe.

---

[71] Herodotus, *The Histories*, 7:2, P. 442

Indeed, sir, H.M. King Xerxes I, soon after subduing Egypt and recovering his income from its people, announced that he "will not rest until I have taken Athens and burnt it to the ground ... we shall so extend the empire of Persia that its boundaries will be God's own sky ... I shall pass through Europe from end to end and make it all one country."[72]

"For the four years following the conquest of Egypt the mustering of troops and the provision of stores and equipment continued, and towards the close of the fifth Xerxes, at the head of his enormous force, began his march ... It dwarfed the army [of] Darius."[73]

Your majesty King Cyrus, your new successor, H.M. King Xerxes I, "then prepared to move forward to Abydos, where a bridge had already been constructed across the Hellespont from Asia to Europe."[74]

Disaster!

Just as it happened in the days of H.M. King Darius I, nature, my lord, conspired once again against the invasion of your people. The platoon bridges, which were tied up with flax, and papyrus cables suffered a major blow.

And so who is to blame here sir?

The answer is more than obvious, my lord: the god of the waters of the narrow channels. The god of the sea straights, which separate Asia from Europe, is the one to be blamed.

And so now what should you do, sir, to tame this god and bring him into submission?

Whip him, of course. What else, my lord, whip him!

"The work was successfully completed, but a subsequent storm of great violence smashed it up and carried everything away. Xerxes was very angry when he learned of the disaster, and gave orders that the Hellespont should receive three hundred lashes and have a pair of fetters [chains] thrown into it. I have heard before now that he also sent people to brand it with hot irons. He certainly instructed the men with the whips to utter, as they wielded them, the barbarous and presumptuous words ""You salt and bitter stream, your master lays this punishment upon you for injuring him, who never injured you. But Xerxes the king will cross you, with or without

---

[72] 7:8a, P. 444
[73] 7:18, P. 452
[74] 7:30, P. 456

308—EARTH OUT OF ORBIT

your permission. No man sacrifices to you, and you deserve the neglect by your acid and muddy waters"".[75]

Your majesty King Cyrus, in addition to punishing the god of the Hellespont, your third successor, H.M. King Xerxes I, gave orders that the men responsible for building the bridges should have their heads cut off.[5] And why not? This is the way it goes.

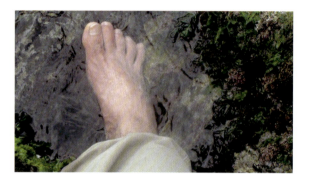

The waters that separate Asia from Europe were whipped and branded (image source: author).

Go ahead now, your majesty, King Xerxes I. Cross the salty waters and march on victorious to the heart of Greece.

"we shall conquer all Europe," said his Iranian majesty.[76]

It took a full seven days, sir, a full seven days for the huge army of your third successor to cross the bridges from Asia to Europe. If this says anything, my lord, it says that the army of your successor was a very huge army, indeed.

And now the feet of your countrymen, sir, and their allies are stomping upon the European soil, while the navy ships of your people, sir, sail abreast along the European shores.

Welcome to the beautiful lands of Europe, my lord, King Xerxes I. Welcome.

Your majesty King Cyrus the great, at this point of time the towns of Greece are being run over one by one, sir, as your successor marches steadily towards the doomed city of Athens.

---

[75] 7:30, P. 457
[76] Herodotus, The *Histories*, 7:49, P. 462

Athens, it is now the time to pray to every available god of yours. But please make reasonable demands on the gods. For it is indeed already too late to ask for preventing troubles; you should be more than happy if the gods could split your troubles by half.

> "A man of Abdera [one of the Greek towns] called Megacreon ... adviced the people of the town to take their wives to the temples and pray heaven to continue to spare them one half of their troubles."[77]

Sir, the armies of the east of H.M. King Xerxes I continue their steady march in close touch with the fleet.

But now the Greeks, who were fighting tooth and nail amongst themselves, sir, had at last sobered up to the imminent danger rushing at them and ended up forging an alliance of their warring regions and cities. Yet, one must say, sir, that the Greek leaders are terribly disheartened and do not believe that their Greece has any chance against the huge Persian Iranian army of armies of the east of your successor.

King Xerxes I, Persepolis ancient capital of Persia/Iran (image source: photographer Jona Lendering; Site: www.livius.org).

---

[77] Herodotus, *The Histories*, 7:121, P. 481

## August/September 480 BC
## The Last Stand

Gradually, your majesty, a strategy is emerging for the Greek alliance.

The good thinking, sir, says that the only hope for Greece and Europe is to block the narrow mountain pass, which leads to Athens—the hallway in the mountains, which your people, sir, must march through in order to reach Athens city.

And in the sea, the Greeks, sir, decided to send the navy to block the narrow straights—the narrow highways of the sea leading to Athens.

These tight spaces on land and in sea, my lord, would allow a small portion of the soldiers of your successor and a small portion of his ships to go through at any one time. And so this Greek strategy, my lord, does somewhat improve the odds for them, sir.

In fact, my lord, it is so happened that this combination of a narrow mountains pass and a narrow sea straight did indeed exist near Thermopylae by Artemisium. Indeed, the mountain pass at Thermopylae is only fifty feet wide to start, but then it narrows down to a width wide enough for a single wagon track and nothing else.

> "These, then, were the places which the Greeks thought would best suit their purpose … the realization that the Persians would be unable to use their cavalry or take advantage of their numbers, determined then to make their stand at this point against the invader."[78]

Good strategy. Good thinking.

Come hail or sunshine, sir, the Persian Iranian army of your third successor, H.M. King Xerxes I, must try to cross the narrow mountain pass by Thermopylae. And his armada must equally try to sail the narrow straits by Artemisium in their way to sack the cultured city of Athens.

Punishment knows the way to you Athens city.

Unfortunately for the Greek alliance, sir, their good and well-thought-out strategy would not work.

It would not work, sir, even though, once again, a sudden storm that lasted three days had played havoc with the fleet of your people.

> "Four hundred ships, at the lowest estimate, are said to have been lost in the disaster, and the loss of life and of treasure was beyond reckoning."[79]

---

[78] Herodotus, *The Histories*, 7:176, P. 504
[79] Herodotus, *The Histories*, 7:187, P. 508

Speaking of the storm, your majesty King Cyrus, the Greeks once again saw in it the hand of God delaying and weakening your countrymen. Maybe so, but the huge number of the soldiers of your successor, sir, is far from depleted.

> "the [Greek] look-out men ... described in detail the destruction of the Persian ships. On hearing the news, they offered prayers of thanksgiving and libations of wine to Poseidon their saviour ... From that day on to this they have always addressed Poseidon by the title of Saviour."[80]

Today, your army of armies, the armies of the east, sir, and all its recruits from all over the empire have reached the pass of Thermopylae [the hot gates] and began assaulting the fierce Greek Spartans who were guarding it.

Your majesty King Xerxes, your advisors should make sure that you know a thing or two about the rugged and courageous Spartans whom you are facing today, sir. At the very least, sir, they should let you know their motto.

> "never ... retreat ... conquer or die."[81]

Two days, your majesty King Cyrus had passed by and the huge armies of the east accompanying your successor cannot make a headway, none whatsoever, against the much smaller Greek contingent led by the brave Spartans and their lion king, King Leonidas. Two days have passed, sir, without any breakthrough whatsoever!

Soon, your majesty, King Xerxes, soon you will hear what all the Greeks think of this brave man, King Leonidas.

But now, your majesty, King Xerxes, what do you think, sir, could be done to take this impregnable mountain pass of Thermopylae?

Well, it takes a Greek, sir.

> "How to deal with the situation Xerxes had no idea; but just then, a man from Malis, Ephialtes, the son of Eurydemus, came, in hope of a rich reward, to tell the king about the track which led over the hills to Thermopylae."[82]

---

[80] Herodotus, *The Histories*, 7:189, P. 189,190
[81] Herodotus, *The Histories*, 7:107, P. 477
[82] Herodotus, *The Histories*, 7:213, P. 515

A traitor! The traitor, your majesty, King Cyrus the Great, has shown your Iranian countrymen a small mountain trail, which would bring your Iranian soldiers behind the small army of the Greek alliance.

The Greeks, including the brave and elite Spartan troops, would be then sandwiched in the back and in the front.

However, my lord, the news of the betrayal had reached the brave King Leonidas. The brave man, your majesty, sprang to action. Do you know, sir, what is happening behind your lines? Do you know what the brave King Leonidas did, sir?

The Spartan lion, sir, sent all the Greek soldiers away while he, himself, remained with three hundred of his elite Spartan soldiers in order to stem the onslaught of the multitude of your people and their recruits—three hundred soldiers, sir, against innumerable multitude.

What a man, sir! What a patriot of his people, sir! His decision is a sentence of death and he very well knew his doomed fate and that of his courageous elite and patriotic fighters. But the Spartans, your majesty, the Spartans never retreat. Conquer or die.

And today sir, in our modern day, they call this event the greatest last stand in history.

> "For not the strength of lions or of the bulls shall hold him,
> Strength against strength; for he has the power of Zeus,
> And will not be checked till one of these two he has consumed."[83]

> "The merits of these men, who would not regard them with wonder?
>     They with one accord did not desert the post to which Greece had assigned them, but gladly offered upon their own lives for the common salvation of all Greeks, and preferred to die bravely rather than to live shamefully.
>     2 The consternation of the Persians also, no one could doubt that they felt it. For what man among the barbarians could have conceived of that which had taken place?
>     ...
>     Consequently what man of later times might not emulate the valour of those warriors who, finding themselves in the grip of an overwhelming situation, though their bodies were subdued, were not conquered in spirit? These men, therefore, alone of all of whom history records, have in defeat been accorded a greater fame than all others who have won the fairest victories
>     ...

---

[83] Herodotus, *The Histories*, 7:220, P.518

Of those who perished at Thermopylae
All glorious is the fortune, fair the doom;
Their grave's an altar, ceaseless memory's theirs
Instead of lamentation, and their fate
Is chant of praise. Such winding-sheet as this
Nor mould nor all-consuming time shall waste."[84]

The ancient historian Plutarch rebuffs historian Herodotus and gives more details of the action of those heroic Spartan men, sir.

"Now Herodotus, in his narration of that fight, hath obscured also the bravest act of Leonidas, saying that they all fell in the straits near the hill. [Herodotus, vii. 225.]

But the affair was otherwise managed. For when they perceived by night that they were encompassed by the barbarians, they marched straight to the enemies' camp, and got very near the King's pavilion [King Xerxes I's], with a resolution to kill him and leave their lives about him.

They came then to his tent, killing or putting to flight all they met; but when Xerxes was not found there, seeking him in that vast camp and wandering about, they were at last with much difficulty slain by the barbarians, who surrounded them on every side."[85]

A cast of Spartan King Leonidas, Museum of Classical Archaeology, University of Cambridge, UK (image source: author).

But your majesty King Cyrus the great, just as the melody arises for the dead heroes, so does the hate settle deep between the Greeks and the "Barbarians"—the two superpowers of the western and eastern worlds.

All said and done, sir, your third successor, H.M. King Xerxes I, the "barbarian" is today the master of the pass that leads to the bedrooms and playgrounds of Europe.

---

[84] Historian Diodorus Siculus, *Bibliotheca Historica [written 60-30 BC]*, Book 11, Ch.11.1, PP. 2, 6
[85] Historian Plutarch, *The Malice of Herodotus*

The ancient poet, Simonidas of Ceos, wrote on the memorial epitaph of the 300 Spartans who died in battle of Thermopylae: "Go tell the Spartans, strangers passing by, that here obedient to their laws we lie."

The sacrifice of the three hundred Spartans are considered the most famous of history's last stands (image source: Wikipedia, Rafal Slubowski, N. Pantelis).

Now that you broke away, your majesty, King Xerxes I, why not rush ahead and eat the beautiful land of Europe inch by inch and yard by yard, all the way to the heart of Greece!

Carry on your majesty, and despair not because of the thunderstorm of the last few days—you have been plagued with those storms.

Indeed, you may wish to know, sir, that after the three days of skirmishes, along with the awful heavy thunderstorm that wrecked many of your ships in Artemisium, the navy of the Greek alliance has at this moment, sir, cleared out and abandoned the strait by Artemisium. It is over for them and they know it; their land soldiers and their ships are all on the run, my lord, like chicken before a fox.

So now sir, having occupied the strategic land passageway at Thermopylae, why not go on and occupy the narrow highway of the sea by Artemisium? Forward you go, sir, whether heavens like it or not. Nothing is left but a total success.

> "a tremendous thunderstorm ... the wind and rain began, and every [Iranian] ship, overpowered and forced to run blind before it, piled up on the rocks.
> Heaven was indeed doing everything possible <u>to reduce the superiority of the Persian fleet and bring it down to the size of the Greeks</u>."[86]

---

[86] Herodotus, *The Histories*, 8:13, P. 529

We know it is somewhat disheartening, sir, that the gods remain relentless in resisting your invasion with a storm after a storm.

> "a great storm arose and destroyed many [Iranian] ships which were anchored outside the harbour, so that it appeared <u>as if Providence were taking the part of the Greeks</u> in order that, the multitude of the barbarians' ships having been lessened, the Greek force might become a match for them and strong enough to offer battle. As a result the Greeks grew ever more bold, whereas the barbarians became ever more timorous before the conflicts which faced them."[87]

As far as we know, your majesty, King Xerxes I, the Greek navy is dashing full sails to Athens city in order to help evacuating and ferrying the residents of the great city to the nearby island of Salamis.

Athens shall soon be a ghost town, my lord. Punishment, Athens, is on the way.

The way of the youngster of Daniel's prophecy is being prepared, my lords.

> "The Athenians, surveying the dangers threatening each and every inhabitant of Athens, put on boats their children and wives and every useful article they could and brought them to Salamis."[88]

Meanwhile, your majesty, King Xerxes I, go ahead, sir, slash and burn and destroy the beautiful towns and landmarks of Greece.

The goddess Athena, the guardian goddess of the city of Athens and the most revered goddess for all Greeks, Naples Archaeological museum, Italy (image source: author).

But keep in mind, sir, that the flames of the temples and the rape of women shall kindle a burning fire of hatred that shall last for hundreds of years, between the Greeks and your people of Iran. Be prepared, sir, that the Greeks will keep looking and waiting for a day to exact their revenge, sir.

My lords, the frightened residents of the little towns and villages can gawk all they want if they can bear the sight of thousands upon thousands of soldiers of many nationalities marching in endless lines down their streets,

---

[87] Ancient historian Diodorus Siculus, *Bibliotheca Historica*, Book 11, Ch. 13:1
[88] Diodorus Siculus, *Bibliotheca Historica*, Book IX, Ch.13:3

wearing strange uniforms and carrying strange weapons. What a scary and frightening sight it is! These are the enemies; these are the future masters forever.

Some soldiers, my lords, such as the Cissians march along wearing turbans. Then, here come the Caspians and the Sarangians who dress in leather jackets. Following them, here come the Ethiopians in their leopard skins and lion skins, and who smear half their bodies with chalk and half with vermilion blood.

How many of you Greek wives and children knew what the headdress of the eastern Ethiopians warriors look like? Today, you will see and learn that their headdress is made of horses' scalps, stripped off the ears but with the mane attached. And now, here come the Thracians, well you are familiar with them; they are your people. Here they come with their headdress of fox skin. The Thracians betrayed you, and whether the betrayal was out of fear or because of bribes of gold, it does not matter, all said and done they are siding with the "barbarians" against you.

> "everywhere they [the armies of Iran] went was devastation by fire and sword, and towns and temples were burnt ... nothing was spared ... all these places were burnt to the ground, including Abae, where there was a temple of Apollo richly furnished, with treasure and offerings of all kinds ... and some women were raped successively by so many Persian soldiers that they died."[89]

Yes, you too can go ahead, historian Diodorus Siculus, whenever you see it fit to add your report.

> "great fear gripped the other Greeks who, driven from every quarter, were now cooped up in the Peloponnesus alone."[90]

> "the army of the Greeks on land was no whit less terrified by the armament of the enemy, and not only the loss at Thermopylae of their most illustrious warriors caused them dismay, but also the disasters which were taking place in Attica before their very eyes were filling the Greeks with utter despair."[91]

My lords, his Iranian Majesty King Xerxes I may not know this, but the populations of the Greek towns have managed to hide their jewelry and

---

[89] Herodotus, *The Histories*, 8:34, P .535
[90] Ancient historian Diodorus Siculus [c. 60 BC], *Bibliotheca Historica*, Book IX, Ch. 15:2
[91] Historian Diodorus Siculus, *Bibliotheca Historica*, Book IX, Ch. 16:2

valuables in caves nestled in the peaks of the nearby mountains, such as what they are doing today in the Corycian cave up in the summits of Parnassus.

Dancing lesson! Athens, your daily routine is interrupted. This is no time to dance. It is time to fear and mourn, 440-430 BC, The Altes Museum, Berlin, Germany (image source: author).

Greek Necklace with butterfly pendant, late second century BC

"As the symbol of the soul, the butterfly was an appropriate motif for a burial gift." This quote is copied from the Walters Museum of Art, Baltimore, USA (image source: author)

And you may not know, too, your majesty, King Xerxes I, but the Greek alliance, having now completed the evacuation of their women and children from Athens city to the Isle of Salamis, are at this moment holding a council of war to decide what to do next.

What can they do, your majesty, after their disasters in the mountain pass of Thermopylae and the narrow sea straights of Artemisium?

Indeed, the news is streaming steadily to them, sir, that their entire beautifully decorated country is on fire in a "wholesale devastation."

Let them panic, sir. But as for you, your majesty, King Xerxes I, the highways are empty and wide open to Athens city and to its Acropolis, which incidentally, sir, the Greeks believe is guarded by a great snake. Let us see what this great snake can do to stop your army of armies, sir.

Snake or not, punishment is on the way.

And you may as well wake up the youngster.

Prophet Daniel, you have seen all of these coming sir—haven't you? But, how?

The Parthenon of the goddess Athena was used as the treasury. It was reconstructed in 447 BC following its destruction by the Persians (image source: author).

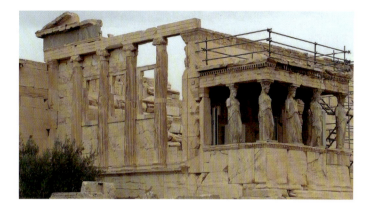

The Erechtheum temple and porch of the Caryatids of the Acropolis is one of the ancient treasures of Athens (421-407 BC) (image source: author).

The Ancient Greek Acropolis of Athens as viewed from the Mouseion Hill (image source: Christophe Meneboeuf).

My lords, it is three months already—three busy months since his majesty's troops of the armies of the east crossed the Hellespont to the shores of Europe.

> "The Persians found Athens itself abandoned except for a few people in the temple of Athens Polias – temple stewards and needy folk, who had barricaded the Acropolis against the invaders with planks and timbers ... The Persians occupied the hill which the Athenians call the Areopagus, opposite the Acropolis."[92]

---

[92] Herodotus, *The Histories*, 8:49, P. 540

Your majesties, the Acropolis, the landmark of Athens, has been sacked.

> "[t]hey stripped the temple of its treasures and burnt everything on the Acropolis. Xerxes, now absolute master of Athens, dispatched a rider to Susa [ancient capital of Iran] with news ... of his success."[93]

Now, my lords, we can tell you that this event alone shall seal itself indelibly in the mind of the did once he comes alive. The world, my lords, has not yet seen his like.

The kid, sculptured around 340-330 BC, Acropolis Museum, Athens, Greece (image source: author).

---

[93] Herodotus, *The Histories*, 8:54, P. 541

But for the moment, do please cut in, prophet Daniel, one more time with your old and unlikely prophecy about the "race of slaves," as the Persians called themselves.

> DAN 8:3 *Then I lifted up mine eyes, and saw, and, behold, there stood before the river a ram [The Persian Iranian Empire] which had two horns [Media and Persia]: and the two horns were high; but one was higher than the other, and the higher came up last [the Medians came first and the Persians revolted and rose to power after].*
> DAN 8:4 *I saw the ram [Media and Persia i.e. Iran] <u>pushing westward</u> [towards Greece and Europe], and northward [towards Armenia], and southward [towards Egypt where part of their army was presumed lost]; so that no beasts [other countries or kingdoms] might stand before him [the Persian Empire of Iran], neither was there any that could deliver out of his hand; but he did according to his will, and became great [the great Persian Empire, one of the greatest in the history of the world. Daniel saw this unlikely rise of Iran, the race of slaves, ahead of time.]*
> DAN 11:2 *Behold, there shall stand up yet three kings in Persia; and the fourth shall be far richer than they all: and by his strength through his riches he shall stir up all against the realm of Grecia.*

King Xerxes I, here is confidential information for you, sir. The panicking generals of the Greek alliance are arguing back and forth trying to agree on a war strategy, but cannot come to an agreement on anything.

Perhaps, sir, this is how panicking people, even hardened generals facing the loss of everything, act.

They are actually shouting at each other sir; the Corinthian Adeimantus is basically telling the most skilled commander of the navy to shut up.

He may shut up if they wish, sir. But as the days and nights change places, the generals' desperate situation is becoming much worse, even though they know it not. They have no inklings, sir, that they are being trapped.

But, your majesty, King Xerxes I, this trap of yours is a terrible mistake––a huge, huge mistake—if we may say so, sir.

Yes, my lords, without any argument the Greeks are superior to the Persians in sea wars, as men are superior to women, if we may, my lords, quote an Iranian Persian commander in the service of his Iranian majesty King Xerxes I.

> "The Greek commanders at [the island of] Salamis were still at loggerheads. They did not yet know that the enemy ships had blocked their escape at both ends of the channel."[94]

Meanwhile, my lords, the cooped-up Greek population, packed together on the island of Salamis, was gripped and frozen with terror. When shall they ever go back home? And how much of home is left?

> "Certainly the fear that was upon them must have made them believe that they saw many things which they saw not, and heard many that they did not hear. What supplications, what reminders of sacrifices, were not sent up to Heaven! What pity was felt for children, what yearning over wives, what compassion for fathers and mothers, in calculating the evils that would result from their ill success!"[95]

The Greek situation on the island of Salamis, trapped by the Persian navy on both ends of the channel, is more than desperate, my lords; it is fatal.

### *Worse than a Woman*

An Iranian commander urged King Xerxes I not to engage the Greeks in a sea battle off the island of Salamis saying,

> "Spare your ships and do not fight at sea, for the Greeks are as far superior to us in naval matters as men are to women."[96]

And there was the incident when one of the sons of King Darius had labeled his defeated general worse than a woman, which is the worst insult for to an Iranian man.

> "To call a man 'worse than a woman' is, of course, the greatest insult one can offer a Persian."[97]

---

[94] Herodotus, *The Histories*, 8:73, P. 548
[95] Ancient Greek speech writer Lysias [b.459 BC] 2:39
[96] Herodotus, *The Histories*, 8:67, P. 547
[97] Herodotus, *The Histories*, 9:105, P. 619

## Hell is Full of Them

Over a thousand years after King Xerxes I, the Arabian prophet Muhammad had an unfavorable take on women as well.

In this instance, Aisha, the child wife of the prophet, admonished him that he had made women equal to dogs, or donkeys for that matter.

> *Bukhari*, 1, 9, 490
>
> Narrated 'Aisha:
> "Prayer is annulled by a dog, a donkey and a woman (if they pass in front of the praying people)."
> I said, "<u>You have made us (i.e. women) dogs</u>.

> *Bukhari*, 9, 486
>
> Narrated 'Aisha:
> Do you make us <u>(women) equal to dogs and donkeys</u>?

Umar in the following quote is one of the two chief believers of Muhammad and was his second successor.

> *Dawud*, 41, 5119
>
> A woman was my wife and I loved her, but Umar hated her. He said to me: Divorce her, but I refused. Umar then went to the Prophet (pbuh) and mentioned that to him. The Prophet (pbuh) said: <u>Divorce her</u>.

> *Dawud*, 11, 2142
>
> The Prophet (pbuh) said: <u>A man will not be asked as to why he beat his wife</u>.

## The Back of the Bus

> *Dawud*, 41, 5252
>
> AbuUsayd heard the Apostle of Allah (pbuh) say when he was coming out of the mosque, and men and women were mingled in the road: Draw back, for <u>you must not walk in the middle of the road; keep to the sides of the road</u>. Then women were keeping so close to the wall that their garments were rubbing against it.

> *Al-Tirmidhi*, 963
>
> Once when Allah's Messenger (pbuh) ... said... If I were to order anyone to prostrate himself before another, I should order a woman to prostrate herself before her husband. If he were to order her to convey stones from a yellow mountain to a black one, or from a black mountain to a white one, it would be incumbent on her to do so."

Yet at least one woman did not fear to confront him while he was on his death bed.

> *Bukhari*, 6, 60, 475
>
> Once Allah's Apostle became sick and could not offer his night prayer (Tahajjud) for two or three nights. Then a lady (the wife of Abu Lahab) came and said, "O Muhammad! <u>I think that your Satan has forsaken you</u>, for I have not seen him with you for two or three nights!"

Yet the man was quite sensual and desired as many women as he could sexually. In fact, he had a very unpleasant encounter with two of them who turned down his sexual advances.

> *Bukhari*, 7, 63, 182
>
> We went out with the Prophet to a garden called Ash-Shaut till we reached two walls between which we sat down.
> The Prophet said, "Sit here," and went in (the garden). The Jauniyya (a lady from Bani Jaun) had been brought and lodged in a house in a date-palm garden in the home of Umaima bint An-Nu'man bin Sharahil, and her wet nurse was with her.
> When the Prophet entered upon her, he said to her, "<u>Give me yourself as a gift</u>."
> She said, "Can a princess give herself in marriage to an ordinary man?"
> The Prophet raised his hand to pat her so that she might become tranquil.
> She said, "I seek refuge with Allah from you."
> ...
> Then the Prophet came out to us and said, "O Abu Usaid! Give her two white linen dresses to wear and let her go back to her family."
> Narrated Sahl and Abu Usaid: The Prophet ... stretched his hand towards her. It seemed that she disliked that, whereupon the Prophet ordered Abu Usaid to prepare her and to provide her with two white linen dresses.

> *Bukhari*, 7, 69, 541
>
> An Arab lady was mentioned to the Prophet so he asked Abu Usaid As-Sa'idi to send for her, and he sent for her and she came and stayed in the castle of Bani Sa'ida. The Prophet came out and went to her and entered upon her. Behold, it was a lady sitting with a drooping head. When the Prophet spoke to her, she said, "<u>I seek refuge with Allah from you</u>."

> *Bukhari*, 8, 73, 123
>
> <u>The Prophet did something and allowed his people to do it, but some people refrained from doing it</u>. When the Prophet learned of that, he delivered a sermon, and after having sent Praises to Allah, he said, "What is wrong with such people as refrain from doing a thing that I do? By Allah, I know Allah better than they, and I am more afraid of Him than they."

Indeed, the prophet allocated the best-looking women that his Mujahedeen have captured in their raids for himself. This included a young Jewish woman, Safiya by name, whose bridegroom husband and her parents were killed in the raid on the Jewish fortress of Khaibar in Saudi Arabia.

The frightened young woman was mourning her losses and was also menstruating. But the prophet wished to have intercourse with her on the same night she was captured.

Nonetheless, his child-wife Aisha reproached him and prevented him from doing so. Indeed, Aisha had sarcastically told him that Allah always hurries to send Koranic verses, allowing him to enjoy women. Indeed, he himself has indicated in the Koran that he has a special privilege from Allah to enjoy whichever woman he desired.

> *Bukhari*, 4, 52, 143
>
> The prophet ... when Allah enabled him to conquer the Fort (of Khaibar), the beauty of Safiya bint Huyai bin Akhtab was described to him. Her husband had been killed while she was a bride. So Allah's Apostle selected her for himself and took her along with him.
>
> *Bukhari*, 1, 8, 367
>
> 'When Allah's Apostle invaded Khaibar ... When he entered the town, he said, 'Allahu Akbar! Khaibar is ruined ... We conquered Khaibar, took the captives, and the booty was collected. Dihya came and said, 'O Allah's Prophet! Give me a slave girl from the captives.' The Prophet said, 'Go and take any slave girl.' He took Safiya bint Huyai.
> A man came to the Prophet and said, 'O Allah's Apostles! You gave Safiya bint Huyai to Dihya and she is the chief mistress of the tribes of Quraiza and An-Nadir and she befits none but you.'
> So the Prophet said, 'Bring him along with her.' So Dihya came with her and when the Prophet saw her, he said to Dihya, 'Take any slave girl other than her from the captives.'
>
> *Bukhari*, 7, 62, 48
>
> Khaula bint Hakim was one of those ladies who presented themselves to the Prophet for marriage.
> 'Aisha said, "Doesn't a lady feel ashamed for presenting herself to a man?"
> But when the Verse: "(O Muhammad) You may postpone (the turn of) any of them (your wives) that you please,' (33.51) was revealed, " 'Aisha said, 'O Allah's Apostle! I do not see, but, that your Lord hurries in pleasing you.' "
>
> *The Koran*, the Clans 33:50
>
> O Prophet! Lo! We have made lawful unto thee thy wives unto whom thou hast paid their dowries, and those whom thy right hand possesseth of those whom Allah hath given thee as spoils of war, and the daughters of thine uncle on the father's side and the daughters of thine aunts on the father's side, and the daughters of thine uncle on the mother's side and the daughters of thine aunts on the mother's side who emigrated with thee, and

> a believing woman if she give herself unto the Prophet and the Prophet desire to ask her in marriage-<u>a privilege for thee only, not for the (rest of) believers</u>
>
> But other than the sexual attraction, the Arabian prophet considered women to be of low intelligence and also evil. Hell will be full of them.
>
> *Bukhari, 1, 6, 301*
>
> Once Allah's Apostle ... passed by the women and said, "O women! Give alms, as I have seen that <u>the majority of the dwellers of Hell-fire were you (women)</u>."
> They asked, "Why is it so, O Allah's Apostle ?"
> He replied, "You curse frequently and are ungrateful to your husbands. I have not seen anyone more <u>deficient in intelligence and religion than you. A cautious sensible man could be led astray by some of you</u>."
> The women asked, "O Allah's Apostle! What is deficient in our intelligence and religion?"
> He said, "Is not the evidence of two women equal to the witness of one man?"
> They replied in the affirmative.
> He said, "This is the deficiency in her intelligence. Isn't it true that a woman can neither pray nor fast during her menses?"
> The women replied in the affirmative.
> He said, "This is the deficiency in her religion."
>
> *Al-Tirmidhi, 927*
>
> Allah's Messenger (pbuh) saw a woman who charmed him, so he went to Sawdah who was making perfume in the company of some women. They left him, and after he had satisfied his desire he said, "If any man sees a woman who charms him he should go to his wife, for she has the same kind of thing as the other woman."
>
> *Bukhari, 8, 73, 97*
>
> Anas bin Malik said, "<u>Any of the female slaves of Medina could take hold of the hand of Allah's Apostle and take him wherever she wished</u>."

Well, if you can believe this, my lords, the commanders of the allied Greek fleet have finally come to an agreement. They have decided to take a risk and fight the larger Iranian fleet in the narrow straight off the island of Salamis. And they had, or so they believed, a good reason for their decision, my lords. And of course you are at liberty, your majesties, and commanders, to judge their reason for yourselves.

> "[w]e shall be fighting in narrow waters, and there, with our inferior numbers, we shall win, provided things go as we reasonably expect.

Fighting in a confined space favours us but the open sea favours the enemy."[98]

## September 480 BC Salamis Says It All

It was bound to happen, my lords. And it had nothing to do with the gods, unless they knew how to disperse wisdom to the Greeks and shortsightedness to the Iranians.

> **Becoming Intelligent**
>
> JAS 1:5 *If any of you lack wisdom, let him ask of God, that giveth to all men liberally [generously], and upbraideth [criticizes] not; <u>and it shall be given him</u>.*

At any rate, my lords, the strategy of his Iranian majesty King Xerxes I has backfired.

"[t]he Greek fleet worked together as a whole, while the Persians had lost formation and were no longer fighting on any plan, that was what was bound to happen ... the Persian fleet had lost all semblance of order."[99]

Please cut in, historian Diodorus Siculus.

"The Persians, as they advanced, could at the outset maintain their line, since they had plenty of space; but when they came to the narrow passage, they were compelled to withdraw some ships from the line, creating in this way much disorder.
    5 The admiral, who was leading the way before the line and was the first to begin the fighting, was slain after having acquitted himself valiantly. When his ship went down, disorder seized the barbarian fleet, for there were many now to give orders, but each man did not issue the same commands. Consequently they halted the advance, and holding back their ships, they began to withdraw to where there was plenty of room.
    6 The Athenians, observing the disorder among the barbarians, now advanced upon the enemy, and some of their ships they struck with their rams, while from others they sheared off the rows of oars; and when the men at the oars could no longer do their work, many Persian triremes [war ships], getting sidewise to the enemy, were time and again severely damaged by the beaks of the ships.

---

[98] Herodotus, *The Histories*, 8:62, P. 543
[99] Herodotus, *The histories*, 8:85, P. 552

Consequently they ceased merely backing water, but turned about and fled precipitately."[100]

Greek warships, ruins of Pompeii, Italy, Naples National Archaeological Museum, Italy (images source: author).

The barbarian enemy was in hopeless confusion. And the Greeks "were forced to the conclusion that the hand of God was in the matter ... the prayers of Greece are being answered."[101]

On the run!

Slow down your Majesty king Xerxes I. Slow down, sir.

No.

Panic is taking hold of his majesty, who is now afraid of getting trapped in Europe.

> "Xerxes, when he realized the extent of the disaster, was afraid that the Greeks ... might sail to the Hellespont [the narrow water strait that separates Europe from Asia] and break the [Persian constructed] bridges here. If this happened, he would be cut off in Europe and in danger of destruction. Accordingly, he laid his plans for escape.
>
> ...

---

[100] Ancient historian Diodorus Siculus, *Bibliotheca Historica*, Book IX, Ch. 18:3
[101] Herodotus, *The Histories*, 8:95, P. 555

> Mardonius [the general of the Iranian army] could see that <u>Xerxes took the defeat at Salamis very hard</u>."[102]

Naturally, my lords, the Persian Iranian commanders did their best to console their heartbroken king.

> "[t]he object of your campaign accomplished – for you have burnt Athens."[103]

But here is the good news, my lords. His majesty and part of the remnant of the mixed armies of the east managed to leave the European shore behind, have safely crossed the Hellespont, gone back to the Asian shore, and finally to the city of Sardis of Lydia.

Rest assured, my lords, H.M. King Xerxes I has not given up on the dream of possessing Europe just yet. His good general Mardonius has asked his master to let him choose 300,000 soldiers to stay behind with him at the borders of Greece. And his plan, my lords, was to reinvade Greece again once the weather allows it.

Meanwhile, these hand-picked 300,000 soldiers would set camp at the borders of Europe, and train and prepare themselves for the next invasion. As for what is left of the navy, it too shall winter nearby and get ready for the return of the good weather. Athens, it is not over yet.

"I am Xerxes, the great king, the king of kings, the king of the lands, king of all the languages, king of the great and large land, the son of king Darius the Achaemenian." King Xerxes, son of King Darius I, sacked and burned Athens City of Greece. WC, <u>Bjørn Christian Tørrissen</u>

---

[102] Herodotus, *The Histories*, 8:97 & 100, P.P. 555, 556
[103] Herodotus, *The Histories*, 8:99, P. 558

## Xerxes, Husband of Esther?

King Xerxes I was about 36-years-old at the time of ascending the throne [October–December 486 BC.].

Almost immediately, he succeeded to subdue Egypt following its previous year rebellion against his father, King Darius I. Indeed, he also appointed his brother Achaemenes as the new governor of Egypt. Thus, his borders, the borders of the Persian Empire, stretched all the way to Ethiopia, south of Egypt [the African region surrounding present-day Sudan, starting at the borders of Egypt, as was called Ethiopia in those days].

He did also manage to quash a rebellion in Babylon, today's southern Iraq [484 BC], where he had angered the population by melting down the golden statue of their main god Bel.

Following these two major successes, he then turned his face to invade Greece.

And so on the third year of his reign, please underline the third year that King Xerxes I began to call himself "king of nations," meaning *king of the world*.

This may line up with the biblical event mentioned in the Book of Esther regarding Persian King Ahasuerus, and thus would lead us to think that the two are one and the same.

The biblical book of Esther does say that by the third year of his reign, King Ahasuerus ruled from India to Ethiopia. And that in his third year, which would be the time he had successfully subdued Egypt, Ethiopia, and Babylon, he held a national feast, perhaps to celebrate those two great victories. His feast lasted six months and gathered important leaders from all over his extended domain.

> Est 1:1 Now it came to pass in the days of Ahasuerus, this is Ahasuerus which reigned, from India even <u>unto Ethiopia</u>, over an hundred and seven and twenty provinces.
> Est 1:3 <u>In the third year of his reign [483 BC]</u>, he made a feast unto all his princes and his servants; the power of Persia and Media, the nobles and princes of the provinces, being before him.
> Est 1:4 When he shewed the riches of his glorious kingdom and the honour of his excellent majesty many days, even an hundred and fourscore [180] days.

Indeed, the ancient Persian Daiva inscription lists the same countries as the Bible to be under the rule of King Xerxes I, thus giving further credence to the possibility that the two names belong to the same king.

**PREVIOUS PAGE:**

The ancient Persian Daiva inscriptions, http://www.livius.org/aa-ac/achaemenians/XPh.html

1. "A great god is Ahuramazda, who created this earth, who created yonder sky, who created man, who created happiness for man, who made Xerxes king, one king of many, one lord of many.

2. I am Xerxes, the great king, king of kings, king of countries containing many kinds of men, king in this great earth far and wide, son of king Darius, an Achaemenian, a Persian, son of a Persian, an Aryan, of Aryan stock.

3. King Xerxes says: By the grace of Ahuramazda these are the countries of which I was king apart from Persia. I had lordship over them. They bore me tribute. What was said to them by me, that they did.

My law, that held them: Media, Elam, Arachosia, Armenia, Drangiana, Parthia, Aria, Bactria, Sogdia, Chorasmia, Babylonia, Assyria, Sattagydia, Lydia, Egypt, Yaunā, those who dwell on this side of the sea and those who dwell across the sea, men of Maka, Arabia, Gandara, India, Cappadocia, the Dahae, the haoma-drinking Sacae, the Sacae wearing pointed caps, Thrace, men of ◆kaufaciy◆, Libyans, Carians, and the Nubians.[104]

## *483 BC  Final Days of Celebration*

*Est 1:5* And when these days were expired, the king made a feast unto all the people that were present in Shushan [Susa, the capital city] the palace, both unto great and small, seven days, in the court of the garden of the king's palace;

*Est 1:6* Where were white, green, and blue, hangings, fastened with cords of fine linen and purple to silver rings and pillars of marble: the beds were of gold and silver, upon a pavement of red, and blue, and white, and black, marble.

*Est 1:7* And they gave them drink in vessels of gold, (the vessels being diverse one from another,) and royal wine in abundance, according to the state of the king.

*Est 1:10* On the seventh day, when the heart of the king was merry with wine [drunk], he commanded Mehuman, Biztha, Harbona, Bigtha, and Abagtha, Zethar, and Carcas, the seven chamberlains that served in the presence of Ahasuerus the king,

*Est 1:11* To bring Vashti the queen before the king with the crown royal, to shew the people and the princes her beauty: for she was fair to look on.

*Est 1:12* But the queen Vashti refused to come at the king's commandment by his chamberlains: therefore was the king very wroth, and his anger burned in him.

*Est 2:2* Then said the king's servants that ministered unto him, Let there be fair young virgins sought for the king:

---

[104] http://www.livius.org/aa-ac/achaemenians/XPh.html

> Est 2:3 *And let the king appoint officers in all the provinces of his kingdom, that they may gather together all the fair young virgins unto Shushan the palace, to the house of the women, unto the custody of Hege the king's chamberlain, keeper of the women; and let their things for purification be given them:*
> Est 2:4 *And let the maiden which pleaseth the king be queen instead of Vashti. And the thing pleased the king; and he did so.*
> Est 2:14 *In the evening she went, and on the morrow she returned into the second house of the women [harem], to the custody of Shaashgaz, the king's chamberlain, which kept the concubines: she came in unto the king no more, except the king delighted in her, and that she were called by name.*

## 480 BC

The king then went on to invade Greece [480 BC]. A couple of years after his return, an exiled Israeli young woman by the name of Esther was brought to him. The king loved her above all the rest and crowned her as his queen.

In summary, King Xerxes ascended the throne in 486/485 BC, had his great celebration in 484/483 BC, invaded Greece in 480 BC, returned to his capital Susa in the same year, and married Esther in the year 478 BC, which is about two years after his defeat in Greece.

> Est 2:16 *So Esther was taken unto king Ahasuerus into his house royal in the tenth month, which is the month Tebeth, in the <u>seventh year of his reign</u> [this would be 478 BC as he became king at the start of 485 BC. The Battle of Salamis took place in 480 BC].*
> Est 2:17 *And the king loved Esther above all the women, and she obtained grace and favour in his sight more than all the virgins; so that he set the royal crown upon her head, and made her queen instead of Vashti.*

## 479 BC
## Foreign Trash

My lords, an opportunity is knocking.

Once again, the fiercest enemies of the Persian Iranians, the brave and hardy Spartans, are celebrating a high religious holiday, which is to last two weeks, and in which they are forbidden to take up arms.

The highway to Athens is now open and the opportunity is tempting.

And here is the strategy for working the opportunity, my lords.

The leaders of the different cities of Greece are back now at each other's throat. Danger unites them; peace divides them. And the Iranians, your majesties, have gold and money to spare. Why not, my lords, bribe Greek leaders and generals against each other? Divide and conquer, my lords.

LEFT: Persian coins from Sardes; gold Daric (from Darius) domination, and silver Siglos of the Persian empire, about 500 BC, British Museum, London (image source: author). RIGHT: Gold Daric from the reign of King Xerxes I, Archaeological Museum of Vienna/Austria (image source: author).

The bribing strategy worked, my lords. Where the sword fails, gold triumphs every time, your majesties.

Today, ten months after H.M. King Xerxes I had captured Athens, General Mardonius and his picked and chosen 300,000 soldiers, along with the navy, are dashing once again through divided and bribed Greece, and heading straight for Athens City while the hardy Spartans are celebrating their feast.

The Iranian army is now in Athens city, my lords.

But the feast is now over, my lords, and the Spartans are taking to the field.

There it goes again, my lords.

A runner is carrying the disappointing message to the Persian general. And the Persian general can do no better than turn on his heel—it is time to leave.

This is not a place for a cavalry war, my lords, and horses, your majesties, are the main strength of the Persian army. Well then, your majesties, there was one thing left to do to Athens and to the Greek population.

The youngster, the kid, is more than one hundred years away now.

"Before he [Persian General Mardonius] went, he burnt Athens and reduced to complete ruin anything that remained standing – walls, houses, temples, and all."[105]

---

[105] Herodotus, *The Histories*, 9:13, P. 581

# THE UNEQUAL TWO HORNS OF IRAN—335

Born July 20/21, 356 BC, the kid still 123 years away, Wien Museum, Vienna, Austria (image source: author).

What now? Who can tell H.M. King Xerxes I what the Europeans and the Greeks really think of the Iranian Persians at heart? Who can?

> "Let us show them that the men they have plotted to murder are Greeks – and they themselves mere foreign trash."[106]

But the strange thing, my lords, and it is the thing that even H.M. King Xerxes I himself has not heard, is that the middle and low ranks of his troops were and are convinced that they will never win against the Greeks. Never! Why? Well, my lords, hear for yourselves the words of one of the Persian commanders and please keep his words, which he is confiding to a Greek, confidential.

> "My friend" rejoined the other, "What God has ordained no man can by any means prevent. Many of us know that what I have said is true; yet, because we cannot do otherwise, we continue to take orders from our commander."[107]

## You Are Not Equal

Foreign trash.
You are not equal. The slave and the free are not equal. Men and women are not equal. Greeks and Barbarians are not equal. The educated and the

---

[106] Herodotus, *The histories*, 9:17, P. 583
[107] Herodotus, *The Histories*, 9:15, P. 583

> uneducated are not equal in God's sight. Jews and Arabs are not equal. No. They are not equal.
>
> You are one. You are one and the same.
>
> Blacks and whites are not equal. They are one and the same in the affection of Christ the Lord.
>
> > <sup>Col 3:11</sup> There is neither Greek nor Jew, circumcision nor uncircumcision [Jews or non-Jews], Barbarian, Scythian, bond [slave] nor free: but Christ is all, and in all.
> > <sup>Gal 3:28</sup> There is neither Jew nor Greek, there is neither bond nor free, there is neither male nor female: for ye are all one in Christ Jesus.
> >
> > <sup>1 Sam 16:7</sup> The LORD said unto Samuel, Look not on his countenance [face and appearance], or on the height of his stature ... for the LORD seeth not as man seeth; for man looketh on the outward appearance, but the LORD looketh on the heart.

# Plataea and Mycale

As for now, my lords, the Greeks are once more united. They are marching right on the heels of the Iranians and intend to sit camp near the city of Plataea.

They had arrived there, my lords.

The two armies are now standing their distance and have been watching each other for the past ten days. Neither side is daring to take any action.

Today, on the eleventh day, your majesties, the Iranians attacked the starving and thirsty Greeks. The Greeks got the worst of it, my lords, but managed to slip away at night to get near waters. And near the waters, my lords, the terrain was not suitable for the deployment of the Iranian cavalry, the horse regiment.

Be that as it may, they are at it again, my lords.

Hold everything now.

Major news, my lords—major!

A fearless Spartan has managed to break through the Iranian ranks and kill the Iranian General Mardonius, no less.

We might as well, my commanders, say it is all over for the Iranian Persians. Not only for the Iranian army but for the Iranian navy as well, and you shall see why, my lords, if you may wait a minute.

Please cut in once again, historian Herodotus, when you feel applicable. Thank you, sir!

"The Persian troops fled in disorder and took refuge in their wooden fort."[108]

Now the fight for the strong Persian camp, or fort, was very violent, my lords, but the Greeks at last sacked it. And what a gold mine this Iranian camp or fort was, my lords!

"[They] went through the whole camp. Treasure was there in plenty––tents full of gold and silver furniture; couches overlaid with the same precious metals, bowls, goblets, and cups, all of gold: and wagons loaded with sacks full of gold and silver basins.

From the bodies of the dead they stripped anklets and chains and golden-hilted scimitars ... When all the stuff had been collected, a tenth was set apart for the God at Delphi, and from this was made the gold tripod which stands next to the altar on the three-headed bronze snake."[109]

Ottoman miniature of the three intertwined snakes carrying the altar, from the Surname-i Vehbi (image source: Wikipedia, Bilkent University).

---

[108] Herodotus, *The Histories*, Book 9, P. 613.
[109] Herodotus, *The Histories*, Book 9, P. 613.

The Serpent Column (Battle of Plataea 479 BC, relocated to Istanbul by Emperor Constantine the Great in 324 BC, Istanbul/Turkey (image source: author).

"This column is formed by three intertwined bronze serpents and was dedicated to Apollo by the 31 Greek city states, which defeated the Persians in the battle of Plataea in 479 BC."

Bronze head of one of the three snakes from the column at the Hippodrome, Istanbul Archaeological Museum (image source: Wikipedia, Gryffindor).

The Iranian army has been wiped out at Plataea, my lords, by the coalition of thirty-one united Greek cities. But what about the Iranian navy, you may ask, your majesties?

Well, the Greek navy prior to the battle of Plataea, my lords, had left the island of Salamis for the second time and went chasing after the Persian navy. Skill was chasing after numbers, my lords.

The Iranians, not willing to have anymore sea battles with the Greek alliance had decided, your majesties, to beach their ships and fence them in near Mycale.

The Persians, because of their huge number of soldiers, my lords, had every intention under the sun to limit their fights on land against the Greeks near Plataea. But unfortunately for the Iranians, this strategy may have worked any day but not today, my lords. We shall let historian Herodotus carry on with what happened next your majesties.

> "[a] rumor flew through the ranks that the Greeks had beaten Mardonius in Boeotia [outside Plataea]. Many things make it plain to me that the hand of God is active in human affairs—for how else could it be, when the Persian defeat at Mycale was about to take place on the same day as his defeat in Plataea, that a rumor of that kind should reach the Greek army [all the way from Plataea to Mycale in the same day], giving everyman greater courage for the coming battle and a fiercer determination to risk his life for the

country? ... once the good news came, they moved to assault with better heart and quicker pace."[110]

It was a close call. It was a near-death experience for the Greeks, my lords. But Greece and Europe were saved to breathe the sweet scent of freedom and keep their culture for yet another day. And who knows how long shall the day be? How long this bloody rivalry between these two strong antagonists could last?

The answer, my lords, is that it shall last until Daniel's prophecy is fulfilled—the prophecy that shall be the first page of three hundred pages or years of prophecies.

It is indeed obvious, my lords, that if you wish to put an end to this bloody rivalry between Iran and Greece, then one of the two antagonists must be totally annihilated. Thus, my lords, we should brace ourselves for more wars and invasions. The Middle East desires what Europe has to offer, but Europe refuses to give.

As for now, my lords, we will have to be the bearers of bad news.

Following this series of disastrous defeats against the Greeks, H.M. King Xerxes I has been assassinated by none less than the commander of his body guard, his son. How sad!

Meanwhile, my lords, Daniel's people say that the plan of God and the schedule of God carry on uninterrupted. They say it is known unto God all His plans from the beginning of the world. And He had decided in advance the boundaries of the Greeks and the boundaries of the Iranians.

> ACTS 15:18 *Known unto God are all his works from the beginning of the world.*
> ACTS 17:26 *[God] hath made of one blood all nations of men for to dwell on all the face of the earth, and <u>hath determined the times [the schedule] before appointed, and the bounds [boundaries] of their habitation [dwelling]</u>*

But it is now time, my lords, that we turn the pages of time fast in order to reach another important date. It is one of those counting dates that we can use to add and subtract in order to reach, once again, the greatest event for mankind—adoption.

---

[110] Herodotus, *The Histories*, 9:99, P. 616

## THE UNEQUAL TWO HORNS OF IRAN—341

One school of thought maintains that this one-of-its kind silver decadrachms was minted to celebrate the Athenians victory in Salamis and Plataea, particularly that it was minted shortly after the two battles. The obverse side shows the goddess Athena, while the reverse side shows the owl, the sacred bird of Athens, in a unique pose. The Numismatic Museum of Athens, Greece (image source: author).

## MONEY IS MIGHTIER THAN THE SWORD

**465-424 BC**
**Artaxerxes I**

Your majesties, following the assassination of H.M. King Xerxes I, his son King Artaxerxes I became the new king of Persia [Iran]—the fifth on the throne of Iran after H.M. King Cyrus the great.

King Cyrus the great, my lords, was followed by his son King Cambyses I, who defeated Egypt but lost an army there; then imposter King Tonyoaxarces, who nearly restored the throne to the Medians out of the hands of the Persians; and then H.M. King Darius I of Marathon, who prepared the Persian armies to attack Greece and Europe; and then H.M. King Xerxes I of Salamis, who failed to defeat Greece and rule Europe.

We can tell you, your majesties, that exhaustion and hopelessness have taken their natural course on the two sordid enemies and that the war efforts are suspended these days between Iran and Greece.

Meanwhile, the prophecies are closing in on the counting date.

**458 BC**

Meanwhile your majesties, the day H.M. King Artaxerxes I took the throne of Iran [465 BC] is the day that marks fifty years since the house of the Lord was completed in Jerusalem city [516 BC], as was permitted by his Iranian majesty, King Darius I, of the Battle of Marathon.

Today, at this point of time your majesties, a high-ranking Israeli priest, exiled in Iran, and whose name is Ezra, has appeared before H.M. King Artaxerxes I.

Priest Ezra is asking his majesty for permission to travel to Israel and take with him as many exiled Israelites as he can, in accordance with the decree of H.M. King Cyrus the great and his successor, King Darius I.

His majesty King Artaxerxes I gave the permission, my lords. And the journey of another wave of the exiled children of Israel began homeward.

It took nearly four months, my lords, for priest Ezra and his company of exiles to reach Jerusalem from Babylon of southern Iraq. However, Ezra and his companions, my lords, are carrying with them a large amount of money in gold and silver coins to pay for the finishing touches of the parliament of God.

This large company of the children of Israel, my lords, is the largest wave of returning exiles. And it took place, my lords, eighty long years after the first one [538 BC], which was authorized by H.M. King Cyrus the great.

We should also add, my lords, that it took place nearly fifty-eight years after the building [516/515 BC] of the house, the parliament of God.

Go ahead, please, Priest Ezra and Governor Nehemiah, whenever you feel it is appropriate.

> EZRA 7:1 Now after these things, <u>in the reign of Artaxerxes king of Persia</u>, Ezra the son of Seraiah, the son of Azariah, the son of Hilkiah,
> EZRA 7:6 This Ezra went up from Babylon; and he was a ready scribe [expert] in the law of Moses ... and the king granted him all his request
> EZRA 7:7 And there went up some of the children of Israel, and of the priests, and the Levites, and the singers, and the porters, and the Nethinims, unto Jerusalem, <u>in the seventh year of Artaxerxes the king</u> [458 BC].
> ...
> EZRA 7:11 Now this is the copy of the letter that the king Artaxerxes gave unto Ezra the priest, the scribe
> EZRA 7:12 Artaxerxes, king of kings, unto Ezra the priest, a scribe of the law of the God of heaven, perfect peace, and at such a time.
> EZRA 7:13 I make a decree, that all they of the people of Israel, and of his priests and Levites, in my realm, which are minded of their own freewill to go up to Jerusalem, go with thee.
> ...
> EZRA 8:36 And they delivered the king's commissions unto the king's lieutenants, and to the governors on this side the river [the Iranian governors of the region]: and they furthered the people [advanced their work], and the house of God.

"Silver bowl with inscription of Artaxerxes I...'Artaxerxes, the great king, king of kings, king of countries, son of Xerxes the king ... son of Darius the king.'" The quote is taken from the British Museum, where the above silver drinking bowl is housed (image source: author).

## 445 BC
## A Counting Date

Thirteen years, my lords, after the scribe and priest Ezra was authorized to return to Israel, another Israelite, a royal valet by the name of Nehemiah, in the service of his kind Iranian majesty King Artaxerxes I, did also ask his sovereign a permission for a time off to travel to Israel.

Nehemiah's intent, my lords, was to rebuild the protective walls of Jerusalem city. This is very important, my lords.

His kind Iranian majesty went ahead with the request and appointed Nehemiah as the new governor of Israel, a position that Nehemiah shall hold for twelve years, my lords, and during which time he would live a simple life full of activity aimed at building and strengthening Jerusalem city and its protective walls.

> NEH 2:1 *And it came to pass in the month Nisan, <u>in the twentieth year of Artaxerxes the king</u> [445 BC, a year to remember], <u>that wine was before him</u>: and I took up the wine, and gave it unto the king. Now I had not been beforetime sad in his presence.*
>
> NEH 2:2 *Wherefore the king said unto me, Why is thy countenance sad, seeing thou art not sick? this is nothing else but sorrow of heart. Then I was very sore afraid,*
>
> NEH 2:3 *And said unto the king, Let the king live for ever: why should not my countenance be sad, when the city [Jerusalem], the place of my fathers' sepulchers [graves], lieth waste, and the gates [the gates of the city] thereof are consumed with fire?*
>
> NEH 2:4 *Then the king said unto me, For what dost thou make request?*

His Iranian majesty King Artaxerxes I directed his officials, my lords, to draft a letter commanding the royal superintendent of the woodland of the region encompassing Israel to supply Governor Nehemiah with logs and timber for the chancellery of the house of the Lord [the Citadel], and for the gates of the wall of Jerusalem, as well as for the governor's residence.

> NEH 2:8 *And a letter unto Asaph the keeper of the king's forest, <u>that he may give me timber to make beams for the gates of the palace which appertained to the house, and for the wall of the city, and for the house that I shall enter into</u>. And the king granted me, according to the good hand of my God upon me.*
>
> NEH 2:17 *Then said I unto them, Ye see the distress that we are in, how Jerusalem lieth waste, and the gates thereof are burned with fire: come, and let us build up the wall of Jerusalem, that we be no more a reproach.*

# THE UNEQUAL TWO HORNS OF IRAN—345

Meanwhile, as expected, my lords, the neighboring nations, such as the Arabs and Iraqis, tried, as in the past, to delay if not completely stop the rebuilding of the walls of Jerusalem and its strong gates.

Indeed, my lords, the standard joke among the surrounding local nationalities went along the line that a fox would be able to knock down the wall the Israelite trying to build. A walled city is a world of its own, as they say, my lords.

Their aim of course, my lords, is to discourage the builders of the wall by inferring that the flimsy wall is not worth the sweat.

> NEH 4:1 *But it came to pass, that when Sanballat [one of the neighboring rulers] heard that we builded the wall, he was wroth [angry-furious], and took great indignation, and mocked [laughed at] the Jews.*
> NEH 4:2 *And he spake before his brethren and the army of Samaria, and said, What do these feeble Jews? [what are they doing ?] will they fortify themselves? will they sacrifice? will they make an end in a day? will they revive the stones out of the heaps of the rubbish which are burned?*
> NEH 4:3 *Now Tobiah the Ammonite was by him, and he said, Even that which they build, if a fox go up, he shall even break down their stone wall.*
> NEH 4:7 *But it came to pass, that when Sanballat, and Tobiah, and the Arabians, and the Ammonites [Jordanians], and the Ashdodites [Philistines], heard that the walls of Jerusalem were made up, and that the breaches began to be stopped, then they were very wroth,*
> NEH 4:8 *And <u>conspired all of them together to come and to fight against Jerusalem</u>, and to hinder it.*
> NEH 4:9 *Nevertheless we made our prayer unto our God, and set a watch against them day and night, because of them.*
> NEH 5:14 *Moreover from the time that I was appointed to be their governor in the land of Judah, from the twentieth year <u>even unto the two and thirtieth year of Artaxerxes the king</u>, that is, twelve years, I and my brethren have not eaten the bread of the governor [we did not live lavishly].*
> NEH 6:15 *<u>So the wall was finished</u> in the twenty and fifth day of the month Elul, in fifty and two days.*

My lords, we wish at this point to remind you of one of Daniel's prophecy.

It is the prophecy, my lords, which gives man the permission and the guarantee for a celestial life after death. It is the prophecy of the greatest event in God's calendar.

Go ahead, please, prophet Daniel, you know, without doubt ,what we are referring to, sir.

> DAN 9:24 *Seventy weeks are determined upon thy people and upon thy holy city, to finish the transgression, and to make an end of sins, and to make reconciliation for iniquity [to forgive sins and reconcile man with God], and to bring in everlasting righteousness, and to seal up the vision and prophecy [to fulfill the prophecy of the crucifixion and resurrection of the Lord], and to anoint [the Lord] the most Holy.*
>
> DAN 9:25 *Know therefore and understand, that from the going forth of the commandment [by King Darius I in 516 BC] to restore and to build Jerusalem unto the Messiah the Prince [Crucified 31 AD] shall be seven weeks, and threescore and two weeks [547 solar years as have been calculated previously]: the street shall be built again, and the wall, even in troublous times.*

As we have shown you before, my lords, the prophet Daniel had prophesied that 547 solar years would pass from the year H.M. King Darius gave orders to build the temple [516 BC] to the death and, more importantly, the resurrection of Christ Jesus the Lord [31 AD]. God's sacrifice of love! God's guarantee of celestial life without end!

It seems, my lords, that the prophet Daniel, considering the importance of the event, and to assure those waiting for the Messiah of the date of His appearance, has provided another date to count from.

This time, my lords, the prophet Daniel prophesied that the death and the resurrection of the Lord would take place 476 solar years after rebuilding the walls of Jerusalem, according to the command of His Iranian Majesty King Artaxerxes I.

Daniel, my lords, made this prophecy 90 years before H.M. King Artaxerxes I gave the command of building the wall.

> DAN 9:25 *Know therefore and understand, that from the going forth of the commandment [by King Artaxerxes 445 BC] to restore and to build Jerusalem unto the Messiah the Prince [Crucified 31 AD] shall be seven weeks, and threescore and two weeks [7 + 60 + 2 = 69 weeks X 7 = 483 prophetical years, which are equivalent to 476 solar years]: the street shall be built again, and the wall, even in troublous times.*

# THE UNEQUAL TWO HORNS OF IRAN—347

And, indeed, all of this happened on time, my lords, as we shall see up the highway of prophecy.

Der Beliner Dom, Berlin Cathedral, Germany (image source: author).

Jon 1:29 Behold the Lamb of God (the sacrifice of God), which taketh away the sin of the world.

> ### Sixty-Two and Seven
>
> As mentioned before, a "score" is twenty. Thus three scores = 60.
>
> The breakdown is [69 weeks X 7] 483 prophetical years X 360 / 365.25 = 476 solar years.
>
> Adding 476 solar years to 445 BC would therefore yield 31 AD.
>
>> Dan 9:25 Know therefore and understand, that from the going forth of the commandment [by King Artaxerxes in 445 BC] <u>to restore and to build Jerusalem</u> unto the Messiah the Prince [Crucified 31 AD] shall be seven weeks, and threescore and two weeks [476 years]: the street shall be built again, and the wall, even in troublous times.

## 424–423 BC
## A Year of Upheaval and Mayhem

Your majesties, the time had come for the friend of Israel, his Iranian majesty King Artaxerxes I, the wall builder, to bid the world farewell, close his book of life, and prepare himself to appear before the judge of the whole earth.

Sadly enough, my lords, all hell broke loose after his death. His one and only legitimate heir, King Xerxes II, was assassinated by his half brother while his new majesty was drunk.

H.M. King Xerxes II sat on the throne of Iran for a mere forty-five days in all.

It did not fare much better for the assassin, my lords. H.M. King Sogdianus did not last many months either, for he too was assassinated by another half brother, who was born from another concubine of H.M. King Xerxes I.

In total, my lords, he managed to sit on the throne of Iran for a mere six months and fifteen days.

What is in store for the superpower of the world, my lords?

The kid is, my lords.

## 423–405 BC

Well, another son of H.M. King Artaxerxes I took his turn. He is H.M. King Darius II. And all we can tell you about him, my lords, is that he took advantage of the fights amongst the Greeks and formed an alliance with the Spartans. This is indeed bad news for all of Greece. But who can blame the Spartans? It is hard to resist taking money, my lords.

At any rate, his majesty died after occupying the throne of Iran for nearly nineteen years.

The days, your majesties, are drawing near for Daniel's opening prophecy.

404–358 BC

After H.M. King Darius II, my lords, came H.M. King Artaxerxes II.

His new majesty carried on with the new strategy of conquering the Greeks without shooting one arrow. Indeed, his majesty handed out fortunes in bribes in order to buy Greeks against Greeks.

At one time, he bought the Athenians against the Spartans. And. in other times he did the reverse, my lords. Basically, his majesty waged a war against Greece with an army of money—an army of gold and silver coins.

Go ahead, please, historian Plutarch, with your ancient record.

> "This being the case, Artaxerxes considered how he must carry on the war with Agesilaüs, and sent Timocrates the Rhodian into Greece with a great sum of money, bidding him use it for the corruption of the most influential men in the cities there, <u>and for stirring up the Greeks to make war upon Sparta</u>. 4 Timocrates did as he was bidden, the most important cities conspired together against Sparta, Peloponnesus was in turmoil, and the Spartan magistrates summoned Agesilaüs home from Asia.
>
> It was at this time, as we are told, and as he was going home, that Agesilaüs said to his friends: "The king has driven me out of Asia with thirty thousand archers"; for the Persian coin has the figure of an archer stamped upon it."[111]

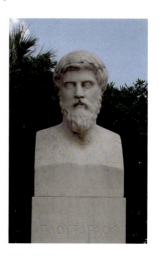

Ancient Greek historian Plutarch, WC

All in all, my lords, his majesty managed to ensure receiving annual taxes from the Greek cities in Ionia. And Ionia, of course, is the old property

---

[111] Ancient Greek historian Plutarch [b. 46 AD.], *The Parallel Lives,* 20:1.1-4

of H.M King Cyrus the great, where he some one hundred fifty years ago occupied it after defeating the fabulously rich Greek King Croesus of Lydia.

However, H.M King Artaxerxes II is known, my lords, more than any of you, to have had many wives and many children, some even say he had 350 wives.

## *The Sea, the Sea*

It works both ways.

King Artaxerxes II had to fight his brother Prince Cyrus for the throne of Iran.

Prince Cyrus recruited a large army of ten thousand Greek mercenaries [401 BC], who indeed won a decisive battle against Artaxerxes II. However, Cyrus died in the battle and the victory was thus a hollow one.

The Greek mercenaries who helped him were then trapped in enemy territory in Iran.

Plutarch one of the commanders of the remaining ten thousand Greek mercenaries detailed in a book how they managed to fight their way back to Greece through arid desert, cold, and snow while the Iranian soldiers and populations were nipping at their heels.

And when at last they reached the sea shore, dotted with Greek towns and villages, the ten thousand could not hold their cry of joy: "the sea, the sea!"

This story is related in Plutarch's famous book the Anabasis.

And so, my lords, King Artaxerxes II's day came, as ours shall one day come, to go the way of the whole earth.

Following him came two minor successors: first, his son King Ochus [358–338 BC] also known as King Artaxerxes III,]; and then after his assassination came his son King Arses [338–336 BC] who in turn was assassinated.

It is a mayhem in Iran, my lords.

But then everything changed.

The time for a prophecy has come. And the next six years would see it fulfilled.

The kid's day has come at last, my lords.

Sometimes, your majesties, we must walk in the alleys of history in order to reach the main highway of prophecy.

# The Sunset of the Kings of the World

Do you remember Balaam, son of Boer your Majesties?

The name of the biblical prophet Balaam was found by archaeologists (see EOOO, Volume One), on March 17, 1967 in an archeological dig in Jordan.

The plastered walls of the building had ancient writings on them, which begin with the following lines:

"Inscription of (Ba)laam (son of Beo)r, the man who was a seer of the gods. Lo, the gods came to him at night and (spoke to) him."

Balaam son of Beor [1397 BC], my sovereign, had nearly 1,065 years earlier prophesied of the coming of the kid and his unstoppable small but fast army.

Go ahead, please, Balaam.

> NUM 24:21 *And he [Balaam] looked on the Kenites [dwellers of the strongholds of the highlands of Jordan, a neighbor of Israel], and took up his parable, and said, Strong is thy dwellingplace, and thou puttest thy nest in a rock [strongly defended on high grounds].*
> NUM 24:22 *Nevertheless the Kenite shall be wasted, until Asshur [Assyria - the Empire of Assyria] shall carry thee away captive.*
> NUM 24:23 *And he took up his parable, and said, Alas, who shall live when God doeth this [brings about the Assyrian Empire]!*

> NUM 24:24 *And ships shall come from the coast of Chittim [Greek ships], and shall afflict Asshur [Assyria], and shall afflict Eber [the Greeks shall defeat the Assyrian Iraqis and the Persian Iranians], and he [the Greek Empire] also shall perish for ever [the Roman leagues were to defeat the Greeks and establish the Roman Empire].*

And beside Balaam, your majesties, the prophet Daniel, too, prophesied [540 BC] that out of Greece shall a leader come, who will march with great speed and in no time at all shall put an end to the great Persian empire of Iran—the deadly threat against Europe.

Go ahead please prophet Daniel.

> DAN 8:3 *Then I lifted up mine eyes, and saw, and, behold, there stood before the river a ram [The Persian Iranian Empire] which had two horns [Media and Persia]: and the two horns were high; but one was higher than the other, and the higher came up last [the Medians came first and the Persians rose to greater power after].*
>
> DAN 8:4 *I saw the ram [Media and Persia i.e. Iran] pushing westward [towards Greece and Europe], and northward [towards Armenia], and southward [towards Israel, Egypt and Ethiopia, or Nubia]; so that no beasts [other countries or kingdoms] might stand before him [the Persian Empire of Iran], neither was there any that could deliver out of his hand; but he did according to his will, and became great [the great Persian Empire, one of the greatest in the history of the world. Daniel saw this far ahead in time.]*

And then Daniel, my lords, went on to prophesy of the clash of the titans. This is clash that some people today, my lords, call "the clash of civilization."

Carry on, sir.

> DAN 8:5 *And as I was considering, behold, an he goat [the Greeks] came from the west on the face of the whole earth, and touched not the ground [dashing extremely fast]: and the goat had a notable horn between his eyes [the Kid].*
>
> DAN 8:6 *And he came to the ram [The Persian Iranians] that had two horns [Media and Persia], which I had seen standing before the river, and ran unto him in the fury of his power.*

*DAN 8:7* And I saw him [the Kid] come close unto the ram [Persian King Darius III and his Iranian army], and he was moved with choler [anger] against him [because of what the Iranians had done to Greece and to the city of Athens], and smote the ram [the Persian Iranian Empire], and brake his two horns: and there was no power in the ram [Iran] to stand before him [the Kid], but he cast him down to the ground, and stamped upon him: and there was none that could deliver the ram [the Iranians] out of his hand [the Kid's hand].

The great Persian (Iranian) Empire, a guardian bull, one of a set of two, guarding the portico of the Persian Hundred, Column Hall, Chicago Oriental Institute (image source: author).

My lords, it is needless to say to mighty men and women such as yourselves that the world does not daily produce combinations of men and circumstances that give us the likes of their majesties King Cyrus the great, King Darius I the great, and King Xerxes I.

To his record, his Iranian majesty King Cyrus undid the Babylonian empire of King Nebuchadnezzar of the hanging gardens of Babylon—the man who exiled the people of Israel into Iraqi and Iranian cities.

And to his record also his Iranian majesty, King Cyrus, freed the exiled children of Israel and allowed them to go back home.

Following his example, his Iranian majesty King Darius I, the friend of Israel, helped the reborn nation against its neighbors and indeed financed and allowed its leaders to build the temple. And it was he also, my lords, who expanded the Persian Iranian Empire to its farthest borders, sacking Egypt and Nubia and attacking Greece, although he lost at Marathon.

And then, my lords, his Iranian majesty King Xerxes I came along and attacked the west and Greece, and, presumably, burned Athens city, destroying some of its great temples and landmarks, although he ended up losing the war at the navy battle of Salamis.

But then, my lords, following these giant Iranian kings came a few unremarkable kings.

Throughout the days of these great kings, Israel, my lords, saw a number of her prophecies fulfilled. Immediately following the edict of H.M. King Cyrus the great, a company of a large number of the children of Israel returned to Jerusalem. This was the first wave, my sovereigns, and it was followed by a couple of more waves.

And when the children of Israel returned to Jerusalem, my lords, they returned to a city that was a mess of burnt rubbles and heaps of trash lining up along burnt homes and shops in ruins—a garbage dump, so to speak, my lords, and a mangled nuisance ground. Worse, it was a defenseless, wide-open city without walls surrounding it. And as you know now, your majesties, the temple was totally destroyed—a heap of rubbish.

The heart desire of the returning children of Israel, my lords, was to rebuild the wall, populate the city, and above all rebuild the house of the Lord on the same spot where it always stood.

And so, my lords, the heavy work of rebuilding the wall, the temple, and the city began. But, as you well remember, your majesties, the neighbors of Israel would not allow any of it and tried their best in every possible occasion to make it impossible for Israel to live again.

Letters and delegations, your majesties, went back and force to the Persian princes and successive Iranian kings, warning them against Israel.

Go ahead please, priest Ezra.

*EZRA 4:4* *the people of the land [the neighbors] weakened the hands of the people of Judah [the Israelites], and troubled them in building,*

The Arabs and the rest of the neighbors threatened and tricked, but at last, your majesties, new houses and homes and streets and market places were built in Jerusalem in troublesome times. The temple, albeit a smaller one than the original, was also rebuilt on its exact spot. And a new city wall was built, complete with the gates.

This then, your majesties, is the second temple [516 BC]. The first one [968–947 BC], of course, my lords, was the one built by the wealthiest man who ever lived, H.M King Solomon, 430 years earlier.

Model of the second temple of Jerusalem made by Michael Osnis from Kedumim, WC, Daniel Ventura

356—EARTH OUT OF ORBIT

"A stone (2.43x1 meters) with the Hebrew language inscription 'To the Trumpeting Place' excavated by B. Mazar at the southern foot of the Temple Mount. It is believed that this was part of the "second Temple," which was built when the children of Israel returned back from Babylon, WC, Talmoryair

# Chapter Six

# Past and Present Abominations

## The Only Two Men in the World Who Count

Sitting amongst you today, my lords, is a great man, a military innovator. This man, my lords, and you know who you are, sir, nearly killed his son in a fit of anger. He was drunk, my lords, a drunk king.

Had he succeeded, my lords, to kill his son, he would have killed a man who later on, and within only ten years from this incident, would rule the largest part of God's earth that was ever ruled by one single man—ever.

But this was not the only coincidence in the life of this king and his son that would have changed the history of our world, my lords. In fact, King Philip II would not have become king except that his two older brothers had died. Strange, strange how life's unnoticeable little coincidences end up, my lords, in great changes—changes that sometimes affect a single person, and at times affect the entire world as in the case of H.M. King Philip II of Macedon in northern Greece.

You do know by now, your majesties, that the children of the Holy One say that there is a steady and invisible hand behind the visible scene.

> DAN 4:17 to the intent that the living may know that the most High ruleth in the kingdom of men, and giveth it to whomsoever he will

Incidentally, your majesties, should you wish to know, it was his Greek majesty King Philip II who changed the name of the town of Crenides to "Philippi" and fortified it to protect the gold mine nearby.

And on a side note, my lords, the Christian apostle Paul visited this city of Philippi and sent a letter to its small Christian fellowship. The letter is called "Philippians."

Go ahead, please, apostle Paul and read to their majesties a few verses of your letter to the Philippians.

> PHIL 3:20 the Lord Jesus Christ:
> PHIL 3:21 shall change our vile [mortal, decaying] body, that it may be fashioned like unto his glorious body [heavenly, celestial]

> PHIL 4:4 *Rejoice in the Lord alway: and again I say, Rejoice.*
> PHIL 4:8 *Finally, brethren, whatsoever things are true, whatsoever things are honest, whatsoever things are just, whatsoever things are pure, whatsoever things are lovely, whatsoever things are of good report; if there be any virtue, and if there be any praise, think on these things.*
> PHIL 4:13 *I can do all things through Christ which strengtheneth me.*
> PHIL 4:23 *The grace of our Lord Jesus Christ be with you all. Amen.*

These gold mines of Philippi were the main source of income for H.M. King Philip II. And as you know, my lords, income means weapons and weapons mean a strong army and a strong army means empires.

Anyway, we mention all of this to you, my lords, because the year that H.M. King Philip II sacked Philippi was also the year his son Alexander was born [356 BC].

Do you wish, my lords, to hear of another incident that changed the history of our world and sealed who we have become? It happened in a wedding, my lords, the wedding of the daughter of H.M. King Philip II.

It was in this wedding, my lords, that H.M. King Philip II was assassinated by none less than one of his own bodyguards. And the murder happened as his majesty was entering into the theater for the wedding celebration. And so, my lords, in October 336 BC his young son became the new king—and the world would never be the same again.

But what does Greek King Philip II have to do with biblical prophecy, you may ask, my lords?

Well, your majesties, may we repeat what the philosopher Isocrates wrote to him, which went like this: if you defeat Persia, there will be nothing left for you to do but to become a god.

This is it, my lords. Iran has now become the target—the reason for living.

Revenge, against what its Kings Darius I of Marathon and Xerxes I of Salamis have done to the Greeks, to Athens, and to the temples, is a fire that has been burning nonstop in the hearts of the Greeks, my lords. The one who could defeat Iran is a god.

And the Greeks, my lords, have by this time decided that they shall no longer sit at home and scuffle to defend themselves whenever the "barbarians" got it into their heads to invade Europe. No, no more!

The Greeks by this time, my lords, have devised a new strategy: they shall henceforth take the war to the soil of Persia [Iran].

And this, my lords, has much to do with us today in our modern times.

We, the living today, my lords, we are digging up the root of the ancient tree.

King Philip II nearly murdered his son "the kid," who was destined to rule the world, the Altes Museum, Berlin, Germany (image source: author).

Do you, my lords, wish to hear of another seemingly insignificant coincidence that ended up shaping our world even to our modern day?

Here it is your majesties: in the same year [336 BC], when King Philip II was assassinated and young Alexander became the king of Greece, King Darius III became the king of Persia.

Consider this, my lords, H.M. King Darius III was not in line for the Persian throne but a set of complicated infightings brought him to the throne of Persia. This is destiny at work, my lords, destiny!

And you may rightfully ask, my lords, why is this worth mentioning that young Alexander and King Darius III became the two rival kings?

We believe, my lords, that the quickest answer we can give you is embedded in the words that young Alexander said at the conclusion of a speech he made to encourage his soldiers for the deadly Iranian battle ahead of them.

Young Alexander said the following to his outnumbered soldiers getting ready to put their lives on the line your majesties:

> "And what, finally, of the two men in supreme command? You have Alexander, they—Darius!"[146]

But if you are wishing for more details, your majesties, well, allow us then to hear what the ancient historian Arrian wrote about his Iranian majesty King Darius III.

---

[146] Ancient historian Arrian. *The Campaigns of Alexander*. P. 112

The notable horn of Daniel's prophecy, Alexander the Great, British Museum, London (image source: author).

Go ahead, sir.

"Darius was always ready to believe what he found it most agreeable to believe, and on this occasion [the first battle of the Greeks against the Persian Iranians - West against East – Europe against the Middle East] flattering courtiers, such as always are, and always will be, the bane of kings, had persuaded him ...First one, then another of them blew up the bladder of his conceit by saying that the Persian cavalry [the horse division – the strength of the Persian army] would ride over the Macedonian [Greek] army and trample it to pieces"[147].

And here once again, my lords, another seemingly insignificant incident took place.

A mercenary Greek general working for H.M. King Darius III tried to convince the Iranian ruler of what indeed could have been a victory plan, yet his good plan was turned down flat. Instead, my lords, H.M. King Darius III took the opposite advice.

Historian Arrian, what is the reason, sir, that his majesty rejected the good advice and accepted the bad one?

"because it told him what at the moment he liked to hear; more than that, there was surely some supernatural power which led Darius to take up a [detrimental] position."[148]

But my lords, one cannot dismiss King Darius III's attitude lightly. Indeed, the Iranian cavalry, the cream of the crop of the Iranian army, was the largest in the world. And the land forces of his majesty were the most numerous ever, even to our modern day. The Iranian army was the largest armed forces on planet earth, my lords. The deck, my lords, was heavily stacked against any king—Greek, European, or otherwise. The deck was stacked against any earthly force whatsoever that dreamt of challenging the might of the Iranian forces. And so was the atmosphere of the day, my lords.

---

[147] Arrian. The Campaigns of Alexander, P.P. 110, 111
[148] Arrian. *The Campaigns of Alexander*, P.P. 110, 111

Cut in, please, ancient historian Josephus.

"for not he only [King Darius III], but all those that were in Asia also, were persuaded that the Macedonians [Greeks] would not so much as come to a battle with the Persians, on account of their multitude]."[149]

## 334 BC
## Let Us Share

No, it is not up to you to share. You cannot share what you do not own.

Within a short two years of inheriting the thrones of Greece and of Persia, the armies of the two most important men on the surface of the earth, their Majesties Greek King Alexander and Iranian King Darius III, would be facing each other, my lords. The world will stop breathing to watch the match your majesties.

Undeterred by the huge odds against him, young King Alexander, my lords, and his small army have ferried across the Hellespont [the strait of Dardanelles] and thus crossed from Europe to Asia aiming for the heart of the Iranian dominion—the heart of the one and mighty Persian Empire founded by H.M. King Cyrus the Great.

Your majesties, it is almost a shame to gloss over the tactics and maneuvers of some of the greatest battles of the world—the battles of young King Alexander the Great. But we are in a hurry, my lords, to reach our modern day.

And indeed, your majesties, each battle was more stunning than the previous one.

To begin, my lords, his Iranian majesty King Darius III sent his large army to stop the 22-year-old Greek young man at the western gate of the Persian Empire, the border between Europe and Asia.

And it was there on the road from Abydos to Dascylium at the crossing of the Granicus River [May 3, 334 BC] that the 22-year-old Greek youngster with an army half the size of that of the Persians sent the Iranians fighters flying for their lives.

It was the first encounter, my lords. And the message was clear: the superiority of young King Alexander and the quality of his Europeans troops and weapons shall defeat the Iranians, no matter how large of an army they will muster. Young Alexander can do anything he wanted.

---

[149] Josephus, *Antiquities of the Jews*, Book XI, Chap. VIII: 3

And this, your majesties, the battle of the Granicus River, was the first of three battles that would take down H.M. King Darius III and the Persian Empire with him.

The 22-year-old came as an unexpected summer storm, your majesties, and hurriedly crashed against fortress Iran. Indeed, the young man's fully loaded army clocked 185 miles of marching in three days—it was that fast of an army, my lords.

### From the West ... and Touched Not the Ground

Alexander the Great had first to defeat and unite the battling Greek cities before venturing out to Asia and Iran.

> "It is said that when asked how he [Alexander] had contrived to subdue Greece <u>so swiftly</u>, he answered, "By never putting off anything till tomorrow."[150]

> Dan 8:5 And as I was considering, behold, an he goat [the Greeks] came from the west on the face of the whole earth, <u>and touched not the ground</u> [dashing extremely fast]: and the goat had a notable horn between his eyes [the kid, young King Alexander the Great].

LEFT: The head of King Alexander the Great, the goat of Daniel's prophecy, is featured wearing royal and divine symbols: the diadem and the horns of the god Zeus Ammon, British Museum (image source: author).

And indeed it happened again, my lords. Young King Alexander the Great fought a second battle, the great Battle of Issus, against the Persian-Iranian army. This time the Iranian army, my lords, was led by H.M. King Darius III himself.

But the Iranians were routed once again, my lords, even though they were in number twice as many as the Greeks.

It was as if the Greek army of young Alexander the Great was fighting two Iranian armies in the same time, my lords. But his tactics and the Iranian mistakes brought him victory after victory your majesties.

---

[150] *The Nature of Alexander* by Mary Renault, Penguin Books, 1975, P.88

Historian and Roman Senator Arrian, [b. 87 BC], would you please, sir, read to their majesties a synopsis of your record regarding the battle of Issus?

"The moment the Persian left [wing] went to pieces under Alexander's attack and Darius in his war-chariot, saw that it was cut off, he incontinently fled – indeed, he led the race for safety... dropping his shield and stripping off his mantle – and even leaving his bow in the war-chariot – he leapt upon a horse and rode for his life. Darkness soon closed in; and that alone saved him from falling into the hands of Alexander.

...

Darius' headquarters were stormed and captured; his mother was taken, together with his wife (who was also his sister) and his infant son; in addition to these, two of his daughters fell into Alexander's hands with a few noble Persian ladies who were in attendance upon them

...

Such, then was the result of the battle of Issus [fought in the month of November 333 BC]."[151]

Alexander the Great, the destroyer of the Persian/Iranian Empire, is the young man whose successors fulfilled many of Daniel's prophecies, British Museum (image source: author).

## I Will Find You Wherever You Hide

My lords, his Iranian majesty King Darius III has by now gotten the clear message that young Greek Alexander is a formidable foe. And so, his majesty, the great ruler of the 200-year-old great Persian Empire decided to send a message of his own to the Greek youngster. At that time, the youngster was in the middle of battles in Lebanon and heading towards Israel and Egypt.

May we, my lords, ask the historian Arrian one more time to read out his record concerning the contents of the message and the response of the young supreme commander of the West!

Go ahead, sir.

---

[151] Arrian. *The Campaigns of Alexander*, translated by Aubrey De Selincourt. Revised by J. R. Hamilton, Penguin Books, 1958, P.P 120-128

"While Alexander was at Marathus, envoys from Darius came with a request for the release of his mother, wife, and children. They also brought a letter from him.

...

Alexander, having written his reply,

...

Your ancestors invaded Macedonia and Greece and caused havoc in our country, though we had done nothing to provoke them. As supreme commander of all Greece I invaded Asia because I wished to punish Persia for this act

...

First I defeated in battle your generals and satraps [provincial governors]; now I have defeated yourself and the army you led.

By God's help I am master of your country … come to me, therefore, as you would come to the lord of the continent of Asia … come then, and ask me for your mother, your wife, and your children and anything else you please; for you shall have them, and whatever besides you can persuade me to give you.

And in future let any communication you wish to make with me be addressed to the King of all Asia. Do not write to me as an equal. Everything you possess is now mine; so, if you should want anything, let me know in the proper terms, or I shall take steps to deal with you as a criminal.

If, on the other hand, you wish to dispute your throne, stand and fight for it and do not run away. Wherever you may hide yourself, be sure I shall seek you out."[152]

Alexander the Great "with the ram's horn of the Egyptian god Ammon in his hair," ca. 90–75 BC, the Archaeological Museum of Philadelphia (image source: author).

Ho, ho, ho, my lords! Have you heard what this youngster was about to call the king of the world, the heir of a 200-year old-empire … he was about to call him a criminal? The youngster tells the king of the world "do not write to me as an equal." What?

---

[152] Arrian. *The Campaigns of Alexander*, translated by Aubrey De Selincourt. Revised by J. R. Hamilton, Penguin Books, 1958, P.P 120-128

And now, my lords, from the great battles of Granicus and Issus, the notable horn, young King Alexander the Great, carried on with his important strategy of securing the east seaboard of the Mediterranean Sea, sacking the cities and the capitals of the Middle East all the way down to Egypt.

And, take this, your majesties: in passing through Jerusalem of Israel, he was shown, or so they say, the book of Daniel in order to read the 215-year-old prophecies concerning him [c. 547–332 BC].

This coin shows Alexander's famous war horse, Boukephalos. Alexander trained this difficult wild horse while he was merely a 16-year-old teenager. He rode the horse the entire time he took down the Persian Empire, and when the horse died, Alexander named a city after it, British Museum (image source: author).

> DAN 8:5 *And as I was considering, <u>behold, an he goat came from the west on the face of the whole earth, and touched not the ground: and the goat had a notable horn between his eyes</u> [Alexander the Great].*
> DAN 8:6 *And he came to the ram that had two horns [The Persian Empire], which I had seen standing before the river, and ran unto him in the fury of his power.*

## I Am Not Parmenio

At this point of time your majesties, the young Greek was besieging the great harbor city of Tyre of Lebanon—a siege, which, incidentally, lasted seven months [from January to August 332 BC].

Now, if you may, my lords, permit the ancient Roman historian Arrian to read out a bit of his record regarding further correspondence from his Iranian majesty King Darius III to the young Greek!

Go ahead please, sir, whenever you have something to add.

> "While Alexander was still occupied with the siege [of the wealthy Tyre city of Lebanon], he was visited by envoys from Darius, who in the king's name offered a sum of 10,000 talents in exchange for his mother, wife, and children; they further proposed that all the territory west of the Euphrates right to the Aegean Sea [Iraq, Syria, Turkey, Lebanon, Israel, Jordan, and Egypt] should belong to Alexander, who should seal his bond of friendship and alliance with Persia by marrying Darius' daughter."

H.M. King Darius III is practically giving the entire Middle East to the young Greek while keeping Iran and a portion of Iraq for himself. The attractive proposal was therefore discussed in the young Greek's inner circle, my lords.

Obviously no one would reject such a proposal, not even General Parmenio.

> "These proposals were made known at a meeting of Alexander's personal advisers, and Parmenio, [one of Alexander's most skilful generals] according to all reports, declared that were he Alexander he would be happy to end the war on such terms and be done with any further adventures.
>
> "That," replied Alexander, "is what I should do were I Parmenio; but since I am Alexander, I shall send Darius a different answer."

And sending a different answer, he did, my lords!

He had no need, he wrote, of Darius' money, nor was there any call upon him to accept a part of the continent in place of the whole. All Asia, including all its wealth, shall be his property and real estate. Furthermore, if he wished to marry Darius' daughter, he would do so, whether Darius liked it or not.

Look at this brash young fellow here, my lords. He was offered half of the Iranian Empire, the half closest to his Greece and Europe. Yet he turns down the man who, a few months earlier, was feared and called "king of the universe." Alas, his universe is shrinking awfully fast.

Allow us to go back again to historian Arrian, my lords.

> "If, moreover, Darius wanted kindness and consideration at his hands, he must come to ask for it in person.
>
> Upon receiving this reply, Darius abandoned all thought of coming to terms and began once more to prepare for war."[153]

Indeed, my sovereigns, his Iranian majesty King Darius III, who managed to escape from the battle of Issus, began immediately to amass the largest army he could possibly assemble together. It was and is the largest army the world has ever seen, my lords.

At that time, my sovereigns, H.M. King Darius III was almost twice as old as his enemy Alexander the Great.

---

[153] Arrian. *The Campaigns of Alexander*, P.P. 143,144

## PAST AND PRESENT ABOMINATIONS—367

**331 BC** After the fall of the besieged Tyre of Lebanon, young King Alexander, my lords, attacked the city of Gaza of the Philistines, and then went down to Egypt.

Leaving Egypt [331 BC], young King Alexander then, my lords, marched towards Babylon and the heart of the Persian Empire chasing after his Iranian majesty King Darius III.

And now, your majesties, the third major battle between the west and the east took place—the battle of Gaugamela, or as it is also called the "battle of Arbela." This great battle, my lords, took place almost two years after the disastrous battle of Issus.

As we have mentioned, my sovereigns, his Iranian majesty King Darius III was ready and had already put together a massive army, which enlisted fighters from all corners of the great Persian Empire.

Some, my lords, estimate his army to be five times that of Alexander's—five times, my lords. Once again, my sovereigns and commanders, it was as if young Alexander were fighting five well-equipped armies all at once.

ABOVE LEFT: Third century BC statue of Alexander the Great, Istanbul Archaeology Museum, WC, Tkbwikmed

LEFT: An ancient large Greek vase called the "vase of the Persians" because it depicts King Darius III sitting on a throne listening to a messenger before his final battle with Alexander the Great (second band from the bottom). The vase is displayed in the National Archaeological Museum of Naples, Italy (image source: author).

Particular thank you for the private viewing granted by the museum to the author

Details of the ancient vase, 340–320 BC, "The central band shows Darius on his throne, behind whom stands figures who are presumably members of his bodyguard, carefully listening to a messenger standing erect in the king's presence on a circular podium, surrounded by seated dignitaries and, it would seem, his pedagogue, who can be identified as the old man leaning on a stick." The quote above is taken from the National Archaeological Museum of Naples; the name of King Darius appears above him (image source: author).

This Bessus, your majesties, declared himself the new king of Persia, but was in turn captured by young Alexander and put to death.

Your majesties, the one and only 200-year-old great Persian Empire came to its end on the hands of a hurried Greek, a notable horn, storming from the west.

Some of you would wonder now, my lords, what happened to young Alexander? How was he like growing old? And what are the names of his children, who inherited his great empire, an empire that swallowed both the Babylonian and Persian Empires?

And for your questions, my lords, we shall let the prophet Daniel of the nation of the prophets give the answer.

Sir!

> DAN 8:8 *the he goat waxed very great: and when he was strong, the great horn [Alexander the Great] was broken; and for it came up four notable ones toward the four winds of heaven.*

More importantly, your majesties, the prophet Daniel said, more than 215 years in advance, that the huge empire of King Alexander the Great shall not be inherited by his children.

> DAN 11:3 *And a mighty king shall stand up, that shall rule with great dominion, and do according to his will.*

*DAN 11:4* *And when he shall stand up [at the peak of his power], his kingdom shall be broken, and <u>shall be divided toward the four winds of heaven</u>; <u>and not to his posterity</u>, nor according to his dominion which he ruled: for his kingdom shall be plucked up, even for others beside those.*

We suspect, my sovereigns, that the question lingers in your minds as it lingered in ours.

Is it possible that prophecies can be real? Is it possible that God does reveal future events in His calendar to tested and chosen men and women?

It is difficult, my lords, to believe that prophecy is real. But it is equally difficult to deny it, my lords, because Daniel, whose writings have been around for more than two thousand years, speak of events that happened in our modern time and only forty years ago, my lords.

Indeed, your majesties, a good number of his prophecies took place in the last seventy years of our modern world of today.

More than that, my lords, Daniel and prophet John, after him, spoke of events, that have not happened yet, but pieces are being put together that indicate that they shall indeed take place. And, yet the two men who foretold of these events are dead and buried long ago, my lords.

Time shall yet pass judgment on what still in store. But even then, my lords, there shall always be those who will find a way not to believe in the timetable of God. Always is the case, my lords.

King Alexander the Great on his famous horse to the left, King Darius III in his chariot to the right.

King Alexander the Great on his famous horse Boukephalos

King Alexander the Great fought many close battles but was never defeated in any; he has fulfilled the prophecy of Daniel

"The mosaic represents the moment in which Alexander the Great (to the left) attacks the chariot of Darius, king of Persians. The scene is commonly identified as one of the decisive battles in the conquest of the East (Issus, Granicus, Gaugamela) …The mosaic is probably a copy, datable between 125 and 120 BC, of a famous Greek picture painted by Philoxenos of Eretria for King Cassander of Macedon at the end of the fourth century BC".

This mosaic is found in ancient Pompeii in the House of the Faun and is now housed in the Museo Archeologico Nazionale, where the quote is taken, Naples, Italy (Images and details source: the author).

# PAST AND PRESENT ABOMINATIONS—371

ABOVE: Details of the mural (previous page, top left) showing King Darius III.

BELOW: Soldiers of King Darius III.

## In the Palace of Nebuchadnezzar

Ancient Babylon! Your story has not finished yet.

Babylon of southern Iraq, home of the Shiite Moslems, the allies of Shiite Iran, your story continues to our day.

But you, your majesty, King Nebuchadnezzar, you have built Babylon to make your name last for generations to come. And it did, sir.

Go ahead please, prophet Daniel, you know what we are after, sir.

> DAN 4:28 *king Nebuchadnezzar.*
> DAN 4:29 *walked in the palace of the kingdom of Babylon.*
> DAN 4:30 *The king spake, and said, Is not this great Babylon [capital city of the Babylonian Empire of southern Iraq – the modern Shiite part of Iraq], that I have built for the house of the kingdom [royal palace] by the might of my power, and for the honour of my majesty?*

And then, your majesty, King Nebuchadnezzar, the Medians united with the Persians under the command of H. M. King Cyrus, the great the liberator of the children of Israel, came and took over your great city and swallowed up the nations you governed and owned. Your majesty King Nebuchadnezzar, those Medians and the Persians of Iran, your conquerors, became the great Persian Empire.

And now this young Greek comes, from the west, sir, from Europe and today he, a 32-year-old man, sits on your throne as the king of Babylon. He is in essence, sir, the king of Greece, the king of Syria, the king of Lebanon, the king of Israel, the king of Egypt, the king of Jordan, the king of Arabia, the king of Iraq, the king of Iran, the king of Afghanistan, the king of Pakistan, the king of India, and sundry.

The king of all resides today in your Babylon, your majesty.

## June 10, 323 BC

But be of good cheers, your majesty, King Nebuchadnezzar, the Greek supreme commander and king is not in a very good shape today—he is ill with high fever. No one knows exactly what befell him, sir.

Has he been poisoned or has he drunk contaminated water, or perhaps too much wine? No one is sure yet, my lord.

But we can tell you, your Babylonian majesty King Nebuchadnezzar, that the answer to this question does not matter to you anymore, sir.

Today, the troops, his beloved Greek and European soldiers, march empty handed, no weapons in their hands; they march in silence by his bed.

## PAST AND PRESENT ABOMINATIONS—373

"These clay tablets come from Babylonia and are written in cuneiform script ... The third text mentions Alexander's defeat of the last Persian king Darius III at Gaugamela on 1 October 331 BC and his later triumphant entry into Babylon." The quote comes from the British Museum, London (image source: author).

Go ahead ancient, historian Plutarch, please.

"they all filed slowly past his bedside one by one, wearing neither cloak nor armour ... On the twenty-eighth towards evening he died."[154*]

My lords and commanders, the Greek king, the young supreme commander of the vastest real estate of planet earth, is dead. He is dead at the age of thirty-three.

He ruled his dominion in the universe unchallenged—a dominion that he had accumulated in ten years of unstoppable victories, and without one single defeat.

The young savior of Europe is dead and gone, my lords.

---

[154] Plutarch, *The Age of Alexander*, P. 333

374—EARTH OUT OF ORBIT

ABOVE RIGHT: "This is a diary of astronomical and meteorological phenomena observed during the second month in the year 323 to 322 BC. Written in cuneiform script, it records the death of Alexander on the 29th day of the lunar month. The author describes Alexander simply as "the king." The quote comes from the British Museum; the underlining and the image source are supplied by the author.

BELOW RIGHT: Alexander the Great in his later years, the Louvre Museum (image source: author).

# PAST AND PRESENT ABOMINATIONS—375

Dying Alexander, a Roman copy of a Hellenistic portrait, Museum of Classical Archaeology, University of Cambridge, UK (image source: author).

Alas, my lords, and commanders, the greatest general who ever lived did not live long enough to enjoy his unmatched achievement, which remains as such in the annals of history up to our modern day. The greatest commander who ever lived died at the peak of his mountain of success.

My sovereigns, perhaps it is worthwhile to check what the prophet Daniel had said over two hundred and fifteen years in advance.

Go ahead please, prophet Daniel, and remind their majesties of your prophecy.

> *DAN 8:1* *In the third year of the reign of king Belshazzar [C.547 BC. In the dying days of the Babylonian Empire, which was founded by the father of King Nebuchadnezzar] a vision appeared unto me, even unto me Daniel, after that which appeared unto me at the first.*
> *DAN 8:2* *And I saw in a vision; and it came to pass, when I saw, that I was at Shushan in the palace, which is in the province of Elam [Iran]; and I saw in a vision, and I was by the river of Ulai.*
> *DAN 8:3* *Then I lifted up mine eyes, and saw, and, behold, there stood before the river <u>a ram [Iran of Persia and Media] which had two horns: and the two horns were high; but one was higher than the other, and the higher came up last.</u>*
> *DAN 8:4* *I saw the ram [Persia and Media] pushing westward, and northward, and southward; so that no beasts might stand before him, neither was there any that could deliver out of his hand; but he did according to his will, and became great [the great Persian Empire].*

> DAN 8:5 *And as I was considering, <u>behold, an he goat [the Greeks] came from the west on the face of the whole earth, and touched not the ground: and the goat had a notable horn between his eyes [Alexander the Great]</u>.*
> DAN 8:6 *And he came to the ram that had two horns [The Persian Empire], which I had seen standing before the river, and ran unto him in the fury of his power.*
> DAN 8:7 *And I saw him come close unto the ram, and he was moved with choler against him, and smote the ram, and brake his two horns [Media and Persia]: and there was no power in the ram to stand before him, but he cast him down to the ground, and stamped upon him: and there was none that could deliver the ram out of his hand.*
> DAN 8:8 *Therefore the he goat waxed very great: and when he was strong, <u>the great horn was broken</u> [King Alexander the Great died, 332 BC]; <u>and for it came up four notable ones toward the four winds of heaven</u>.*
> ...
> DAN 8:19 *And he said, Behold, I will make thee know what shall be in the last end of the indignation [the return of the Children of Israel from the Babylonian exile by the order of King Cyrus the Great]: for at the time appointed [seventy years] the end shall be.*
> DAN 8:20 <u>*The ram which thou sawest having two horns are the kings of Media and Persia.*</u>
> DAN 8:21 <u>*And the rough goat is the king of Grecia [Greece]: and the great horn that is between his eyes is the first king*</u> *[Alexander the Great].*
> DAN 8:22 <u>*Now that being broken [died], whereas four stood up for it, four kingdoms shall stand up out of the nation [the empire – the Grecian Empire], but not in his power.*</u>

Who now, my lords, shall inherit the largest real estate of the world, the holdings of the great Grecian Empire, a holding of many countries, languages, nationalities, religions, and cultures stretching from India to Greece to Egypt?

The answer, which the prophet Daniel gives in advance, my lords, is that H.M. King Alexander the Great shall not be succeeded by his own offspring, even though he had left behind a pregnant young wife.

Go ahead, sir, please cut in when appropriate.

> DAN 11:4 *And when he shall stand up [at the peak of his power], his kingdom shall be broken, <u>and shall be divided toward the four winds of heaven</u>; <u>and not to his posterity</u> [not given to his children],*

Who then shall inherit him, prophet Daniel?

His vast and great empire would end up divided between four royal dynasties besides lesser ones.

> DAN 8:21 *And the rough goat is the king of Grecia: and the great horn that is between his eyes is the first king [King Alexander the Great].*
> DAN 8:22 *Now that being broken [died], whereas four stood up for it, four kingdoms shall stand up out of the nation [the empire – the Grecian Empire], but not in his power.*

Would you also, prophet Daniel, quote your second prophecy please!

> DAN 11:1 *Also I in the first year of Darius the Mede [A Median governor of Babylonia under Cyrus the great?]*
> DAN 11:2 *Behold, there shall stand up yet three kings in Persia; and the fourth shall be far richer than they all: and by his strength through his riches he shall stir up all against the realm of Grecia [King Xerxes I].*
> DAN 11:3 *And a mighty king [Alexander the Great] shall stand up, that shall rule with great dominion, and do according to his will.*
> DAN 11:4 *And when he shall stand up [at the peak of his power], his kingdom shall be broken, and shall be divided toward the four winds of heaven [the four directions]; and not to his posterity [not given to his children], nor according to his dominion [none of the new four kingdoms would be as vast as his empire] which he ruled: for his kingdom shall be plucked up, even for others beside those [besides the main four dynasties].*

Alexander's domain stretching from Greece to India and to Egypt, http://www.bible-history.com/maps/map-alexander-the-great.html

The empire of Alexander the Great stretched from Greece to Egypt to India and Afghanistan, WC, Captain Blood

The death of his majesty, my lords, is the opening chapter of three hundred years of prophecies centered on two of his heirs, two of the four royal families, which indeed inherited his vast domain. Soon, my lords, we shall meet with the four royal houses.

And we can tell you, my sovereigns, that even today, in our modern time, we still have some of their great monuments and the carvings of their faces. We know, my lords, how these famous royals, the inheritors of H.M. King Alexander the Great looked like.

And if anyone, my lords, was expecting the four main dynasties to take over immediately upon the death of H.M. King Alexander the Great [June 10, 323 BC], then he or she would have been terribly disappointed. In fact, for a while, my lords, it seemed that a team of a father and a son would inherit all his majesty's belongings.

At any rate, my lords, it took nearly fifty years, forty-eight years to be exact, to fulfill the prophecies of Daniel. This was a long wait for those watching the for Daniel's prophecies.

## Four Royal Houses: First and Second

His majesty died and friends became enemies. The jostling, my lords, for ruling the world pitted companions in arms against each other. All of them were heavy-weights, my lords, and of strong personalities. And none of them was below the ranks of powerful and ambitious generals, governors. And of course the pushing and shoving rallied the immediate members of the royal family of H.M. King Alexander, including his own strong-willed mother,

Olympias. None of the barons of the world stood quietly watching on the sidelines.

Did you foresee all of these, prophet Daniel?

When his majesty died, my lords, he left behind a pregnant Iranian wife, Roxana, whom he had married shortly before his death.

As some of you may know or recall, my lords, H.M. King Alexander, shortly before his death, had encouraged his generals and commanders to intermarry with the local royalties, Iranians, Iraqis, and Indians in order to create a stable empire of a melting pot of mixed races. His sudden and inexplicable death, my lords, has indeed put a stop to the melting pot idea.

Medallion of Olympias, mother of King Alexander the Great, the Walters Museum of Art, Baltimore (image source: author).

Be that as it may, your majesties, if we may digress for a minute, all the major generals did obey his order, although they all, with one exception, dropped their Iranian and Iraqi wives upon the death of his majesty.

The only one who kept his Iranian wife is the commander whose descendant will put an abomination in the temple of the Lord in Jerusalem of Israel and thus fulfill an important prophecy of Daniel's.

All in all, my sovereigns, in addition to the pregnant young wife Roxana, H.M. King Alexander had also left behind a half brother, Arrhidaeus, who was physically handicapped and just as much mentally.

And so, my lords, on one hand you have a pregnant wife, whom we do not know if she is carrying a male or a female child. And on the other hand you have a man considered unsuitable for the burden of a large empire, basically the inhabitable world.

No worries, my lords! We can tell you, your majesties, that the two most influential men, the two strongest generals of the great army of his majesty, have today reached a solution and settled on an agreement.

Commander Perdiccas, the commander of the cavalry, and Commander Meleager, the commander of the infantry and the navy, have agreed, my lords, amongst themselves to make King Alexander's half brother the new king, King Philip III, named after his father King Philip II.

Furthermore, my lords, they decided that the new king of the world, H.M. King Philip III, must rule jointly with Roxana's expected child, provided of course that the expected child is a male.

Tetradrachm of King Philip III, 323–316 BC, half brother of King Alexander the Great, Altes Museum, Berlin (image source: author).

As for the two powerful military men themselves, my lords, the severe Commander Perdiccas was appointed as the regent, the guardian of the entire empire and the supreme commander of its forces.

On the other hand, Commander Meleager was appointed as the guardian of the royal family of his dead majesty King Alexander.

Settled!

Where are the four main dynasties prophet Daniel prophesied about?

They are nowhere in sight.

Has the prophecy failed?

It appears to be.

The leadership of the world is settled, my lords.

We are now awaiting the birth of his majesty's child.

In addition, my lords, the two great military men have further agreed to divide the great empire into small governable domains, and install some twenty-five men to rule them [Edit: This agreement is known as the "partition of Babylon"].

We can tell you ahead of time, my lords, that of all of these twenty-five governors, there are two important ones whose successors would be involved in the prophecies of Daniel—only two out of the mass of twenty-five.

The first one is the governor of Egypt. He was, my lords, one of the most capable and important generals of H.M. King Alexander the Great. His name is Commander Ptolemy.

And the second, my lords, would come later and his name is Commander Seleucus.

These, my lords, are two dynasties that shall occupy us for nearly three hundred years. At the end of these three hundred years, my lords, we shall have a newcomer who would last for over two thousand years. He is with us today the minute we opened our eyes this morning.

## PAST AND PRESENT ABOMINATIONS—381

Commander Ptolemy, 305-283 BC, whose dynasty would fulfill the prophecies of Daniel, Altes Museum, Berlin, Germany (image source: author).

Tetradrachm of Commander Seleucid, one of his successors, would fulfill a major prophecy of Daniel's, which would be repeated in our modern day, Susa/Iran, c. 300 BC, Altes Museum, Berlin, Germany (image source: author).

Unfortunately, my lords, the arrangement that the two powerful commanders agreed upon did not last.

The fact of the matter, my lords, is that each of these two men, Perdiccas and Meleager, were in deadly competition amongst themselves, each buying time to root in and increase his power in order to snap the top prize and rule the world all alone.

You can also say the same, your majesties, of the twenty-five governors. Every single one of them has his own dream to dream and his own ambition to fulfill. These are, my sovereigns, twenty-five men of strong personalities, of big ambitions, and of high energy, with circles of connections and friendships. All of them were subtly competing and building their bases in order to swallow the next domain over and add it to theirs and thus increase their wealth and prestige and satisfy their inflated pride.

The pot at this time, my lords, is boiling with too many competitors.

May we, your majesties, call upon the Jewish historian Josephus to report on the inheritors of H.M. King Alexander the Great!

Go ahead, please, historian Josephus.

> "NOW when Alexander, king of Macedon, had put an end to the dominion of the Persians, and had settled the affairs in Judea [Israel] after the fore mentioned manner, he ended his life.
>
> And as his government fell among many, Antigonus obtained Asia [or Anatolia, present day Turkey, but later lost it to the Attalid dynasty], Seleucus Babylon [ruled Iran, Iraq and Syria out of Babylon to begin]; and of the other nations which were there, Lysimachus governed the Hellespont [Asia Minor], and Cassander possessed Macedonia [northern Greece]; as did Ptolemy the son of Lagus seize upon Egypt.
>
> And while these princes [including the Greek Seleucids and Ptolemies] ambitiously strove one against another, every one for his own principality, it came to pass that there were continual wars, and those lasting wars too; and the cities were sufferers, and lost a great many of their inhabitants in these times of distress."[155]

But, my lords, the one who can solve this steaming competition began to solve it. Death! Death, my lords, whether by natural causes or by the sword began to thin down the tangled rivalry.

Within two years of the death of H.M. King Alexander, Commander Perdiccas succeeded to have his main competition, Commander Meleager, assassinated, my lords.

And then a few months later, Commander Perdiccas, who became the most important man of the empire, was himself assassinated [321 BC] by his own officers while he was on his way to eliminate his next strong competitor, Commander Ptolemy, who became the governor of Egypt.

---

[155] Historian Josephus, *Antiquities of the Jews*, Book XII, Chap. I: 1

Greek generals were eliminating Greek generals, your majesties, as they marched towards Daniel's prophecy!

Oh, if H.M. King Alexander the Great could have seen this happening!

One of the three officers who assassinated Commander Perdiccas, your majesties, is Commander Seleucus, whom we had mentioned earlier. And as a result of this assassination, your majesties, Commander Seleucus became the governor of Babylonia.

Congratulations governor Seleucus, Babylonia is a fat, rich province, a good piece of real estate. You will do mighty well there, sir.

Do you hear this, your majesty, King Nebuchadnezzar? The governor of southern Iraq, your rich Babylonia, home of the hanging gardens, is not an Iraqi, neither a Persian Iranian; he is a Greek man, although married to an Iranian woman.

But we can tell you, your majesty King Nebuchadnezzar that Governor Seleucus's ambition is much greater, much more greater, sir, than just owning your Iraq, wealthy as it may be.

And today your majesties, Governor Ptolemy of Egypt and Governor Seleucus of Iraq, have become good friends after having helped each other to assassinate the strong Commander Perdiccas.

This friendship, my lords, shall end with their death. Their children shall fight tooth and nail over Israel and its surrounding region. And as you may have rightly suspected, my lords, their wars shall indeed fulfill Daniel's 300-year-long prophecies, and all the way to Queen Cleopatra.

Meanwhile, my lords, death, the king of all, continued his untiring work of thinning down the ranks of the fierce and ambitious competitors.

Olympias, the mother of H.M. King Alexander had King Philip III, King Alexander's half brother, killed [317 BC]. And then soon after, she herself was killed [316 BC].

And then Roxana, the Iranian wife of H.M. King Alexander, and his child, which indeed turned out to be a son and was crowned King Alexander IV, were both killed.

Young King Alexander IV, your majesties, who was born a few months after his father's death [August, 323 BC], was a twelve-year-old teenager by the time of his death [311/310 BC]. He did not make it. But at least the first part of Daniel's prophecy concerning the offspring of King Alexander the Great has been fulfilled almost twelve years after the death of his majesty.

As of the four main dynasties, this prophecy remains in jeopardy, my lords.

Go ahead, please, prophet Daniel.

*DAN 11:4 And when he shall stand up [at the peak of his power], his kingdom shall be broken, <u>and shall be divided toward the four winds of heaven</u>; <u>and not to his posterity</u> [not given to his children],*

And so, your majesties, as the battlefield began to eliminate one competitor after another; a few of the stronger governors who were left began to boil up to the top of the steaming stew and strengthen their rising domains.

General Ptolemy, governor of Egypt, sent his navy up the Mediterranean Sea and added the island of Cyprus, plus several harbors on the Syrian coast, to his growing account of islands, harbors, and cities.

As some of you may know, my lords, the large island of Cyprus, halfway between Egypt and Italy, is very important for the Egyptian cargo ships plying the Mediterranean Sea with Egyptian grain and goods to the rising but grains-hungry Roman republic.

Besides Governor Ptolemy of Egypt, your majesties, Governor Seleucus of Babylonia Iraq is marching east and adding Iranian lands and fields and towns and taxes, soldiers and manpower to his bulging account.

The two governors have increased their power, my lords. Yet, they were only governors. They were not kings with dynasties to endure. And their enemies were not asleep; they too were building up their strength, my lords, in order to take away what these two had.

## The Third Kingdom —Macedonia

At this point of time, my lords, the strongest threat, which all the governors fear is a team of an ambitious father and his military brilliant son.

The father, my lords, is a one-eyed general who served under H.M. King Philip II, the father of H.M. King Alexander the Great, and who became a governor, Governor Antigonus.

Now his son's name, my lords, is Demetrius. They, father and the son, aimed, my lords, at reuniting the empire of H.M. King Alexander the Great under their joint rule, and theirs only.

First, my lords, they established their base in Greece, where the father was a governor. Then they began to move east [315 BC], intending to take over the rich provinces of Syria, Iraq, and Iran from Governor Seleucus.

Governor Seleucus of Babylon could do no more than abandon Babylon city and flee to his friend Governor Ptolemy of Egypt for shelter and help.

One-eyed Governor Antigonus and his son Commander Demetrius, having secured Syria and Iraq, my lords, turned their armies south towards Egypt to fight Governor Ptolemy and his protégée, Governor Seleucus.

If they succeed to take Egypt, your majesties, then they would be well on their way to inherit the empire of H.M. King Alexander the Great. And at the same time, Daniel's would fail.

They are doing fine at the moment, my lords.

In their way south to Egypt, they sacked the wealthy city of Tyre of Lebanon and also took Israel [314 BC].

Governor Seleucus I Nicator of Babylon, the Louvre Museum, Paris (image source: author).

So far, so good for the father and son team, my lords!

Then the father-son team split, your majesties. The father returned to Greece for more battles there. And the son was left with an army to protect the new acquisitions in Lebanon and Israel near Egypt.

Governor Ptolemy of Egypt and his protégée, Governor Seleucus, of Iraq responded, my lords, by attacking Commander Demetrius near Gaza, north of the Egyptian borders.

The Egyptians won, your majesties, [the Battle of Gaza 312 BC]. But young Commander Demetrius survived the battle and retreated farther north into Lebanon.

But his defeat, my lords, was a major reversal to the ambitions of the father and son team.

It is far from over, my lords. In fact, the enemies shall intermarry—anything for power, my lords. We do not have to tell you this your majesties, do we?

Come springtime, your majesties, Governor Ptolemy [early spring 311 BC] provided his protégé, Governor Seleucus of Iraq, with about 800–1000 foot soldiers and 200–300 horses, to conduct him safely back to Babylon, where he may regroup and continue the war against Governor Antigonus, the one-eyed governor.

The war lasted two years, my lords, and Governor Seleucus became steadily stronger.

The father and the son team began to give up hope on the dream of reuniting the empire, my lords, and instead sued for peace.

Tetradrachm of Commander Demetrios I Poliorketes of Macedonia, he and his father, the one-eyed general, intended to eliminate all competitors and inherit the empire of King Alexander the Great, 306-283 BC. They will end up building the third of the four kingdoms Daniel prophesied of, British Museum, London (image source: author).

However, my lords, after broken peace agreements and yet more wars, Governor Antigonus I Monophthalmus, the one-eyed general, succeeded to take the island of Cyprus from General Ptolemy of Egypt [306 BC]. Now this was a major setback for Governor Ptolemy of Egypt.

And then with this success, my lords, a major change took place. We are now, my sovereigns, beginning to see the faint lines of the prophecies of Daniel.

With his latest success, Governor Antigonus I Monophthalmus, my lords, crowned himself, and his son Demetrius I. Poliarcetes, joint kings of Macedonia of Greece. Macedonia, my lords, is of course the birthplace kingdom of H.M. King Alexander the Great.

The two men are no longer governors, my lords. They are kings. They shall therefore establish a royal house, heirs and a kingdom.

The precedent is now set, my lords.

And so, in turn, Governor Ptolemy responded by calling himself King Ptolemy I Soter of Egypt. And so did Governor Seleucid, who now is calling himself "King Seleucid I Nicator of Babylonia Iraq," ruling from Iran to Syria.

Three dynasties have been established at this moment, my lords: Macedonia, Syria, and Egypt.

And with this your majesties, with the generals crowning themselves kings [306/305 BC, seventeen years after the death of King Alexander the

Great in 323 BC] and establishing their dominions as kingdoms, you may as well, my lords, say that any hope of one man inheriting the unified empire of H.M. King Alexander the Great is now dead and buried.

Daniel's prophecy, my lords, stands a good chance of fulfillment.

But big dreams do not die in a hurry, my lords; they keep watching for opportunities and chances, and build on small successes towards greater ones.

H.M. King Demetrius I. Poliarcetes, the son of the one-eyed general and now king of northern Greece, managed to defeat the navy of H.M. King Ptolemy I Soter of Egypt and added the Mediterranean island of Salamis to his previous winning of the island of Cyprus.

He now owns the highways of the sea.

And springing from this success, my lords, his majesty sailed on to Egypt in order to eliminate his strong rival, King Ptolemy I Soter.

Daniel's prophecy is once again put at risk.

Stop the sailing.

My lords, a storm put an end to the Armanda of H.M. King Demetrius I. Poliarcetes of Macedonia.

Daniel's prophecy of the four main dynasties survived for yet another day.

Each of these developments, my lords, tested those who believed in Daniel's prophecies and cheered up those who could not believe in them.

Another image of the brilliant commander Demetrius I. Poliarcetes son of Governor Antigonus I Monophthalmus (one-eyed), National Archaeological Museum of Naples, Italy (image source: author).

Even with the storm setback, the threat of the one-eyed King Antigonus and his son King Demetrius remains strong, my lords.

And this why, your majesties, a few years after the battle of Salamis, and yet another one for the island of Rhodes [301 BC], that three kings—H.M. King Lysimachus, H.M. King Cassander and, of course, H.M. King Seleucus I Nicator of Iraq—with the help of others such as H.M. King Ptolemy I Soter of Egypt, rallied up their forces against the 81-year-old, one-eyed King Antigonus I Monophthalmus and his son, King Demetrius I. Poliarcetes.

> *Misunderstanding*
>
> A peace agreement followed the victory of the alliance. The agreement was vague. The successors of King Seleucus believed that Israel belonged to them; whereas the successors of King Ptolemy believed that it was theirs. This misunderstanding led to the 300-year-old wars between them—a series of wars that shall fulfill Daniel's prophecies.

The allies, my lords, succeeded to defeat father and son in the battle of Ipsus [301 BC].

In fact, my lords, the allies managed to kill the one-eyed King Antigonus. Now only the son is left to fend for himself.

And here, your majesties, the tide of history gets closer to the shore.

Having very little options, King Demetrius I. Poliarcetes of Macedonia, of northern Greece, has reconciled with King Seleucus I Nicator of Babylonia Iraq. In fact, my lords, H.M. King Demetrius gave King Seleucus I his teenage daughter as a wife [300 BC].

Alas, my lords, this political marriage did not work. A few years, later King Seleucus I Nicator, as a result of another war [286 BC], captured his father-in-law King Demetrius I. Poliarcetes, who eventually died in captivity [284 BC].

Tetradrachm of Antigonos Gonatas, King of Macedonia and successor of King Demetrius I Poliarcetes, c. 270. Their royal house lasted nearly 130 years, Altes Museum, Berlin, Germany (image source: author).

Has this third dynasty of Macedonia of northern Greece then come to an end? No, it did not your majesties.

King Seleucus of Iraq has allowed the royal family of his father-in-law to continue as the rulers of Macedonia, of northern Greece—the birthplace kingdom of H.M. King Alexander the Great.

And this dynasty, my lords, of the one-eyed king and his son, lasted until the Roman legions came and invaded Macedonian nearly one hundred thirty-three years after the death of the one-eyed founder. The dynasty of the one-eyed-king had a good run on royal life your majesties.

And so, my lords, this was the third notable dynasty, along with those of H.M. King Ptolemy I Soter of Egypt and H.M. King Seleucus I Nicator of Iraq and Iran.

## The Fourth Kingdom —Anatolia [Asia Minor]

And so, my lords, besides the two superpower dynasties of Egypt in the south—and the united Iran, Iraq, and Syria in the north—a third royal family has now emerged in Macedonia of northern Greece, as you have seen.

And so now we go to the fourth dynasty, your majesties, Anatolia or Asia Minor [Edit: today's Turkey].

As you may recall, my lords, Anatolia, is the region where the wars between the Iranian Persians and the Greek cities in Turkey began.

In those long ago days, my lords, the region, as some of you may recall, was called Ionia.

Those were your days, your majesties King Cyrus the Great, King Darius I, King Xerxes I and, your majesty, King Darius III. Those were the days of wealthy King Croesus, the battles of Marathon and Thermopylae, of the Spartans last stand, the days of the burning of Athens city, and the naval battle of Salamis.

And there in this Ionia, or Asia Minor, or as we today call it, "Turkey," there, your majesties, could find the great Greek cities of Delphi, Corinth, Ephesus, and Pergamon.

Some of you, my lords, may not know that the Greek city of Ephesus is home of the goddess Artemis, whose statue fell from the sky, according to her devoted and sincere worshippers.

And as for Pergamon city, my lords, it is home of the great Pergamon Altar, which partially survives to our modern day, my lords.

ABOVE: The Pergamon Altar built during the reign of King Eumenes II of Asia Minor, Anatolia, the fourth major kingdom after the death of King Alexander the Great, 197-159 BC, Pergamon Museum, Berlin (image source: author).

RIGHT: The goddess Artemis of Ephesus, 2nd century AD, Naples Archaeological Museum, Italy (image source: author).

In the year when many governors declared themselves kings [306 BC, about seventeen/eighteen years after the death of Alexander the Great], Governor Lysimachus did so as well, my lords, and crowned himself king in Asia Minor of Turkey. And indeed, my lords, the new king fought hard for his territory, which expanded and shrank from fight to fight.

In those days there were many young bloods, my lords, in the fights that followed the death of his young majesty King Alexander the Great.

Tetradrachm of Lysimachus, c .297–281, founder of the fourth dominion. The Greek kings for many years styled themselves after Alexander the Great, Bode Museum, Berlin, Germany (image source: author).

Stater (coin domination) of Lysimachus, c. 297-281, Bode Museum, Berlin, Germany (image source: author).

H.M. King Lysimachus, my lords, married a young Iranian princess, who in fact—take this—my lords, was a niece of King Darius III, who lost the Persian Empire to the one and only King Alexander the Great. Unfortunately, this political marriage to the Iranian princess Amastris did not last.

ABOVE LEFT: Queen Amastris, c.300–285 BC, born a Persian princess, a niece of King Darius III, being the daughter of Oxyathres who is King Darius's brother, married Greek King Lysimachus in 302 BC, Altes Museum, Berlin, Germany (image source: author).

ABOVE RIGHT: Statuette of Greek Queen Arsinoe II, daughter of Greek King Ptolemy I Soter of Egypt, and his wife Bernice I, married King Lysimachus King of Anatolia, Turkey, when she was 15 years' old, the Louvre Museum, Paris, France (image source: author).

Upon divorcing his Persian-born Queen Amastris, H.M. King Lysimachus of Anatolia Turkey then married the daughter of King Ptolemy I Soter of Egypt—another political marriage, my lords.

Queen Arsinoe II, Bode Museum, Berlin, Germany (image source: author).

Another image of Greek Queen Arsinoe II, this time with her second husband Greek King Ptolemy II of Egypt, whom she married after the death of King Lysimachus, coin c. 260-240, Bode Museum, Berlin, Germany (image source: author).

King Lysimachus' marriage to the Iranian-born princess and then to the Egyptian-born Queen Arsinoe II caused a rift in the military ranks of his majesty. One officer, in charge of the city of Pergamon, revolted, my lords, and succeeded to take the reins of the government of Anatolia Turkey, following the death of H.M. King Lysimachus.

The officer, who then became the new king of Asia Minor of Turkey, is Philetaerus your majesties.

Tetradrachm of Philetairos (or Philetaerus) of Pergamon, who will go on to establish the fourth kingdom following the death of King Alexander the Great, 270 BC, Bode Museum, Berlin, Germany (image source: author).

Now, my lords, H.M. King Philetaerus, and his successors, King Eumenes I and Attalus I, went on to establish a dynasty in Asia Minor of Turkey. Their dynasty, my lords, lasted until the newcomer, the Roman legions, wrestled the world from Greece, as Balaam son of Boer had prophesied nearly two thousand years ago if, your majesties, may recall.

Tetradrachm of Eumenes I of Pergamon, one of the founding fathers of the fourth major kingdom of the divided empire of King Alexander the Great, 262-241, Bode Museum, Berlin, Germany (image source: author).

Tetradrachm of Attalos I, king of Pergamon, portraying King Philetairos, the founding father of the Attalid dynasty of Asia Minor, 241-197 BC, British Museum, London, UK (image source: author).

## The Final Count

My lords, after forty-eight hectic years in a boiling caldron and endless wars, the vast earthly holdings of H.M. King Alexander the Great settled into the hands of four major dynasties and negligible minor ones.

King Ptolemy I Soter had taken the wealthy lands of Egypt, Palestine, and Israel [Coele-Syria]. He is the king of the south.

King Seleucus I Nicator took possession of the vast territory of Iran, Iraq, and Syria. His majesty is the king of the north, that is, north of Israel, my lords.

The one-eyed H.M. King Antigonus and his descendants took Macedon, birthplace of H.M. King Alexander the Great.

And the fourth dynasty, the Attalid dynasty, was established in Asia Minor, Turkey.

Your majesties, the prophet Daniel foretold all of this in more than one prophecy.

"This coin bears an image of King Ptolemy I. It was designed by a famous craftsman in Alexandria whose "signature" is the Greek letter (Δ) seen behind Ptolemy's ear." The quote is copied from the Metropolitan Museum of Art where the coin is preserved, NY (image source: author).

And the prophecies were repeated more than once, your majesties, in order to assure him, and further explain to him, what his eyes of the day have not and could not see. And his responsibility, my lords, was to write down these events in order to strengthen the faith of future generations so that all may come to know that God has a plan and a timetable for the beautiful but doomed earth, as His people preach, my lords.

Prophet Daniel, did you foresee all of this nearly 265 years in advance? Please, tell their majesties, sir, all you saw about the inheritors of H.M. King Alexander the Great.

> DAN 7:1 *In the first year of Belshazzar king of Babylon [before the fall of the Babylonian Empire, before the rise and fall of the Persian Empire, and before the birth and death of King Alexander the Great] Daniel had a dream and visions of his head upon his bed: then he wrote the dream, and told the sum of the matters.*
> DAN 7:2 *Daniel spake and said, I saw in my vision by night, and, behold, the four winds of the heaven strove upon the great sea [Mediterranean Sea].*

*DAN 7:3* And four great beasts came up from the sea, diverse one from another.
*DAN 7:4* The first was like a lion [Babylonian Empire of King Nebuchadnezzar reached the Mediterranean Sea], and had eagle's wings: I beheld till the wings thereof were plucked, and it was lifted up from the earth, and made stand upon the feet as a man, and a man's heart was given to it [weakened].
*DAN 7:5* And behold another beast a second [the Median-Persian Empire of King Cyrus the Great], like to a bear, and it raised up itself on one side, and it had three ribs [Media, Elam and Persia, the three regions of Iran] in the mouth of it between the teeth of it: and they said thus unto it, Arise, devour much flesh.
*DAN 7:6* After this I beheld, and lo another, like a leopard [the fast and agile Grecian Empire of King Alexander the Great], which had upon the back of it four wings of a fowl [the four main kingdoms born of the divided Grecian Empire of Alexander the Great]; <u>the beast had also four heads; and dominion was given to it</u>.

What else did you see, prophet Daniel, two years after?

*Dan 8:1* In the third year of the reign of [Babylonian] king Belshazzar a vision appeared unto me, even unto me Daniel, after that which appeared unto me at the first.
*Dan 8:2* And I saw in a vision; and it came to pass, when I saw, that I was at Shushan in the palace, which is in the province of Elam [in Iran]; and I saw in a vision, and I was by the river of Ulai.
*Dan 8:3* Then I lifted up mine eyes, and saw, and, behold, there stood before the river a ram which had two horns [Media and Persia]: and the two horns were high; but one was higher than the other, and the higher came up last.
*Dan 8:4* I saw the ram pushing westward, and northward, and southward; so that no beasts might stand before him, neither was there any that could deliver out of his hand; but he did according to his will, and became great.
*Dan 8:5* And as I was considering, behold, an he goat came from the west on the face of the whole earth, and touched not the ground: and the goat had a notable horn between his eyes [King Alexander the Great].
*Dan 8:6* And he came to the ram that had two horns [the Median-Persian Empire], which I had seen standing before the river, and ran unto him in the fury of his power.

*Dan 8:7* And I saw him come close unto the ram, and he was moved with choler against him, and smote the ram, and brake his two horns: and there was no power in the ram to stand before him, but he cast him down to the ground, and stamped upon him: and there was none that could deliver the ram out of his hand.
*Dan 8:8* Therefore the he goat [the Greeks] waxed very great: and when he was strong, <u>the great horn was broken; and for it came up four notable ones toward the four winds of heaven</u>.
...
*Dan 8:19* And he said, Behold, I will make thee know what shall be in the last end of the indignation [at the end of the Babylonian Exile of the Children of Israel]: for at the time appointed the end shall be [seventy years of exile as per the prophecy of the prophet Jeremiah].
*Dan 8:20* The ram which thou sawest having two horns are the kings of Media and Persia.
*Dan 8:21* And the rough [strong] goat is the king of Grecia: and the great horn that is between his eyes is the first king.
*Dan 8:22* <u>Now that being broken, whereas four stood up for it, four kingdoms shall stand up out of the nation [Greece], but not in his power</u>.

Would you also please, prophet Daniel, tell their majesties of your third prophecy!

*DAN 11:3 a mighty king shall stand up [another vision that speaks of King Alexander the Great with additional details], that shall rule with great dominion, and do according to his will.*
*DAN 11:4 And when he shall stand up [at the peak of his power], his kingdom shall be broken, <u>and shall be divided toward the four winds of heaven</u>; <u>and not to his posterity</u> [not given to his children], nor according to his dominion [none of the new dominions would be as strong as Alexander's dominion] which he ruled: for his kingdom shall be plucked up, even for others beside those [besides the main four kingdoms or dynasties].*

And now, my lords, we go on for nearly three hundred years of prophecies.

# Marriages and Divorces Peace and War

The great and experienced commanders, my lords, began to leave the scene one by one. The founding fathers of the main Greek royal families, the undisputed masters of our world, began to bow out in their way to the heavenly court of justice of the universe.

The giants died, my lords, but the prophecies lived on in order to illuminate future days in God's calendar.

The first to go, my lords, was H.M. King Ptolemy I Soter of Egypt, whose body was left in the ground but his soul went to his maker. His majesty walked amongst us commoners for nearly eighty-four years and ruled his plot of earth for about forty solid years. Farewell your majesty.

LEFT: One of Alexander's main and capable generals, who later became King Ptolemy I Soter, king of Egypt (305/4–283/2 BC), is the ancestor of the famous Greek Queen Cleopatra of Egypt, British Museum (image source: author).

BELOW: A statue of King Ptolemy I Soter of Egypt, Numismatic Museum of Athens, Greece (image source: author).

Following the departure of H.M. King Ptolemy I Soter of Egypt came the turn of his protégé H.M. King Seleucus I Nicator. The number of the days of H.M. king Seleucus I Nicator, king of the united Iran, Iraq, and Syria ran out, my lords, by the time he reached fifty-two years of age and ruled his assigned piece of the earth for twenty-five years.

And with the death of these two kings, my lords, the friendship between their two royal houses died as well. But the prophecies will come alive. And the prophecies, my lords, will give life to those in the grip of doubts.

King Seleucus I Nicator, the founder of the Seleucid royal family, married an Iranian, Princess Apama in 324 BC.

One of his offspring fulfilled a very important event in God's timetable for the earth, National Archaeological Museum of Naples, Italy (image source: author).

## Egypt Takes Israel

During the forty-eight years when the great generals of Alexander were trying to carve kingdoms for themselves, King Ptolemy I Soter of Egypt managed to invade his neighboring nation of Israel and add it to his domain of Egypt.

This fact does not seem important at this point of time.

But later on, the Greek royals of Iraq and Iran would insist that Israel belonged to them and not to Egypt. And this dispute amongst the royals of the north and the royals of the south would then ignite six wars. And in turn, these six wars would fulfill many prophecies, including the enigmatic one about the "daughter of the women."

> ### 320 BC
>
> According to historian Josephus, King Ptolemy I Soter of Egypt managed to take Jerusalem city, the seat of the government of Israel by ruse, attacking it during its day of rest—the Sabbath day.
>
>> "*Ptolemy the son of Lagus ... seized upon Jerusalem, and for that end made use of deceit and treachery; for as he came into the city on a sabbath day, as if he would offer sacrifices he, without any trouble, gained the city,*
>> ...
>> Ptolemy had taken a great many captives, both from the mountainous parts of Judea [Sothern province of Israel], and from the places about Jerusalem and Samaria [capital city of northern Israel], and the places near Mount Gerizzim, *he led them all into Egypt, and settled them there.*
>> And as he knew that the people of Jerusalem were most faithful in the observation of oaths and covenants; and this from the answer they made to Alexander, when he sent an embassage to them, after he had beaten Darius in battle; so he distributed many of them into garrisons, and at Alexandria gave them equal privileges of citizens with the [Greek] Macedonians themselves; and required of them to take their oaths, that they would keep their fidelity to the posterity of those who committed these places to their care.
>> Nay, there were not a few other Jews who, of their own accord, went into Egypt, as invited by the goodness of the soil, and by the liberality of Ptolemy.[156]"

## 280 BC Who Owns Israel?

As you may recall, my lords, H.M. King Ptolemy I Soter of Egypt had sheltered and assisted H.M. King Seleucus I Nicator of Iraq and Iran. And then later on, he further lent him a hand in defeating the one-eyed King Antigonus I Monophthalmus and his son King Demetrius I. Poliarcetes.

The peace agreement, which followed the victory, left everyone confused, my lords.

The royal family of H.M. King Seleucus I Nicator of Syria, Iraq, and Iran believed that Israel was allocated to them, but that H.M. King Seleucus did not claim it from Egypt out of gratitude to his protector H.M. King Ptolemy I Soter who, occupied it [since 320 BC].

---

[156] Josephus, *Antiquities of the Jews*, Book XII, Chapter: 1:1

On the other hand, my lords, the royal Ptolemaic house of Egypt insisted that their founder, H.M. King Ptolemy I Soter, had never agreed to give Israel to his protégée King Seleucus I Nicator of Iraq and Iran.

And so, my lords, a bit over a year after the death of H.M. King Seleucus I Nicator, his son, H.M. King Antiochus I, went on the attack against King Ptolemy I Soter's son, H.M. King Ptolemy II Philadelphus of Egypt [First Syrian War 280–279, first part].

Unfortunately, my lords, the royal house of the Seleucids lost. Five years later H.M. King Antiochus I tried again to take Israel, but was defeated once again by H.M. King Ptolemy II Philadelphus of Egypt.

King Antiochus I, Numismatic Museum of Athens (image source: author)

ABOVE: Intellectual Greek King Ptolemy II Philadelphus of Egypt, 284-246 BC, founder of the Library of Alexandria, home of great thinkers and scientists and mathematicians such as Euclid, Archimedes, and Eratosthenes of Cyrene (who with a great accuracy calculated the circumference of the earth and the tilt of its axis). It is said that an inscription above the shelves of the great library read: "The place of the cure of the soul," Numismatic Museum of Athens, Greece (image source: author).

LEFT: King Ptolemy II Philadelphus of Egypt inherited the southern part of the Grecian Empire. He was attacked by King Antiochus I of Iraq and Iran, who wanted to wrestle Israel from him, the National Archaeological Museum of Naples, Italy (image source: author).

## The Greatest Library of the Ancient World – Home of the Book of Daniel in Greek

King Ptolemy II Philadelphus of Egypt, the second ruler of the Ptolemaic dynasty, was a scholarly and intellectual man. Indeed, his drive to collect as many books as possible included the Old Testament of the Bible, which he had translated to Greek 2,500 years ago. The Old Testament of the Bible does of course include the book of Daniel.

> "1. WHEN Alexander [the Great] had reigned twelve years, and after him Ptolemy Soter forty years, [King Ptolemy II] Philadelphus then took the kingdom of Egypt, and held it forty years within one.
>
> He procured the law to be interpreted [the entire Old Testament of the Bible, including the Book of Daniel – or its first five books only?], and set free those [Israelites] that were come from Jerusalem into Egypt, and were in slavery there, who were a hundred and twenty thousand.
>
> The occasion was this: Demetrius Phalerius, who was library keeper to the king, was now endeavoring, if it were possible, <u>to gather together all the books that were in the habitable earth, and buying whatsoever was any where valuable, or agreeable to the king's inclination, who was very earnestly set upon collecting of books</u>, to which inclination of his Demetrius was zealously subservient.
>
> And when once Ptolemy asked him how many ten thousands of books he had collected, he replied, that he had already about twenty times ten thousand; but that, in a little time, he should have fifty times ten thousand.
>
> <u>But he said he had been informed that there were many books of laws [the entire Old Testament?] among the Jews worthy of inquiring after, and worthy of the king's library</u>, but which, being written in characters and in a dialect of their own, will cause no small pains in getting them <u>translated into the Greek tongue</u>; that the character in which they are written seems to be like to that which is the proper character of the Syrians, and that its sound, when pronounced, is like theirs also; and that this sound appears to be peculiar to themselves.
>
> Wherefore he said that nothing hindered why they might not get those books to be translated also; for while nothing is wanting that is necessary for that purpose, we may have their books also in this library. So the king thought that Demetrius was very zealous to procure him abundance of books, and that he suggested what was exceeding proper for him to do; <u>and therefore he wrote to the Jewish high priest</u>, that he should act accordingly."[157]

And so the head of the library did then formerly advice King Ptolemy II Philadelphus on the best way to bring, and interpret, the Old Testament into Greek.

---

[157] Josephus, *Antiquities of the Jews*, Book XII, Chapter II: 1

4." Now when this had been done after so magnificent a manner, according to the king's inclinations, he gave order to Demetrius to give him in writing his sentiments concerning the transcribing of the Jewish books; for no part of the administration is done rashly by these kings, but all things are managed with great circumspection.

...

Now the copy of the epistle was to this purpose: "Demetrius to the great king. When thou, O king, gavest me a charge concerning the collection of books that were wanting to fill your library, and concerning the care that ought to be taken about such as are imperfect, I have used the utmost diligence about those matters. And I let you know, that we want the books of the Jewish legislation, with some others [again, the Entire Old Testament, including Daniel's Book?]; for they are written in the Hebrew characters, and being in the language of that nation, are to us unknown. It hath also happened to them, that they have been transcribed more carelessly than they ought to have been, because they have not had hitherto royal care taken about them. <u>Now it is necessary that thou shouldst have accurate copies of them. And indeed this legislation is full of hidden wisdom, and entirely blameless</u>, as being the legislation of God; for which cause it is, as Hecateus of Abdera says, that the poets and historians make no mention of it, nor of those men who lead their lives according to it, since it is a holy law, and ought not to be published by profane mouths.

<u>If then it please thee, O king, thou mayst write to the high priest of the Jews, to send six of the elders out of every tribe [72 men in total], and those such as are most skillful of the laws, that by their means we may learn the clear and agreeing sense of these books, and may obtain an accurate interpretation of their contents, and so may have such a collection of these as may be suitable to thy desire.</u>"[158]

King Ptolemy II Philadelphus accepted the advice of the head of his royal library of Alexandria and wrote a letter to Eleazar the high priest of Israel.

"<u>I have determined to procure an interpretation of your law, and to have it translated out of Hebrew into Greek, and to be deposited in my library</u>. Thou wilt therefore do well to choose out and send to me men of a good character, who are now elders in age, and six in number out of every tribe. <u>These, by their age, must be skillful in the laws, and of abilities to make an accurate interpretation of them; and when this shall be finished, I shall think that I have done a work glorious to myself</u>. And I have sent to thee Andreas, the captain of my guard, and Aristeus, men whom I have in very great esteem; by whom I have sent those first-fruits which I have dedicated to the temple, and to the sacrifices, and to other uses, to the value of a hundred talents. And if thou wilt send to us, to let us know what thou wouldst have further, thou wilt do a thing acceptable to me."[159]

---

[158] Josephus, *Antiquities of the Jews*, Book XII, Chapter II: 4
[159] Josephus, *Antiquities of the Jews*, Book XII, Chapter II: 5

In no time, high priest Eleazar gave his answer to King Ptolemy II Philadelphus.

> "Eleazar the high priest to King Ptolemy, sendeth greeting. If thou and thy queen Arsinoe, and thy children, be well, we are entirely satisfied.
>
> ...
>
> and that the translation of our law may come to the conclusion thou desirest, and be for thy advantage. We have also chosen six elders out of every tribe, whom we have sent, and the law with them.
>
> ...
>
> Farewell."[160]

**Octodrachm of Queen Arsinoe II of Egypt, c.253–246 BC, wife of King Ptolemy II, Altes Museum, Berlin, Germany (image source: author).**

> "Now when the law was transcribed, and the labor of interpretation was over, which came to its conclusion in seventy-two days, Demetrius [the head of the library] gathered all the Jews together to the place where the laws were translated, and where the interpreters were, and read them over.
>
> The multitude did also approve of those elders that were the interpreters of the law.
>
> They withal commended Demetrius for his proposal [of having the translation read before many people], as the inventor of what was greatly for their happiness; and they desired that he would give leave to their rulers also to read the law.
>
> Moreover, they all, both the priest and the ancientest of the elders, and the principal men of their commonwealth, made it their request, that since the interpretation was happily finished, it might continue in the state it now was, and might not be altered. And when they all commended that determination of theirs, they enjoined, that if any one observed either anything superfluous, or anything omitted, that he would take a view of it again, and have it laid before them, and corrected; which was a wise action of theirs, that when the thing was judged to have been well done, it might continue for ever."[161]

---

[160] Josephus, *Antiquities of the Jews*, Book XII, Chapter II: 6
[161] Josephus, *Antiquities of the Jews*, Book XII, Chapter II: 13

Prophet Daniel, would you please inform their majesties of what you said will happen after the death of H.M. King Ptolemy I Soter of Egypt and his protégé, H.M. King Seleucus I Nicator of Syria and Iraq?

But please begin your prophecy from a point of time known to their majesties.

> DAN 11:3 *a mighty king [King Alexander the Great] shall stand up, that shall rule with great dominion, and do according to his will.*
> DAN 11:4 *And when he shall stand up, his kingdom shall be broken, and shall be divided toward the four winds of heaven; and not to his posterity, nor according to his dominion which he ruled: for his kingdom shall be plucked up, even for others beside those.*

Excuse us for the interruption, sir; we need to caution their majesties.

My lords, we caution you that the prophecy may sound very enigmatic at this point of time. But perhaps you may nonetheless wish to try and see for yourselves how much you can glean from it.

And so now, prophet Daniel, what did you see next, sir, after the birth of the four main kingdoms?

> DAN 11:5 *And the king of the south [King Ptolemy I, the most able of King Alexander's generals, ruled Egypt, south of Israel] shall be strong, and <u>one of his princes; and he shall be strong above him</u>, and have dominion; his dominion shall be a great dominion.*
> DAN 11:6 *And in the end of years <u>they shall join themselves together; for the king's daughter of the south shall come to the king of the north to make an agreement: but she shall not retain the power of the arm; neither shall he stand, nor his arm: but she shall be given up, and they that brought her, and he that begat her, and he that strengthened her in these times.</u>*
> DAN 11:7 *But out of a branch of her roots shall one stand up in his estate, which shall come with an army, and shall enter into the fortress of the king of the north, and shall deal against them, and shall prevail:*
> DAN 11:8 *And shall also carry captives into Egypt their gods, with their princes, and with their precious vessels of silver and of gold; and he shall continue more years than the king of the north.*
> DAN 11:9 *So the king of the south shall come into his kingdom, and shall return into his own land.*

Prophet Daniel, sir, please once again accept our apology, for we know next to nothing of those royals mentioned in your prophecy nor of the events you are prophesying—nothing. And, therefore sir, we must admit that your prophecy is an enigma to most of us.

But in the same time, sir, we do realize that this prophecy must have meant much for the people of the Holy One in the trying times they went through amongst the clashing of swords all around their homes and families. Those days must have seen their shares of impoverished widows, inconsolable orphans, maimed and handicapped men, and broken-hearted grandparents—all confused and in doubt of the care and the abilities of their eternal guardian above.

> HEB 1:1 God, who at sundry [different] times and in divers manners spake in time past unto the fathers by the prophets,
> ACTS 14:15 the living God, which made heaven, and earth, and the sea, and all things that are therein:
> ACTS 14:16 Who in times past
> ACTS 14:17 left not himself without witness.

But for us, here and now, sir, we still need to understand these prophecies in order to decipher the ones dealing with us—especially the one that speaks of the little horn and the dreadful beast.

And so with your permission, prophet Daniel, we shall stop you here, sir, and ask the ancient men who lived in those olden days, in the days of the fulfillment of your prophecies, to tell us what exactly happened.

My lords, time passed, and the second ruler of Syria, Iran, and Iraq—H.M. King Antiochus I Soter—died. But his intellectual counterpart, the second ruler of Egypt H.M. King Ptolemy II Philadelphus of Egypt, lives still at this point of time. He is the man of the library, my lords.

Now your majesties, the new Seleucid comer, the third ruler of Iraq and Iran, H.M. King Antiochus II Theos, began his reign by attacking the nearby Egyptian holdings on the Syrian coast, the profitable shipping harbors, and succeeded to take them from the Egyptian garrisons stationed there.

But soon the wedding music began to play, my lords.

Tetradrachm coin of King Antiochus II Theos, third ruler of Syria, Iran, and Iraq, who defeated the second ruler of Egypt, King Ptolemy II Philadelphus, Alts Museum, Berlin (image source: author).

Bridal attire, 4th–3rd Cent BC, Altes Museum, Berlin (image source: author).

Now aging H.M. King Ptolemy II Philadelphus of Egypt did the best he could under the circumstances and struck a peace treaty with his victorious majesty King Antiochus II Theos of the Seleucids Empire [253 BC] of the north.

And to cement the treaty, his Egyptian majesty did what some of you, my lords, had done in your day. He turned to his daughter.

Indeed, nearly a year after the peace treaty, H.M. King Antiochus II of the north divorced his Iranian wife, Queen Laodice, and agreed to marry

408—EARTH OUT OF ORBIT

Princess Berenice II Phernephorus, daughter of his Egyptian Majesty, the intellectual King Ptolemy II Philadelphus.

Now, as you see, my lords, the prophecy is beginning to clear up a bit.

LEFT: Princess Berenice Phernophorus (?), daughter of intellectual King Ptolemy II Philadelphus of Egypt, married King Antiochus II Theos of the North (Iran, Iraq, and Syria) and became the queen of the Seleucids Empire, the National Archaeological Museum of Naples, Italy (image source: author).

RIGHT: Scholar King Ptolemy II Philadelphus of Egypt, above, gave his daughter Bernice in marriage to King Antiochus II, The National Museum of Denmark, Copenhagen (image source: author).

Tetradrachm of King Antiochus II Theos, grandson of the founder of the Seleucids Empire, King Seleucus I Nicator, who divorced his partially Iranian wife, Queen Laodice, and married Princess Berenice, daughter of King Ptolemy II of Egypt, Altes Museum, Berlin, Germany (image source: author).

# PAST AND PRESENT ABOMINATIONS—409

Bad mistake, your majesties! Bad mistake!

To clarify, my lords, it was a bad mistake to humiliate the partly Iranian Queen Laodice.

On the other hand, this humiliation, my lords, did eventually lead to fulfilling and clarifying another part of Daniel's prophecy.

The spurred queen, my lords, had her chance to revenge her humiliation six years after she was repudiated —six years after the Egyptian princess Berenice Phernophorus married her ex-husband, the victorious King Antiochus II Theos.

For, it so happened, my lords, that at that time more than one important event took place simultaneously.

One of these events, my lords, was the death of his Egyptian majesty intellectual King Ptolemy II Philadelphus [January 28, 246 BC]. And his death, your majesties, began the chain of events mentioned in Daniel's prophecy, which we could not understand.

Immediately, my lords, his son-in-law, H.M. King Antiochus II Theos of the north, dropped Queen Berenice II, daughter of the now-deceased King Ptolemy II Philadelphus, and went back to his partly Iranian, partly Greek wife, Laodice.

He went to die, my lords.

Was his return good enough for the woman he humiliated your majesties?

The answer took a few months to surface.

In about seven months [early July 246 BC] the story goes, my lords, that Queen Laodice managed to poison and kill her repentant husband.

Gold pentadrachm of intellectual Greek King Ptolemy II of Egypt, 285–246 BC, wearing a royal diadem, University of Pennsylvania Archaeological Museum, Philadelphia, USA (image source: author).

What then would happen to the Egyptian-born Queen Berenice II and her son, the crown prince and the heir of the Seleucid Empire of the North [Iran, Iraq, and Syria]?

In fact, your majesties, we now have two youngsters; each is fully qualified to be the crown prince and the heir of the vacant Seleucids throne of the north.

We have here, my lords, the son of the partly Iranian Queen Laodice, 19-year-old Seleucus II Callinicus. And we also have the son of the Egyptian-born Queen Berenice, 5-year-old Antiochus.

And as may be expected, my lords, the two mothers of the two apparent heirs are, at this point of time, fighting tooth and nail for their perspective son and the royal throne of the wealthy empire of the north.

Now, my lords, you can imagine the reaction in Egypt to the rumors that the partly Iranian Queen Laodice is preparing the way for her son to inherit the empire, which naturally means, my lords, that H.M. Queen Berenice Phernophorus and her infant son, Antiochus, are in a real and mortal danger up there.

May we now, my lords, call on ancient historian Apian to further detail you on the situation!

Go ahead, sir.

> "After the death of Seleucus, the kingdom of Syria passed in regular succession from father to son as follows: the first was the same Antiochus who fell in love with his stepmother, to whom was given the surname of *Soter*, 'Savior', for driving out the Gauls who had made an incursion into Asia from Europe.
>
> The second was another Antiochus, born of this marriage, who received the surname of *Theos*, 'Divine,' from the Milesians in the first instance, because he slew their tyrant, Timarchus.
>
> <u>This Theos was poisoned by his wife. He had two wives, Laodice and Berenice, the former a love-match, the latter a daughter pledged to him by [the Ptolemaic Egyptian king] Ptolemy [II Philadelphus]</u>.[162]

The wheels are spinning fast in Egypt, my lords, and the chariots are on the move.

Queen Bernice's brother, the new king of Egypt, H.M. King Ptolemy III Euergetes, is on the move to ensure that the Seleucid Empire would remain in the Ptolemaic family and that his sister and his young nephew, the new king, would live on to rule it.

## September 246 BC
## Greater Than His Father

His majesty, the new 38-year-old monarch of Egypt, King Ptolemy III Euergetes has mobilized both the army and the navy, my lords, [The Laodicean War, named after Queen Laodice, or the Third Syrian War]. The Egyptian army, my lords, is sailing north full steam to deal with Queen Laodice and her army.

---

[162] Apian [c. 95–c. 165], *The Roman History*, *Syrian Wars*: 65, translated by Horace White, and the additions in green by Jona Lendering.

Shall he succeed, my lords?

Enormously in one objective, my sovereigns, but fail miserably in another. But in both instances, my lords, the prophecy of Daniel came though.

LEFT: Silver Tetradrachm c. 230–222 BC, of Greek King Ptolemy III of Egypt, University of Pennsylvania Archaeological Museum, Philadelphia, USA (image source: author).

BELOW: Bust of King Ptolemy III who attacked Queen Laodice and her son Seleucus II Callinicus of the north in order to rescue his sister Berenice Phernophorus and her 5-year-old son Antiochus, (L) National Archaeological Museum of Naples, Italy, (R) Neues Museum, Berlin, Germany (images source: author).

If you can believe this, my lords, and we have the records to prove it, H.M. King Ptolemy III Euergetes has indeed surpassed the achievements of his formidable grandfather, King Ptolemy I Soter.

As you may recall, my sovereigns, H.M. King Ptolemy I Soter was one of the most able generals of H.M. King Alexander the Great. Yet, today, the grandson has excelled above his formidable grandfather.

The Egyptian army and navy under his majesty's command had succeeded, my lords, to capture both capital cities of the mighty Seleucid Empire of the north.

Your majesty King Ptolemy I Soter, you, sir, have not accomplished such a success as your grandson. Have you, sir?

And furthermore, sir, may we inform you that the army of your grandson, H.M. King Ptolemy III Euergetes, has conquered Seleucid's towns and cities, one after another, and, sir, if you can believe this: the army has indeed marched all the way east right to Babylon itself and conquered it [December 246 BC].

Have you heard our conversation, your majesty, King Nebuchadnezzar? In your day, sir, you defeated his Egyptian majesty King Necho II, who defeated King Hezekiah of Israel in the Battle of Armageddon.

But today, sir, a Greek Egyptian king has captured your Babylon, the city that had bowed and knelt down before his Iranian majesty King Cyrus the great, and then lay prostrate before his Grecian Majesty King Alexander the Great, and today, sir, it is still flat on the ground before the Greek Egyptian King Ptolemy III Euergetes.

However, your majesty, King Nebuchadnezzar, despair not, sir; indeed, the city has been taken, but the palace is still under heavy fighting.

This, my lords, was the remarkable success.

And we shall now, your majesties; call upon the ancient historian Polybius to verify the core of these events.

Go ahead please, sir.

> "Seleucia [one of the capital cities of the Greek Seleucid Empire of Iran, Iraq and Syria] had been garrisoned by the kings of Egypt ever since the time of <u>Ptolemy Euergetes</u>, when that prince, <u>owing to his indignation at the murder of Berenice, invaded Syria and seized on this town</u>."[163]

---

[163] Polybius, *The Histories*, Book 5:58:10, 11

But then there was also the heartbreaking failure, my lords. His majesty could not save his sister or his young nephew—both were assassinated.

Please, historian Apian, cut in with your record.

> "[246] Laodice assassinated him [her repentant husband King Antiochus II Theos] and afterward Berenice and her child.
> Ptolemy [III Euergetes], the son of [Ptolemy II] Philadelphus, avenged these crimes by killing Laodice. He invaded Syria and advanced as far as Babylon."[164]

Has the prophecy of Daniel become a bit clearer now, my sovereigns? Indeed, it has, my lords. There is more yet, my lords, which should make it crystal clear.

King Ptolemy III Euergetes had done greater than his grandfather, Numismatic Museum of Athens, Greece (image source: author).

## 246 BC
## The Gods Came Home

H.M. King Ptolemy III Euergetes of Egypt, my lords, did more than conquer towns and cities, including the great city of Babylon. He also brought back to Egypt its stolen gods. This fact is important for us to know, my lords, in order to understand prophet Daniel.

---

[164] Apian [c.95-c.165], *The Roman History, Syrian Wars*: 65, translated by Horace White, and the additions in green by Jona Lendering

King Ptolemy III Euergetes of Egypt, 246–221 BC, The Louvre Museum, Paris (image source: author)

Indeed, my lords, there is an ancient inscription, the Adoulis inscription, which parallels what prophet Daniel had foreseen nearly three hundred years in advance [540 BC–246 BC].

With your permission, my sovereigns, we shall now read this ancient inscription to you.

"Great King Ptolemy [III Euergetes], son of King Ptolemy [II Philadelphus] and Queen Arsinoe, the Brother and Sister Gods, the children of King Ptolemy [I Soter] and Queen Berenice the Savior Gods, descendant on the paternal side of Heracles the son of Zeus, on the maternal of Dionysus the son of Zeus, having inherited from his father the kingdom of Egypt and Libya and Syria and Phoenicia and Cyprus and Lycia and Caria and the Cyclades islands, led a campaign into Asia with infantry and cavalry and fleet and Troglodytic and Ethiopian elephants, which he and his father were the first to hunt from these lands and, bringing them back into Egypt, to fit out for military service.

Having become master of all the land this side of the Euphrates and of Cilicia and Pamphylia and Ionia and the Hellespont and Thrace and of all the forces and Indian elephants in these lands, and having made subject all the princes in the (various) regions, he crossed the Euphrates river and after subjecting to himself Mesopotamia and Babylonia and Sousiana and Persis and Media and all the rest of the land up to Bactria and having sought out all the temple belongings that had been carried out of Egypt by the Persians and having brought them back with the rest of the treasure [note the word "treasure"] from the (various) regions he sent his forces to Egypt through the canals that had been dug."[165]

---

[165] http://www.livius.org/cg-cm/chronicles/bchp-ptolemy_iii/bchp_ptolemy_iii_01.html, Bagnall, Derow 1981, No. 26

PAST AND PRESENT ABOMINATIONS—415

May we now, my lords, go back to Daniel's ancient and enigmatic prophecy of 540 BC!

> DAN 11:3 *a mighty king [King Alexander the Great] shall stand up, that shall rule with great dominion, and do according to his will.* DAN 11:4 *And when he shall stand up, his kingdom shall be broken, and shall be divided toward the four winds of heaven; and not to his posterity, nor according to his dominion which he ruled: for his kingdom shall be plucked up, even for others beside those.*
> DAN 11:5 <u>*And the king of the south [King Ptolemy I, the most able of King Alexander's generals, ruled Egypt, which is located south of Israel] shall be strong, and one of his princes [his grandson King Ptolemy III Euergetes]; and he [the grandson] shall be strong above him, and have dominion; his dominion shall be a great dominion [King Ptolemy III Euergetes conquered more territory than his grandfather King Ptolemy I ever did].*</u>

The Ptolemy III Chronicle is a Babylonian text that documents the invasion of the Greek Egyptian king against Iraq, British Museum. The top is the obverse side and bottom is the reverse side of the chronicle (image source: http://www.livius.org/cg-cm/chronicles/bchp-ptolemy_iii/bchp_ptolemy_iii_01.html).

DAN 11:6 *And in the end of years they shall join themselves together; for the king's daughter of the south [Princess Berenice Phernophorus, daughter of King Ptolemy II of Egypt or the south] shall come to the king of the north [King Antiochus II Theos of Syria or the north] to make an agreement [peace agreement]: but she shall not retain the power of the arm ; neither shall he stand [King Antiochus II Theos was poisoned by his repudiated wife Laodice], nor his arm: but she shall be given up [Queen Bernice Phernophorus was murdered], and they that brought her, and he that begat her [her father, intellectual King Ptolemy II Philadelphus, died and his death precipitated her death and the death of her son, who was to inherit the Seleucids Empire], and he that strengthened her in these times [her brother King Ptolemy III Euergetes].*

DAN 11:7 *But out of a branch of her roots shall one stand up in his estate [her brother, King Ptolemy III Euergetes], which shall come with an army, and shall enter into the fortress of the king of the north [the Seleucids of Iran, Iraq, and Syria], and shall deal against them, and shall prevail:*

DAN 11:8 <u>*And shall also carry captives into Egypt their gods*</u>, *with their princes, and with their precious vessels of silver and of gold; and he shall continue more years than the king of the north.*

DAN 11:9 *So the king of the south shall come into his kingdom, and shall return into his own land.*

A period sample of "their precious vessels of silver and of gold"; a cosmetic medallion with the bust of Eros, 2nd half of 3rd century BC, the Louvre Museum, Paris (image source: author).

## Another Great One

The days stole away unnoticed as usual, my lords, and the nights slipped away in the dark while the high and low slept, your majesties. Meanwhile, a few of the potentates and masters of our world entered the ground one after another.

Laodice's son, King Seleucus II Callinicus, ruled Syria, Iraq, and parts of Iran for twenty-one years, [246–225 BC] and then his turn came to enter the ground, carrying along with him the sealed biography of his days on the beautiful planet earth.

His elder son H.M. King Seleucus III, my lords, held on to the Seleucid throne of the north for short three years [225–222 BC] and was assassinated by his own army.

And today, my lords, following the assassination and sudden death of King Seleucus III of the north, comes his younger brother, 18-year-old King Antiochus III. Later, my lords, he would be called King Antiochus III the great—the great lord of the Seleucid empires of the north, which spans God's lands from Syria to Iraq and to Iran. And his title, your majesties, says it all.

It is now twenty-five years since H.M. King Ptolemy III Euergetes of Egypt had invaded the north to save his sister and nephew but failed.

Octadrachm (c. 204–197 BC) of King Antiochus III the great, the Greek king of Syria, Iraq, and Iran, Altes Museum, Berlin, Germany (image source: author).

Meanwhile the ground in Egypt, my lords, had welcomed into its bosom an empty royal body as well. For it is so happened, my lords, that within a few months after H.M. King Antiochus III the great became king of the North [222 BC] that the great King Ptolemy III Euergetes entered the ground, while his soul went to its Maker. His successor on the throne of Egypt today, your majesties, is the fourth monarch of the Ptolemaic Dynasty of Egypt, H.M. King Ptolemy IV Philopator.

The above image belongs to either King Ptolemy IV Philopator or King Ptolemy VI of Egypt, the Louvre Museum, Paris (image source: author).

Octadrachm (203-201 BC) of Queen Arsinoe III, wife of King Ptolemy IV Philopator, the Greek king of Egypt, Altes Museum, Berlin, Germany (images source: author).

## Royals in Review

And so, if we may, with your permission, my lords, take a very quick minute here to march before your eyes the royals, the kings, who were to pave the way to the "Little Horn," the "Man of Sin," the man of the past, and the man of tomorrow.

## King Alexander the Great

*DAN 11:3 And a mighty king shall stand up [Alexander the Great], that shall rule with great dominion, and do according to his will.*

*DAN 11:4 And when he shall stand up [at the peak of his power], his kingdom shall be broken, and shall be divided toward the four winds of heaven [four main kingdoms]; and not to his posterity [children], nor according to his dominion which he ruled [none of the new kingdoms would be as vast as his]: for his kingdom shall be plucked up, even for others beside those [four].*

## Ptolemy II of Egypt [His Daughter Marries King of the North]

*DAN 11:5 And the king of the south [King Ptolemy I of Egypt] shall be strong, and one of his princes [King Ptolemy III]; and he shall be strong above him [stronger than his grandfather King Ptolemy I], and have dominion; his dominion shall be a great dominion [King Ptolemy III conquered Syria and Iraq].*

*DAN 11:6 And in the end of years they shall join themselves together [the kings of Syria and of Egypt]; for the king's daughter of the south [Princess Berenice Phernophorus, daughter of King Ptolemy II of Egypt, marries King Antiochus II of the north i.e. Syria-Iran] shall come to the king of the north to make an agreement: but she shall not retain the power of the arm [was killed along with her husband King Antiochus II and their crown prince]; neither shall he stand [King Antiochus II], nor his arm [his crown prince born of Egyptian Princess Berenice Phernophorus]: but she shall be given up, and they that brought her, and he that begat her [her father King Ptolemy II died at the same time. Indeed she was assassinated as a result of his death and demise], and he that strengthened her in these times.*

# Ptolemy III of Egypt [Attacks the North to Revenge his Sister]

*DAN 11:7* But out of a branch of her roots shall one stand up in his estate [King Ptolemy III inherits the throne of Egypt from his deceased father King Ptolemy II], which shall come with an army, and shall enter into the fortress of the king of the north [invades Syria and Iraq], and shall deal against them, and shall prevail:

*DAN 11:8* And shall also carry captives into Egypt their gods [which the historians did indeed mention], with their princes, and with <u>their precious vessels of silver and of gold</u>; and he shall continue more years than the king of the north.

*DAN 11:9* So the king of the south shall come into his kingdom, and shall return into his own land.

Another period sample of precious silver and gold items; earrings, end of fourth-start of third century BC, the Louvre Museum, Paris (image source: author).

And now, my lords, we come to the new crop of royalties and their fights and marriages.

And so at this point of time, we wish, my lords, to call once again on prophet Daniel to tell you what else he had seen three hundred years in advance.

And once again, my lords, we would like to issue our usual warning here that it shall be a challenge to understand what Daniel is prophesying. And it shall remain so, my lords, until we call on the contemporaries of their majesties King Ptolemy IV Philopator, and King Antiochus III the great to tell us what happened in their days of old.

Meanwhile, my lords, we hereby present you with the enigmatic prophecy. But in order to make it less difficult to understand, we shall, my lords, return to a familiar time. We shall return to the days of H.M. King Ptolemy III, the avenger of his sister.

Go ahead, please, prophet Daniel.

> *DAN 11:7 out of a branch of her roots shall one stand up in his estate [King Ptolemy III Euergetes inherits the throne of his father King Ptolemy II, whose daughter, Ptolemy III' sister, married the king of the North], which shall come with an army, and shall enter into the fortress of the king of the north, and shall deal against them, and shall prevail [he reached all the way to Babylon city of Iraq]:*
> *DAN 11:8 And shall also carry captives into Egypt their gods, with their princes, and with their precious vessels of silver and of gold; and he shall continue more years than the king of the north.*
> *DAN 11:9 So the king of the south shall come into his kingdom, and shall return into his own land.*

So far, so good! Carry on, sir.

> *DAN 11:10 But his sons shall be stirred up, and shall assemble a multitude of great forces: and one shall certainly come, and overflow, and pass through: then shall he return, and be stirred up, even to his fortress.*
> *DAN 11:11 And the king of the south shall be moved with choler [great anger], and shall come forth and fight with him, even with the king of the north: and he shall set forth a great multitude; but the multitude shall be given into his hand.*
> *DAN 11:12 And when he hath taken away the multitude, his heart shall be lifted up; and he shall cast down many ten thousands: but he shall not be strengthened by it.*

At this point, we do not know exactly what happened, your majesties. All what we can glean here out of these words is that another war has broken out.

And so, my lords, we shall go back in time and read the ancient documents, the newspapers of the past in order to know the names of the mighty men included in the prophecy.

It is our fervent desire, my lords, to know their names. And, indeed, it would be yet more interesting to look at their faces—and as it turned out, my lords, many of them were handsome men and women.

But for now, your majesties, do please allow prophet Daniel to recite the remainder of his prophecy regarding the events that shall herald the days of trouble and finally the end of an era for Israel.

Go ahead, please, prophet Daniel.

> DAN 11:13 *the king of the north shall return, and shall set forth a multitude greater than the former, and shall certainly come after certain years with a great army and with much riches.*

It looks like another war has taken place, my lords. But we cannot tell exactly who is winning and who is losing. Carry on, sir.

> DAN 11:14 *And in those times there shall many stand up against the king of the south: also the robbers of thy people shall exalt themselves to establish the vision; but they shall fall.*
> DAN 11:15 *So the king of the north shall come, and cast up a mount, and take the most fenced cities: and the arms of the south shall not withstand, neither his chosen people, neither shall there be any strength to withstand.*
> DAN 11:16 *But he that cometh against him shall do according to his own will, and none shall stand before him: and he shall stand in the glorious land, which by his hand shall be consumed.*
> DAN 11:17 *He shall also set his face to enter with the strength of his whole kingdom, and upright ones with him; thus shall he do: and he shall give him the daughter of women, corrupting her: but she shall not stand on his side, neither be for him.*
> DAN 11:18 *After this shall he turn his face unto the isles, and shall take many: but a prince for his own behalf shall cause the reproach offered by him to cease; without his own reproach he shall cause it to turn upon him.*

And here is the finale, my lords: the great has fallen.

> DAN 11:19 *Then he shall turn his face toward the fort of his own land: but he shall stumble and fall, and not be found.*

What exactly is prophet Daniel saying, my lords, and where is the "Little Horn," the "Man of Sin"?

## 219/218 BC
## The Fight to Own Israel

My lords, young 24-year-old King Antiochus III, the future great, acting upon the advice of his counselors, set his heart to do what his fathers had tried to do before him and wrestle away Israel and the entire region of Cole-Syria, southern Syria, out of the hands of Egypt and its Ptolemaic royal family.

It has been nearly eighty-five long years, my lords, since the Seleucids kings of the north have been complaining that Israel, and southern Syria, belonged to them and not to the Ptolemies of Egypt.

Today, my lords, this brash youngster is determined to make the old dream a reality, intends to make history.

King Antiochus III the great, the Louvre Museum, Paris (image source: author).

And as it happens, my lords, at this point of time on earth, the major three kingdoms born of King Alexander's empire are ruled by young men.

The Egyptian King Ptolemy IV Philopator is merely two years older than H.M. King Antiochus III of the north. And both of these two men, my lords, are in the hands of shrewd handlers and advisors looking out for their own narrow interests.

Your majesties, without offense, it will make it much clearer if we avoid politeness and tell you straight out that H.M. King Ptolemy IV Philopator of Egypt is a drunken delinquent and a sensual youngster.

It is also more to the point, your majesties, if we tell you straight out that the Egyptian army is out of practice and out of shape—aged and bloated.

And with your permission, my lords, we shall call on the ancient historian Polybius to relate a story to you, which will go a long way, my lords, to show you what the people—Romans, Greek, and Egyptians—thought of the young Egyptian monarch, King Ptolemy IV Philopator!

Historian Polybius' story, my lords, deals with a merchant who brought a cargo of horses to sell in Alexandria, the capital of Egypt.

Go ahead, please, historian Polybius.

"This Nicagoras had <u>arrived not long ago at Alexandria with a cargo of horses</u> and on disembarking he found Cleomenes, with Panteus and Hippitas, walking on the quay.

When Cleomenes saw him he came up to him and greeted him affectionately and asked him on what business he had come.

When he told him he had brought horses to sell, Cleomenes said, "I very much wish you had brought catamites and sackbut <u>girls instead of the horses, for those are the wares this king is after</u>."

Nicagoras at the time smiled and held his tongue."[166]

Marble portrait of King Ptolemy IV Philopator, third century BC, Benaki Museum, Athens, Greece (image source: author).

---

[166] Polybius, *The Histories*, Book 5:37:7-11.
http://penelope.uchicago.edu/Thayer/E/Roman/Texts/Polybius/5*.html

But Egypt's bad news, my lords, does not stop with its delinquent monarch and out-of-shape army.

Listen to this, my lords, the Egyptian, yes, my lords, the Egyptian governor of the contested Israel and southern Syrian region, whose name is Governor Theodotus, has apparently sent a letter to the enemy, his young majesty King Antiochus III of the north.

And what is his letter about, my lords?

This capable Egyptian governor, a Greek by race, and the entire Egyptian army under his command would be more than glad to defect to H.M. King Antiochus III of Iran, Iraq, and Syria.

Silver Didrachm 221-180 BC, delinquent King Ptolemy IV, fulfilled Daniel's prophecy, University of Cambridge Archaeology Museum, UK (image source: author).

So now, my lords, we have a delinquent and drunken Egyptian king, an aged and bloated Egyptian, army, and also a treachery to boot.

In other words, your majesties, the old dream of taking Israel and southern Syria will be fulfilled on the cheap. And Daniel's prophecy would fail.

But on second thought, can the treachery be true? Or is it a ploy by the Egyptian Governor Theodotus?

Carry on please, historian Polybius.

> "The next conspiracy shortly after this was that of Theodotus the governor of Coele-Syria [Israel and southern Syria], and [a Greek] Aetolian by birth. Holding the [Egyptian] king [Ptolemy IV Philopator] in contempt owing to his debauched life and general conduct and mistrusting the court circles, because after recently rendering important service to Ptolemy in various ways and especially in connexion with the first attempt of Antiochus [III the Great] on Coele-Syria, he had not only received no thanks for this but on the contrary had been recalled to Alexandria [capital of Egypt] and had barely escaped with his life, he now formed the project of entering into communication with Antiochus and handing over to him the cities of Coele-Syria. Antiochus gladly grasped at the proposal and the matter was soon in a fair way of being accomplished."[167]

---

[167] Polybius, *The Histories*, Book 5:40:1-3

It is a ploy. His majesty King Antiochus III is too clever to fall for it. Time will tell.

Be that as it may, his majesty is marching on from a place to a place in southern Syria and heading in the direction of Israel and Egypt.

He has already taken some villages and towns and cities by force. Others have simply surrendered and opened their gates in welcome, and handed out provisions of food and drink for the thousands of soldiers and the war animals of his majesty king of the north.

King Antiochus III, University of Pennsylvania Archaeological Museum, Philadelphia, USA (image source: author).

The Egyptian advisers have been alerted, my lords, of the movements of his majesty. And they are in the middle of figuring out what to do, my lords. And they are indeed very cunning men, especially the top two royal advisors of his young majesty, drunken and womanizer King Ptolemy IV Philopator.

These two cunning men, my lords, have sent a message to their enemy H.M. King Antiochus III of the north. The message says: hold it, sir. Let us negotiate a settlement and come to a compromise and share Israel and southern Syria between us.

Fair enough. Let us negotiate. Winter is coming and so the season is too late for wars anyway.

And so, my lords, his young Majesty King Antiochus III the great of the north has agreed to an armistice of four months and moved his army to winter quarters.

Meanwhile, the cunning Egyptian advisers, the real power behind the drunken throne, my lords, have removed the Egyptian king and the royal court from the capital city of Alexandria to Cairo. Why? Top secret, my lords. Top secret!

His delinquent majesty King Ptolemy IV Philopator of Egypt would from now on meet all foreign dignitaries and delegations in Cairo only. The city of Alexandria from this point on and until further notice shall be closed off and out of boundary for any foreigner, whoever he may be.

They are cunning men, my lords, those two advisors; they are. But their cunning, my lords, may indeed help with prophet Daniel's old prophecy.

And the shrewd moves keep adding up, my lords.

His delinquent majesty King Ptolemy IV Philopator and his cunning advisors have hired two of the best and most experienced Greek generals from Macedonia, the birthplace of H.M. King Alexander the Great.

These two great Macedonian generals, my lords, have now brought with them thousands of Macedonian mercenaries to train and beef up the unfit Egyptian army.

Daily, my lords, daily the Egyptian soldiers are being drilled and trained under the skilled Greeks in the closed-off city of Alexandria. At the same time, my lords, weapons and war materials are being manufactured at a feverish pace, although out of the eyes of any prying foe.

(L) Bronze Cuirass, body armor, 6th–5th century BC, New York Metropolitan Museum of Art (image source: author).

(R) Bronze greave, shin guard, 4th century BC, New York Metropolitan Museum of Art (image source: author).

And then, your majesties, a new idea cropped up—an idea, which in due time shall fulfill and clarify another line in Daniel's prophecy.

Go ahead, historian Polybius please.

> "At length, however, Agathocles and Sosibius, who were then the king's chief ministers, took counsel together and decided on the only course possible under present circumstances. For they resolved to occupy themselves with preparations for war, but in the meanwhile by negotiations to make Antiochus relax his activity, pretending to fortify him in the opinion of Ptolemy he had all along entertained, <u>which was that he would not venture to fight</u>, but

would by overtures and through his friends attempt to reason with him [with King Antiochus III] and persuade him to evacuate Coele-Syria [Israel and southern Syria].

On arriving at this decision Agathocles and Sosibius, who were charged with the conduct of the matter, began to communicate with Antiochus, and dispatching embassies at the same time to Rhodes, Byzantium, Cyzicus, and Aetolia invited these states to send missions to further the negotiations.

The arrival of these missions, which went backwards and forwards between the two kings, gave them ample facilities <u>for gaining time to prosecute at leisure their warlike preparations</u>.

Establishing themselves at Memphis [Cairo] they continued to receive these missions as well as Antiochus' own envoys, replying to all in conciliatory terms.

Meanwhile they recalled and assembled at Alexandria the mercenaries in their employment in foreign parts, sending out recruiting officers also and getting ready provisions for the troops they already had and for those they were raising. They also attended to all other preparations, paying constant visit to Alexandria by turns to see that none of the supplies required for their purpose were wanting.

The task of providing arms, selecting the men and organizing them they entrusted to Echecrates the Thessalian and Phoxidas of Melita, assisted by Eurylochus the Magnesian, Socrates the Boeotian, and Cnopias of Allaria. <u>They were most well advised in availing themselves of the services of these men, who having served under Demetrius and Antigonus</u> [two great kings and military commanders, mentioned previously] <u>had some notion of the reality of war of campaigning in general. Taking the troops in hand they got them into shape by correct military methods.</u>"[168]

In the way of reminder, my lords, the unfit Egyptian army was an army made up entirely of Greek soldiers who had settled in Egypt. Indeed, my lords, restricting the privilege of serving in the army to Greeks only gave assurance of loyalty to the Greek Ptolemaic rulers of Egypt.

But now, my lords, in the face of this major danger, his delinquent majesty King Ptolemy IV Philopator and his two Greek advisors came up with the new and untested idea of recruiting 20,000 native Egyptians to join the army.

A Mistake! A grave mistake, my lords!

Go ahead, historian Polybius.

---

[168] Polybius, *The Histories*, Book 5:63:1-14

"<u>The total native Egyptian force</u> consisted of about twenty thousand heavy-armed men, and was commanded by Sosibius."[169]

A bust, part of a statue of decadent King Ptolemy IV Philopator (r.221/1–205/4 BC), British Museum, London (image source: author).

My lords, think about it. The native Egyptians are now being trained in the army as foot soldiers. They are being trained in the Greek art of war and its efficient tactics and maneuvering. And then there are hundreds of them, my lords, who are also being assigned to the cavalry, the cream of the crop of the army. And there, in their regiments, they are to be trained by seasoned Greeks generals, such as Polycrates of Argos. And so the question is, my lords, where is this going to go?

---

[169] Polybius, *The Histories*, Book 5:65:9

Meanwhile, your majesties, the devious Egyptian advisors and their delegations ensured that the negotiations with his young majesty King Antiochus III the great stay difficult and prolonged.

But at last, the intentionally prolonged negotiations came to an end—useless negotiation as far as his young Majesty King Antiochus III is concerned, but very successful from the point of view of his delinquent majesty King Ptolemy IV Philopator.

The time has come for the swords to clash against each other, my lords. The time to make widows and orphans is calling.

> GEN 6:11 *The earth also was corrupt before God, and the earth was filled with violence.*
> GEN 6:6 *and it grieved him at his heart.*

## The Battle of Raphia
## June 13–22, 217 BC

Go ahead, please, historian Polybius.

"By the beginning of spring Antiochus and Ptolemy had completed their preparations and were determined on deciding the fate of the Syrian expedition by a battle.

Now Ptolemy started from Alexandria with an army of seventy thousand foot, five thousand horse, and seventy-three elephants, and Antiochus, on learning of his advance, concentrated his forces. These consisted first of Daae, Carmanians, and Cilicians, light-armed troops about five thousand in number organized and commanded by Byttacus the Macedonian. <u>Under Theodotus the Aetolian, who had played the traitor to Ptolemy, was a force of ten thousand selected from every part of the kingdom</u> and armed in the Macedonian manner, most of them with silver shields. The phalanx was about twenty thousand strong and was under the command of Nicarchus and Theodotus surnamed Hemiolius. There were Agrianian and Persian bowmen and slingers to the number of two thousand, and with them two thousand Thracians, all under the command of Menedemus of Alabanda.

...

The whole army of Antiochus consisted of sixty-two thousand foot, six thousand horse, and a hundred and two elephants."[170]

---

[170] Polybius, *The Histories*, Book 5:79:1-6 & 13

The two armies, my lords, are now on the move and steadily approaching each other. It is now time for courage and time for the soldiers' hearts to beat faster and louder. It is time to look for the soldier beside you for solidarity.

Carry on, historian Polybius please.

> "Ptolemy, marching on Pelusium [Egyptian frontier city on the border with southern Syria and Israel], made his first halt at that city, and after picking up stragglers and serving out rations to his men moved on marching through the desert and skirting Mount Casius and the marshes called Barathra.
>
> Reaching the spot he was bound for on the fifth day he encamped at a distance of fifty stades from Raphia, which is the first city of Coele-Syria on the Egyptian side after Rhinocolura.
>
> Antiochus was approaching at the same time with his army, and after reaching Gaza and resting his forces there, continued to advance slowly. Passing Raphia he encamped by night at a distance of ten stades from the enemy."[171]

Historian Polybius, please, cut in when it is appropriate, sir.

> "The kings after remaining encamped opposite each other for five days both resolved to decide matters by a battle."[172]

> "Ptolemy being supported by Andromachus, Sosibius and his sister Arsinoë and Antiochus by Theodotus and Nicarchus, these being the commanders of the phalanx on either side."[173]

The blood was shed, my lords, and the soldiers, faces buried in the soil, bid the world farewell. Their families would in due time water this soil with their tears.

The ruse worked, my lords. The boot camp of closed-off Alexandria brought results. The Egyptian army took the prize.

And as you may be able to see, my lords, one part of the prophecy of prophet Daniel has been fulfilled.

> "But [King Antiochus III of the North] finding that his whole army had taken to flight, he retired to Raphia, in the confident belief that as far as it depended on himself he had won the battle [he won in the

---

[171] Polybius, *The Histories*, Book 5:80:1-4
[172] Polybius, *The Histories*, Book 5:82:1
[173] Polybius, *The Histories*, Book 5:83:1

quarters he was fighting in], but had suffered this disaster owing to the base cowardice of the rest.

Ptolemy having thus obtained a decisive victory by his phalanx [the outside wings of the army], and having killed many of the enemy in the pursuit by the hands of the cavalry and mercenaries of his right wing, retired and spent the night in his former camp.

Next day, after picking up and burying his own dead and despoiling those of the enemy [stripping them of their weapons and valuables], he broke up his camp and advanced on Raphia."[174]

"Such was the result of the battle of Raphia fought by the kings for the possession of Coele-Syria.

After paying the last honours to the dead Antiochus returned to his own kingdom with his army, and Ptolemy took without resistance Raphia and the other towns, each community endeavouring to anticipate its neighbours in going over to him [King Ptolemy IV Philopator] and resuming its allegiance.

…

But at this juncture it was only to be expected that they should act so, as their affection for the Egyptian kings was of no recent growth; for the peoples of Coele-Syria [including Israel] have always been more attached to that house [the Ptolemaic Royal Egyptian family] than to the Seleucidae.

…

[Delinquent King Ptolemy IV Philopator] Sending back Sosibius with the ambassadors the ratify the treaty, he remained himself for three months in Syria and Phoenicia [Lebanon] establishing order in the towns, and then, leaving Andromachus behind as military governor of the whole district, he returned with his sister and his friends to Alexandria, having brought the war to an end in a manner that astonished his subjects in view of his character in general."[175]vi

Once again, Lebanon, Israel, and Palestine of southern Syria are all now in the hands of Egypt and its new military governor of the region.

## 205 BC
## The Delinquent Gone

Merely twelve years after his great and unexpected victory at the battle of Raphia, the soul of the debauched king veered off his body in its way to wait for the day of judgment.

---

[174] Polybius, *The Histories*, Book 5:85:13, 86: 1 & 2
[175] Polybius, *The Histories*, Book 5:87:7, 8 & 10 and 87:6 & 7

This was the best thing he could do, my lords, because troubles were now brewing in southern Egypt.

> MAT 16:26 *For what is a man profited, if he shall gain the whole world, and lose his own soul? or what shall a man give in exchange for his soul?*

His death, my lords, is rumored to have been instigated by his favorite mistress, a noble woman by the name of "Agathoclea."

Be that as it may your majesties, do you still remember the 20,000 well-trained native Egyptian soldiers?

Well, your majesties, this is a well-trained and fair-sized army.

We can tell you, my lords, that soon after returning from the battle of Raphia, the Egyptians broke out in street riots and uprisings in the southern half of the country.

Indeed, the population dared to rebel against their victorious Greek king, my lords, because they were now supported by these well-trained native Egyptian soldiers. And these native soldiers, my lords, were led by two nationalistic leaders, Hyrgonaphor [A.K.A. Haronnophris] and Chaonnophris.

In response, my lords, his delinquent majesty King Ptolemy IV Philopator had then directed his people to crush the demonstrators. And the man he had assigned to crush the rebellion, my lords, was the man who shared in training the 20,000, and whose name was Polycrates of Argos.

## 205–186 BC
## The Egyptian Secession

If we may jump ahead of ourselves for a minute, your majesties, then we can tell you that the native Egyptian uprising did spread quickly in several towns and cities. The aim of the national rebellion, my lords, was to separate the southern half of Egypt, from the northern half where the Greek rulers, their entourage, and their Greek army were stationed, particularly in Alexandria and Memphis/Cairo.

The rebellion did last, my lords, for nearly twenty years [205–186 BC] as the Greek army struggled year after year to crush it [It is known in history as the Egyptian secession, or the great Egyptian rebellion].

And so now, my lords, it is time that we once again wish to call on prophet Daniel to repeat his enigmatic prophecy.

Go ahead, prophet Daniel, but one more time, sir, please begin from a period familiar to their majesties.

*DAN 11:7* But out of a branch of her roots shall one stand up in his estate [King Ptolemy III Euergetes inherits the throne of his father King Ptolemy II], which shall come with an army, and shall enter into the fortress of the king of the north [the Seleucids royal family], and shall deal against them, and shall prevail [he reaches all the way to Babylon city of Iraq].

*DAN 11:8* And shall also carry captives into Egypt their gods, with their princes, and with their precious vessels of silver and of gold; and he shall continue more years than the king of the north.

*DAN 11:9* So the king of the south [King Ptolemy III Euergetes] shall come into his kingdom, and shall return into his own land.

*DAN 11:10* But his sons [there were two who were then followed by King Antiochus III the Great] shall be stirred up, and shall assemble a multitude of great forces: and one shall certainly come, and overflow [takes many cities and towns in the neighborhood of Israel and Lebanon], and pass through: then shall he return, and be stirred up, even to his fortress [Raphia, June 22, 217 BC].

*DAN 11:11* And the king of the south [the decadent King Ptolemy IV Philopator] shall be moved with choler, and shall come forth and fight with him, even with the king of the north [King Antiochus III the Great]: and he [King Antiochus III the Great] shall set forth a great multitude; but the multitude shall be given into his hand [King Ptolemy IV defeats King Antiochus III the great at the Battle of Raphia].

*DAN 11:12* And when he [King Ptolemy IV Philopator] hath taken away the multitude, his heart shall be lifted up; and he shall cast down many ten thousands: but he shall not be strengthened by it [troubles will be brewing in Egypt].

…

*DAN 11:14* <u>And in those times there shall many stand up against the king of the south</u> [King Ptolemy IV of Egypt, the Great Egyptian Revolt 205-186 BC]: also the robbers of thy people shall exalt themselves to establish the vision; but they shall fall.

# PAST AND PRESENT ABOMINATIONS—435

"Ring with Ptolemy IV as Dionysus," third century BC. Ptolemy IV identified himself with the wine god and assumed the title "the New Dionysus." This quote is copied from the Walters Museum of Art, Baltimore, USA (image source: author).

Indeed, your majesties, the revolt has picked up momentum, and at this point of time, is spreading from the cities of southern Egypt to the northern half of the country and heading straight for Cairo and Alexandria, the seats of the Greek rulers. Furthermore, my lords, the population is now totally enraged on account of the rising taxes, which are needed in order to pay off the thousands Greek mercenaries whom H.M. King Ptolemy IV Philopator has hired against King Antiochus III.

In those days, my lords, if we may digress for a second, H.M. King Ptolemy IV Philopator collected the taxes through the temples; thus, your majesties, the sacred temples, the taxation centers, were at this point of time the targets of the leaders of the Egyptian uprising.

Historian Polybius, tell us what you know please.

"The war against the Egyptians started shortly after the battle at Raphia (in 217 BC) in which Ptolemy IV by gaining an unexpected victory on the Seleucid Antiochos III managed to keep control over Palestine. By arming the Egyptians for his war against Antiochos, Ptolemy had an excellent idea for the short time, but he did not take into account the future.

Priding themselves upon their victory at Raphia, the soldiers [native Egyptian soldiers] were no longer disposed to obey orders, but they sought out a leader and figure-head, in the opinion that they could come up for themselves. And shortly afterwards, they did indeed do so.

...

After the end of the war for Coele-Syria king Ptolemy Philopator <u>entirely abandoned the path of virtue and took to a life of dissipation</u> such as I have described above."

May we interrupt here, my lords, to reintroduce a couple of verses from Daniel's prophecy!

DAN 11:11 *And the king of the south [King Ptolemy IV Philopator] shall be moved with choler, and shall come forth and fight with him [King Antiochus III the Great], even with the king of the north: and he shall set forth a great multitude; but the multitude shall be given into his hand [King Ptolemy IV defeats King Antiochus III the great at the Battle of Raphia].*
DAN 11:12 *And when he hath taken away the multitude, <u>his heart shall be lifted up [entirely abandoned the path of virtue and took to a life of dissipation]</u>*

Carry on, sir.

"After the end of the war for Coele-Syria king Ptolemy Philopator entirely abandoned the path of virtue and took to a life of dissipation such as I have described above.

"Late in his reign he was forced by circumstances into the above-mentioned war [the Egyptian Rebellion], which, apart from the mutual savagery and lawlessness of the combatants, contained nothing worthy of note, no pitched battle, no naval battle, no siege [a guerilla war]."[176]

---

[176] Polybius, *Historiae* V 107.1 and XIV 107.1. http://tebtunis.berkeley.edu/lecture/revolt

## The Great Egyptian Rebellion

> Dan 11:14 <u>And in those times there shall many stand up against the king of the south</u> [King Ptolemy IV of Egypt, the Great Egyptian Revolt 205-186 BC]: also the robbers of thy people shall exalt themselves to establish the vision [shall be made clear]; but they shall fall.

There are several ancient Egyptian records that document the great Egyptian revolt, which gathered strength in the final days of victorious but decadent King Ptolemy IV Philopator and continued during the reign of his son King Ptolemy V.

One of these records of the Egyptian rebellion can be found documented on the walls of the temple of Edfu. It should be remembered that the temples were the target for the rebellion because it was there that taxes were collected by the Greek rulers of Egypt.

> "So was the temple built, the inner sanctuary being completed for the golden Horus, up to the year 10, Epiph the 7th, in the time of King Ptolemy Philopator. The wall in it was adorned with fair writing, with the great name of his Majesty and with pictures of the gods and goddesses of Edfu, and its great gateway completed, and the double doors of its broad chamber, up to the year 16 of his Majesty [207/206 BC]. <u>Then there broke out a rebellion, and it came to pass that bands of insurgents hid themselves in the interior of the temple. . . .</u>"[177]

Temple of Edfu
(image source: WC, Than 217).

More documents can be also found on the outside wall of the *mammisi* (temple of royal birth) at <u>Philae</u>.

---

[177] *The House of Ptolemy*, E. R. Bevan, published by Methuen Publishing, London, 1927, Chapter VII, Page 240. http://penelope.uchicago.edu/Thayer/E/Gazetteer/Places/Africa/Egypt/_Texts/BEVHOP/7*.html

> "The rebel against the gods, Hr–wnf, he who had made war in Egypt, gathering insolent people from all districts on account of their crimes, they did terrible things to the governors of the nomes [provinces], <u>they desecrated (?) the temples, they damaged (?) the divine statues, they molested (?) the priests and suppressed (?) the offerings on the altars and in the shrines</u>. They sacked (?) the towns and their population, women and children included, committing all kinds of crimes <u>in the time of anarchy</u>. They stole the taxes of the nomes [provinces], they damaged the irrigation works."[178]

But perhaps the most famous document that speaks of the uprising, or as Daniel phrases it: "<u>And in those times there shall many stand up against the king of the south</u> [King Ptolemy IV Philopator]" is the very famous Rosetta stone, which is a temple stele, or inscribed slap.

**The famous Rosetta stone, 196 BC, (and details) is preserved in the British Museum, London.**

**The Rosetta stone was issued on behalf of King Ptolemy V (205/204-181 BC) and speaks of one of his victories against the native Egyptian rebels (images source: author).**

Indeed, it took over nineteen years to finally capture and put to death the leaders of the uprising and their Sudanese supporters [August 27, 186 BC]. The name of the governor of southern Egypt who crushed the rebellion is Komanos [or Comanos].

---

[178] W.M. Müller, Egyptological Researches III. The bilingual decrees of Philae (Washington 1920), pp. 59–88

## 198 BC
## Battle of Panium—
## The Tide Turns

Whichever way H.M. King Ptolemy IV Philopator died, my lords, whether in a natural death or otherwise, one thing remains certain. The vouchers at home are circling today around his new successor H.M. King Ptolemy V Epiphanes. And besides them there is also the ever-present outside voucher who is never too far, and who knows that the new king, the fifth ruler of the Ptolemaic dynasty of Egypt, is a child, a 5-year-old infant, in the middle of a raging storm of riots and uprisings at home.

Who is exactly steering the ship of Egypt these days? How many men of different interests and opinions are steering it? And the calculations from this point on become very simple, my lords.

LEFT: Silver Tetradrachm, 204–180 BC, of King Ptolemy V, University of Cambridge Archaeological Museum, UK (image source: author).

RIGHT: King Ptolemy V Epiphanes, Numismatic Museum of Athens, Greece (image source: author)

H.M. King Antiochus III the great, king of the north, has now a much better chance of achieving that old Seleucids dream of wrenching Israel and southern Syria, Coele-Syria, from the Egyptian Ptolemies.

Indeed, my lords, his majesty had in the course of the past eighteen or nineteen years, since the battle of Raphia, made himself a name as a great military commander winning battles after battles all the way to India. His majesty has indeed merited his title of greatness.

In fact, my lords, with the circumstances in Egypt now being what they are, H.M. King Antiochus III would not only fulfill but would possibly exceed his ancestors' dream and become the king of Iran, Iraq, Syria, Israel, Lebanon, Jordan, Egypt, and the island of Cyprus.

440—EARTH OUT OF ORBIT

And towards this shinning goal, my lords, his majesty had approached and finalized an alliance with King Philip I of Macedon of northern Greece. The two kings have agreed to divide the old empire of H.M. King Alexander the great amongst the two of them. King Philip I takes Europe, his majesty takes the Middle East.

Nearly seven years after the death of his delinquent majesty King Ptolemy IV, his mature, experienced majesty King Antiochus III is marching his formidable army south towards Israel and Egypt, accompanied by his son as a commander.

Go ahead, prophet Daniel, reboot and go on and tell their majesties the outcome that you had seen 342 years in advance.

> DAN 11:7 *But out of a branch of her roots shall one stand up in his estate [King Ptolemy III inherits the throne of his father King Ptolemy II], which shall come with an army, and shall enter into the fortress of the king of the north, and shall deal against them, and shall prevail [he reaches all the way to Babylon city of Iraq].*
> DAN 11:8 *And [King Ptolemy III] shall also carry captives into Egypt their gods, with their princes, and with their precious vessels of silver and of gold; and he shall continue more years than the king of the north.*
> DAN 11:9 *So the king of the south [King Ptolemy III] shall come into his kingdom, and shall return into his own land.*
> DAN 11:10 *But his sons [sons of the king of the north; King Antiochus III the Great] shall be stirred up, and shall assemble a multitude of great forces: and one shall certainly come, and overflow [takes many cities and towns in the neighborhood of Israel], and pass through: then shall he return [after the winter quarter], and be stirred up, even to his fortress [Raphia, June 17-22, 217 BC].*
> DAN 11:11 *And the king of the south [the decadent King Ptolemy IV] shall be moved with choler, and shall come forth and fight with him, even with the king of the north: and he shall set forth a great multitude [King Antiochus had soldiers from many parts of his kingdom as mentioned previously]; but the multitude shall be given into his hand [decadent King Ptolemy IV defeats King Antiochus III the great at the Battle of Raphia].*
> DAN 11:12 *And when he [King Ptolemy IV] hath taken away the multitude, his heart shall be lifted up; and he shall cast down many ten thousands: but he shall not be strengthened by it [Egypt rises in revolt].*

And now, my lords, here comes the new.

## PAST AND PRESENT ABOMINATIONS—441

> DAN 11:13 *For the king of the north [King Antiochus III the Great] shall return, and shall set forth a multitude greater than the former, and shall certainly come after certain years [19 years] with a great army and with much riches.*
>
> DAN 11:14 *And in those times there shall many stand up against the king of the south [The great Egyptian revolt, 205-186 BC, which began during the reign of decadent King Ptolemy IV of Egypt and continued unabated during the reign of his son King Ptolemy V Epiphanes]: also the robbers of thy people shall exalt themselves to establish the vision; but they shall fall.*
>
> DAN 11:15 *So the king of the north shall come, and cast up a mount, and take the most fenced cities: and the arms of the south shall not withstand, neither his chosen people, neither shall there be any strength to withstand.*
>
> DAN 11:16 *But he that cometh against him shall do according to his own will, and none shall stand before him: and he shall stand in the glorious land, which by his hand shall be consumed.*
>
> DAN 11:17 *He shall also set his face to enter with the strength of his whole kingdom, and upright ones with him; thus shall he do: and he shall give him the daughter of women, corrupting her: but she shall not stand on his side, neither be for him.*
>
> DAN 11:18 *After this shall he turn his face unto the isles, and shall take many: but a prince for his own behalf shall cause the reproach offered by him to cease; without his own reproach he shall cause it to turn upon him.*

Once again, my sovereigns, we will need to call on the ancient historians, the reporters and journalists of the ancient newspapers, to tell us what has happened in their days of old.

And while we are getting ready to do so, we can tell you, my lords, that the Egyptian army of the teen-aged King Ptolemy V Epiphanes has now been mobilized. And the general in command of its armed forces is an exiled Greek by the name of General Scopas.

The two great armies, one under the command of H.M. King Antiochus III of the north and the second led by General Scopas have at this point of time, my lords, gathered in a battlefield by the fountains of the Jordan River.

When the dust settled, my lords, the defeat was total.

Where is historian Flavius Josephus? There you are, sir. Please recount to their majesties what you have gleaned.

> "Now it happened that in the reign of Antiochus [III] the Great, who ruled over all Asia, that the Jews, as well as the inhabitants of Celesyria, suffered greatly, and their land was sorely harassed; for while he was at war with [decadent] Ptolemy [IV] Philopater, and

442—EARTH OUT OF ORBIT

> with his son, who was called [Ptolemy V] Epiphanes, it fell out that these nations were equally sufferers, both when he [Antiochus III] was beaten, and when he beat the others: so that they were very like to a ship in a storm, which is tossed by the waves on both sides; and just thus were they in their situation in the middle between Antiochus's prosperity and its change to adversity.
>
> But at length, when Antiochus [III] had beaten Ptolemy [V Epiphanes], he seized upon Judea [Israel]; and when [King Ptolemy IV] Philopater was dead, his son [King Ptolemy V Epiphanes] sent out a great army under Scopas, the general of his forces, against the inhabitants of Celesyria, who took many of their cities, and in particular our nation; which when he fell upon them, went over to him."[179]

Hear now, my lords, the report of the battle by the fountains of the Jordan River, near the town of Panium.

And please accept my apology for the interruption, historian Josephus. Do carry on, please, sir.

> "Yet was it not long afterward when Antiochus [III] overcame Scopas [the chief commander of the Egyptian army], in a battle fought at the fountains of Jordan, and destroyed a great part of his army.
>
> But afterward, when Antiochus subdued those cities of Celesyria which Scopas had gotten into his possession, and Samaria with them [capital of northern Israel], the Jews, of their own accord, went over to him [King Antiochus III], and received him into the city (Jerusalem), and gave plentiful provision to all his army, and to his elephants, and readily assisted him when he besieged the [Egyptian] garrison which was in the citadel of Jerusalem."

His Majesty King Antiochus III, my lords, has fulfilled his fathers' dream. He wrote history. It took over 120 years to fulfill the dream. His majesty has decisively beaten the Egyptian army and took full position of Israel and of the surrounding region of southern Syria along the borders of Egypt. Israel, at this point of time [198 BC.], my lords, and for the first time ever, is ruled by the king of Iran, Iraq, and Syria [Israel was an Egyptian property since 320 BC].

But yet, my lords, the victorious king of the north would surprise his watchers.

---

[179] Josephus, *Antiquities of the Jews*, Book XII, Chapter III: III.

With your permission, your majesties, we wish to go back to the battle of Panium for a minute.

Historian Josephus, my sovereigns, in support of his report, he refers to what historian Polybius wrote. Unfortunately, my lords, what is left to us from historian Polybius are just a few fragments. These fragments mainly criticize another historian, Zeno, for his inaccurate description of the deployment of the forces in the battlefield of Panium and the sequel of the events that took place there.

Please, go ahead, historian Josephus, finish your report, which we shall sort out later for the benefit of their majesties.

> "[I] will produce first the testimony of Polybius of Megalopolis; for thus does he speak, in the sixteenth book of his history:
>
> "Now Scopas, the general of Ptolemy's [Egyptian] army, went in haste to the superior parts of the country, and in the winter time overthrew the nation of the Jews"
>
> He also saith, in the same book, that "when Scopas was conquered by Antiochus, Antiochus received Batanea, and Samaria, and Abila, and Gadara; and that, a while afterwards, there came in to him those Jews that inhabited near that temple which was called Jerusalem; concerning which, although I have more to say, and particularly concerning the presence of God about that temple, yet do I put off that history till another opportunity." This it is which Polybius relates."[180]

All right then, my lords, here are then a few lines from book sixteen of Polybius, which historian Josephus referred to:

> "I will attempt to make my meaning clear by the following instance.
>
> The above-mentioned author [historian Zeno] in narrating the siege of Gaza and the engagement between Antiochus and Scopas at the Panium in Coele-Syria has evidently taken so much pains about his style that the extravagance of his language is not excelled by any of those declamatory works written to produce a sensation among the vulgar [Zeno's record is just as bad as the sensational reports that meant to excite the ignorant].
>
> He [historian Zeno] has, however, paid so little attention to facts that his recklessness and lack of experience are again unsurpassed.
>
> Undertaking in the first place to describe [Egyptian General] Scopas's order of battle he tells us that the phalanx with a few horsemen rested its right wing on the hills, while the left wing and all the cavalry set apart for this purpose stood on the level ground.
>
> ...

---

[180] Josephus, *Antiquities of the Jews*, Book XII, Chapter III: III

> Scopas ... when he saw the younger Antiochus [son of King Antiochus III, and who was a commander in the Battle of Panium along with his father] returning from the pursuit and threatening the phalanx from the rear he [the Egyptian general] despaired of victory and retreated.
>
> ...
>
> Writers it seems to me should be thoroughly ashamed of nonsensical errors like the above.
>
> They should therefore strive above all to become masters of the whole craft of history, for to do so is good; but if this be out of their own power, they should give the closest attention to what is most necessary and important.
>
> I was led to make these observations, because I observe that at the present day, as in the case of other arts and professions, what is true and really useful is always treated with neglect, while what is pretentious and showy is praised and coveted as if it were something great and wonderful, whereas it is both easier to produce and wins applause more cheaply, as is the case with all other written matter."[181]

And so, my lords, nearly nineteen years after his surprising defeat in the Battle of Raphia [217 BC] on the hands of decadent King Ptolemy IV Philopator, H.M. King Antiochus III the Great returns to Israel and the surrounding region and decisively beats the Egyptian forces of the young King Ptolemy V Epiphanes of Egypt [198 BC].

Prophet Daniel, your 342-year-old prophecy, one more time, please, [540 BC–198 BC].

> DAN 11:13 *For the king of the north [King Antiochus III the Great] shall return, and shall set forth a multitude greater than the former, and shall certainly come after certain years [nearly nineteen years] with a great army and with much riches.*
> DAN 11:14 *And in those times there shall many stand up against the king of the south [The great Egyptian revolt, 205-186 BC]: also the robbers of thy people shall exalt themselves to establish the vision; but they shall fall.*
> DAN 11:15 *So the king of the north [King Antiochus III] shall come, and cast up a mount, and take the most fenced cities: and the arms of the south [the armies of King Ptolemy V Epiphanes] shall not withstand, neither his chosen people, neither shall there be any strength to withstand.*

---

[181] Polybius, *The Histories*, Book XVI: 18–20

PAST AND PRESENT ABOMINATIONS—445

*DAN 11:16 But he [King Antiochus III] that cometh against him [King Ptolemy V Epiphanes] shall do according to his own will, and none shall stand before him: and he shall stand in the glorious land [King Antiochus III takes Israel], which by his hand shall be consumed [would be fulfilled in the days of one of King Antiochus III's successors].*

*DAN 11:17 He shall also set his face to enter with the strength of his whole kingdom, and upright ones with him; thus shall he do: and he shall give him the daughter of women, corrupting her: but she shall not stand on his side, neither be for him.*

*DAN 11:18 After this shall he turn his face unto the isles, and shall take many: but a prince for his own behalf shall cause the reproach offered by him to cease; without his own reproach he shall cause it to turn upon him.*

## Why Not King of Europe Too?

And here comes a difficult question, my lords, who is the daughter of the women, which prophet Daniel speaks of?

We can tell you, my lords, that at this point of time, H. M. King Antiochus III of the north is at the summit of his success. He is the one and undisputed king of lands stretching from India to the shores of Europe and from the Arabian Gulf to the shores of the Mediterranean. He is the king of Iran and the Middle East.

But, my lords, his majesty is not the lord of Europe; rising Rome is contesting it, your majesties.

And he is not the king of Egypt, and he is not the king of Greece, and why can he not? Why an ambitious and great man cannot be the king of all? Especially that his majesty knows that there are regions in Europe and in Anatolia of Turkey that belong to his family; at least according to him, they do.

My lords, these days his majesty is sleeping with a new dream—crossing to Europe. And he finds it hard to understand why the Romans should stop him from taking the lands that supposedly belong to his family and royal house.

### Forever Kings in Roman Times

The Assyrians of northern Iraq, home of the Sunni Muslims, ruled the world. Then their kingdom came to an end when the Babylonians of southern Iraq,

> home of the Shiite Muslims, obliterated them. The Babylonians ruled the world until the Persians of Iran came and ended their empire. The Persians of Iran, home of the Shiite Muslims, ruled the world until the Greeks came and demolished them. The Greeks would then rule the world until the Romans come. The Romans came and ruled the world. But at the start of their rule, the seed of a new kingdom was planted—totally different kingdom with a different king.
>
>> Ps 72:6 *He shall come down like rain upon the mown grass: as showers that water the earth.*
>> Ps 72:7 *In his days shall the righteous flourish; and abundance of peace so long as the moon endureth.*
>> Ps 72:8 *He shall have dominion also from sea to sea, and from the river unto the ends of the earth.*
>>
>> Isa 9:6 *For unto us a child is born, unto us a son is given: and the government shall be upon his shoulder: and his name shall be called Wonderful, Counsellor, The mighty God, The everlasting Father, The Prince of Peace.*
>> Isa 9:7 *Of the increase of his government and peace there shall be no end.*
>
> ## *Be Very Ambitious*
>
> And this shall be the time when His people shall rule. Each shall hold a different rank. And this is why the apostle Paul encourages the people of God to be ambitious, very ambitious.
>
>> Lk 22:29 *And I appoint unto you a kingdom*
>> Mat 25:21 *His lord said unto him, Well done, thou good and faithful servant: thou hast been faithful over a few things, I will make thee ruler over many things: enter thou into the joy of thy lord.*

But first things first—one step at a time! Let the acquisition of the world be done systematically.

And so, my lords, his majesty began to mop all the maritime cities, the commercial and shopping harbors along the eastern Mediterranean, which for a long time belonged to the now defeated Egypt.

Shipping, my lords, which made Egypt wealthy, would now be his private export-import company.

And so it goes without saying, my lords, that the large and important islands of Cyprus and Euboea on the shipping sea lane, the corn highway, between Egypt and Rome are two of his majesty's targets.

# PAST AND PRESENT ABOMINATIONS—447

And so now we can report to you, my lords, that two years after his victory in the battle of Panium over Egypt, H.M. King Antiochus III the great, king of Iran, is crossing to Thrace and to Europe [196 BC].

He claims, my lords, that he is doing so in order to free his Greek kin from the rule of the Romans whose military bases indeed fill many Greek cities.

No doubts, my lords, the Greek cities and their leaders would be more than happy to rally around him and strengthen him against the Romans.

Think again, my lords.

Meanwhile we can tell you, your majesties, that the Roman Senate is now quite worried about this adventurous Greek king of many lands.

## 195–193 BC
## An Astonishing Move

And, today, in line with his ambition, my lords, his majesty makes an unexpected but a very pragmatic move.

Five years, your majesties, after he defeated young King Ptolemy V Epiphanes of Egypt, he offers the young Egyptian king [almost fifteen or sixteen years' old] his ten-year-old daughter, Princess Cleopatra I Syra, as a wife—a ten-year-old child is given away as a wife [she was about eight or nine years old when betrothed in 195 BC and about ten or eleven years old when married 193 BC].

There is more yet, my sovereigns.

As a dowry for his juvenile daughter, H.M. King Antiochus III the great proposes to share half the taxes of the wealthy Israel and Coele-Syria and the surrounding region with the 16-year-old defeated king of Egypt. Why? Why would he do such a thing?

Historian Josephus, please cut in where you have information to provide, sir.

The above image belongs to either Cleopatra I (the daughter of the women) or Cleopatra III), Louvre Museum, Paris (image source: author).

> "Antiochus made a friendship and league with Ptolemy [V Epiphanes], and gave him his daughter Cleopatra to wife, and yielded up to him Celesyria, and Samaria [northern half of Israel], and Judea [southern half of Israel], and Phoenicia [Lebanon], by way of dowry. And upon the division of the taxes between the two kings, all the principal men [tax collectors] farmed the taxes of their several countries, and collecting the sum that was settled for them, paid the same to the [two] kings.
>
> ...
>
> And when the day came on which the king was to let the taxes of the cities to farm [the king auctions the taxes of the cities and the towns. The local leaders of these cities and towns make bids on the taxes. They bid as low as they possibly can [payable taxes] and demand as high as they could from the locals, and thus make their profit], and those that were the principal men of dignity in their several countries were to bid for them, the sum of the taxes together, of Celesyria, and Phoenicia, and Judea, with Samaria, (as they were bidden for,) came to eight thousand talents."[182]

Why, my lords, why would H.M. King Antiochus III the great give his infant daughter to the man he defeated, King Ptolemy V Epiphanes of Egypt? And why would he be willing to share the taxes of Israel and the surrounding region with a conquered enemy? You may ask, my lords. And we in our turn shall let ancient historian Appian answer your question.

Go ahead, sir.

> "[193 BC] Now, determining no longer to conceal his intended war with the Romans, he [King Antiochus III the Great] formed alliances by marriage with the neighboring kings. <u>To Ptolemy [V Epiphanes] in Egypt he sent his daughter Cleopatra, surnamed Syra, giving with her Coele-Syria as a dowry, which he had taken away from Ptolemy himself, thus flattering the young king in order to keep him quiet during the war with the Romans.</u>"[183]

---

[182] Josephus, *Antiquities of the Jews*, Book XII, Chapter 4:1 & 4

[183] Appian's *History of Rome*: The Syrian Wars 1:5. http://www.livius.org/ap-ark/appian/appian_syriaca_01.html

## PAST AND PRESENT ABOMINATIONS—449

The reign of King Ptolemy V Epiphanes, Numismatic Museum of Athens, Greece (image source: author).

King Ptolemy V of Egypt, became the son-in-law of King Antiochus III when he married the "daughter of the women" and yet sided with the Romans against his powerful father-in-law, Numismatic Museum of Athens, Greece (image source: author)

And here, my lords, we once again call upon prophet Daniel.

*DAN 11:17* *He [King Antiochus III the Great] shall also set his face to enter with the strength of his whole kingdom, and upright ones with him; thus shall he do: and he shall give him [King Ptolemy V Epiphanes of Egypt] the daughter of women [a child, an eleven-year old girl], corrupting her: but she shall not stand on his side, neither be for him [King Ptolemy V Epiphanes of Egypt, the husband of the child Princess Cleopatra I Syra, still ended up siding with the Romans against his father-in-law, Antiochus III].*

My lords, at this time, H.M. King Antiochus III, the king of the Middle East, is invading Europe and Greece proper, and promising freedom to the Greek cities from their Roman rulers and overlords.

Being in Greece, my lords, he is therefore not far away from Italy. And Rome, my lords, is worried. The senate has taken keen notice of the fiercely ambitious leader of the Middle East and Asia.

Go ahead, please, historian Appian.

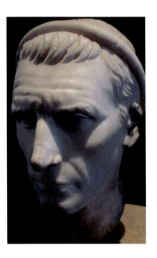

Prophet Daniel prophesied of King Antiochus III the great, the Greek king of the Middle East and Asia, Louvre Museum, Paris (image source: author).

"[November 192] When the Romans heard of the eruption of Antiochus into Greece and the killing and capture of Romans at Delium, they declared war. In this way the war between them [between the Romans and King Antiochus III], which had been smouldering a long time, first actually broke out.

So great was the dominion of Antiochus, ruler of many powerful nations of upper Asia, and of all but a few on the sea-coast [Mediterranean harbors], who had now invaded Europe; so formidable was his reputation and so complete his preparation, so many and so famous had been his exploits against other peoples, from which he had earned the title of *Great*, that the Romans anticipated that this war would be long and severe for them."[184]

Historian Cassius Dio, can you, sir, confirm the record of historian Appian?

---

[184] Appian's *History of Rome*, the Syrian Wars: 15

"The fame of Antiochus occupied a large share of Rome's attention and caused the Romans no small degree of uneasiness. Many rumours were rife regarding him: some reported that he already held the whole of Greece, others that he was hastening toward Italy."[185]

As you saw, my lords, H.M. King Antiochus III made a great strategic move by giving away half his taxes from Israel and Coele-Syria in order to enlist Egypt against Rome.

But this strategic move by the fox of the Middle East, my lords, was in fact a response to a strategic move by the Italian king of foxes.

The Italian king of foxes, my lords, is a 30-year old Roman Governor [consul] whose appointment as a governor was illegal, my lords, but the Roman senate did allow it by overruling the constitution in order to grant him the position, or so they say, my lords. Whatever the case maybe, he is one of the men who shall fulfill the prophecy of Daniel.

And so, your majesties, H.M. King Antiochus III knew fairly well that he could invade Greece and challenge the powerful Roman legions without support. He needed above all, my lords, to win the hearts and souls of the citizens of the Greek cities along with their leaders. Therefore, his message to the Greek leaders and to the Greek population, my lords, was that he, a Greek like them and their kin, is coming to free them from their Roman taxing masters.

And we can tell you here, my lords, that indeed a Greek province and all of its cities and allies were more than happy to welcome him and supply his army with the necessary provision, and even fight along his troops. They did so, my lords, for the simple reason that they, the Aetolians and their league of cities, were indeed feeling enslaved by Rome and the annual taxes they had to pay her year after year.

But yet the situation was somewhat complicated, my lords, because not all the Greeks hated the Romans. Or maybe we should say, your majesties, that the population of some Greek cities hated the Romans less than they hated a neighboring Greek king.

Indeed, it was only a few months ago that this Greek king, H.M. King Philip V of Macedon had invaded many neighboring Greek cities and added them to his domain. He too taxed these cities.

---

[185] Cassius Dio, *Roman History,* Vol. II, Loeb Classical Library edition, 1914, introduction

Gold coin of King Philip V of Macedonia, 221-179 BC, Louvre Museum, Paris, (image source: author)

And therefore, Greek King Philip V of Macedon has now, my lords, made himself an enemy to the rest of the Greek provinces and cities besides, of course, being an enemy of Rome.

As a result, my lords, many Greek cities had been communicating and sending ambassadors to the Roman senate asking for their help to free them from this rising Greek star in their neighborhood.

And so, my lords, in response to the request of these Greek cities, the senate sent its mighty Roman legions, which indeed succeeded to defeat his Greek majesty King Philip V and restrict him to his own kingdom of Macedon.

So you can see, my lords, that the Romans were more or less loved by those Greek cities, which they freed. Or did they?

No, my lords, the Romans were not loved by all. Some Greeks leaders thought that the Romans played favoritism among the Greeks and did not grant a blanket freedom to all.

Greek King Philip V (221-179 BC) of Macedon conquered many Greek cities of his neighboring provinces and opened the door to the fulfillment of one of Daniel's prophecies, British Museum, London (image source: author).

My lords, the Aetolian Greeks and their allies are complaining that the Roman senate was selective in their treatment of the Greek cities they freed from King Philip V.

And it is true, my lords, the Romans pulled away their military garrisons from some cities and granted them complete freedom from taxes, but they also kept their troops in other cities, including those belonging to the Aetolian Greeks.

Thus, my lords, the Aetolians and their allies were not happy with Rome, the pretentious savior of all Greek cities. And thus, too, my lords, they were more than willing to deal with H.M. King Antiochus III the great against Rome.

Go ahead, please, historian Titus Livius.

> "[196 BC] peace was granted to Philip on these terms: that all the Greek cities which were in Europe or in Asia should enjoy their liberty and laws; that, whatever cities had been under the sway of Philip, from these Philip should withdraw his garrisons and should hand

them over to the Romans, free of his troops, before the time of the Isthmian Games."[186]

Carry on, sir.

"While all the Greek cities approved this settlement, only the Aetolians with secret grumblings criticized the decision of the ten commissioners [appointed by the Roman senate]: mere words had been trimmed up with the empty show of liberty; why were some cities delivered to the Romans [to become Roman properties] without being named, others specified and ordered to be free ... to wit, [the Greek cities, which were not granted their freedom were] Corinth and Chalcis and Oreus along with Eretria and Demetrias?

Their complaint [their reproach of the Romans empty words, as they said above] was not altogether groundless. For there was some uncertainty with respect to [important cities such as] Corinth and Chalcis and Demetrias, because in the decree of the senate, under which the ten commissioners were sent from Rome, the other cities of Greece and Asia were beyond question set free, but regarding these three [important] cities the commissioners were [ambiguous, and there was a good reason for the commissioners to keep the statues of these important cities ambiguous.].There was King Antiochus, who, there was no doubt, would invade Europe as soon as his forces seemed adequate; they did not wish to leave these cities, so favourably located, open to his occupancy [the Romans wanted these cities occupied by their own troops without plainly saying so]."[187]

So this is then, my lords, the idea that the Roman commissioners had in mind when they kept their legions garrisoned in these grumbling Greek cities. They wanted the legions to stay there in order to fight the ambitious Greek king when he comes by. And if the garrisons must remain in these cities, then these cities must pay taxes for their keep.

And, indeed, all the Roman commissioners of the senate, my lords, had supported this plan with the exception of one commissioner whose name is Quinctius. This man, my lords, shall lead the way to fulfilling Daniel's prophecy.

What is his line of reasoning?

Well, Commissioner Quinctius, your majesties, argued that the Roman senate should do the very opposite and pull the army, and grant these Greek

---

[186] Titus Livius (Livy), *The History of Rome*, Book 33:30.
http://www.perseus.tufts.edu/hopper/text?doc=Perseus%3Atext%3A1999.02.0164%3Abook%3D34s
[187] Titus Livius (Livy), *The History of Rome*, Book 33:31

cities their freedom so that they would not, out of anger, side with H.M. King Antiochus against Rome. He meant, my lords, that the population can do more harm than the good the legions can do.

Please, go ahead, historian Titus Livius.

> "<u>Quinctius urged repeatedly that all Greece should be set free</u>, if they wished to stop the muttering [the complaining, the reproaching] of the Aetolians and to create genuine affection and respect for the Roman name among all the Greeks, and if they wished to convince them that they had crossed the sea to liberate Greece and not to transfer dominion from Philip to themselves.
>
> The others said nothing opposed to this as regards the freedom of the cities, but <u>they believed it safer for the Greeks themselves to remain for a while under the protection of Roman garrisons than to receive Antiochus as lord in place of Philip</u>.
>
> Finally, this decision was reached: Corinth should be given over to the Achaeans, a garrison, however, to be retained in Acrocorinthus; Chalcis and Demetrias should be held until the anxiety about Antiochus should have passed."[188]

Not good enough, my lords. The Greek Aetolians kept up their grumblings and reproach of the Romans.

Now enter Governor Flamininus, my lords. This man, my lords, will cap off what is needed to clarify and fulfill Daniel's prophecy.

Governor Flamininus, my lords, was waiting for an important occasion, the Isthmian Games, to make his important announcement in the crowded sports arena. [The Isthmian Games were held the year before and the year after the Olympic Games]. And his announcement, my lords, was meant to take the wind out of the grumblings and the reproaching of the Greek Aetolians, who wanted to take their chances with King Antiochus III against them.

Now, your majesties, the trumpet had sounded in the crowded stadium and then fell silent. So let us listen together to the words of the herald.

No, this cannot be true!

Recall the herald for an encore.

Let us hear him one more time.

Another line in prophet Daniel's prophecy is being fulfilled before our own eyes, my lords.

Carry on please, historian Titus Livius.

---

[188] Titus Livius (Livy), *The History of Rome*, Book 33:31

# PAST AND PRESENT ABOMINATIONS—455

"[196 BC] The appointed time of the Isthmian Games was at hand, a spectacle always, even on other occasions, attended by crowds, on account of the fondness, native to the race, for exhibitions in which there are trials of skill in every variety of art as well as of strength and swiftness of foot [the Greeks loved competitions of different skills];

...

But at this time they had assembled from all quarters not only for the usual purposes, but especially because <u>they were consumed with wonder</u> what thenceforth the state of Greece would be, and what their own condition; they not only had their own silent thoughts, some believing one thing and others another, but discussed openly what the Romans would do; <u>almost no one was convinced that they would withdraw from all Greece</u>.

They had taken their seats at the games and the herald with the trumpeter, as is the custom, had come forth into the midst of the arena, where the games are regularly opened with a ritual chant, and proclaiming silence with a trumpet-call, the herald read the decree:

"The Roman senate and Titus Quinctius, *imperator*, having conquered King Philip and the Macedonians, <u>declare to be free, independent, and subject to their own laws</u>, the Corinthians, the Phocians, all the Locrians, the island of Euboea, the Magnesians, the Thessalians, the Perrhaebians, and the Phthiotic Achaeans."

My lords, the herald named all the states, which had been subject to King Philip V of Macedon.

"When the herald's voice was heard there was rejoicing greater than men could grasp in its entirety. <u>They could scarce believe that they had heard aright, and they looked at one another marvelling as at the empty vision of a dream; they asked their neighbours what concerned each one, unwilling to trust the evidence of their own ears.</u>

<u>The herald was recalled, each one desiring not only to hear but to behold the man who brought the tidings of his freedom, and again the herald read the same decree</u>. Then, when the ground for their joy was certain, such a storm of applause began and was so often repeated that it was easily apparent that of all blessings none pleases a throng more than liberty. The contests were then rapidly finished, no man's eyes or thoughts being fixed upon the sight [they were completely distracted from watching the competetions]; joy

alone had so completely replaced their perception of all other delightful things."[189]

May we, my lords, let ancient historian Cassius Dio confirm the move by the Romans to end the Greeks reproach against them!
Sir!

> "[Quinctius] Flamininus at this time set all the Greeks free, and later he summoned them together and after reminding them of the benefits they had received urged them to maintain friendship with Rome [against Antiochus III]; he then withdrew all the garrisons and departed with his entire army.
>
> ...
>
> the Romans had no hope of overcoming Antiochus, but were content if only they could preserve their former conquests. For he was regarded as a mighty ruler even by virtue of his own power, by which he had subjugated Media [Iran] among other exploits; but he became far mightier still through having gained as sons-in-law Ptolemy, king of Egypt, and Ariarathes, king of Cappadocia.
>
> ...
>
> Antiochus did, at any rate, succeed in crossing into Europe twice, and in reaching Greece.
>
> ...
>
> The Romans and he both now sent envoys to each other submitting mutual complaints; in order that they might find an excuse for war and also that they might observe conditions on the other side before the conflict began."[190]

And now, my lords, we have another ancient historian, historian Appian who would like to add more details.
Sir!

> "When he [Quinctius Flamininus] had arranged these things with them he went to the Isthmian games, and, the stadium being full of people, he commanded silence by trumpet and directed the herald to make this proclamation, 'The Roman people and Senate, and Flamininus, their general, having vanquished the Macedonians and Philip, their king, <u>order that Greece shall be free from foreign garrisons, not subject to tribute [annual taxes], and shall live under her own customs and laws.</u>'

---

[189] Titus Livius (Livy), *The History of Rome*, Book 33:32
[190] Cassius Dio, *Roman History,* Vol. II, Loeb Classical Library edition, 1914, introduction

> Thereupon there was great shouting and rejoicing and a scene of rapturous tumult; and groups here and there called the herald back in order that he might repeat his words for them.
> They threw crowns and fillets upon the general and voted statues for him in their cities. They sent ambassadors with golden crowns to the Capitol at Rome to express their gratitude, and inscribed themselves as allies of the Roman people."[191]

Prophet Daniel, the floor is yours, one more time, sir.

> DAN 11:17 *He [King Antiochus III the Great] shall also set his face to enter with the strength of his whole kingdom, and upright ones with him; thus shall he do: and he shall give him [King Ptolemy V Epiphanes] the daughter of women [Cleopatra I Syra; a child, an eleven-year old girl], corrupting her: but she shall not stand on his side, neither be for him [Her husband King Ptolemy V Epiphanes of Egypt ended up siding with the Romans against his father-in-law, King Antiochus III the Great].*
> DAN 11:18 *After this shall he [King Antiochus III] turn his face unto the isles, and shall take many: but a prince [the Roman governor Quinctius Flamininus] for his own behalf [because of him, because of Antiochus III] shall cause the reproach offered by him to cease [Flamininus freed all the Greek cities under Roman control and dismantled the Roman military garrisons in them thus he took away Antiochus's reproach of the Romans that they are enslaving the Greeks and their cities after freeing them from King Philip V]; without his own reproach he shall cause it to turn upon him [as a result; the Greek cities would now side with the Romans against their own kin Greek King Antiochus III the Great].*

Nonetheless, my lords, H.M. King Antiochus III, went on to invade Greece.

In turn, your majesties, the Roman legions were dispatched to confront him at that old blood-stained narrow way, the doorway of Europe—the hot gates. It is the same passageway in the mountains where the great last stand of Spartan King Leonidas took place nearly 290 years ago [480 BC] against H.M. King Xerxes I of Iran.

---

[191] Appian's History of Rome: The Macedonian Wars (2): 13. http://www.livius.org/ap-ark/appian/appian_macedonia2.html

General T. Quinctius Flamininus "issued his famous declaration of freedom of the Greek people." The quote is taken from the British Museum, London, where the left side coin is preserved, the right side coin is housed in the Louvre Museum, Paris (images source: author).

We can tell you, my sovereigns, a few outcomes ahead of time.

We can tell you that at the end of his ambitions, H.M. King Antiochus III will be riddled with debt. We can tell you that he will end up robbing banks, that is to say temples, my lords. And we can also tell you that his successor would do anything to get money, a drive that will lead him to Jerusalem and its temple. And finally, my lords, we can tell you that his successor not only ransacked the temple but also became intent on changing the "religion," the faith of Israel. Meaning, my lords, that he wanted to destroy the nation of the prophets and put an end to the spreading of the good tidings concerning the plan and the schedule of God.

> ROM 6:23 *For the wages of sin is death; but the gift of God is eternal life through Jesus Christ our Lord.*
> 1 JN 2:25 *And this is the promise that he hath promised us, even eternal life.*

# Hot Gates Again —Thermopylae

This piece of land, my lords, is a maker and breaker of dreams. It is the piece of land that votes on the championship of the world.

Five years had passed, my lords, since each side had made his intentions clear. Five years had passed while the two sides were busy reinforcing their positions and engaging in futile negotiations of a cold war.

At last the time had come to unsheathe the sharp swords, shed some blood, and break up families.

## PAST AND PRESENT ABOMINATIONS—459

And so with your permission, my lords, we shall point to several historians to read out their records as we go.

"The Aetolians had gone over to Antiochus and were forming a union out of various states with or without their consent.

...

The people at Rome, learning that he was in Greece and that he had captured Chalcis, took up the war openly ... and sent Manius Glabrio [191 BC] with a large army into Greece.

...

Antiochus meanwhile was remaining at Chalcis and keeping quiet. Afterward he went into Boeotia and <u>awaited the advance of the Romans at Thermopylae</u>; for he believed, in view of his small numbers, that the natural advantages of the place would be of assistance to him. But in order to avoid repeating the experience of the Greeks who had been arrayed there against the Persian [Iranians] he sent a division of the Aetolians up to the summit of the mountains to keep guard there [to guard the pass, which the Persian Iranians had used to encircle the Greeks]."[192]

"The passage at Thermopylae is long and narrow, flanked on the one side by a rough and inhospitable sea and on the other by a deep and impassable morass. It is overhung by two mountain peaks, one called Tichius and the other Callidromus. The place also contains some hot springs, whence comes the name *Thermopylae*, 'hot gates.'

There Antiochus built a double wall on which he placed engines. He sent Aetolian troops to occupy the summits of the mountains to prevent anybody from coming around secretly by way of the hill called Atropos, as **Xerxes** had come upon the Spartans under Leonidas, the mountain paths at that time being unguarded. One thousand Aetolians occupied each mountain. The remainder encamped by themselves near the city of Heraclea."[193]

## 188 BC
## A Debt to Pay

The Romans' large army, my lords, engaged the army of H.M. King Antiochus III and routed it. But this was nothing but the first encounter. A couple more followed, my lords, and the outcome of each was the same.

---

[192] Cassius Dio, *Roman History*, Vol. II: 19, Loeb Classical Library edition, 1914
[193] Appian's *History of Rome*: The Syrian Wars 17, 18

"So they routed Antiochus and captured his camp. The king forthwith retired to Chalcis, but learning that the consul [the Roman general] was approaching, he retired secretly to Asia.

...

Then crossing into Asia, they [King Antiochus and his army] found most of the coast districts already occupied by the Romans who had gone there first.

...

Eumenes and his brother Attalus were injuring the country of Antiochus, and [Greek] <u>cities kept coming over to the Romans, some under compulsion, some voluntarily, with the result that Antiochus was obliged to abandon Europe entirely.</u>

...

After this, upon overtures made by Antiochus, an armistice was arranged.

...

consequently they [the Roman Senate] laid upon Antiochus conditions no more severe than those they had originally made before the battle."[194]

"King Antiochus, learning that <u>the [Greek] cities of Thessaly had gone over to the Romans</u>, that his Asiatic forces were slow in arriving, and that the Aetolians [his Greek Allies] were negligent and full of excuses, was deeply distressed. He was, in consequence, angry with those who, on the strength of the Aetolian alliance, had induced him to embark upon a war for which he was not prepared.

...

Antiochus, on learning that the Romans had crossed to Asia, sent Heracleides of Byzantium to the consul to sue for peace, offering to pay half the costs of the war, and also to give up the cities of Lampsacus, Smyrna, and Alexandria, which had, it was thought, been responsible for bringing on the conflict. Of the Greek cities in Asia these were, in fact, the first to dispatch embassies to the senate, invoking its aid in behalf of their independence.

...

After the defeat of Antiochus envoys presented themselves from all the cities and principalities of Asia, some suing for independence, others for a return for their good services to Rome in the common struggle against Antiochus."[195]

---

[194] Cassius Dio, *Roman History*, Fragments of Book XIX, Zonaras section, 19.1, 20.1
http://penelope.uchicago.edu/Thayer/E/Roman/Texts/Cassius_Dio/19*.html

[195] Diodorus Siculus Book 29:3:1, 7:1 & 11:1.
http://penelope.uchicago.edu/Thayer/E/Roman/Texts/Diodorus_Siculus/29*.html#15

Prophet Daniel, it is your turn, go ahead, sir.

DAN 11:17 *He [King Antiochus III the Great] shall also set his face to enter with the strength of his whole kingdom, and upright ones with him; thus shall he do: and he shall give him the daughter of women, corrupting her: but she shall not stand on his side, neither be for him [King Ptolemy V Epiphanes of Egypt, the husband of the child Cleopatra I, still ended up siding with the Romans against his father-in-law, Antiochus III].*

DAN 11:18 *After this shall he turn his face unto the isles, and shall take many: but a prince [the Roman governor Flamininus] for his own behalf [because of him, because of Antiochus III] shall cause the reproach offered by him to cease [Flamininus frees all the Greek cities under Roman control and dismantles the Roman military garrisons in them thus takes away Antiochus's reproach of the Romans that they are enslaving the Greeks and their cities]; without his own reproach he shall cause it to turn upon him [as a result; the Greek cities would now side with the Romans against their own kin Antiochus III].*

## 187 BC
## The Great Has Fallen

Some of you, my lords, know exactly what you need to do when you are short of money. Some of you, my lords, knew exactly where the treasure troves of surrounding nations were hidden.

His majesty King Esarhaddon sitting among you today, my lords, may wish to whisper to your ears what he has done and how his action started a revolution. We may tell him today that after his death, that revolution ended up destroying his empire and fueled a new one. It is a dangerous move to make, my lords, but you end up sacking temples when it is your last resource.

And to no one's surprise, my lords, H.M. King Antiochus III did the same as H.M. King Esarhaddon has done. And in doing so, my lords, he set a precedence for his successor—the "small horn," the "man of sin"—to copy his action.

After a series of engagements, the war with the Romans had come to an end, my lords.

"Antiochus, abandoning the conflict in despair, dispatched an embassy to the consul [Roman governor], requesting pardon for his errors and the granting of peace on whatever terms possible.

The consul, adhering to the traditional Roman policy of fair dealing ... granted peace on the following terms: the king must

> withdraw, in favour of the Romans, from Europe ... he must surrender his [war] elephants and warships, <u>and pay in full the expenses incurred in the war</u>, which were assessed at 5,000 Euboean talents; and he must deliver up Hannibal the Carthaginian, Thoas the Aetolian, and certain others, together with twenty hostages to be designated by the Romans.
>
> In his desire for peace Antiochus accepted all the conditions and brought the fighting to a close."[196]

The ancient historian Appian, your majesties—he too gives more details on the peace conditions and the payment schedule.

> "He [King Antiochus III the Great] must abandon Europe altogether and all of Asia this side of the <u>Taurus</u> ... he shall surrender all the elephants he has, and such number of ships as we may prescribe, and for the future keep no elephants and only so many ships as we allow ... and pay for the cost of the present war, incurred on his account, 500 Euboic talents down and 2500 more when the <u>Senate</u> ratifies the treaty; <u>and 12,000 more during twelve years, each yearly installment to be delivered in Rome.</u>
> ...
> If Antiochus accepts these conditions without guile we will grant him peace and friendship subject to the Senate's ratification."[197]

The Roman senate, my lords, has ratified the agreement, and a treaty was written with a few changes here and there, as advised by the respected Scipio.

According to the agreement, my lords, H.M. King Antiochus III of the north is not allowed to have more than twelve warships, which were allowed only for the purpose of keeping his subjects under control. However, he may also be allowed to have more if he were attacked.

He should not recruit mercenaries from Roman territory nor entertain fugitives from the same, and the hostages should be changed every third year, except the son, the crown prince of Antiochus, who must remain hostage while his father lives.

> "This treaty was engraved on brazen tablets and deposited in the Capitol (where it was customary to deposit such treaties) [188 BCE],

---

[196] Diodorus Siculus *Library of History* Fragments of Book XXIX, Chapter 10. http://penelope.uchicago.edu/Thayer/E/Roman/Texts/Diodorus_Siculus/29*.html

[197] Appian's *History of Rome*: The Syrians War, Book 1:38

and a copy of it was sent to Manlius Vulso, Scipio's successor in the command.

...

This was the end of the war between Antiochus the Great and the Romans."[198]

A newcomer has now firmly entered the scene, my lords—a dreadful and terrible beast—a beast that shall eventually grow ten horns and live long, my lords. But yet, your majesties, this newcomer is not a stranger. He was longtime expected. And he arrived on time. And his remnant is still here with us today as we speak with you.

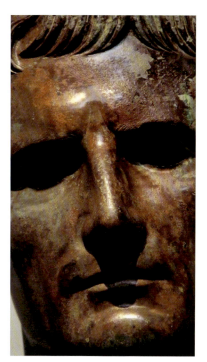

The newcomer, the beast out of whom another small horn should come in the last days of the earth, the National Museum of Greece, Athens (Image source: the author).

Dan 7:7 After this I saw in the night visions, and behold a fourth beast, dreadful and terrible, and strong exceedingly; and it had great iron teeth: it devoured and brake in pieces, and stamped the residue (of the Babylonian, Persian and Greek Empires) with the feet of it: and it was diverse from all the beasts that were before it; and it had ten horns.

Dan 7:8 I considered the horns, and, behold, there came up among them <u>another little horn</u>, before whom there were three of the first horns plucked up by the roots: and, behold, in this horn were eyes like the eyes of man, and a mouth speaking great things (this prophecy will reach its end in 1945 of our modern day, which will then be followed by another prophecy fulfilled in 1967; other prophecies of Daniel shall yet take place in the future, although their settings, such as the siege of Jerusalem, are being assembled as we speak).

## Pillaging Temples

You all know, your majesties, what the strongest weapon of wars is. You do all know, my lords and my commanders, that money is the "sinews of war," and that without money, no victory is guaranteed.

---

[198] Appian's *History of Rome*: The Syrians War, Book 1:39

Would you agree with this statement, historian Diodorus Siculus?

> "In warfare a ready supply of money is needed, as the familiar proverb has it, the sister of success [others called it sinews of war"], since he who is well provided with money never lacks men able to fight.
>
> So, for example, the Carthaginians recently brought the Romans to the brink of disaster, yet it was not with an army of citizens that they won their victories in those great engagements, but by the great number of their mercenary soldiers [hired foreign combatants]. An abundance of foreign troops is, in fact, very advantageous to the side that employs them, and very formidable to the enemy, inasmuch as the employers bring together at trifling cost men to do battle in their behalf, while citizen soldiers, even if victorious, are nevertheless promptly faced with a fresh crop of opponents.
>
> In the case of citizen armies, a single defeat spells complete disaster, but in the case of mercenaries, however many times they suffer defeat, none the less the employers maintain their forces intact as long as their money lasts."[199]

And so now, my lords, H.M. King Antiochus III has an urgent problem to deal with before dreaming about future and glorious victories. His majesty has only closed his forties and began to step on the threshold of fifty years old—there is time yet to change his fortune.

But for today, he must find a way to lay his hands on gold and silver in order to pay the Roman senate for the cost of the war and stop their legions from chasing him to the ends of the world.

Would you please, historian Diodorus Siculus, tell their majesties how his majesty managed to get funds? We ask you this question, sir, because we know that his son, a vile person, would do the same in Jerusalem.

> "Antiochus, pressed for funds and hearing that the temple of Bel in Elymaïs had a large store of silver and gold, derived from the dedications, resolved to pillage it. He proceeded to Elymaïs and after accusing the inhabitants of initiating hostilities, pillaged the temple; but though he amassed much wealth he speedily received meet punishment from the gods."[200]

Time ran out.

---

[199] Diodorus Siculus, *Library of History*, Fragments of Book 29:6
[200] Diodorus Siculus, Book 29:15.
http://penelope.uchicago.edu/Thayer/E/Roman/Texts/Diodorus_Siculus/29*.html#15

> As for Antiochus, his project of pillaging the sanctuary of Zeus at Elymaïs brought him to appropriate disaster, and he perished with all his host [army]."[201]

My lords, H.M. King Antiochus III the great is dead [187 BC]. His dreams rested in peace with him.

But the prophecy of prophet Daniel, my lords, takes life steadily. Go ahead, please, prophet Daniel.

Gold Octadrachm of King Antiochus III the great (223-187 BC), father of King Antiochus IV Epiphanes, the British Museum, London (image source: author).

> DAN 11:17 He [King Antiochus III the Great] shall also set his face to enter with the strength of his whole kingdom, and upright ones with him; thus shall he do: and he shall give him the daughter of women, corrupting her: but she shall not stand on his side, neither be for him.
> DAN 11:18 After this shall he turn his face unto the isles, and shall take many: but a prince for his own behalf shall cause the reproach offered by him to cease; without his own reproach he shall cause it to turn upon him.
> DAN 11:19 Then he [King Antiochus III the Great] shall turn his face toward the fort of his own land: but he shall stumble and fall, and not be found.

## 187-175 BC
## The Tax Collector

My lords, his great majesty has died but the indemnity, the cost of the war he began, remains to be paid now and annually for the next twelve years, as stipulated in the peace treaty.

Now, his son and successor, H.M. King Philopator, must find a way to pay it.

And finding a way, he did, my lords.

---

[201] Diodorus Siculus Book 29.3:1

Silver tetradrachm of King Seleucus IV, the tax collector of Daniel's prophecy, Pennsylvania Archaeological Museum, Philadelphia, USA (image source: author).

H.M. King Seleucus IV Philopator of the north is sending an envoy to Jerusalem, capital of Israel.

Jerusalem city, my lords, has been under his father's control since his great victory in the battle of Panium [c. 198 BC].

The envoy and the soldiers of his new majesty have arrived to Jerusalem.

And, of course, the taxation money, which they are after, my lords, is stored in the temple of Jerusalem—the Parliament of God.

It is reported, my lords, that the envoy, upon his return from Jerusalem, had a falling out with his master, H.M. King Seleucus IV Philopator, and indeed assassinated him.

And even though his dead majesty had only retained the throne for a short period of twelve years, he, nonetheless, succeeded in clarifying and fulfilling another line in Daniel's prophecy.

Go ahead, please, prophet Daniel.

DAN 11:20 *Then shall stand up in his estate [King Antiochus III shall be succeeded by] a raiser of taxes in the glory of the kingdom: but within few days he shall be destroyed, neither in anger, nor in battle.*

King Seleucus IV, the collector of taxes of the prophecy of Daniel, Numismatic Museum of Athens, Greece (image source: author)

And so, my lords, while the young crown prince, Demetrius I Soter, was kept as a hostage in Rome in order to insure compliance with the terms of the peace treaty, the younger brother of his slain majesty King Seleucus IV Philopator went after the killer of his older brother, Heliodorus.

And yes, in time, my lords, the younger brother has managed to capture and slay the usurper Heliodorus.

The little horn, my lords, is entering the highway of kings.

The younger brother did not stop at justice. Indeed, my lords, he went on to commit a crime and assassinate his brother's son, his nephew, the crown prince and legitimate new king of the Seleucids kingdom of Iran, Iraq, Syria, Lebanon, and Israel—the king of the North.

And so at this point of time, my lords, the successor of H.M. King Antiochus III the great is his younger son, a killer, H.M. King Antiochus IV Epiphanes, who some on a play of his name, later on called him "Epimanes," meaning *the Mad One*.

Go ahead, please, historian Appian.

The Heliodorus stele, 178 BC, Israel Museum; the inscription on the stele informs Heliodorus that King Seleucus has appointed a certain Olympiodoros to be in charge of the temples of Coele-Syria (Israel) and Phoenicia (Lebanon); the edited quote and the image's source are Wikipedia.

> "Thus Antiochus [IV], the son of Antiochus [III] the Great, ascended the throne of Syria. He was called *Epiphanes*, "the Illustrious", by the Syrians, because when the government was seized by usurpers he showed himself to be their true sovereign. By cementing the friendship and alliance of Eumenes he governed Syria and the neighboring nations with a firm hand."[202]

As some of you, my lords, may know, H.M. King Antiochus IV Epiphanes is of a mixed Greek and Iranian race, being a descendant of the first Seleucids Greek king, H.M. King Seleucus I Nicator, and his Iranian

---

[202] Ancient historian Appian of Alexandria [c .96–c. 165], *Roman History, Syrian Wars*, Part 10, 45

wife, Apama. Indeed, his majesty was born in Iran where his father, King Antiochus III the great, was residing at the time.

And as a reminder, my lords, King Seleucus I Nicator, the founder of the Seleucids royal house of the north, was one of the close companions and generals of H.M. King Alexander the Great.

At any rate, H.M. King Antiochus IV Epiphanes, the killer of his nephew, the mad one, has at this point of time inherited from his deceased father, King Antiochus III, the great one of the strongest armies in the region. But he also inherited a large debt to be paid annually to Rome and its senate.

His new majesty has a financial problem, my lords. This is a big problem for all time. He needs to become a thief.

Fortunately for him, my lords, the guardians, the top-ranking keepers of one of the greatest treasure coves in the region, would do the thieving for him. The thieves, my lords, are some of the top-ranking priests of Israel—robbers, as prophet Daniel had prophesied about them over 360 years ahead of time.

## Family Feud in Israel

Meanwhile, your majesties, an important family feud was heating up in Israel.

And this feud, my lords, was taking place amongst the highest ranks of the leadership of the nation of the prophets, the calendar of the earth.

If one can believe it, my lords, the family feud in Israel was taking place within the family of the high priest of Israel itself. And it is a family feud, which shall lead us to meet the "Little Horn."

But to be fair, the disputed issue, your majesties, was a great one.

One group of leaders wanted to "westernize" Israel, while the opposing group wanted to maintain the old traditions of Israel—a mixture of biblical expectations and manmade rules.

The citizens of Israel, your majesties, were divided in their opinions. Meanwhile, the heated arguments among the leaders became blows, and the blows turned to blood.

> MK 3:24 *if a kingdom be divided against itself, that kingdom cannot stand.*

The feud in Israel began, my lords, when the country's high priest, a godly and loved man by the name of Onias, died. Following his death, the leaders gave the highest position in the land to his brother Jason.

The position of high priest in Israel, my lords, makes the holder the de facto king, but without that title because Israel considers the Lord to be its one and only king.

At any rate, my lords, H.M. King Antiochus IV Epiphanes, who inherited Israel from his father H.M. King Antiochus III the great, did not like the new high priest Jason, and replaced him with a new high priest by the name of Menelaus.

Money, my lords, played a big part in this transfer of title, especially that his majesty needed a lot of it in order to pay the Roman senate.

And besides money, my lords, his majesty wanted a trusted and friendly Israeli leader. He wanted a high priest who was the most willing to westernize, "hellenize," Israel and shape it into the Greek way of life.

We shall now and then, my lords, call on the writer of the books of the Maccabees to give you some details.

> "King Seleucus died and Antiochus (known as Epiphanes) became king, Jason the brother of [now deceased high priest] Onias became High Priest by corrupt means.
>
> He went to see the king and offered him [360 talents of silver] ... with [80 talents of silver] ... to be paid later.
>
> Jason also offered him an additional [150 talents of silver] ... for the authority to establish a stadium where young men could train [in the nude following the Greek manner]."[203]

As for the stadium, or the gymnasium, my lords, it was built. And the leader of Israel, who is its high priest, did everything in his power to westernize and hellenize his nation of the prophets and the promised Savior of the world.

So far, my lords, the Greek sovereign, H.M. King Antiochus IV Epiphanes, should be happy.

> "With great enthusiasm he [High Priest Jason] built a stadium near the Temple hill and led our finest young men to adopt the Greek custom of participating in athletic events [in the nude].
>
> Because of the unrivaled wickedness of Jason, that ungodly and illegitimate High Priest, the craze for the Greek way of life and for foreign customs reached such a point that even the priests lost all interest in their sacred duties. They lost interest in the Temple services and neglected the sacrifices.
>
> Just as soon as the signal was given, they would rush off to take part in the games ... they prized only Greek honors."[204]

---

[203] II *Book of Maccabees*, new English translation, Ch. 4:7-9.
[204] II *Book of Maccabees*, Ch. 4:12-15.

Bronze statue of a young Greek athlete, about 340–330 BC, the National Archaeological Museum of Greece, Athens (image source: author).

In fact, my lords, it is said that high priest Jason, "the wretch, who is no high priest," sent three hundred drachms of silver to pay for the sacrifices offered in honor of the Greek god Hercules in a festival in Tyre of Lebanon. This was an important festival, and was attended by H.M. King Antiochus IV Epiphanes.

Allow us to repeat ourselves, my lords: the religious leader of one religion is sacrificing, that is to say, worshipping the god of another religion. Which god is his?

## The Nephew Is Unhappy

About this time, my lords, H.M. King Ptolemy V of Egypt, who was defeated by King Antiochus III the great, has died and the country was crowning his successor, H.M. King Ptolemy VI Philometor.

He is therefore, your majesties, the sixth ruler of the Greek Ptolemaic dynasty of Egypt.

Now, H.M. King Antiochus IV Epiphanes of the north sent one of his representatives to Egypt in order to attend the coronation ceremony.

After all, the new king is his majesty's nephew, the son of his sister, "the daughter of the women," daughter of King Antiochus III the great.

Hercules at rest. Roman copy, 2nd- to early-3rd century AD, from a Greek original from the second half of 4th century BC, Naples National Museum, Italy (image source: author).

# PAST AND PRESENT ABOMINATIONS—471

The representative of his majesty, my lords, came back with unsettling news.

King Ptolemy VI Philometor, Numismatic Museum of Athens, Greece (image source: author).

> "When Apollonius son of Menestheus was sent to Egypt to attend the crowning of Philomotor as king, Antiochus learned that Philometor was opposed to his policies. Antiochus became concerned about the security of his own kingdom."[205]

H.M. King Antiochus IV Epiphanes' assessment of the sentiment of the royal court in Egypt was a correct one, my lords. His nephew, the new king of Egypt, wants Israel back.

His majesty began to plan.

He does not need to plan too long.

Another storm of Daniel's prophecies is building up all the way to Rome.

Go ahead, please, historian Josephus.

> "At the same time that Antiochus [IV], who was called Epiphanes, had a quarrel with the sixth Ptolemy [VI Philometor] about his right to the whole country of Syria [including Israel], a great sedition [a great quarrel] fell among the men of power in Judea [Israel], and they had a contention about obtaining the government; while each of those that were of dignity could not endure to be subject to their equals."[206]

---

[205] II *Book of Maccabees*, Ch. 4:21
[206] Josephus, *The Wars of the Jews*, Book 1, Chapter. 1:1

King Antiochus IV Epiphanes (image source Wikipedia Commons, Classical Numismatic Group, Inc. http://www.cngcoins.com)

## 170 BC
## The King Is Taken Hostage

My lords, the new and young King Ptolemy VI Philometor was led by his counselors to believe that the Egyptian army was strong enough to face off against H.M. King Antiochus IV Epiphanes and wrestle back the wealthy region of Israel and southern Syria.

But then again, my lords, young King Ptolemy VI Philometor was also emboldened to face off against H.M. King Antiochus IV Epiphanes because the Romans were on Egypt's side.

Go ahead, please, historian Diodorus of Sicily.

> "Ptolemy [VI Philometor], king of Egypt, knowing that his ancestors had held Coelê Syria [Israel and southern Syria. Indeed, Egypt had held the region for all the years following the death of Alexander the Great. As mentioned earlier King Ptolemy I Soter had invaded Jerusalem city and taken it by ruse during a Sabbath day], made great preparations for war in support of his claim, hoping that since it had been detached in times past through an unjust war [by King Antiochus III the great at the battle of Apamea] he might now justly recover it on the same terms.
>
> Antiochus [IV Epiphanes], learning of this, dispatched envoys to Rome bidding them call the senate to witness that Ptolemy [VI Philometor], without just cause, was bent on making war.
>
> Ptolemy, however, also sent off envoys to speak in his defense, and to inform the senate that Coelê Syria had belonged to his forebears and that its subjection to Antiochus was contrary to all

justice. He also instructed them to renew friendly relations with the Romans."[207]

And so, my lords, the war between the king of the north and the king of the south broke out one more time. Indeed, my lords, this will be one of the last two wars, and soon we shall see why.

But briefly, your majesties, the wars between the king of the north and the king of the south shall end soon because of a message, a message that came on the hands of an old man, an arrogant old man.

For now, my lords, the war [sixth Syrian war] took place in the same old battle field along the frontiers between Egypt and Israel. And the final outcome of the war, my lords, was a decisive one.

A ring bearing the image of King Ptolemy VI, (181–145 BC), who wanted to wrestle Israel and the surrounding region back from the king of the north, the Louvre Museum, Paris (image source: author).

The young Egyptian king, H.M. King Ptolemy VI Philometor, who was egged along by his own guardians and advisors to take Israel, was in no way a match to his uncle, H.M. King Antiochus IV Epiphanes, the brother of his mother, "the daughter of the women."

The soldiers of H.M. King Antiochus IV Epiphanes not only have soundly defeated the army of Egypt but have also captured young King Ptolemy VI Philometor himself.

Yet, my lords, the victory was a hollow victory. Thanks to the arrogant old man.

## A Shifty Lawyer Destroys by Peace

It was in the fortress town of Pelusium, my lords, that we came to have a good look at the character of H.M. King Antiochus IV Epiphanes, the murderer of his nephew.

---

[207] Diodorus of Sicily, *Library of World History*, 30.2

The man, to say the least, is fascinating, my lords. He is a study of contrast. But yet he is the man who shall soon attempt to turn Israel from being the preacher of the Holy One to the preacher of the Greek gods.

The ancients used to say, my lords, that if you do not have enough of a lion's skin, then you could finish off the job with a fox's skin. And so did his majesty.

My lords, on his way to Egypt, H.M. King Antiochus IV Epiphanes must pass through the strong fortress of Pelusium on the frontier of Egypt. It was very important, my commanders, that he must sack the city before he could move along to Egypt and leave his back vulnerable to enemies.

But there was a problem, my commanders. Pelusium city was a well-fortified city—a fortress. Thus, it was not easy for him, a man who was in a hurry to get to the big prize of Egypt, to take the time to besiege the city. There simply was not enough of a lion skin to sack the city, and sack it quickly.

Luckily enough, a favorable opportunity presented itself to a fox worthy of the name.

It was at that time, my lords, that H.M. King Antiochus IV Epiphanes encountered Egyptians troops and captured many of their soldiers. Those captured soldiers were the means, which his majesty used, my lords, to stitch in the fox's skin and trick the keepers of the walled city of Pelusium.

His Majesty ordered his men to spare the lives of the captured Egyptian soldiers. The word spread to the keepers of Pelusium. This is a clement warrior. This king is a kind and generous king.

The leaders of the fortress, my lords, were convinced of his majesty's generous and good character, and so they agreed to strike a truce with him. And then the fox was inside the coop.

More lines of Daniel's prophecy would become clearer, my lords.

Meanwhile, do not judge the fooled leaders harshly, my lords, because indeed H.M. King Antiochus IV had built a good reputation of himself, as he marched down from Syria through Lebanon, Israel, and Gaza. His majesty peppered the crowds with money everywhere he went.

Hear for yourselves, my lords, what the ancient historian Polybius says. Please go ahead, historian Polybius.

> "After showing kindness to the people there, and making a present of a gold stater [coin money] to each of the Greek residents, he advanced towards Alexandria."[208]

---

[208] Polybius, *The Histories*, Fragments of Book XXVIII, 20

And so, my lords, in addition to the trail of coins he left behind him, now came the clemency towards the captured Egyptian soldiers, which historian Diodorus of Sicily had recorded.

Go ahead, sir.

> "Though Antiochus was in a position to slaughter the defeated Egyptians, he rode about calling to his men not to kill them, but to take them alive. Before long he reaped the fruits of his shrewdness, since this act of generosity contributed very greatly to his seizure of Pelusium, and later to the acquisition of all Egypt."[209]

From ancient times, my lords, even before the days of many of you, your majesties, there were war traditions, which could not under any circumstances be broken.

There were those hallowed traditions regarding the safety of war messengers and the recovering of dead soldiers on the battlefields. These honored war traditions, my lords, helped facilitating negotiations, ending wars, and establishing peace agreements between warring nations, as you all know, my sovereigns.

But look here, my commanders, what his majesty has done at the fortress of Pelusium.

Shame! Shame! Shame!

At the fortified fortress of Pelusium, my lords, his majesty tore up all these old and hallowed war traditions, which were obeyed by all nations.

> "Antiochus showed himself a true statesman, and a man worthy of the royal dignity, except in the stratagem [the ploy] that he employed at Pelusium."[210]

His behavior, my lords, was that of an adult who managed to befriend an innocent trusting child, a lad, and then proceeded to murder him. Shame!

> "Antiochus got possession of Pelusium by means of a questionable bit of strategy.
> 
> For though all warfare is an exception to humane standards of law and justice, even so it has certain quasi-laws of its own: a truce, for example, may not be broken; heralds [the messengers] must not be put to death; a man who has placed himself under the protection of a superior opponent may not be visited with punishment or vengeance.

---

[209] Diodorus of Sicily, *Library of World History*, 30.14
[210] Diodorus of Sicily, Library of World History, 30.18

These and similar matters... ... one might fairly say that Antiochus, in making the seizure after the truce, rather like a pettifogging [unethical, shifty] lawyer held fast to the letter of the law but not to justice and honour, which are bonds of social life. For on the grounds of kinship he should, as he said himself, have spared the lad, but on the contrary after winning his confidence he deceived him and sought to bring him to utter ruin."[211]

Prophet Daniel, my lords, 370 years in advance [540 BC–170 BC], described his majesty in similar terms.

Go ahead, please, prophet Daniel.

DAN 8:25 And through his policy also he [King Antiochus IV Epiphanes] shall cause craft to prosper in his hand; and he shall magnify himself in his heart, and by peace shall destroy many: he shall also stand up against the Prince of princes; but he shall be broken without hand.

And more than being shifty, my lords, H.M. King Antiochus IV Epiphanes, the mad one, was considered also to be too base to be called king to begin with. If you wish, my lords, his majesty is a man who walks around with a sorry horse—a horse in bad shape, my lords.

## A Vile Person —Cheap, Flashy and Base

Go ahead, please, historian Diodorus, and describe the man to their majesties.

"Certain of the enterprises and acts of Antiochus were kingly and altogether admirable, while others again were so cheap and so tawdry [gaudy, showy] as to bring upon him the utter scorn of all mankind.

For example, in celebrating his festal games he adopted, in the first place, a policy contrary to that of the other kings.

They, while strengthening their kingdoms both in arms and in wealth, as far as possible tried to conceal their intentions because of the superiority of Rome. He, however, taking the opposite approach, brought together at his festival the most distinguished men from virtually the whole world, adorned all parts of his capital in magnificent fashion, and having assembled in one spot, and, as it were, put upon the stage his entire kingdom, left them [the watchful Romans] ignorant of nothing that concerned him.

---

[211] Diodorus Siculus, *Library of History*, Fragments of Book XXX: 18, 19

# PAST AND PRESENT ABOMINATIONS—477

In putting on these lavish games and this stupendous festival Antiochus outdid all earlier rivals. <u>Yet for him personally to manage the affair was a shabby business, worthy of contempt.</u>

<u>He would, for example, ride at the side of the procession [parade] on a sorry nag [a horse in a bad shape or old], ordering these men to advance, those to halt, and assigning others to their posts, as occasion required; consequently, but for the diadem [crown], no one who did not already know him would have believed that this person was the king, lord of the whole domain, seeing that his appearance was not even that of an average subordinate.</u>

<u>At the drinking parties, stationing himself at the entrance [a door-greeter] he would lead some of the guests in, seat others at their places, and assign to their posts the attendants who were serving food.</u>

<u>Continuing in the same vein he would, on occasion, approach the banqueters, and sometimes sit down, sometimes recline beside them; then, laying aside his cup or tossing away his sop, he would leap to his feet and move on, and making the rounds of the whole party accept toasts even while he stood and jested with the entertainers.</u>

<u>Indeed once, when the merrymaking was well advanced and the greater part of the guests had already departed, he made an entrance, all bundled up and carried in procession by the mimes [actors]. Placed on the ground by his fellow actors, as soon as the symphony sounded his cue he leapt to his feet naked, and jesting with the mimes performed the kind of dances that usually provoke laughter and hoots of derision — to the great embarrassment of the company [basically acting like a bum], who all left the party in haste.</u>

Each and every person, in fact, who attended the festival found that when he regarded the extravagance of the outlay and the general management and administration of the games and processions, he was astounded, and that he admired both the king and the kingdom; when, however, he focused his attention on the king himself and his unacceptable behaviour, he could not believe that <u>it was possible for such excellence and such baseness to exist in one and the same character.</u>

After the games had ended, the embassy of Gracchus [a Roman envoy] arrived to investigate the kingdom. The king held friendly conversations with them, with the result that they caught no hint of intrigue on his part, nor anything to indicate such enmity as might be expected to exist covertly after the rebuff that he had received in Egypt [an incident, which will be mentioned soon]. His true policy was not, however, what it appeared to be; on the contrary he was deeply disaffected toward the Romans."[212]

King Antiochus IV intended to exterminate Israel, Altes Museum, Berlin, Germany (image source: author).

And again, my lords, prophet Daniel, a long time in advance, 370 years, had similar words to describe his majesty. Go ahead, please, sir.

DAN 11:18 *After this shall he [King Antiochus III the Great] turn his face unto the isles, and shall take many: but a prince for his own behalf [the Roman Flamininus] shall cause the reproach offered by him to cease; without his own reproach he shall cause it to turn upon him [the allied Greek cities abandon him].*
DAN 11:19 *Then he shall turn his face toward the fort of his own land: but he shall stumble and fall, and not be found.*
DAN 11:20 *Then shall stand up in his estate a raiser of taxes in the glory of the kingdom [the assassinated King Seleucus IV Philopator, son of King Antiochus III the Great]: but within few days he shall be destroyed, neither in anger, nor in battle.*
DAN 11:21 *And in his estate shall stand up a vile person [King Antiochus IV Epiphanes, the younger brother of the assassinated King Seleucus IV Philopator], to whom they shall not give the honour of the kingdom: but he shall come in peaceably, and obtain the kingdom by flatteries [he cheated his nephew, the legitimate crown prince, being the son of his older brother, the assassinated King Seleucus IV Philopator].*

Indeed, as we have already mentioned, my lords, certain people had made a turn on his name "Epiphanes" to mean *the mad one*. We understand

---

[212] Diodorus of Sicily, *Library of World History* 31:16-18

too, my lords, that while he was the king, he nonetheless and senselessly ran in the elections for small municipal offices—this is quite true, my lords.

At any rate, please, go ahead, historian Diodorus, and finish off your report.

King Antiochus IV Epiphanes a bum? Altes Museum, Berlin, Germany (image source: author).

> "Antiochus [IV Epiphanes] on first succeeding to the throne, embarked upon a quixotic mode of life foreign to other monarchs.
>
> To begin with, he would often slip out of the palace without informing his courtiers, and wander at random about the city with one or two companions.
>
> Next, he took pride in stooping to the company of common people, no matter where, and in drinking with visiting foreigners of the meanest stamp.
>
> In general, if he learned that any young men were forgathering at an early hour, he would suddenly appear at the party with a fife and other music; so that in their astonishment some of the commoners who were guests would take to their heels and others be struck dumb with fear.
>
> Finally, he would at times put off his royal garb, and wrapping himself in a toga, as he had seen candidates [running in election] for office do at Rome [when he was held hostage there], would accost the citizens, saluting and embracing them one by one, and ask them to give him their vote, now for the office of aedile, and again for that of tribune.
>
> Upon being elected, he would sit on an ivory chair, and in the Roman fashion listen to the opposing arguments in ordinary cases of contract. He did this with such close attention and zeal that all men of refinement were perplexed about him, some ascribing his behaviour to artless simplicity, others to folly, and some to madness."[213]

---

[213] Diodorus of Sicily, *Library of World History*, 29:32

# 170 BC
# Incomplete Victory

As we have already mentioned, your majesties, the victory of H.M. King Antiochus IV Epiphanes of the north over his nephew, King Ptolemy VI Philometor of Egypt, was not a complete one.

Indeed, H.M. King Antiochus IV Epiphanes succeeded to sack the important city of Cairo, but unfortunately he could not do the same to Alexandria, the capital city of Egypt, and the seat of its Greek royal family.

And yet this royal family of Egypt, my lords, was in the middle of a heated sibling rivalry.

At the time, my lords, there were three royal siblings vying for the Greek Ptolemaic throne of Egypt.

First, there was H.M. King Ptolemy VI Philometor.

But against him was his sister, Princess Cleopatra II, paired with their younger brother, Prince Ptolemy VIII Euergetes II Physcon.

These last two siblings, my lords, were firmly entrenched behind the walls of Alexandria city, which H.M. King Antiochus IV Epiphanes, king of the north, could not penetrate. The two royals were safe inside its walls.

LEFT: Queen Cleopatra II, Numismatic Museum of Athens (image source: author). RIGHT: Older King Ptolemy VIII Euergetes II, Numismatic Museum of Athens, Greece (image source: author).

You asked your majesties: why the sister and the younger brother did not come out and bring the rest of the Egyptian army with them in order to join their older brother against H.M. King Antiochus IV Epiphanes? And the answer now is clear to you your majesties. The two of them wanted their brother dead so that they could share the throne of Egypt all alone. Those who ate at the same table, my lords, were plotting madly against each other. A throne thins the blood, my lords.

# PAST AND PRESENT ABOMINATIONS—481

Prophet Daniel, go ahead, please, sir.

> DAN 11:21 *And in his estate [in place of King Seleucus IV Philopator] shall stand up a vile person [King Antiochus IV Epiphanes], to whom they shall not give the honour of the kingdom: but he shall come in peaceably, and obtain the kingdom by flatteries.*
> ...
> DAN 11:25 *And he [King Antiochus IV Epiphanes] shall stir up his power and his courage against the king of the south [King Ptolemy VI Philometor of Egypt] with a great army; and the king of the south shall be stirred up to battle with a very great and mighty army; but he [King Ptolemy VI Philometor of Egypt] shall not stand: for they shall forecast devices [plot] against him.*
> DAN 11:26 <u>*Yea, they that feed of the portion of his meat shall destroy him*</u>, *and his army shall overflow [scatter]: and many shall fall down slain.*

And so now H.M. King Antiochus IV, my lords, is wondering what to do with his high value hostage, the captured King Ptolemy VI Philopator of Egypt.

And the answer to his reflections became quite clear, my lords.

In his pondering, my lords, his majesty had to consider an important factor.

Mad or not, his majesty was not inclined to repeat his father's mistake and antagonize the mighty Romans, the allies of Egypt—the country, the farm, that supplies them with corn and food among other needed goods.

So what did his majesty do, my lords, with his high value hostage?

His majesty reinstalled King Ptolemy IV Philometor as the king of Egypt. And in order to encourage his protégée, the young Egyptian monarch, to fight for his throne, his majesty promised to back him up with his army against his rivals, Princess Cleopatra II and Prince Ptolemy VIII Physcon.

You most certainly can see what he is doing at this time, my lords.

However, H.M. King Ptolemy VI is no one's fool either. Indeed, my lords, he became suspicious of his uncle's motives. The reason for the suspicion, my lords, is that his uncle King Antiochus IV has indeed removed his army from every city he occupied in Egypt, yet made sure to occupy the fortress at the border with a garrison of his soldiers. He is gone, but not too far.

Deceptions and treachery on all sides, my lords! Treaties and alliances mean nothing your majesties. Nothing but duplicity, my lords! For, in reality, all what H.M. King Antiochus IV wanted was to have the Egyptian royals deplete and finish one another off so that he could go after the last depleted one standing. Alexandria, and with it all of Egypt, would at last fall into his hands.

And so, my lords, on his part, young King Ptolemy VI Philometor tried to convince his sister and younger brother that it would be to their advantage to shelter him inside Alexandria city. And that without him and without his remaining troops, King Antiochus IV would, sooner or later, be able to besiege the city and breach it.

Greek King Ptolemy VI Philometor of Egypt (181-145 BC). During his contested rule, King Antiochus IV Epiphanes invaded Egypt; the Louvre Museum, Paris (images source: author).

May we now bring the ancient historian Livy into our conversation your majesties?

Go ahead, please, historian Livy.

> "Antiochus was now master of the rest of Egypt, but after his check before Alexandria he retired from its walls.
>
> The elder Ptolemy [VI Philometor], whose restoration to his throne Antiochus pretended was his sole object in invading Egypt was left at Memphis [Cairo city], and Antiochus withdrew his army into Syria, prepared to attack whichever brother should prove victorious.

Ptolemy was quite aware of his intention, and hoped that by playing upon his brother's fears [Ptolemy VIII Euergetes II Physcon] and holding out the prospect of a siege [of Alexandria city] he might possibly, with the active assistance of his sister [Cleopatra II] and the acquiescence of his brother's friends, be admitted into Alexandria.

He began a correspondence with his sister and his brother's friends, and continued to write to them until he had come to terms with them.

What made him suspicious of Antiochus was that after handing over the rest of Egypt he had left a strong garrison in Pelusium [the fortress city at the entrance of Egypt as you come south from Syria]. It was obvious that Antiochus was holding the key of Egypt in order to make a fresh invasion whenever he chose, and for Ptolemy to engage in intestine strife with his brother would prove to be his ruin, since, even if victorious, he would be no match for Antiochus after an exhausting war.

The above image belongs either to Cleopatra II, or Cleopatra I (daughter of the women), Louvre Museum, Paris (image source: author)

These wise reflections met with the approval of his brother and his friends, and his sister helped him very largely by her advice and her appeals to the brother. So peace was made, and he was admitted into Alexandria with everybody's consent; even the populace manifested no opposition, though they had suffered severely both during the investment and after the retirement of the enemy, as no supplies were being brought in from the rest of Egypt.

This [peace between the Egyptian fighting royals] ought to have given the liveliest satisfaction to Antiochus [should have pleased Antiochus IV Epiphanes], had his motive for bringing his army into Egypt really been the restoration of Ptolemy [VI Philometor]. For this was the pretext he alleged in all his communications to the cities of Greece and Asia, and in his replies to their deputations.

But he was so intensely annoyed at what had happened that he began to make preparations for war in a much more aggressive and ruthless temper against the two brothers than he had previously shown against the one.[214]

---

[214] Livy, *The History of Rome*, 45 [XLV]: 11&12. http://mcadams.posc.mu.edu/txt/ah/livy/Livy45.html

Prophet Daniel, please recite your prophecy one more time, sir.

> DAN 11:25 And he [King Antiochus IV Epiphanes] shall stir up his power and his courage against the king of the south [King Ptolemy VI Philometor] with a great army; and the king of the south shall be stirred up to battle with a very great and mighty army; but he [King Ptolemy VI Philometor] shall not stand: for they shall forecast devices against him [plot against him. His siblings left him all alone against Antiochus IV Epiphanes].
> DAN 11:26 Yea, they that feed of the portion of his meat [his guardians and siblings] shall destroy him, and his army shall overflow [scatter]: and many shall fall down slain.
> DAN 11:27 And both these kings' hearts shall be to do mischief, and they shall speak lies at one table; but it shall not prosper: for yet <u>the end shall be at the time appointed</u> [according to the timetable of God].
> DAN 11:28 Then shall he [King Antiochus IV Epiphanes] return into his land with great riches; and his heart shall be against the holy covenant; and he shall do exploits, and return to his own land.

Indeed, my lords, while H.M. King Antiochus IV Epiphanes and his army were in Egypt, several of the Greek cities had consulted together to send him a delegation. The delegation's task, my lords, was to persuade his majesty to return the disputed region of Coele-Syria, which includes Israel, to the Greek Egyptian rulers–the Ptolemies.

Is this correct, historian Polybius?

> "At the time when Antiochus occupied Egypt, those of the envoys from Greece who were sent to make peace joined him.
>
> Giving them a kind reception he entertained them splendidly on the first occasion of his meeting them, and on the second granted them an audience, and bade them tell him what their instructions were.
>
> ...
>
> They all ascribed the fault for what had happened to [they blamed the war on] Eulaeus [a guardian and a royal advisor of the Egyptian young king Ptolemy VI Philometor who stirred him to fight King Antiochus IV Epiphanes, instead of suing for peace], and, pleading Ptolemy's kinship with the king and his youth, attempted to appease the wrath of Antiochus."

May we interrupt for a second, my lords, in order to reflect once more on Daniel's prophecy?

*DAN 11:26* *Yea, they that feed of the portion of his meat [the royal advisors such as Eulaeus mentioned above] shall destroy him [the young king of Egypt], and his army shall overflow [scatter]: and many shall fall down slain.*

Carry on, sir.

"The king [Antiochus IV Epiphanes] accepted all these pleas, even attaching greater weight to them than they did, but began to speak about his original rights, attempting to convince them that the district of Coele-Syria [including Israel] was the property of the kings of Syria ... Further he rested his case on the occupation of the country by his father Antiochus [King Antiochus III the great] after a war [Battle of Panium c.198 BC.]; and finally denied the existence of the agreement stated by those in Alexandria to have been made between his father [King Antiochus III the Great] and the Ptolemy [King Ptolemy V Epiphanes] recently deceased, <u>by which the latter [King Ptolemy V Epiphanes of Egypt] should receive Coele-Syria as a dowry when he married Cleopatra [Cleopatra I Syra, daughter of King Antiochus III the Great], the mother of the present king [King Ptolemy VI Philometor]</u>.

After speaking in this sense, and convincing not only himself but his auditors that he was right, he crossed to Naucratis."[215]

## The Bank

Once again, my lords, we repeat the slogan that wars breathe, inhale, and exhale money, and cannot survive without it. And H.M. King Antiochus IV needs money badly in order to feed the Romans and feed his army. And it is rumored, my lords, that Jerusalem of Israel has a cove of treasure, a bank full of money. How can he not be tempted to find out my lords?

And yet, if it is true, how can he lay his hands on it without enraging the population?

Fortune, my lords, so to speak, came knocking at the door of his majesty, bringing along more than one charm. It came in bringing information that, yes, there was money to be had—lots of money.

But fortune did not stop there: it also brought along a strong man who would help his majesty lay his hand on the gold and silver coins.

And fortune, so to speak, my lords, came to his majesty in the shape of a man, an envoy from the high priest of Israel, the de facto king of Israel.

---

[215] Polybius, *The Histories*, Fragments of Book XXVIII, 20

Silver Staters (coin domination), buried c. 440 BC and found in a black-gaze olpe, The Numismatics Museum of Athens, Greece (image source: author).

And it came to fulfill the prophecy of Daniel.

And the name of the envoy of fortune was "Menelaus." And this Menelaus and his brother are thieves, my lords. But they are his majesty's thieves, and this is all that counts.

> "Three years later, Jason [the high priest who bribed King Antiochus to become the high priest and build a gymnasium in Jerusalem] sent Menelaus ... to take some money to the king and to get his decision on several important matters.
>
> But when he [envoy Menelaus] stood before the king, Menelaus impressed him with his show of authority and offered ... [300 talents, coin domination, of silver] more than Jason had offered for his appointment to the office of High Priest.
>
> As a result Menelaus returned to Jerusalem with papers from the king, confirming him as High Priest. But he possessed no other qualifications; he had the temper of a cruel tyrant and could be as fierce as a wild animal."[216]

---

[216] II *Book of Maccabees*, new English translation, Ch. 4:23-25

## Thieves and Robbers

And when his position was later challenged, this Menelaus, the new high priest of Israel, went right ahead and stole money from the temple of the Lord, the parliament of God, and gave it to the representative of H.M. King Antiochus IV in order to help him keep his position as the ruler of Israel.

Yes, my lords, he did so. He stole. The high priest of Israel, the representative of the kindness of the Holy One, stole treasures from the temple of the Lord. And he did so along with his brother Lysimachus, my lords.

> "Menelaus took advantage of this opportunity and presented Andronicus [the representative of King Antiochus IV] with some of the gold objects he had removed [robbed] from the Temple in Jerusalem. He had already sold some of them to the city of Tyre and to other nearby cities [he has been stealing from the temple for some time already]."[217]

The highest ranks of clergy, my lords, the examples for the flock of God, were nothing more than thieves and robbers. The sheep were better than the shepherds. But his majesty liked the shepherds and befriended them.

> "Meanwhile, with the support of his brother Menelaus [the new high priest and thief], Lysimachus had on numerous occasions robbed the Jerusalem Temple and had taken many of its gold objects.
> 
> When word of this spread around, crowds began to gather in protest against Lysimachus.
> 
> Finally, the crowds were becoming dangerous and were beginning to get out of control, so Lysimachus sent 3,000 armed men to attack them. They were led by Auranus, a man as stupid as he was old.
> 
> When the Jews in the Temple courtyard realized what was happening, they picked up rocks, pieces of wood, or simply handfuls of ashes from the altar and threw them at Lysimachus and his men in the confusion. They killed a few of Lysimachus' men, wounded many of them, and all the rest ran for their lives. Lysimachus himself, that temple robber, was killed near the Temple treasury."[218]

---

[217] II *Book of Maccabees*, new English translation, Ch. 4:32
[218] II *Book of Maccabees*, new English translation, Ch. 4:39-42

## 170 BC A Date to Remember

My lords, his majesty's father had done it before when he needed to. And so why can his majesty not do it as well? His father raided a temple full of gold and silver to pay his soldiers and keep them. He paid for the money with his life and blood.

Be that as it may, his son will try to do the same and remain alive.

> "Now when the kingdom was established before Antiochus [IV Epiphanes], he thought to reign over Egypt that he might have the dominion of two realms [the north and the south – The Ptolemaic and Seleucid dominions].
> 
> Wherefore he entered into Egypt with a great multitude [170 BC.], with chariots, and elephants, and horsemen, and a great navy,
> 
> And made war against Ptolemee [VI Philometor] king of Egypt: but Ptolemee was afraid of him, and fled; and many were wounded to death.
> 
> Thus they got the strong cities in the land of Egypt and he took the spoils thereof.
> 
> And after that Antiochus had smitten Egypt, he returned again in the hundred forty and third year [of the Seleucid dynasty = 170/169 BC.], and went up against Israel and Jerusalem with a great multitude,
> 
> And entered proudly into the sanctuary [into the Temple and into the Holy of Holiness part of it – the Parliament of the Holy One], and took away the golden altar, and the candlestick of light, and all the vessels [all made of gold] thereof,
> 
> And the table of the shewbread, and the pouring vessels, and the vials. and the censers of gold, and the veil, and the crown, and the golden ornaments that were before the temple, all which he pulled off.
> 
> He took also the silver and the gold [coins?], and the precious vessels: also he took the hidden treasures which he found.
> 
> And when he had taken all away, he went into his own land, having made a great massacre, and spoken very proudly.
> 
> Therefore there was a great mourning in Israel, in every place where they were;"[219]

We can tell you, your majesties, that he shall come back in two years. He shall come back humiliated and angry. And he shall unleash his anger on Israel. And against all those who resist his rule and the rule of his appointees.

---

[219] I Macc 1:16-25

He shall bury them all and he shall put his own gods in their most sacred shrine.

Coins minted in Alexandria/Egypt 54 AD –285 AD, British Museum (image source: author).

## 168 BC Round Two— A Line in the Sand

As we have mentioned already, my lords, H.M. King Antiochus IV Epiphanes of Syria, Iraq, and Iran had made it clear to the world leaders ahead of his first campaign that his intention of marching against Egypt was to defend and establish its legitimate young ruler, H.M. King Ptolemy VI Philometor.

In reality, my lords, every world leader, and particularly the Roman senate, suspected that his majesty intended all along to swallow and occupy Egypt with all its wealth and riches.

Possibly Queen Cleopatra II (172–116 BC.), who fought her brother King Ptolemy VI Philometor and thus gave King Antiochus IV Epiphanes a reason to invade Egypt for a second time, and in turn fulfilled Daniel's prophecy; the Louvre Museum, Paris (image source: author).

Egypt, your majesties, is one of the finest farms money can buy, so to speak. And it is the number one, bar none, supplier of corn to the rising power of Rome. Egypt puts bread on Rome's daily table, my lords. Without Egypt, Rome would go to bed hungry. And so, my lords, once you own Egypt, then you are in a position to force Rome to negotiate with you on your own terms. And this is why H.M. King Antiochus IV Epiphanes, my lords, took the islands of the sea, the relay grain shipping stations between Rome and Egypt. Today, my lords, we say that that the fastest and cheapest highways of old were made of water.

## Grain to Rome

Egypt continued to ship grains to Rome for a long time.

Nearly two hundred years after King Antiochus IV, the apostle Paul, taken as a prisoner, was a passenger in one of the ships carrying grain from Alexandria to Rome. The ship was caught in a storm and heavy seas; thus, the passengers had to throw the grain to the sea in order to lighten the load of the ship.

> Acts 27:6 *the centurion [Roman soldier] found a ship of Alexandria sailing into Italy; and he put us therein.*
> ...
> Acts 27:37 *And we were in all in the ship two hundred threescore and sixteen [276] souls.*
> Acts 27:38 *they lightened the ship, and cast out the wheat into the sea.*

Egypt was a major exporter of grain. Above is a gold ring carrying the image of a rat, with ears of corns in its mouth, tied to a column, 300–250 BC, the ring presumed to be found in Alexandria, British Museum (image source: author).

At any rate, my lords, the shifty lawyer who walks around with the sorry horse was disappointed that King Ptolemy VI Philometor of Egypt, his sister Princess Cleopatra II, and younger brother Prince Ptolemy VIII had made peace amongst themselves. Basically, they took away his pretended excuse to invade Egypt. Egypt and its wealth were now slipping away from between his fingers.

And so, my lords, pretext or not, his majesty at this point of time has decided to make his way for the second time to invade Egypt [168 BC.].

We can jump ahead, your majesties, and tell you that on his way back, he will fulfill more lines of Daniel's prophecy.

Please, lead the way, historians Livy and Diodorus.

> "This [peace between the fighting Egyptian royals] ought to have given the liveliest satisfaction to Antiochus[ should have made him happy], had his motive for bringing his army into Egypt really been the restoration of Ptolemy. For this was the pretext he alleged in all his communications to the cities of Greece and Asia, and in his replies to their deputations.
>
> But he was so intensely annoyed at what had happened [the reconciliation of the Egyptian royals] that <u>he began to make preparations for war in a much more aggressive and ruthless temper against the two brothers than he had previously shown against the one</u>."[220]

> "<u>Antiochus at first put up a fine front, asserting that no thought of taking the throne of Egypt lay behind his extensive military preparations, and that his only motive was to assist the elder Ptolemy in securing the position that was his by right of inheritance.</u>
>
> This was by no means true; on the contrary, he conceived that by presiding over a dispute between the youths [King Ptolemy VI Philometor and his younger brother King Ptolemy VIII Euergetes II (Physcon)] and so making an investment in goodwill <u>he should conquer Egypt without a blow [the fighting amongst the Egyptian royals would deplete them and reduce the winner to an easy target unable to fight Antiochus].</u>
>
> But when Fortune put his professions [pretence] to the test and deprived him of the pretext he had alleged, he stood revealed as <u>one of the many princes who count no point of honour more important than gain [the shifty lawyer].</u>"[221]

Prophet Daniel, your prophecy please.

---

[220] Livy, *The History of Rome*, 45 [XLV]:12
[221] Diodorus of Sicily, Library of World History, 31.1

> *DAN 11:29* <u>At the time appointed</u> [in accordance with the timetable of God] he [King Antiochus IV Epiphanes] <u>shall return, and come toward the south</u> [Egypt]; <u>but it shall not be as the former</u> [invasion], <u>or as the latter</u> [it is different this time because of an arrogant old man].

First things first, my lords.

His majesty King Antiochus IV Epiphanes had first of all sent his fleet to capture the island of Cyprus in the Mediterranean Sea—a stepping stone in his way to attack Alexandria city, Egypt's main harbor and now home of its three royals.

This is not the first time, my lords, that the Greek kings of Syria, the Seleucids, attack the islands.

King Antiochus III the great had done the same before.

And so once again, my lords, H.M. King Antiochus IV Epiphanes, travelling on land from the eastern borders of Egypt towards its western borders, took villages and towns and then occupied Cairo. This is basically a straight copy of his first invasion.

Now, from Memphis Cairo, my lords, he then marched his armies in a northwesterly direction, heading for Alexandria, home of the greatest library in the world and its lighthouse, the Pharos, the tallest skyscraper of the time, my lords. And it was there, as we have already mentioned, my lords, that the Greek translation of the Book of Daniel of the Old Testament of the Bible was kept secure in the royal library.

Yes, you may go ahead, historian Livy.

> "He [King Antiochus IV Epiphanes] marched through the desert of Arabia [Sinai, the entrance of Egypt coming from the north], while his fleet was sailing up the mouth of the Nile to Pelusium [the fortress city by the border of Israel and Egypt]. After receiving the submission of the inhabitants of Memphis [Cairo city] and of the rest of the Egyptian people, some submitting voluntarily, others under threats, he marched by easy stages towards Alexandria. After crossing the river at Eleusis, about four miles from Alexandria"[222]

About four miles from Alexandria city, yes, my lords, about four short miles from the top prize, trouble showed up in order to fulfill Daniel's prophecy.

---

[222] Livy, History of Rome, XLV: 12

The Lighthouse of Alexandria, Numismatic Museum of Athens, Greece (image source: author).

Prophet Daniel, your 372-year-old prophecy, please.

DAN 11:29 *At the time appointed he shall return, and come toward the south; but it shall not be as the former, or as the latter.*

And why not sir?

## 168 BC
## No Handshakes

A snag! A spoiler, your majesties!

An arrogant old man stood in the way and made the outcome of attacking Egypt a different outcome from the previous successful invasion. And we may as well say, my lords, that it will never be the same again for the Greeks.

The old man was carrying a message.

And the name of the old man, my lords, is Gaius Popillius Laenas.

Perhaps his name does not mean much to any of you, my lords. His name certainly does not mean anything to our modern population. Nonetheless, Gaius Popillius Laenas is a Roman senator and he had a simple message for H.M. Majesty King Antiochus IV Epiphanes of the north.

The Roman senator had sailed from Rome and was in Alexandria, awaiting the arrival of his majesty in order to deliver his message from the Roman senate.

Indeed, your majesties, Senator Gaius Popillius Laenas was not a stranger to H.M. King Antiochus IV Epiphanes, for the two men had met previously in Rome when his majesty, a youngster at the time, was kept there as a hostage while his defeated father, King Antiochus III the great, ruled over Syria, Iraq, and Iran.

At any rate, my lords, the clear and simple message from the Roman Senate to his majesty was: leave Alexandria and Egypt, as well as the island of Cyprus, immediately, and go back home.

Pardon me!

Is this how anyone should order a king commanding one of the strongest armies in the world, my lords? Even though he may at occasions walk around with a sorry horse, which may have a reason for his great sorrow!

Fine!

His majesty replied that he shall take up the matter of withdrawing from Egypt with his council before giving an answer to the august Roman Senate.

Not a chance!

Not a chance?

No.

The Roman envoy—take this, my lords—drew a circle in the sand around his majesty, a line in the sand, my lords, and told H.M. King Antiochus IV Epiphanes that he has to give a reply to the Roman Senate before he steps out of the circle—a line is drawn in the sand—the time for a decision is here and now.

Historian Polybius, it is your turn, sir.

> "At the time when Antiochus approached Ptolemy and meant to occupy Pelusium [the frontier fortress at the entrance of Egypt], Caius Popilius Laenas, the Roman commander, on Antiochus greeting him from a distance and then holding out his hand, handed to the king, as he had it by him, <u>the copy of the senatus-consultum</u>, and told him to read it first, not thinking it proper, as it seems to me, to make the conventional sign of friendship [of shaking hands] before he knew if the intentions of him who was greeting him were friendly or hostile.

Shaking hands is an ancient gesture, Berlin Museum (image source: author).

## PAST AND PRESENT ABOMINATIONS—495

But when the king, after reading it, said he would like to communicate with his friends [advisors] about this intelligence [information], Popilius acted in a manner which was thought to be offensive and exceedingly arrogant.

He was carrying a stick cut from a vine, and with this he drew a circle round Antiochus and told him he must remain inside this circle until he gave his decision about the contents of the letter [this incident is the origin of the expression "drawing a line in the sand"].

The king was astonished at this authoritative proceeding, but, after a few moments' hesitation, said he would do all that the Romans demanded.

Upon this Popilius and his suite [delegation] all grasped him by the hand and greeted him warmly.

The letter ordered him to put an end at once to the war with Ptolemy.

So, as a fixed number of days were allowed to him, he led his army back to Syria [crossing Israel on his way home], deeply hurt [note this expression, my lords] and complaining indeed, but yielding to circumstances for the present."[223]

Prophet Daniel, please go ahead!

DAN 11:29 *At the time appointed [168 BC.] he [King Antiochus IV Epiphanes] shall return [once again to attack Egypt], and come toward the south [Egypt]; but it shall not be as the former, or as the latter.*
DAN 11:30 *For the ships of Chittim [the Roman sea-crossing ships] shall come against him: therefore he shall be grieved [deeply hurt, as the ancient historian Polybius puts it], and return.*

Historian Polybius, please carry on, sir.

"[The Roman Senator] Popilius after arranging matters in Alexandria and exhorting the two kings [the two brothers vying for the throne of Egypt: Ptolemy VI Philometor and Ptolemy VIII Euergetes] there to act in common, ordering them also to send Polyaratus to Rome, sailed for Cyprus [the island taken by Antiochus' navy], wishing to lose no time in expelling the Syrian troops [of King Antiochus IV Epiphanes] that were in the island.

When they arrived, finding that Ptolemy's generals [in the island of Cyprus] had been defeated and that the affairs of Cyprus were generally in a topsy-turvy state, they soon made the Syrian army retire from the country, and waited until the troops took ship for Syria.

---

[223] Polybius, *The Histories*, Book 29:27

In this way the Romans saved the kingdom of Ptolemy [Egypt], which had almost been crushed out of existence: Fortune having so directed the matter of Perseus and Macedonia [Perseus is a Greek king who was engaged in war with Rome and who was a potential alley of Antiochus IV] that when the position of Alexandria and the whole of Egypt was almost desperate, all was again set right simply owing to the fact that the fate of Perseus had been decided [he was defeated by the Roman leagues]. For had this not been so, and had not Antiochus been certain of it, <u>he would never, I think, have obeyed the Roman behests</u> [to depart from Egypt and thus the 372-year-old prophecy of Daniel would have failed]."[224]

A Tetradrachm of King Perseus, 179-168 BC, a relative and ally of King Antiochus IV Epiphanes and whose defeat forced Antiochus IV to retreat from Egypt; Altes Museum, Berlin (image source: author).

## 168/167 BC
## He Is Alive

And so, fortune, as the ancient historian put it, had it, my lords, that H.M. King Antiochus IV Epiphanes realized in the right moment that he stood all alone against the rising might of the legions of Rome. And thus, he was left with no choice but to surrender to its orders and retreat his mighty army from Egypt.

The man, my lords, was left hurt, humiliated and grieved.

And his anger and his hurt were still boiling hot as he retraced his steps and reached Israel.

Somewhere on the road, my lords, somewhere, he received news that his appointee, his puppet high priest of Israel has been booted out by an old

---

[224] Polybius, *The Histories*, Book 29:27

rival. This is insulting. This is a challenge to his authority. And if the news is true, then he is bound to lose his financiers, his faithful and loyal thieves.

And then the rumors got even worse, my lords. Now they say that the entire population of Jerusalem is up in arms, rioting against his authority. They do not want him and they do not like him or like his people in their country. The angry population and its new leader, Jason, shall lock up Jerusalem and bar his troops from entering the city.

And the news was true, my lords.

Jason, the high priest who had years ago lost his position by the orders of his majesty, and who subsequently had escaped to Jordan next door, had emerged again. Jason returned with an army and took Jerusalem city.

Apparently, he was encouraged to attack the city, my lords, because he had heard a rumor that his majesty was killed in fighting in Egypt.

But there was another strong reason for his bold move and courage to stand against one of the strongest armies in the world: Jason relied on an old prophecy, my lords.

The prophecy, your majesties, was almost three hundred and fifty-four years old, [522 BC]. And it took place in the days when the leaders of Israel began to build the walls of Jerusalem in the days of his Persian majesty, King Ahasaoirous.

Jason, my lords, believed that his supporters shall be like a strong bow filled with arrows, and like a great sword. He and they, together, can and shall defeat the mighty Greeks.

He "mis-timed" the prophecy, my lords, of the prophet Zechariah of old.

Go ahead, please, prophet Zechariah.

> ZECH 9:13 *When I have bent [like a bow] Judah [the southern half of Israel] for me, filled the bow with Ephraim [the northern half of Israel], and raised up thy sons, O Zion [Jerusalem], <u>against thy sons, O Greece</u>, and made thee as the sword of a mighty man.*
> ZECH 9:14 *And the LORD shall be seen over them, and his arrow shall go forth as the lightning: and the Lord GOD shall blow the trumpet, and shall go with whirlwinds of the south.*
> ZECH 9:15 *The LORD of hosts shall defend them; and they shall devour, and subdue with sling stones; and they shall drink, and make a noise as through wine [rejoicing].*
> ZECH 9:16 *And the LORD their God shall save them in that day as the flock of his people: for they shall be as the stones of a crown, lifted up as an ensign upon his land.*

Jason succeeded, my lords. But it was a brief success. It was not the right time for this prophecy. Its time was yet to come.

Indeed, he, on the head of a thousand soldiers, plus his many supporters in the city, have managed to boot out high priest Menelaus, the appointee of H.M. King Antiochus IV Epiphanes.

The news reached his grieved majesty. He now faces the prospect of not only losing Egypt but also Israel. There flies away a lot of needed income.

No, this will not happen. His majesty shall decimate this insubordinate nation.

> "[Puppet Menelaus and his supporters] … fled to Antiochus, and besought him to make use of them for his leaders, and to make an expedition into Judea [Israel].
>
> The king being thereto disposed beforehand, complied with them, and came upon the Jews with a great army, and took their city [Jerusalem] by force, and slew a great multitude of those that favored Ptolemy [King VI Philometor of Egypt], and sent out his soldiers to plunder them without mercy."[225]

Yes, your majesties, ever since his first invasion of Egypt, H.M. King Antiochus IV had it on his mind to sack Jerusalem and take complete control of it, or as historian Josephus puts it "The king being thereto disposed beforehand."

Sir!

> DAN 11:25 *And he [King Antiochus IV Epiphanes] shall stir up his power and his courage against the king of the south [Egypt] with a great army; and the king of the south [King Ptolemy VI Philometor of Egypt] shall be stirred up to battle with a very great and mighty army; but he [King Ptolemy VI] shall not stand: for they shall forecast devices [plot] against him.*
> DAN 11:26 *Yea, they that feed of the portion of his meat [Ptolemy VIII and Cleopatra II] shall destroy him, and his army shall overflow [scatter and flee]: and many shall fall down slain.*
> DAN 11:28 *Then shall he [King Antiochus IV Epiphanes] return into his land with great riches; and his heart shall be against the holy covenant [against Jerusalem city]; and he shall do exploits, and return to his own land.*

> "But now, 'When a false report began to spread that Antiochus had died, Jason [the high priest exiled to nearby Jordan] took more than a thousand men and suddenly attacked Jerusalem. They drove back those stationed on the city walls and finally captured the city.

---

[225] Josephus, *Wars of the Jews*, Book.1, Chapter.1, 1

Menelaus [Antiochus' appointed high priest] fled for safety to the fort [a Greek fortress and a garrison], near the Temple hill.

...

When the news of what had happened in Jerusalem reached Antiochus, he thought the whole country of Judea [Israel] was in revolt, and he became as furious as a wild animal. <u>So he left Egypt and took Jerusalem by storm</u> giving his men orders to cut down without mercy everyone they met and to slaughter anyone they found hiding in the houses. They murdered everyone—men and women, boys and girls; even babies were butchered. Three days later Jerusalem had lost 80,000 people: 40,000 killed in the attack and at least that many taken away to be sold as slaves.

But Antiochus was still not satisfied. He even dared to enter the holiest Temple in all the world, guided by [High Priest] Menelaus, who had become a traitor both to his religion and to his people. With his filthy and unholy hands, Antiochus swept away the sacred objects of worship and the gifts which other kings had given to increase the glory and honor of the Temple."[226]

## ABOMINATION, TRIBULATION, AND DESOLATION

### 167 BC A Year for the Counting

My lords, his majesty came. And the few Greek soldiers stationed in the castle he had built near the temple opened the gates of the city of Jerusalem for him. And of course the Greek soldiers did so, my lords, with the help of the "hellenized" supporters of the booted-out high priest Menelaus.

Go ahead, please, historian Flavius Josephus, give their majesties the summary of what happened.

"Now Antiochus, upon the agreeable situation of the affairs of his kingdom, resolved to make an expedition against Egypt, both because he had a desire to gain it, and because he contemned [despised] the son of Ptolemy [son of King Ptolemy V, i.e. young King Ptolemy VI Philometor], as now weak, and not yet of abilities to manage affairs of such consequence; so he came with great forces to Pelusium, and circumvented Ptolemy [VI] Philometor by treachery, and seized upon Egypt.

---

[226] II Macc, Chapter 5:5-16

> He then came to the places about Memphis [Cairo]; and when he had taken them, he made haste to Alexandria, in hopes of taking it by siege, and of subduing Ptolemy, who reigned there.
>
> But he was driven not only from Alexandria, but out of all Egypt, by the declaration of the Romans, who charged him to let that country alone; according as I have elsewhere formerly declared.
>
> I will now give a particular account of what concerns this king, how he subdued Judea [Israel] <u>and the temple</u>; for in my former work I mentioned those things very briefly, and have therefore now thought it necessary to go over that history again, and that with great accuracy.
>
> "<u>King Antiochus returning out of Egypt for fear of the Romans, made an expedition against the city Jerusalem; and when he was there, in the hundred and forty-third year of the kingdom of the [Seleucids], he took the city without fighting, those of his own party opening the gates to him.</u> And when he had gotten possession of Jerusalem, <u>he slew many of the opposite party</u>; and when he had plundered it of a great deal of money, he returned to Antioch [his capital city]."[227]

My lords, this was not the first time that H.M. King Antiochus Epiphanes entered temples to rob their riches and wealth in order to pay his army and support his campaigns.

Where is historian Appian? Here you are, sir; please tell, my lords, what you know about his majesty.

> "Antiochus [IV Epiphanes] reigned not quite twelve years, in the course of which he captured Artaxias the Armenia and made an expedition into Egypt against Ptolemy [VI Philometor] … <u>and robbed the temple of Venus Elymais; then died of a wasting disease</u>, leaving a son nine years of age, the Antiochus [V] Eupator.[228]"

## Abomination of Desolation

Now please, carry on, historian Josephus, and tell their majesties what happened two years after his majesty's first invasion of Jerusalem and robbing its temple of everything that is gold and silver.

But do first allow us a minute here, please, historian Josephus.

We do, sir, believe that the books of Maccabees sort out the events more accurately than you do.

---

[227] Flavius Josephus, *Antiquities of the Jews*, Book 12, Chapter 5:2-4
[228] Appian of Alexandria, *Roman History, Syrian Wars*, Parts 10, 66

# PAST AND PRESENT ABOMINATIONS—501

By that, sir, we mean that you bundle together the events of the first invasion with those of the second one. Nonetheless, sir, we shall attempt here to marry your accurate portions with theirs. So now do, please, sir, go ahead with your record.

> "<u>Now it came to pass, after two years</u> [first invasion 170 BC, the second, two years after 168 BC], in the hundred forty and fifth year, on the twenty-fifth day of that month which is by us called Chasleu [Nov/Dec], and by the Macedonians [the Greeks] Apelleus, in the hundred and fifty-third olympiad, that <u>the king came up to Jerusalem, and, pretending peace, he got possession of the city by treachery</u>; at which time he spared not so much as those that admitted him into it, <u>on account of the riches that lay in the temple</u>; but, led by his covetous inclination, <u>(for he saw there was in it a great deal of gold, and many ornaments that had been dedicated to it of very great value,) and in order to plunder its wealth, he ventured to break the league he had made.</u>
>
> So he left the temple bare, and took away the golden candlesticks, and the golden altar [of incense], and table [of show-bread], and the altar [of burnt-offering]; and did not abstain from even the veils, which were made of fine linen and scarlet.
>
> <u>He also emptied it of its secret treasures, and left nothing at all remaining; and by this means cast the Jews into great lamentation, for he forbade them to offer those daily sacrifices which they used to offer to God, according to the law.</u>
>
> And when he had pillaged the whole city, some of the inhabitants he slew, and some he carried captive, together with their wives and children, so that the multitude of those captives that were taken alive amounted to about ten thousand.
>
> <u>He also burnt down the finest buildings; and when he had overthrown the city walls</u> [broke down the walls], he built a citadel in the lower part of the city, for the place was high, and overlooked the temple; on which account he fortified it with high walls and towers, and put into it a garrison of Macedonians.
>
> However, in that citadel dwelt the impious and wicked part of the [Jewish] multitude, from whom it proved that the citizens suffered many and sore calamities.
>
> <u>And when the king had built an idol altar upon God's altar, he slew swine upon it</u>, and so offered a sacrifice neither according to the law, nor the Jewish religious worship in that country."[229]

"<u>And after two years fully expired</u> the king sent his chief collector of tribute unto the cities of Judah [Israel], who came unto Jerusalem with a great multitude,

---

[229] Flavius Josephus, *Antiquities of the Jews*, Book 12, Chapter 5:2-4

And spake peaceable words unto them, but all was deceit: for when they had given him credence, he fell suddenly upon the city, and smote it very sore, and <u>destroyed much people of Israel</u>.

And when he had taken the spoils of the city, <u>he set it on fire</u>, and pulled down the houses and walls thereof on every side.

But <u>the women and children took they captive</u>, and possessed the cattle.

Then built they the city of David [the castle] with a great and strong wall, and with mighty towers, and made it a strong hold for them [a military garrison full of Greek soldiers and other nationals].

And they put therein a sinful nation, wicked men, and fortified themselves therein.

They stored it also with armour and victuals, and when they had gathered together the spoils of Jerusalem, they laid them up there, and so they became a sore snare [a base for raids and ambushing]:

For it was a place to lie in wait against the sanctuary [temple], and an evil adversary to Israel.

Thus they shed innocent blood on every side of the sanctuary, and defiled it:

Insomuch that the inhabitants of Jerusalem fled because of them [Jerusalem desolated – it shall happen in our time]: whereupon the city was made an habitation of strangers, and became strange to those that were born in her; and her own children left her. "[230]

Historian Josephus, my apology, sir, for the interruption, but we wish also at this point to allow the prophet Daniel to repeat the words of his 370-year-old prophecy.

Go ahead, please, prophet Daniel, and begin from a place where their majesties can now relate to, sir.

> DAN 8:8 *Therefore the he goat waxed very great [King Alexander the Great]: and when he was strong, the great horn was broken; and for it came up four notable ones toward the four winds of heaven.*
> DAN 8:9 *And out of one of them [the Seleucids kings of the north, Iran, Iraq, and Syria] came forth a little horn, which waxed exceeding great, toward the south, and toward the east, and toward the pleasant land.*
> DAN 8:10 *And it waxed great, even to the host of heaven; and it cast down some of the host and of the stars to the ground, and stamped upon them.*

---

[230] I Macc 1:29-38

## PAST AND PRESENT ABOMINATIONS—503

> DAN 8:11 Yea, he magnified himself even to the prince of the host [high priest], <u>and by him the daily sacrifice was taken away, and the place of his sanctuary [the temple, the house of communion with the Holy One] was cast down</u>.
> DAN 8:12 <u>And an host was given him against the daily sacrifice</u> by reason of transgression [the Hellenization of the population], and it cast down the truth to the ground; and it practised, and prospered.

All right, prophet Daniel, you may now, sir, recite your other prophecy, which you wrote in chapter eleven of your book of the prophecies of the Lord.

> DAN 11:20 Then shall stand up in his estate [King Antiochus III the Great] a raiser of taxes in the glory of the kingdom [King Seleucus IV Philopator, son of King Antiochus III the Great]: but within few days he shall be destroyed, neither in anger, nor in battle.
> DAN 11:21 And in his estate shall stand up a vile person [King Antiochus IV Epiphanes], to whom they shall not give the honour of the kingdom: but he shall come in peaceably, and obtain the kingdom by flatteries.
> DAN 11:22 And with the arms of a flood shall they be overflown [take flight] from before him, and shall be broken [defeated]; yea, also the prince of the covenant [the high priest].
> DAN 11:23 And after the league made with him he shall work deceitfully: for he shall come up, and shall become strong with a small people.
> DAN 11:24 He shall enter peaceably even upon the fattest places of the province; and he shall do that which his fathers have not done, nor his fathers' fathers [he occupied Egypt]; he shall scatter among them the prey, and spoil, and riches [peppered the conquered population with gold and silver coins]: yea, and he shall forecast his devices against the strong holds, even for a time.

Thank you, sir, but we are also interested to hear you repeat the rest of the details you saw.

> DAN 11:29 At the time appointed he [King Antiochus IV Epiphanes] shall return, and come toward the south [attack Egypt for the second time]; but it shall not be as the former, or as the latter.

DAN 11:30 *For the ships of Chittim [the Romans] shall come against him: therefore he shall be grieved, and return, and have indignation against the holy covenant [Jerusalem]: so shall he do; he shall even return, and have intelligence with them that forsake the holy covenant [strike an alliance with the westernized, or hellenized, high priest and his hellenized segment of the population of Israel].*

DAN 11:31 *And arms shall stand on his part [he sent a general of his who sacked and burned Jerusalem], and <u>they shall pollute the sanctuary of strength [the temple], and shall take away the daily sacrifice, and they shall place the abomination that maketh desolate [an idol on the altar, which shall be worshipped by many willing Israelites, but the majority of the population would abandon the city out of fear of the Greek occupation. "He plundered the city and put it to the torch. He tore down houses and leveled the walls. He took women and children captives…the inhabitants of Jerusalem fled away and the city became the dwelling place of strangers,"</u> 1 Maccabees 1:32, 39]*

DAN 11:32 *And such as do wickedly against the covenant shall he corrupt by flatteries: but the people that do know their God shall be strong, and do exploits [the Maccabees, as shall yet be seen, won their battles against the Greeks].*

DAN 11:33 *And they that understand among the people shall instruct many [the prophecies of Daniel were the source of encouragement during this great tribulation time]: yet they shall fall by the sword, and by flame, by captivity, and by spoil, many days [this shall be repeated in our modern day].*

DAN 11:34 *Now when they shall fall, they shall be holpen [sustained] with a little help: but many shall cleave to them with flatteries.*

DAN 11:35 *And some of them of understanding shall fall, to try them, and to purge, and to make them white, even to the time of the end: <u>because it is yet for a time appointed</u>.*

My lords, the cup before his majesty is half full, and half empty.

For simplicity's sake, my lords, let us say that half of the population of Israel is westernized, modern, and wants to live the modern Greek way of life and worship the Greek gods—they want to become Greek and not Jews. These citizens, my lords, are his majesty's friends. They are more than willing to have him as the king of Israel.

The other half of the population, my lords, does not like the changes they see. They consider the Greek ideas and way of life to be immoral, improper, and unsuitable for their children and families. This part of the population, my lords, wants his majesty and his Greek soldiers out of the country, and as far away as possible—they do not want the Greek ideas anywhere near their families and children.

And so, my lords, the solution for Israel, as far as his majesty is concerned, is to convert the "faithful ones" by force, by the edge of the sword. Hear what he said, my lords.

"When I get to Jerusalem, I will make it a cemetery for the Jews," said H.M. King Antiochus Epiphanes.[231]

Historian Josephus, you may now finish off your account, sir.

<u>"He also compelled them to forsake the worship which they paid their own God, and to adore those whom he took to be gods; and made them build temples, and raise idol altars in every city and village, and offer swine upon them every day</u>.

He also commanded them not to circumcise their sons, and threatened to punish any that should be found to have transgressed his injunction. He also appointed overseers, who should compel them to do what he commanded.

And indeed <u>many Jews there were who complied with the king's commands, either voluntarily, or out of fear of the penalty that was denounced</u>. But the best men, and those of the noblest souls, did not regard him, but did pay a greater respect to the customs of their country than concern as to the punishment which he threatened to the disobedient; on which account they every day underwent great miseries and bitter torments; for <u>they were whipped with rods, and their bodies were torn to pieces, and were crucified, while they were still alive, and breathed</u>. They also strangled those women and their sons whom they had circumcised, as the king had appointed, hanging their sons about their necks as they were upon the crosses.

And if there were any sacred book of the law found, it was destroyed, and those with whom they were found miserably perished also. [232]

<u>"Antiochus Epiphanes, who, when he had taken the city, offered swine upon the altar, and sprinkled the temple with the broth of their flesh.</u>"[233]

But let us go back, my lords, to the placing of an abomination, the statue of the often-depicted naked Greek god Zeus on the altar of the temple of the Holy One.

---

[231] 2 Macc 9:4

[232] Flavius Josephus, *Antiquities of the Jews*, Book 12, Chapter 5:2-4

[233] Josephus, *Antiquities of the Jews*, Book 13, Chap. 8:2

May we then, my lords, enlist historian Agapius to tell us something about these sacred statues!

Go ahead please, sir.

> "In the year 14 of the reign of Ptolemy and 145 of the Greeks, in the second indiction, Antiochus Epiphanes ascended the throne and reigned for eight years.
>
> <u>He sent a general from his companions with a strong army against Jerusalem. Capturing it by trickery</u>, on the 25 of the month of Kanoun I (Dec.), <u>he entered the Temple and defiled it; he set up on the altar of the Temple the desolation and ruin about which the prophet Daniel speaks. It was a statue of Olympian Zeus</u>. He also placed an(other) statue of Zeus Xenios, on Mt. Garizim. He had the Books of the Law burned. He oppressed all the Israelites until they followed the path [of the gentiles] and adhered to their errors."[234]

The god Zeus, 2nd half of 2nd century BC, the National Archaeological Museum of Greece, Athens (image source: author).

Both these two historians, my lords, Flavius Josephus and Agapius, are religious men. And although what they say of H.M. King Antiochus IV Epiphanes matches the ancient secular historians, we suspect, my lords, that some of you may not be inclined to accept their records. For this reason, my lords, we would like you to hear from two gentlemen who decidedly hate the nation of Israel and the laws of Israel. They will tell you, my lords, of his majesty's drive to exterminate the noncomplying segment of Israel.

> "A great part of <u>Judœa</u> [Israel] consists of scattered villages. They have also towns. <u>Jerusalem</u> is the capital. <u>There stood a temple of immense wealth</u>. First came the city with its fortifications, then the royal palace, then, within the innermost defences, the temple itself.
>
> Only the Jew might approach the gates; all but priests were forbidden to pass the threshold.
>
> While the East was under the sway of the Assyrians, the Medes, and the Persians, Jews were the most contemptible of the subject tribes.

---

[234] *Universal History*, Agapius, 239, 240.

# PAST AND PRESENT ABOMINATIONS—507

When the Macedonians [Greeks] became supreme, <u>King Antiochus strove to destroy the national superstition</u> [the preaching of the plan of the Holy One]<u>, and to introduce Greek civilization</u>, but was prevented by his war with the Parthians from at all improving this vilest of nations; for at this time the revolt of Arsaces had taken place [this revolt would prevent King Antiochus from taking complete control of Israel and destroying it]."[235]

## *National Superstition*

It works both ways.

The Greek philosophers, unaware of the plan of God and His verifiable timetable, considered the message of Israel to be a national superstition.

On the other hand, the children of God consider the teachings of the Greek gods to be no more than good philosophical arguments. After all, these gods have no plan, nor timetable.

> Rom 16:18 *they ... by <u>good words and fair speeches</u> deceive the hearts of the simple.*
> 1 Tim 6:19 *lay hold on eternal life.*
> 2 Tim 2:10 *eternal glory.*
> Rev 3:20 *Behold, I stand at the door, and knock: if any man hear my voice, and open the door, I will come in to him*

Apostle Paul had an encounter with Greek philosophers while he was in Athens.

> Acts 17:16 *Now while Paul waited for them at Athens*
> ...
> Acts 17:18 *certain philosophers of the Epicureans, and of the Stoicks, encountered him. And some said, What will this babbler say? other some, He seemeth to be a setter forth of strange gods: because he preached unto them Jesus, and <u>the resurrection</u>.*
> ...
> Acts 17:32 *And when they heard of <u>the resurrection of the dead</u>, some mocked: and others said, We will hear thee again of this matter.*

The great Greek philosophers, whose philosophical schools survive to our own modern day, mocked the apostle Paul when he spoke of resurrection.

---

[235] Tacitus Cornelius, Book 5, Chap. 8, *Complete Works of Tacitus*. Tacitus. Alfred John Church. William Jackson Brodribb. Sara Bryant. edited for Perseus. New York: Random House, 1873, reprinted 1942.

> Yet, resurrection was taking place all day around them and by the millions.
>
> And it is taking place around us, and by the millions, yet it happens unnoticed.

The second secular historian, your majesties, is the ancient historian Diodorus Siculus.

Please go ahead with your report, sir.

"King Antiochus [Antiochus VII Sidetes, 138-129 BC, a successor of King Antiochus IV Epiphanes] besieged Jerusalem. The Jews withstood the siege for some time; but when all their provisions were used up, they were forced to send ambassadors to him, to seek terms for a truce.

Many of his friends urged him to storm the city, and to root out the whole nation of the Jews; for they only of all people hated to mix with any other nations, and treated them all as enemies.

They suggested to him that the ancestors of the Jews were driven out of Egypt, as impious and hateful to the gods: for seeing that their bodies were infected with white marks and leprosy, by way of expiation the Egyptians gathered them all together, and expelled them out of their county, as profane and wicked wretches.

After they were thus expelled, they settled around Jerusalem, and were afterwards united into one nation, called the nation of the Jews; but their hatred of all other men descended with their blood to their posterity. And therefore they made strange laws, and quite different from other people; they never will eat nor drink with any of other nations, or wish them any prosperity.

His friends reminded him that Antiochus surnamed Epiphanes, after subduing the Jews, entered into the temple of God, into which none was allowed to enter by their law except the priest. When he found in there the image of a man with a long beard, carved in stone sitting upon an ass, he took it to be Moses, who built Jerusalem and brought the nation together, and who established by law all their wicked customs and practices, abounding in hatred and enmity to all other men.

Antiochus therefore, abhorring their antagonism to all other people, tried his utmost to abolish their laws.

To that end he sacrificed a great swine at the image of Moses, and at the altar of God that stood in the outward court, and sprinkled them with the blood of the sacrifice.

He commanded likewise that the books, by which they were taught to hate all other nations, should be sprinkled with the broth made of the swine's flesh. And he put out the lamp (called by them immortal) which burns continually in the temple. Lastly he forced the high priest and the other Jews to eat swine's flesh.

When Antiochus' friends [Antiochus VII Sidetes'] had spoken about all these things, they earnestly advised him to root out the whole nation, or at least to abolish their laws, and compel them to change their former manner of living.

But the king, being of a generous spirit and mild disposition, received hostages and pardoned the Jews: but he demolished the walls of Jerusalem, and took the tribute that was due."[236]

## The Maccabees—Pushing Back

It was a tribulation time for Israel, my lords.

But a resistance to the Greek persecution was also bound to happen.

King Antiochus IV Epiphanes' madness of torturing and killing thousands of innocent citizens, mothers and their babies, and splitting Israeli families and hauling them away, could not go on unchallenged forever, my lords. His daily sacrifices of swine on the altar of the Holy One in the parliament of God had to stop. Someone had to have the courage to rally a resistance.

Terracotta pig dedication, c. 300 BC; "Pigs were often sacrificed to Demeter," British Museum (image source: author).

---

[236] Diodorus Siculus, *The Library of History*, Books 34:1-5

And then there was also the old prophecy, my lords, which not only foretold of this hard time of tribulation, but that someone would indeed raise a challenge to the unstoppable Greek king and his thugs.

The prophet who made this prophecy nearly 355 years before [c. 522 BC–167 BC] is the man by the name of Zechariah, my lords, whom we had already introduced to you.

Yet what man can dare challenge the Greeks? Where would this leader come from? And how can he free the occupied temple and Jerusalem from an outraged and mighty king who was able to beat Egypt and its army?

An old man and his sons can.

Please go ahead with your prophecy, prophet Zechariah.

> ZECH 9:12 *Turn you to the strong hold, ye prisoners of hope: even to day do I declare that I will render double unto thee [I give you twice as much hope].*
>
> ZECH 9:13 *When I have bent Judah for me [like a bow], filled the bow with Ephraim [with the children of Israel North], and raised up thy sons, O Zion [Jerusalem. That is, when I have filled my bow with the children of Israel as darts from north to south and from Jerusalem city], against thy sons, O Greece, and made thee [Israel] as the sword of a mighty man [made the children of Israel strong enough to challenge the might of Greece].*

And now, my lords, we must stop here and let you know that we have no records from ancient secular historians or any of those who hate Israel to back up the claims of what happened next.

Therefore, my lords, we shall rather offer you a quick brief, which the ancient religious historians have reported.

## 167 BC
## A Guerrilla Warfare

The boiling resentment, my lords, needed a leader. And the leader turned to be an old man who originally lived in Zion, which is Jerusalem. He was, my lords, a priest by the name of Mattathias Asamoneus.

Today, your majesties, in our modern times, the Jewish people around the globe celebrate the courageous acts of this man and his family on an annual basis in a feast called "Hanukkah."

Indeed, my lords, if we can jump ahead of ourselves, we can tell you that the family of the old man Mattathias Asamoneus would become the royal family of Israel. And when its royal days came to an end, it did so on the hands of half an Arab whose name is King Herod—a man known throughout history and up to our modern days, my lords, as the killer of the

# PAST AND PRESENT ABOMINATIONS—511

babies of Bethlehem. An incident, my lords, that took place two years after the Messiah, Christ Jesus, the Babe of Bethlehem, was born into the world that waited for Him and needed Him.

> MAT 2:1 *Now when Jesus was born in Bethlehem of Judaea in the days of Herod the king, behold, there came wise men from the east to Jerusalem,*
> ...
> MAT 2:11 *And when they were come into the house, they saw the young child with Mary his mother, and fell down, and worshipped him: and when they had opened their treasures, they presented unto him gifts; gold, and frankincense, and myrrh.*

Go ahead, historian Josephus, you have in the past, sir, proved yourself to be reasonably comparable in your reports of the events that you shared with the secular historians; so go ahead, sir, and relay your record of the revolt to their majesties.

> "NOW at this time there was one whose name was Mattathias, who dwelt at Modin [by the borders of the northern province Ephraim], the son ... of Asamoneus, a priest ... a citizen of Jerusalem.
> 
> He had five sons; John, who was called Gaddis, and Simon, who was called Matthes, and Judas, who was called <u>Maccabeus</u>
> ...
> Now this Mattathias lamented to his children the sad state of their affairs, and the ravage made in the city, and the plundering of the temple, and the calamities the multitude were under
> ...
> <u>when those that were appointed by the king</u> [a Greek army general accompanied by soldiers] <u>were come to Modin</u>, that they might compel the Jews to do what they were commanded, and to enjoin those that were there to offer sacrifice, as the king had commanded, <u>they desired that Mattathias, a person of the greatest character among them</u>, both on other accounts, and particularly on account of such a numerous and so deserving a family of children, <u>would begin the sacrifice</u> [sacrificing of swine], because his fellow citizens would follow his example, and because such a procedure would make him honored by the king.
> 
> But Mattathias said he would not do it ... his sons, who had swords with them ... slew ... Apelles the king's general, who compelled them to sacrifice, with a few of his soldiers.
> ...
> He [Mattathias] made haste into the desert with his sons, and left all his substance in the village. Many others did the same also,

and fled with their children and wives into the desert, and dwelt in caves.

But when the king's generals heard this, <u>they took all the forces they then had in the citadel at Jerusalem, and pursued the Jews into the desert</u>.

...

They burnt them as they were in the caves.

...

There were about a thousand, with their wives and children, who were smothered and died in these caves; but <u>many of those that escaped joined themselves to Mattathias, and appointed him to be their ruler, who taught them to fight</u>

...

So Mattathias got a great army about him, and overthrew their [Greeks'] idol altars

...

But when he had ruled one year, and was fallen into a distemper [fell ill]."[237]

We understand, historian Josephus, that you added further details in another account of yours. Please, sir, relate those details as well to their majesties.

"Matthias, the son of Asamoneus, one of the priests who lived in a village called Modin, armed himself, together with his own family, which had five sons of his in it, and slew Bacchides with daggers; and thereupon, out of the fear of the many garrisons [Greek garrisons scattered throughout Israel], he fled to the mountains; and so many of the people followed him, that he was <u>encouraged to come down from the mountains, and to give battle to Antiochus's generals, when he beat them, and drove them out of Judea</u>. So he came to the government by this his success, and became the prince of his own people by their own free consent, and then died, leaving the government to Judas, his eldest son."[238]

# 164 BC
# Short Calculation
# Hanukkah

The old priest Matthias died, my lords. But the uprising he began went on unabated. Indeed, his grown sons and their fellow fighters have on account of many fights become an accomplished army that managed to

---

[237] Josephus, *Antiquities of the Jews*, Book 12, Ch. 6:1-3
[238] Josephus, *Wars of the Jews*, Book 1, Ch. 1:3

beat the Greeks once and again. The old prophecy of Zechariah was becoming true, my lords.

> ZEC 9:13 When I have bent [like a bow] Judah [the southern half of Israel] for me, filled the bow with Ephraim [the northern half of Israel], and raised up thy sons, O Zion [Jerusalem], <u>against thy sons, O Greece</u>, and made thee as the sword of a mighty man.

And so, at long last, my lords, it was time for the Maccabees fighters to retake Jerusalem city and cleanse the temple.

As you may recall, my lords, the temple was sacked in 170 BC, at the time of his majesty's first invasion of Egypt. And then two years after, at the time of the second invasion of Egypt, the statue of the Greek god Zeus, the abomination, was erected, and swine were sacrificed on the ancient altar of the parliament of the Holy One.

My lords, the temple—these fighters—the Maccabees, came to cleanse today what was not a glorious sight to see; it was an abandoned building run over by nature. Very sad!

Carry on please, historian Josephus.

"A Roman portrait bust said to be of Josephus, though this identification reflects an anti-Semitic trope that assumes that Jews have large noses. In the absence of any epigraphic evidence, this attribution cannot be supported." WC, Jack1956

"When therefore the generals of Antiochus's armies had been beaten so often, Judas assembled the people together, and told them, that <u>after these many victories which God had given them, they ought to go up to Jerusalem, and purify the temple</u>, and offer the appointed sacrifices.

But as soon as he, with the whole multitude, was come to Jerusalem, and <u>found the temple deserted, and its gates burnt down, and plants growing in the temple of their own accord, on account of its desertion</u> ... and were quite confounded at the sight of the temple; so he chose out some of his soldiers, and gave them order to fight against those guards that were in the citadel [the Greek garrison near the temple], until he should have purified the temple.

When therefore he had carefully purged it, and had brought in new vessels, the candlestick, the table [of shew-bread], and the altar [of incense], which were made of gold, he hung up the veils at the gates, and added doors to them. He also took down the altar [of burnt-offering], and built a new one of stones that he gathered together, and not of such as were hewn with iron tools.

So on the five and twentieth day of the month Casleu, which the Macedonians call Apeliens, they lighted the lamps that were on the candlestick, and offered incense upon the altar [of incense], and laid the loaves upon the table [of shew-bread], and offered burnt-offerings upon the new altar [of burnt-offering].

Now it so fell out, that these things were done on the very same day on which their Divine worship had fallen off, and was reduced to a profane and common use, after three years' time; for so it was, that <u>the temple was made desolate by Antiochus, and so continued for three years</u>. This desolation happened to the temple in the hundred forty and fifth year, on the twenty-fifth day of the month Apeliens, and on the hundred fifty and third olympiad: but it was dedicated anew, on the same day, the twenty-fifth of the month Apeliens, on the hundred and forty-eighth year, and on the hundred and fifty-fourth olympiad. And this desolation came to pass according to the prophecy of Daniel, which was given four hundred and eight years before; for he declared that the Macedonians would dissolve that worship [for some time].

...

And from that time to this we celebrate this festival, and call it Lights.

...

Judas also rebuilt the walls round about the city, and reared towers of great height against the incursions of enemies, and set guards therein. He also fortified the city Bethsura, that it might serve as a citadel against any distresses that might come from our enemies."[239]

Prophet Daniel, please cut in with your old prophecy.

*DAN 8:13* Then I heard one saint speaking, and another saint said unto that certain saint which spake, How long shall be the vision concerning the daily sacrifice, and the transgression of desolation, to give both the sanctuary and the host to be trodden under foot?

*DAN 8:14* And he said unto me, Unto two thousand and three hundred days [six years and a few months. 2,300 days / 360 day per year]; then shall the sanctuary be cleansed [170–164 BC].

---

[239] Josephus, *Antiquities of the Jews*, Book 12, Ch.7:6, 7

## 164 BC
## Dust to Dust

Israel, my lords, was no longer an easy target for the Greeks to bleed and fleece on account of the strong Maccabees. And there was nothing more, my lords, that H.M. King Antiochus IV Epiphanes can haul away from the parliament of the Holy One anyway. Yet his majesty still needed money; gold and silver coins, to pay his men, and above all, his hired mercenaries. Fortunately and unfortunately for him, my lords, another treasure cove came to his knowledge.

Carry on, please, historian Josephus.

> "When king Antiochus heard of these things, he was very angry at what had happened; so he got together all his own army, with many mercenaries, whom he had hired from the islands, and took them with him, <u>and prepared to break into Judea about the beginning of the spring</u>.
>
> But when, upon his mustering his soldiers, he perceived that <u>his treasures were deficient</u>, and there was a want of money in them, for all the taxes were not paid, by reason of the seditions there had been among the nations he having been so magnanimous and so liberal, that <u>what he had was not sufficient for him</u>, he therefore resolved first to go into Persia, and collect the taxes of that country."[240]

> "King Antiochus, as he was going over the upper countries, heard that there was a very rich city in Persia, called Elymais; <u>and therein a very rich temple of Diana</u>, and that it was full of all sorts of donations dedicated to it; as also weapons and breastplates, which, upon inquiry, he found had been left there by Alexander [the Great], the son of Philip, king of Macedonia.
>
> And being incited by these motives, he went in haste to Elymais, and assaulted it, and besieged it. But as those that were in it were not terrified at his assault, nor at his siege, but opposed him very courageously, he was beaten off his hopes; for they drove him away from the city, and went out and pursued after him, insomuch that he fled away as far as Babylon, and lost a great many of his army."[241]

The sun, my lords, sat on the man who fulfilled the old prophecies of the Holy One.

---

[240] Josephus, *Antiquities of the Jews*, Book 12, Ch.7:2
[241] Josephus, *Antiquities of the Jews*, Book 12, Ch. 9:1

# Farewell, My Lords

My lords, we have met Babylon, home of today's Shiite Muslims of southern Iraq.

We have met Assyria, home of today's Sunni Muslims of northern Iraq.

And then we met the ram, which had two horns, Iran.

> DAN 8:3 *Then I lifted up mine eyes, and saw, and, behold, there stood before the river <u>a ram which had two horns: and the two horns were high; but one was higher than the other, and the higher came up last.</u>*
> DAN 8:20 <u>*The ram which thou sawest having two horns are the kings of Media and Persia*.</u>

And then we met the goat with the notable horn, Greece, and its great commander, King Alexander the Great.

> DAN 8:5 *And as I was considering, behold, an he goat came from the west on the face of the whole earth, and touched not the ground [very fast]: and the goat had a notable horn between his eyes.*

Next, my lords, we shall meet the fearful beast with ten horns.

> PREVIOUS PAGE: The Ribchester helmet, 1st–2nd century AD, British Museum (image source: author).
>
> Dan 7:7 After this I saw in the night visions, and behold <u>a fourth beast, dreadful and terrible, and strong exceedingly</u>; and it had great iron teeth: it devoured and brake in pieces, and stamped the residue with the feet of it: and it was diverse from all the beasts that were before it; <u>and it had ten horns</u>.
>
> Dan 7:8 I considered the horns, and, behold, there came up among them <u>another little horn, before whom there were three of the first horns plucked up by the roots</u>: and, behold, in this horn were eyes like the eyes of man, and <u>a mouth speaking great things</u>.
>
> Dan 7:21 I beheld, <u>and the same horn made war with the saints, and prevailed against them</u>;

We can tell you, my lords, that the dreadful beast did come on time. And we can tell you that the little horn, who had "a mouth speaking great things," has also come and gone.

At the present time, my lords, and with the light your humble servants have, we believe that the old ram has risen once again from death. He is here today, my lords.

The old ram, who had two horns, Persia and Media [Iran], has risen again, my lords. Except that this time he is pretending to be a peaceful lamb, while he is in fact a ferocious dragon.

Go ahead please, apostle John.

> REV 13:11 *And I beheld another beast coming up out of the earth [coming out from the ground] and <u>he had two horns like a lamb, and he spake as a dragon</u>.*
> REV 13:13 *And he doeth great wonders, so that he maketh fire come down from heaven on the earth in the sight of men [nuclear explosion?].*

And so, next, your majesties, we anticipate the siege of Jerusalem and then the day of rapture, the day of the resurrection of the children of the mighty God.

The Greek philosophers of old, my lords, mocked the apostle Paul when he preached to them about the resurrection.

Yet, you majesties, resurrection takes place before our eyes every day. Go ahead, apostle Paul.

> 1 COR 15:35 *But some man will say, How are the dead raised up? and with what body do they come?*

Look at seeds, your majesty. Look how small, insignificant and plain they are. Indeed, there is not much to behold there, my commanders—is there?

The small and humble seeds, (image source: author's home).

Yet, my lords, if you bury these seeds in the ground, and when their outer body dies, then life, a new life, emerges from the dead husk, the outer body. A grand life emerges from what was buried in soil. A totally new life, with a totally different body, rises to the sky from the outer dead body of the seed, which housed the life inside it.

## PAST AND PRESENT ABOMINATIONS—519

The Cecrus Atlantica tree is similar to the Cedar of Lebanon. Great and magnificent trees rise out of small and plain seeds, Cambridge University, Botanic Garden, UK (image source: author).

*1 COR 15:36* that which thou sowest [that, which you plant] is not quickened [does not come alive], except it die:
*1 COR 15:37* And that which thou sowest, thou sowest not that body that shall be [you do not plant the final grown tree], but bare grain, it may chance of wheat, or of some other grain.
…
*1 COR 15:40* There are also celestial bodies, and bodies terrestrial.
*1 COR 15:42* So also is the resurrection of the dead. It is sown in corruption [mortal]; it is raised in incorruption [immortal].
…
*1 COR 15:44* It is sown a natural body; it is raised a spiritual body. There is a natural body, and there is a spiritual body.
…
*1 COR 15:51* We shall all be changed.

We shall be changed. God can transform a lowly worm to a moth or a colorful butterfly. He can transform man from earthly to a spiritual being like the angels; Museum of Nature History, Vienna, Austria (image source: author).

Alas, the time has come, my sovereigns to bid you farewell. But we must meet again, my lords. We must relate to you the unprecedented cosmic events of the great tribulation, of earth out of orbit, the day of rapture, the first resurrection—the resurrection of the children of God, the one thousand years of the millennium of peace, the black holes, and what shall follow.

But yet, my lords, we cannot help but remember the sober words of the man of God—Joshua.

Ladies and gentlemen, you have heard what you need to hear. It is now for you to choose. And your choice is final. It is eternal.

> JOSH 24:15 *Choose you this day whom ye will serve; whether the gods which your fathers served ... or the gods of the ... land ye dwell: <u>but as for me and my house, we will serve the LORD</u>.*

Until then, may the Lord bless you, may He keep you, and may He ever hold you in the palm of His hands! Salaam, shalom, peace and grace from the Prince of Peace!

From all my heart, with all of my love, and all that I am,

Yours,

*Sanctus Est Adonai*

# Bibliography and Notes

CHAPTER ONE

http://www.nasa.gov/topics/universe/features/universe20110722.html
Tacitus, *Histories*, Kenneth Wellesley [translator] London: Penguin Books, P.81
*The Literature of Ancient Egypt*, translated and edited by: Robert K. Ritner, Vincent A. Tobin, Edward F. Wente, JR. and William Kelly Simpson, Yale University, PP.35
*The Christian Science Monitor*, Jamey Keaten, *Associated Press* / December 7, 2010
*Bukhari*: 9.536
*Muslim*: 40. 6798
*Bukhari*: 4.544
*Qudsi*: Ch.1. 91
*Muslim*: 40. 6792
*Dawud*: 41 – Number 4759
*Muslim*: 32. 6222
*Dawud*: 14. 2599
*Dawud*: 3. 1078
*Dawud*: 28.3852
*Muslim*, 1316
*Bukhari*: 9.610
*Bukhari*: 3.538
*Sunan Ibn Majah*: Ch: 14. 2306
*Bukhari*: 54. 474
*Bukhari*: 6.402
*Al-Tirmidhi*, 1482
*Bukhari*: 4. 55: 553
*Dawud*: 37: 4306
*Dawud*: 37. 4311
*Muslim*: 41. 7028
*Muslim*: 31. 6165
*Muslim*: 31. 6162
*Bukhari*, 8, 73, 188

CHAPTER TWO

*Ancient Records of Egypt*, James Henery Breasted, University of Illinois Press, 2001, V.2, 570, P.P 226

*Al-Tirmidhi Hadith* (Hadith 1452)

CHAPTER THREE

*Ancient Iraq*, 256.
*Ancient Records of Assyria and Babylonia* – Part One, Daniel David Luckenbill, Ch. XIV. 815, 816, P.P. 292.
*Ancient Records of Assyria and Babylonia* – Part One, Daniel David Luckenbill, 1989, 778, 279.
*Ancient Records of Assyria and Babylonia* – Part Two, Daniel David Luckenbill, 1989, 155, PP.82, 83.
*ARAB* – Part Two, 4, P. 2
*AB*-Part Two, 80, P.40
*ARAB*-Part Two, 118, P.61
*Ancient Records of Assyria and Babylonia* – Part Two, Daniel David Luckenbill, Histories & Mysteries of Man LTD., London, England, 1989, 236 & 237, P. 117
*ARAB* – Part two, 133, P.69
*ARAB* – 154, P.82
*ARAB* – Part Two, 172, P.95
*ARA*- Part Two, 240, P.119       p.82
ARAB-Part Two, 327, P.148
ARAB-Part Two, 312, P.143
The ancient *Babylonian Chronicles*, Column III: 34, 35
http://www.sacred-texts.com/ane/rp/rp201/rp20109.htm
*ARAB* Part-Two, 554-556 & 564, P.219 &220
*ARAB* Part-Two, 580, P.226, 227
*ARAB*, 583, P.228
*ARAB* Part-Two, 770, 771, P.292-294
*ARAB*,778, P.296       p.93
*ARAB*-Part Two, 55, P.26
*ARAB* – Part Two, 4, P. 2
*ARAB*-Part Two, 17, P.7
*ARAB*, Part Two, 117, P.61
*Ancient Iraq*, Georges Roux, Penguin Books, 1966, P.278
*ARAB*, Part Two, 66, P.P 33
*ARAB*, Part Two, 257, P.P 128
*ARAB*, Part Two, 260, P.P 130
*ARAB*, Part Two, 234, P.P 116
*ARAB*, Part Two, 345, P.P 153
*The Library of History of Diodorus Siculus*, Book 2, 23: 1-4

http://penelope.uchicago.edu/Thayer/E/Roman/Texts/Diodorus_Siculus/2 A*.html#23

## CHAPTER FOUR

Herodotus, *The Histories*, by Aubrey de Selincourt, Penguin Books, 2:159, P.P 193
*The Babylonian Chronicle*, (ABC) 5, http://www.livius.org/cg-cm/chronicles/abc5/jerusalem.html , obverse, 1-7
*The Ancient Near East, An Anthology of Texts and Pictures (ANT)*, James B. Pritchard, Princeton University Press, P.P 203
*ANT*, P.P 205
*ANT*, P.P 203
https://en.wikipedia.org/wiki/Lachish_letters
http://Cojs.org
http://www.huffingtonpost.com/2012/05/25/jesus-crucifixion-date-possible_n_1546351.html
Herodotus, *the Histories*, P.83

## CHAPTER FIVE

Herodotus, *the Histories*, P.81
Herodotus, *the Histories*, P.83
Herodotus, *the Histories*, P.83
Herodotus, *the Histories*, P.83, 84
Herodotus, *the Histories*, 126, P.94
Herodotus, *the Histories*, P.94, 95
Herodotus, *the Histories*, Book One, P.95
Herodotus, the *Histories*, Book.1, P.95
Herodotus, *the Histories*, 3:65, P. 231
Herodotus, *the Histories*, 1:70, 71, P.68
Herodotus, *the Histories*, 1.89, P.77
Herodotus, *the Histories*, 1:154, P.103
Herodotus, *the Histories*, 1:113, P.181
Herodotus, *the Histories*, 1.192, P.117
Herodotus, *the Histories*, 1.192, P.117
*The verse account of Nabonidus*, http://www.livius.org/ct-cz/cyrus_I/babylon03.html
http://www.livius.org/cg-cm/chronicles/cm/nabonidus.html
Herodotus, *the Histories*, 1:191, P.118
Herodotus, 3: 90, P.243

*Plutarch. The Age Of Alexander*, translated and annotated by Ian Scott-Kilvert, Penguin Books1973, P.326

Strabo's *Geography*, Book Fifteen, Chapter.3:7, http://rbedrosian.com/Classic/strabo15f.htm

Herodotus, *the Histories*, 3:16, P.P 209

*Sahih Bukhari*, 009, 093, 532B

*The Koran*, Surah 78, The News, Verse 31-33

*Hadith Al-Tirmidhi, Jami` at-Tirmidhi*

*Hadith Al-Tirmidhi,*

Herodotus, *the Histories* 3:25, 26

Herodotus, the *Histories*, Book.1:211

Herodotus, *the Histories*, 3:65, P. 231

The *Behistun inscription,* http://www.livius.org/be-bm/behistun/behistun-t05.html#1.36-43

Justin, *Epitome of the Philippic History of Pompeius Trogus,* Book 1:9

Herodotus, *the Histories*, 3:66, P.232

*The Story of Civilization, Our Oriental Heritage,* Will Durant, Simon and Schuster, P 355, 356

Herodotus, *the Histories*, 3:70, P.233

*Justin, 1:9*

Herodotus, *the Histories*, 3:75, P.235

Josephus, *Antiquities of the Jews,* Book XI, Chapter III: 1

Latin historian Justin, 9:10

*Behistun Inscription,* Livius.org

*Behistun Inscription,* Livius.org

*Behistun Inscription,* Livius.org

Latin historian Justin, 1:10

*Sahih Bukhari. 9. 87. 111*

*Muslim*, 1, 199

*Bukhari*, 7, 65, 343

*Bukhari*, 8, 76, 459

*Bukhari*, 5, 57, 57

*Bukhari*, 5, 59, 647

*Muslim*, 40, 6853

*Sahih Bukhari. 9. 92. 461*

*Hadith Bukhari. 5. 58.280*

*Dawud*: 19. 3044

*Bukhari*: 9. 88. 199

*Bukhari*: 9. 93. 539

*Bukhari*: 7: 62. 115

*Malik*: 15.4.9

*Dawud*: Book 19. 3074

*Muslim*, 3, 671
*Muslim*: 2. 504
*Bukhari*: 7. 69. 534
*Bukhari*: 9. 92. 411
*Bukhari*: 5. 58. 199
*Sahih Bukhari*. 7. 62. 133
*Bukhari*, 3, 39,514
*Dawud*, 1, 28
*Muslim*, 2, 504
*Muslim*, 2, 516
*Dawud*, 16, 2840
*Dawud*, 26, 3708
*Dawud*, 32, 4123
*Bukhari*, 7, 72, 746
*Bukhari*, 7, 72, 747
*Dawud*, 1, 42
*Muslim*, 1, 131
*Bukhari*: 54. 506
*Sahih Bukhari*. 9. 87.128
*Maliks Muwatta* , 050, 001.
*Bukhari*, 7, 63, 229
*Dawud*, 40. 4731
*Sahih Muslim*. 30. 5776
*Muslim*: 1. 380
*Qudsi*: 36
*The Koran*, Surah 7. The Heights
*Hadith Muslim*, 8, 3467
*Hadith Bukhari*, 7, 62, 114
Herodotus, *the histories*, 3:74, PP 70
Herodotus, *the Histories*, 4:92, P 301
Herodotus, *the Histories*, 1:70, 71, P.68
Herodotus, *the Histories*, 5:1, P 341
Herodotus, *the Histories*, 5:27, P 350
Herodotus, *the Histories*, 7:30, P.456
Herodotus, *the Histories*, 5:96, PP 379
Herodotus, *the Histories*, 6:28, P 398
Herodotus, *the Histories*, 5:105, PP 382
Herodotus, *the Histories*, 6:41, P 42&43
Herodotus, *the Histories*, 6:94, P 421
Herodotus, *the Histories*, 6:100, P 424
Herodotus, *the Histories*, 6:105, P 425
*Dawud*: 41. 4909

*Dawud*: 41. 4920
*Dawud*: 26. 3677
*Malik*: 52. 52.2.7
*Malik*: 52. 52.2.6
*Muslim*: 28. 5612
Herodotus, *the Histories*, 6:109, P 427
Herodotus, *the Histories*, 6:109, P 428&429
Herodotus, *the Histories*, 7:139, P. 487
Herodotus, *the Histories*, 6:115, P 429
*Pro Lapsu Inter Salutandum*, A Slip of the Tongue in Salutation, Lucian of Samosata, translated by Fowler, H W and F G Oxford, The Clarendon Press 1905, 3
Plutarch, On the Fame of Athens, C
Herodotus, *the Histories*, 7:1&4, P 441, 442
Herodotus, *the Histories*, 7:2, P.442
    7:8a, P.444
    7:18, P.452
    7:30, P.456
    7:30, P.457
Herodotus, *the Histories*, 7:121, P.481
Herodotus, *the Histories*, 7:49, P.462
Herodotus, *the Histories*, 7:176, P.504
Herodotus, *the Histories*, 7:187, P.508
Herodotus, *the Histories*, 7:189, P.189&190
Herodotus, *the Histories*, 7:107, P.477
Herodotus, *the Histories*, 7:213, P.515
Herodotus, *the Histories*, 7:220, P.518
Diodorus Siculus, *Bibliotheca Historica [written 60-30 BC]*, Book 11, Ch.11.1, 2& 6
Plutarch, The malice of Herodotus
Herodotus, *the Histories*, 8:13, P.529
Diodorus Siculus, *Bibliotheca Historica*, Book 11, Ch. 13:1
Herodotus, *the histories*, 8:34, P.535
Diodorus Siculus [c. 60 BC], *Bibliotheca Historica*, Book IX, Ch. 15:2
Diodorus Siculus, *Bibliotheca Historica*, Book IX, Ch. 16:2
Herodotus, *the Histories*, 8:49, P.540
Herodotus, *the Histories*, 8:54, P.541
Lysias [b.459 BC] 2:39
Herodotus, *the Histories*, 9:105, P.619
*Bukhari*, 1, 9, 490
*Bukhari*, 9, 486
*Dawud*, 41, 5119

*Dawud*, 11, 2142
*Dawud*, 41, 5252
*Bukhari*, 6, 60, 475
*Bukhari*, 7, 63, 182
*Bukhari*, 7, 69, 541
*Bukhari*, 8, 73, 123
*Sahih Bukhari*. 4. 52. 143
*Bukhari*, 1, 8, 367
*Sahih Bukhari*. 7. 62. 48
*The Koran, the Clans* 33:50
*Sahih Bukhari*. 1. 6. 301
*Bukhari*, 8, 73, 97
Herodotus, *the Histories*, 8:99, P.558
Herodotus, *the Histories*, 8:97 & 100, P.555 & 556
Herodotus, *the Histories*, 9:13, P.581
http://www.livius.org/aa-ac/achaemenians/XPh.html
Herodotus, *the Histories*, 9:15, P.583
Herodotus, *the Histories*, 9:17, P.583
Herodotus, *the Histories*, 9:99, P.616
Plutarch [b.46 AD.], *the Parallel Lives*, 20:1.1-4

CHAPTER SIX

Arrian. *The Campuigns of Alexander, p. 110, 111*
Arrian. *The Campaigns of Alexander, p. 110, 111*
Josephus, *Antiquities of the Jews*, Book XI, Chap. VIII: 3
*The Nature of Alexander* by Mary Renault, Penguin Books, 1975, P.88
Arrian. *The Campaigns of Alexander*, translated by Aubrey De Selincourt. Revised by J. R. Hamilton, Penguin Books, 1958, p 120-128
Arrian. *The Campaigns of Alexander*, P.143, 144
Josephus, *Antiquities of the Jews*, Book XII, Chapter: 1:1
Josephus, *Antiquities of the Jews*, Book XII, Chapter II: 1
Josephus, *Antiquities of the Jews*, Book XII, Chapter II: 4
Josephus, *Antiquities of the Jews*, Book XII, Chapter II: 5
Josephus, *Antiquities of the Jews*, Book XII, Chapter II: 6
Apian [c.95-c.165], the *Roman History, Syrian Wars*: 65, translated by Horace White, and the additions in green by Jona Lendering, note 4: Incorrect Laodice was still alive in 236
Apian [c.95-c.165], the *Roman History, Syrian Wars*: 65, translated by Horace White, and the additions in green by Jona Lendering

http://www.livius.org/cg-cm/chronicles/bchp-ptolemy_iii/bchp_ptolemy_iii_01.html, Bagnall, Derow 1981, No. 26

Polybius, *the Histories*, Book 5:37:7-11

http://penelope.uchicago.edu/Thayer/E/Roman/Texts/Polybius/5*.html

Polybius, the Histories, Book5:40:1-3

Polybius, *the Histories*, Book5:63:1-14

Polybius, *the Histories*, Book5:65:9

Polybius, *the Histories*, Book 5:79:1-6 & 13

Polybius, *the Histories*, Book 5:80:1-4

Polybius, *the Histories*, Book 5:82:1

Polybius, *the Histories*, Book 5:83:1

Polybius, *the Histories*, Book 5:85:13, 86: 1 & 2

Polybius, *the Histories*, Book 5:87:7, 8 & 10 and 87:6 & 7

Polybius, *Historiae* V 107.1 and XIV 107.1

http://tebtunis.berkeley.edu/lecture/revolt

*The House of Ptolemy*, E. R. Bevan, published by Methuen Publishing, London, 1927, Chapter VII, Page 240

http://penelope.uchicago.edu/Thayer/E/Gazetteer/Places/Africa/Egypt/_Texts/BEVHOP/7*.html

W.M. Müller, *Egyptological Researches III. The bilingual decrees of Philae* (Washington 1920), pp. 59–88

Josephus, *Antiquities of the Jews*, Book XII, Chapter III: III

Polybius, *the Histories*, Book XVI: 18 – 20

Josephus, *Antiquities of the Jews*, Book XII, Chapter 4:1 & 4

Appian's *History of Rome: The Syrian Wars* 1:5

http://www.livius.org/ap-ark/appian/appian_syriaca_01.html

Appian's *History of Rome, the Syrian Wars*: 15

Titus Livius (Livy), *the History of Rome*, Book 33:30

http://www.perseus.tufts.edu/hopper/text?doc=Perseus%3Atext%3A1999.02.0164%3Abook%3D34s

Titus Livius (Livy), *the History of Rome*, Book 33:31

Titus Livius (Livy), *the History of Rome*, Book 33:31

Titus Livius (Livy), *the History of Rome*, Book 33:32

Cassius Dio, *Roman History*, Vol. II, Loeb Classical Library edition, 1914, introduction

Appian's *History of Rome: The Macedonian Wars* (2): 13.

http://www.livius.org/ap-ark/appian/appian_macedonia2.html

Cassius Dio, *Roman History*, Vol. II: 19, Loeb Classical Library edition, 1914

Appian's *History of Rome: The Syrian Wars* 17, 18

Diodorus Siculus Book 29:3:1, 7:1 & 11:1

BIBLIOGRAPHY AND NOTES—529

http://penelope.uchicago.edu/Thayer/E/Roman/Texts/Diodorus_Siculus/29*.html#15
Diodorus Siculus *Library of History* Fragments of Book XXIX, Chapter 10,
http://penelope.uchicago.edu/Thayer/E/Roman/Texts/Diodorus_Siculus/29*.html
Appian's *History of Rome*: The Syrians War, Book 1:38
Diodorus Siculus *Library of History* Fragments of Book 29:6
http://penelope.uchicago.edu/Thayer/E/Roman/Texts/Diodorus_Siculus/29*.html#15
Ancient historian Appian of Alexandria [c.96-c.165], *Roman History, Syrian Wars*, Part 10, 45
II Book of Maccabees, new English translation, Ch.4:7-9
II Book of Maccabees, Ch.4:12-15
II Book of Maccabees, Ch.4:21
Josephus, *the Wars of the Jews*, Book 1, Chapter. 1:1
Diodorus of Sicily, *Library of World History*, 30.2
Polybius, *the Histories*, Fragments of Book XXVIII, 20
Diodorus of Sicily, *Library of World History*, 30.14
Diodorus of Sicily, *Library of World History,* 30.18
Diodorus Siculus, *Library of History*, Fragments of Book XXX: 18, 19
Diodorus of Sicily, *Library of World History* 31:16-18
Diodorus of Sicily, *Library of World History*, 29:32
Livy, *the History of Rome*, 45 [XLV]: 11&12
http://mcadams.posc.mu.edu/txt/ah/livy/Livy45.html
Polybius, *the Histories*, Fragments of Book XXVIII, 20
II Book of Maccabees, new English translation, Ch.4:23-25
II Book of Maccabees, new English translation, Ch.4:39-42
I Maccabees 1:16-25
Livy, *the History of Rome*, 45 [XLV]:12
Diodorus of Sicily, *Library of World History*, 31.1
Livy, *History of Rome*, XLV: 12
Polybius, *the Histories*, Book 29:27
Polybius, *the Histories*, Book 29:27
Josephus, *Wars of the Jews*, Book.1, Chapter.1, 1
II Maccabees, Chapter 5:5-16
Flavius Josephus, *Antiquities of the Jews*, Book 12, Chapter 5:2-4
Appian of Alexandria, *Roman History, Syrian Wars*, Part 10, 66
Flavius Josephus, *Antiquities of the Jews*, Book 12, Chapter 5:2-4
I Maccabees 1:29-38
2 Maccabees 9:4
Flavius Josephus, *Antiquities of the Jews*, Book 12, Chapter 5:2-4

Josephus, *Antiquities of the Jews*, Book 13, Chap. 8:2

*Universal History*, Agapius, 239, 240.

Tacitus Cornelius, Book 5, Chap. 8, *Complete Works of Tacitus*. Tacitus. Alfred John Church. William Jackson Brodribb. Sara Bryant. edited for Perseus. New York. : Random House, Inc. Random House, Inc. 1873. reprinted 1942.

Diodorus Siculus, *the Library of History*, Books 34:1-5

Josephus, *Antiquities of the Jews*, Book 12, Ch.6:1-3

Josephus, *Wars of the Jews*, Book 1, Ch.1:3

Josephus, *Antiquities of the Jews*, Book 12, Ch.7:6, 7

Josephus, *Antiquities of the Jews*, Book 12, Ch.7:2

Josephus, *Antiquities of the Jews*, Book 12, Ch.9:1